. . . .

"Williams has produced a bracing guide to Lewis as theological writer. The sweep of the book delves into timely themes: imagination's relation to theology, Lewis's misunderstanding of Fundamentalism, Hamartiology (you'll see), an investigation into Lewis's "trilema," Soteriology, meaning and function of the Church, and Theological Aesthetics—just to name a few. The work is, in short, a crash-course in Evangelical theological doctrine illuminated and constantly grounded in Lewis's (and others's) writings. All is composed in Williams's strong voice and with the same useful plain-spoken clarity as Lewis. *Deeper Magic* accomplishes what tragically few writers today accomplish: deeper instruction."
　—Rod Miller
　　Professor of Art History, Hendrix College, and editor of
　　C. S. Lewis and the Arts: Creativity in the Shadowlands

. . . .

"C. S. Lewis's best books are his works in literary criticism; but most people do not read them. Perhaps it is because most people are unfamiliar with medieval literature specifically and literary criticism generally. But, what would happen if there was a guide to walk you through the riches of this particular Lewis material? Professor Donald Williams, a top flight medievalist, is such a trailblazer and guide. Lewis opens more than wardrobe doors, but for most, the door has been locked. Williams has picked the lock and allows readers to see how Lewis—the great Oxford and Cambridge scholar—made his faith the means to an integrated scholarship. It is a model for all who want to see an embodiment of what it is to actually think Christianly about any given topic. I highly recommend this book!"
　—Jerry Root
　　C. S. Lewis Scholar and Professor, Wheaton College

. . . .

"Williams has done the impossible: he has written a highly readable overview of C. S. Lewis's theology. He draws from the deep well of a lifetime spent studying literature and theology and Lewis. My understanding has been greatly enriched; yours will be, too. This book is a marvel. I am happy to recommend it."
　—Diana Pavlac Glyer
　　Professor and author of *Bandersnatch: C.S. Lewis, J.R.R. Tolkien,*
　　and the Creative Collaboration of the Inklings

. . . .

. . . .

"In *Deeper Magic: The Theology Behind the Writings of C.S. Lewis*, Donald Williams writes with a clarity, freshness, fairness, and welcome worthy of his subject. Readers will find both breadth and depth in this very comprehensive and insightful analysis. One of the best-written books on Lewis's theology."
—Devin Brown
Professor and author of *A Life Observed: A Spiritual Biography of C. S. Lewis*

. . . .

"This is the best book in print on the greatest Christian writer of our times by a noted C. S. Lewis scholar. It is a treasure trove of systematized information—a must for every C. S. Lewis fan, and all the rest of us who should be."
—Norman Geisler, Ph.D.
Author and founder of Southern Evangelical Seminary

. . . .

DEEPER MAGIC

....

THE THEOLOGY BEHIND THE WRITINGS OF

....

C.S. LEWIS

DEEPER MAGIC

THE THEOLOGY BEHIND THE WRITINGS OF

C.S. LEWIS

DONALD T. WILLIAMS

SQUARE HALO
BOOKS

In Christian art, the square halo identified a living person presumed to be a saint. Square Halo Books is devoted to publishing works that present contextually sensitive biblical studies and practical instruction consistent with the Doctrines of the Reformation. The goal of Square Halo Books is to provide materials useful for encouraging and equipping the saints.

First Edition 2016
Second Printing 2024

Copyright ©2016 Square Halo Books
P.O. Box 18954, Baltimore, MD 21206
ISBN 978-1-941106-05-1
Library of Congress Control Number: 2016956369

All rights reserved. No part of this book may be reproduced without permission from the publisher, except by a reviewer, who may quote brief passages in a review; nor may any part of this book be reproduced, stored in a retrieval system, or transmitted in any form by any means (electronic, mechanical, photocopying, recorded, or other), without permission from the publisher.

CONTENTS

ACKNOWLEDGEMENTS

LIST OF ABBREVIATIONS

INTRODUCTION 13

CHAPTER 1: Prolegomena A: *What Is Truth?* 23

CHAPTER 2: Prolegomena B: *The Task of Theology* 41

CHAPTER 3: Bibliology: *The Doctrine of Scripture* 59

CHAPTER 4: Theology Proper: *The Existence and Nature of God* 75

CHAPTER 5: Anthropology and Hamartiology: *The Nature of Man and His Fall* 103

CHAPTER 6: Christology: *The Person of Christ* 117

INTERLUDE: Excursus on the Trilemma 129

CHAPTER 7: Soteriology: *The Atonement and Salvation* 149

CHAPTER 8: Ecclesiology: *The Church* 173

CHAPTER 9: Sanctification: *The Christian Life* 187

CHAPTER 10: Theological Aesthetics: *Christianity and Culture* 201

CHAPTER 11: Poimenics: *Evangelism and Apologetics* 215

CHAPTER 12: Eschatology: *The Second Coming, Heaven, and Hell* 233

CONCLUSION 251

BIBLIOGRAPHY 255

INDEX OF SCRIPTURE PASSAGES 275

GENERAL INDEX XXX

ACKNOWLEDGEMENTS

Grateful acknowledgement is due first to Toccoa Falls College, whose granting of a half sabbatical a few years ago got the research for this project kick-started, and whose honoring me as its R. S. Forrest Scholar has provided relief from committee work that helped it continue to fruition. The college has also provided me with a steady stream of students who have populated my biennial Lewis course with their inquisitive enthusiasm for and love of Lewis and of truth. This book is for them and the many like them who could not be part of those classes.

A few parts of this discussion have appeared in print before. A version of chapter one appeared as a chapter in my discussion of Lewis's philosophy of beauty, truth, and goodness in *Reflections from Plato's Cave: Essays in Evangelical Philosophy* (Lynchburg: Lantern Hollow Press, 2012). A version of Chapter three appeared as "Text vs. Word: C. S. Lewis's Doctrine of Inspiration and the Inerrancy of Scripture," in *I Am Put Here For the Defense of the Gospel: A Festschrift for Nom Geisler,* ed. Terry L. Miethe (Eugene, Or.: Wipf and Stock, 2016): 153-68. The section on the ontological argument in chapter four appeared as "Anselm and Aslan: C. S. Lewis on the Ontological Argument," *Touchstone: A Journal of Mere Christianity* 27:6 (Nov./Dec. 2014): 36-39. A shorter, popularized version of the Excursus on the Trilemma was published as "Identity Check: Are C. S. Lewis's Critics Right, or Is His 'Trilemma' Valid?" *Touchstone: A Journal of Mere Christianity* 23:3 (May-June 2010): 25-29. A fuller, more scholarly paper was published in *Midwestern Journal of Theology* 11:1 (Spring 2012): 91-102. It was reprinted with permission in *Global Journal of Classical Theology* 11:1 (Spring, 2013): 1-13, and also as chapter four of my book *Reflections from Plato's Cave: Essays in Evangelical Philosophy* (Lynchburg: Lantern Hollow Press, 2012). That material was significantly revised and expanded for the book *C. S. Lewis's Apologetic: Pro and Con,* ed. Gregory Bassham (Rodolpi, 2015), and that version appears here. All these are used here by permission, with thanks.

Friends, theologians, and Lewis scholars such as Michael Bauman, Devin Brown, Ruby Dunlap, Diana Glyer, David Stott Gordon, Brian Melton, and Jerry Root have read bits of this material and made valuable suggestions. Any errors that remain are assuredly my own.

ABBREVIATIONS

AoL	*The Allegory of Love*	**OOW**	*Of Other Worlds*
AoM	*The Abolition of Man*	**Pa**	*Perelandra*
B&F	*Brothers and Friends: The Diaries of Major Warren Hamilton Lewis*	**PC**	*Prince Caspian: The Return to Narnia*
		PoP	*The Problem of Pain*
CR	*Christian Reflections*	**PPL**	*A Preface to Paradise Lost*
DI	*The Discarded Image: An Introduction to Medieval and Renaissance Literature*	**PR**	*Pilgrim's Regress*
		Ps	*Poems*
		RotP	*Reflections on the Psalms*
EiC	*An Experiment in Criticism*	**SbJ**	*Surprised by Joy: The Shape of My Early Life*
FL	*The Four Loves*	**SiW**	*Studies in Words*
GD	*The Great Divorce*	**SL**	*The Screwtape Letters* and *Screwtape Proposes a Toast*
GiD	*God in the Dock*		
GO	*A Grief Observed*		
L	*The Collected Letters of C. S. Lewis*, 3 vol.	**SLE**	*Selected Literary Essays*
		TH&HB	*The Horse and His Boy*
LtM	*Letters to Malcolm, Chiefly on Prayer*	**THS**	*That Hideous Strength*
		TLB	*The Last Battle*
LWW	*The Lion, the Witch, and the Wardrobe*	**TMN**	*The Magician's Nephew*
		TSC	*The Silver Chair*
M	*Miracles: A Preliminary Study*	**TWHF**	*Till We Have Faces: A Myth Retold*
MC	*Mere Christianity*	**VDT**	*The Voyage of the Dawn Treader*
OHEL	*Oxford History of English Literature: English Literature in the Sixteenth Century, Excluding Drama*	**WLN**	*The World's Last Night and Other Essays*
		WoG	*The Weight of Glory and Other Addresses*
OotSP	*Out of the Silent Planet*		

INTRODUCTION

Lewis's Life
and Influence

"Use your specimens while you can. There are not going to be many more dinosaurs" ("De Descriptione Temporum," 14).

THE PURPOSE OF THE BOOK

When George Sayer's first meeting with his new Oxford tutor C. S. Lewis ended, another Oxford faculty member named J. R. R. Tolkien was waiting to see Lewis next. How did the new fresher get on with Lewis, Tolkien wanted to know. Rather well, Sayer figured, adding that he thought Lewis was going to make quite an interesting mentor. "Interesting?" Tolkien replied. "Yes, he's certainly that. You'll never get to the bottom of him" (Sayer xx).

This book is not going to get to the bottom of Lewis either. It mainly deals with Lewis's theology, only one of many aspects of his rich and fertile thought. It won't even get to the bottom of that. It will, though, try to go deeper than other books on Lewis's theology have gone.

There is only one popular book currently on the market that tries to survey Lewis's theology as a whole (Vaus), and it consists almost entirely of summary (albeit accurate), with relatively little analysis or critique. Other book-length studies focus on Lewis's approach to only one doctrine (e.g. Christensen, bibliology; Payne, pneumatology), or a few interrelated doctrines (e.g., Brazier, revelation, theology, Christology) or one area (e.g., Purtill, Burson and Walls, Markos, apologetics), or one idea (e.g., Reppert, the argument from reason). We do not yet have a book that looks at Lewis's presentation of Christian doctrine as a unified whole and critically asks what are its strengths and weaknesses as a guide to biblical faith from a conservative Evangelical perspective. That is the hole this book will try to fill.

It is a strange hole to find in Lewis studies. For while he was not a professional theologian, Lewis might well have gotten more Christian doctrinal content into more heads than anyone who was a professional theologian in his day or since. He saw himself as a "translator," putting abstruse theological ideas back into the language of the people because the professional theologians had forgotten that these truths were *for* the people of God. He said, with excessive self-deprecation, "If the real theologians had tackled this laborious work of translation about a hundred years ago, when they began to lose touch with the people (for whom Christ died), there would have been no place for me" ("Rejoinder" 183). Well, the place was there, and we may be glad for the way Lewis filled it.

Lewis then may be the most important *amateur* theologian ever. Many people (including famously Charles Colson) testify to having been brought to Christ by Lewis's writings, and many more to having been preserved in the faith by discovering him in a period of doubt and questioning. The "Broadcast Talks" which became *Mere Christianity* made Lewis one of the most recognizable voices on the BBC in the 1940's (after Winston Churchill), and his influence has only grown. Half a century after his death, almost all his books are still in print (those which briefly go out tend to cycle back in), and his popularity, especially with American Evangelicals, shows no signs of fading.

As an evangelist (indirectly), an apologist, an expounder, and an incarnater in fiction of the faith, Lewis was one of the most imaginatively winsome and logically forceful ambassadors for Christianity we have seen. For that very reason it behooves us to cultivate a critically sound judgment about his influence. What is the theology that lies behind the popular apologetics, the Narnia books, and the Space Trilogy? How biblical is it? What are its strengths and weaknesses? Where does Lewis succeed in explaining and portraying the truth about Christ, and where in those presentations should we be wary or withhold our judgment? Those are the questions we will try to answer in the following pages.

THE LIFE

Who was this man who became the most important amateur theologian in the history of the church? The outlines of his life are well known. C. S. Lewis was born in 1898 in Northern Ireland. He lost his mother to cancer as a young lad and was sent to a series of horrible boarding schools where he lost the nominal faith of his childhood. He was tutored by William T. Kirkpatrick, who taught him logic and classical languages and an uncompromising love of debate and loyalty to truth. He served in the trenches of World War I and was wounded in action. He took a triple first at Oxford in classics, philosophy, and English.

While there, his reading and his friends undermined his atheism (the story is told in full in *Surprised by Joy*), and he reluctantly became a theist and then a Christian. He became tutor in English at Magdalen College, Oxford, where he became known as a Christian apologist, founded with J. R. R. Tolkien the writers group The Inklings, and was president of the Socratic Club, devoted to debates between Christians and atheists. He became Professor of Medieval and Renaissance Literature at Cambridge. At both schools he wrote literary scholarship that is still read today. He married Joy Davidman and lost her to cancer, inspiring a play and movie very loosely based on their love story. He wrote the Narnia books, one of the most popular series of children's books of all time, and one of the most enjoyed by adults as well as children. He died on November 22, 1963, the same day President Kennedy was shot.

The story is told in detail elsewhere (best by Green and Hooper and by Sayer, and by Lewis himself in *Surprised by Joy*). What interests us here is the consistent manifestation in it of two traits which rarely appear in such strength in the same person, and which in combination are what make Lewis a theologian still worthy of our attention half a century after his death, despite his lack of formal training in that field. These two traits were a fertile imagination alive to the beauty and mystery of life, along with a sharp logical mind capable of deep critical analysis. It was precisely this combination that, in his atheist phase, would not let him rest content in his unbelief. He writes in his autobiography of the frustration of believing only in atoms in motion while caring only about gods and heroes and the great myths (*SBJ* 174). A lesser man might have just given up on the gods and myths and become cynical. Lewis could not. He wrote to his friend Arthur Greeves on 23 May 1918:

> Faeries must be in the woods
> Or the satyr's merry broods,
> Tritons in the summer sea,
> Else how could the dead things be
> Half so lovely as they are? ...
>
> Atoms dead could never thus
> Move the human heart of us,
> Unless the beauty that we see
> Part of endless beauty be. (*L* 1:373)

"Atoms dead could never thus / Move the human heart of us." Lewis saw a contradiction in the philosophy he had accepted—not yet a contradiction in its logic (that would come later), but a contradiction between his reductionistic, materialist philosophy and life itself. It would take him some time to realize how to resolve that impasse, with many false starts. He wrote to Greeves on 29 May 1918, "The conviction is gaining ground on me that after all Spirit does exist.... I fancy there is Something right outside time & place, which did not create matter as the Christians say, but is matter's great enemy: and that Beauty is the call of the spirit in that something to the spirit in us" (*L* 1:374). The full Christian resolution would be some time in coming. But when it came it would come in the form precisely of a healing of the troubling dichotomy: He would write his brother, Warnie, on 24 Oct. 1931 that William Law's *Appeal to All that Doubt or Disbelieve* is "one of those rare works which make you say of Christianity, 'Here is the very thing you like in poetry and the romances, only this time it's true'" (2:5).

Poetry... romance... true. Yes.

The thing to see here is that it was the dual impulse to both imagination and reason, plus the compulsion to find some kind of unity between them that would not be in conflict with life as we actually experience it, that drove Lewis long before he concluded that the answer to this problem is found in Christ.

We can see it coming already: rational apologetics that is full of apt analogy that could only come from the imagination, and imaginary worlds of haunting beauty that contain as integral components set pieces of logical reasoning like Professor Kirk's use of the Trilemma to evaluate Lucy's truthfulness or Puddleglum's refutation of the Green Witch. We step from one to the other seamlessly. And that is why Lewis's theology matters: it is a theology for a Christian life that refuses to be reduced either to cold reason or passionate emotion, and also refuses to compromise either to get the other. With whatever flaws we may discover it to have, it is a theology that flows from the drive to wholeness. Its ability to lead us in the direction of wholeness is a significant reason why we are still reading it. And it is the reason why, in this book, we want to study it.

THE STUDY

The task we have set before us is not an easy one. One might think it would be, given the admirable clarity of Lewis's prose and the aptness of his analogies. But a few difficulties arise to complicate things.

The first is that, ironically, given his commitment to "mere" Christianity, Lewis is a surprisingly polarizing force. It is hard to get an objective handle on him. He has attracted on the one hand an almost idolatrous type of admiration from a certain kind of Evangelical and been the subject of writings from that group that can only be called hagiography. In reaction to this, on the other hand, one finds a certain kind of scholar who thinks he will get instant academic "street cred" if he can find fault with Lewis. He gets almost canonized by the one group and sometimes glibly patronized by the other.

Meanwhile, people of almost every theological persuasion—fundamentalist, Evangelical, neo-orthodox, liberal, Protestant, Roman Catholic, Orthodox—want to enlist Lewis on their "side." One can read tortured attempts by all these groups to claim that Lewis was really one of them—or would have been had he just lived a bit longer! Emotions get involved pretty quickly in some of these turf battles because there is genuinely a lot at stake. This situation alerts us to the danger that many people are more interested in *using* Lewis than in truly understanding him. It is a real temptation because where Lewis is really an ally, he is a formidable one. I will try to resist the temptation to make Lewis more of a conservative Evangelical (to give full disclosure about my own position) than he really was. He is often an ally of that camp, as it rightly perceives—but not always. To honor Lewis, in other words, we have first to honor truth.

A second difficulty arises from the fact that Lewis's most popular books, and among his most theologically influential, are fiction. They are fiction, but they are not allegory (except for *The Pilgrim's Regress*), despite many careless statements by Lewis's readers to the contrary. An allegory is a work of symbolic fiction in which there is a fairly simple correspondence between items or characters in the story and what they represent in the "real" world. (I know there are more sophisticated allegories in which the relationships are not *that* simple—but I'm giving a rough definition here to make a point.) For example, in Bunyan's *Pilgrim's Progress*, the characters have names like "Mr. Worldly Wise Man" or "Faithful." It is not hard to tell what they represent, and their words and actions are intended as direct illustrations of the concepts that they picture. One is on pretty safe ground then talking about Bunyan's theology based on *Pilgrim's Progress*. But Lewis's fictional writings are mostly not like that. Aslan is not simply Christ; he is Christ as he *might* have been *if* God had created a world of talking animals and been incarnated there.

Lewis referred to the things that happen in Narnia or the Space Trilogy as "supposals" as distinguished from "allegories." He explained to Edward T. Dell in a letter of 4 Feb. 1949, "You must not confuse my romances with my theses. In the latter I state and argue a creed. In the former, much is merely supposed for the sake of the story" (*L* 2:914). Similarly, he wrote to a Fifth-Grade Class in Maryland on 24 May 1954:

> You are mistaken when you think that everything in the book "represents" something in this world. Things do that in *Pilgrim's Progress* but I'm not writing in that way. I did not say to myself "Let us represent Jesus as He really is in our world by a Lion in Narnia": I said, "Let us *suppose* that there were a land like Narnia and that the son of God, as He became a

Man in our world, became a Lion there, and then imagine what would happen." (L 3:479-80; cf. 3:1004; emphasis in the original)

In the same vein, Lewis wrote to Tony Pollock on 3 May 1954 that his stories were not about facts at all, though he hoped they contained truth. "That is, they may be regarded as imaginative hypotheses illustrating what I believe to be theological truths" (L 3:465).

The most important passage for understanding the relation of the fiction to Lewis's theological beliefs may be this one:

> I saw how stories of this kind could steal past a certain inhibition which had paralyzed much of my own religion in childhood. Why did one find it so hard to feel as one was told one ought to feel about God or about the sufferings of Christ? I thought that the chief reason was that one was told one ought to.... But supposing that by casting all these things into an imaginary world, stripping them of their stained-glass and Sunday school associations, one could make them for the first time appear in their real potency? Could one not thus steal past those watchful dragons? ("Sometimes" 37)

The fiction then is relevant to understanding Lewis's theology; there is theology there, sneaking past watchful dragons to appear in potency. But one has to be careful about deriving theology from fiction. On the one hand, the children learn to know Aslan in Narnia so that they might learn his other name here. "There I have another name. You must learn to know me by that name. This was the very reason you were brought into Narnia, that by knowing me here for a little you may know me better there" (VDT 270). Therefore, we are intended to see parallels between Aslan (or Maleldil, in the Space Trilogy) and Christ. But we cannot assume that any given detail in the stories necessarily carries a doctrinal meaning. Rather, we should expect the parallels to be on the level of major motifs: incarnation, sacrifice, substitution, etc. As Lewis reminds us, "The only moral [or doctrinal lesson] that is of any value is that which arises inevitably from the whole cast of the author's mind" ("Three Ways" 33). We want to know the theology that lies behind Narnia and the Field of Arbol. But if Lewis gave us an accurate description of what he was doing, we should expect first to find it *taught* it in expository works like *Mere Christianity* and *Miracles*, and then see it *illustrated* by Narnia and the Space Trilogy. And his description was accurate, for it is consistent with the nature of the kind of fiction he wrote.

A third complication arises from Lewis's strategy of focusing only on what he called "mere Christianity." In the book of that name he deliberately tries to avoid giving any advice to people who are hesitating between two "rooms" of the "house" of Christianity; he only wants to get them into the "hall." (He does tell them to look for truth rather than nice paneling or a charismatic doorkeeper, but gives no guidance as to which room best fits that criterion.) This is a strategy he tried to follow in all of his writing and public speaking on behalf of the faith. As he wrote to Edward T. Dell on 29 April 1963, "A great deal of my utility has depended on my having kept out of all dog-fights between professing schools of 'Christian' thought" (*L* 3:1425).

My point here is not to criticize Lewis for this strategy. It was what he took to be his calling, and he was certainly right that it contributed in significant ways to his usefulness. It has its advantages, and I follow it in some circumstances myself. But it does present some challenges for those wishing to study Lewis's theology. For Christian doctrine is not just a random set of unrelated propositions, but an integrated whole in which every part is related to every other part and all find their center in the very character of the God who revealed Himself in Christ to the Prophets and the Apostles. To leave something out because it is controversial or thought (by some) not to be central, is not necessarily just to leave something out; the omission might have an unintended effect on what is left in. And while many denominational differences are indeed over tragically peripheral matters, not all are. Some on both sides have thought that some of the questions at issue between Protestants and the Church of Rome, for example, go right to the heart of what the Gospel is.

Lewis's "mere Christian" stance then was both an asset and a liability to his ministry, and both sides of that equation need to be taken into account. It is something we must remember in evaluating his teaching. One of the problems it creates is that it opened up space for speculation by those who would like to enlist Lewis as allies for their own traditions. Fortunately, he sometimes allowed himself in private correspondence to take positions he would not have taken publicly, and we can use these moments to fill in gaps in the picture. They not only serve to eliminate certain unfruitful speculations; they can also provide context that illuminates his public theology at certain points. Thus the new expanded three-volume edition of Lewis's letters is indispensable to anyone who wishes to get a complete view of Lewis's thinking.

Another challenge is the sheer volume and range of Lewis's writing. Popular apologetics, fiction, poetry, works of literary scholarship, letters, volumes of essays collected by Walter Hooper—there are well over forty books all told, and none of them irrelevant. For Lewis's mind, and consequently his work, was all of a piece. His friend and fellow Inkling Owen Barfield said that the unity of Lewis's thought came from a quality Barfield called "presence of mind." By this he meant that "somehow what [Lewis] thought about everything was secretly present in what he said about anything" (Edwards, *Pineapple* 2). He did not expound Christian doctrine in his literary scholarship, but his views there were informed by the same Christian world view that he expounded directly elsewhere. When we add to that the fact that he was often commenting on Christian writers, trying to win a sympathetic hearing for writers like Milton, for example, we realize that there is nothing in his body of writing so technical or obscure that it might not contain something relevant to our topic. One of the fringe benefits of this study then will be the way in which it illustrates the truth of Barfield's claim.

A final consideration is the development of Lewis's theology. The unity of Lewis's mind and his concentration on the central doctrines of "mere Christianity" make it easy to ignore this question; indeed, it often makes little difference if one does. But one cannot assume this to be the case. One of the virtues of Vaus's study is the fact that he treats Lewis's writings chronologically under each topic, so that where there was development the reader can see it unfolding. Here we are going to be more interested in the interrelationships of Lewis's ideas than in their development, but we will take note of that development when it is relevant.

CONCLUSION

By calling C. S. Lewis an "amateur" theologian I do not mean to imply that he was not a good one or in any way an unimportant one. The word should be taken in its etymological sense of one who does something, not for a living, but for the *love* of it. Love for God, love for God's truth, love for God's people: apart from these loves, no one should presume to handle sacred things. In this sense, all the laity should be theologians and all the clergy amateurs.

That Lewis had the right loves for the job is evident. His love of God helped him to keep himself out of the center and Christ in it. He wrote to Mary Margaret McCaslin on 2 Aug. 1954 that he was shocked to hear that her friends were following him. "I wanted them to follow Christ. But they'll get over this confusion soon, I trust" (*L* 3:501). His love of the truth made him value faithfulness: "If any parts of the book are 'original,' in the sense of being novel or unorthodox, they are so against my will and as a result of my ignorance" (*PoP* viii). His love of God's people sent him to the BBC and to many RAF camps during the Second World War and made him work hard at the task of "translation." His love of good English didn't hurt either. He wrote to Jocelyn Gibb on 11 July 1959, lamenting that so many people who get involved in academic research seem to lose both the desire and the ability to write "clear, sharp, and unambiguous English. Hold onto your finite transitive verb, your concrete nouns, and the muscles of the language (*but, though, for, because,* etc.). The more abstract the subject, the more our language shd. avoid all unnecessary abstraction" (*L* 3:1069).

All these loves, combined with the drive for the integration of reason and imagination we discussed above, contributed to Lewis's greatness as a writer and a theologian. I think they also helped him see clearly what is at stake in our theology:

> Here is a door, behind which, according to some people, the secret of the universe is waiting for you. Either that's true, or it isn't. And if it isn't, then what the door really conceals is simply the greatest fraud, the most colossal "sell" on record. Isn't it obviously the job of every man (that is a man and not a rabbit) to try to find out which, and then to devote his full energies either to serving this tremendous secret or to exposing and destroying this gigantic humbug? ("Man or Rabbit" 111-12)

Lewis so devoted his energies, and he can help us to do so too.

I've been talking throughout this introduction about why we should care about Lewis as a theologian and care about his theology. Perhaps I can best sum it up by applying to him words he wrote about John Milton. For in the final analysis, we only honor Lewis's memory to the extent that we do not really care that these ideas were Lewis's. We will only please his departed spirit if we care about them to the extent that they are *true*. And so I think he would be pleased if we see him as a guide who can point beyond himself, as Beatrice did for Dante, and as Milton did for Lewis himself:

> We are summoned not to hear what one particular man thought and felt about the Fall, but to take part, under his leadership, in a great mimetic dance of all Christendom, ourselves soaring and ruining from Heaven, ourselves enacting Hell and Paradise, the Fall and the repentance. (PPL 60).

In that spirit, let us begin.

CHAPTER I

Prolegomena A
What is Truth?

What I like about experience is that it is such an honest thing. You may take any number of wrong turnings; but keep your eyes open and you will not be allowed to go very far before the warning signs appear. You may have deceived yourself, but experience is not trying to deceive you. The universe rings true wherever you fairly test it. (SbJ, 177)

The word theology (θεολογια) comes from two Greek words: θεοσ (*theos*), God, and λογοσ (*logos*), word or reason. Hence theology is most basically words about God or reasoning about God. For historic Christians it is usually understood to involve a systematic attempt to exhibit what we know about God and His relationship to His creation, particularly His actions to bring salvation to His fallen creatures, human beings. (By "historic Christians" here, I mean people, whether Protestant, Roman Catholic, or Orthodox, who affirm historic Christianity as it is summarized in the ecumenical creeds. They are Trinitarians who believe in the deity and humanity of Christ, and that He died for our sins and rose again. They basically trust the Bible as teaching truth when rightly interpreted, though they may differ on the role of the Church in that interpretation. Classical Protestant liberalism, which denies the core content of the historic faith while still clinging to the name "Christian," is not included in these generalizations.)

A systematic attempt to exhibit what we know about God: If that is indeed the theologian's task, then the very first question we have to answer in doing it is, how in God's name do we dare? How do we presume to say we know anything about Him at all? What *can* finite creatures claim to know about the Infinite Creator? How do they know it? On what basis do they validate that knowledge? What are the correct and fruitful methodologies for pursuing it? Such questions constitute a theological topic called "Prolegomena"—things that come first. In other words, before you can ask what is true about God, you first have to have an understanding of what is truth. Pilate asked the right question. His mistake was not waiting for the answer.

So, how *do* we presume? Historic Christians believe that God has revealed Himself in nature, in history, and in Christ, and that this revelation is authoritatively recorded, focused, and interpreted for us in Scripture. This gracious self-revelation by God is the only thing that makes theology possible. Finite and fallen human beings could never find Him out by seeking; He must stoop to us. Therefore, historic Christians conceive of theology as the explication of that revelation, especially as it is recorded in and interpreted by Scripture. Consequently, theology, when pursued professionally and academically by historic Christians, tends to have a structure something like this:

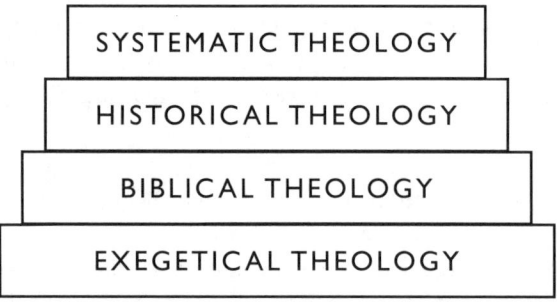

Exegetical theology, the foundation, is the study of individual passages of Scripture (ideally in the original languages using grammatico-historical exegesis) to determine their meaning in context. Biblical theology puts those passages together into larger units to determine themes and motifs and see the development of doctrine through progressive revelation within the biblical canon. Historical theology concerns itself with how various theological questions have been answered in the history of the church, both to discern historical consensus and to avoid reinventing the wheel. Systematic theology then tries to synthesize all of that into a unified presentation of the content of what Christians believe about God and man. When fully developed, it might look something like this:

SYSTEMATIC THEOLOGY {
- **PROLEGOMENA**
  The Nature of Truth
  "What is Truth?"

- **DOGMATICS**
  The Content of Truth
  "What is true?"

- **APOLOGETICS**
  The Defense of the Truth
  "Why is it True?"

- **ETHICS**
  The Application of Truth
  "So What if it's True?"

- **POIMENICS**
  (Practical Theology)
  The Inculcation of the Truth
  "How do we feed on the Truth?"

C. S. Lewis as an intelligent Christian asked the questions; as a Christian trained in philosophy and literature who was a humble student of Scripture and tradition, he had something to say about the answers. Because he was not a professional theologian, he did not give systematic treatments of methodology, nor did he lay the substance of those answers out in a systematically structured form as I have done above. But in many occasional writings, and in others that attempt systematic treatments of limited topics (e.g., miracles, the moral argument for theism, theodicy), he manages to touch on each one of the topoi above—indeed, to say quite a bit about them. So let us assume the basic structure of theological prolegomena and focus in on Pilate's question and the implications that flow from its answer: What is truth? Can we have truth about God? Is theological truth a special kind of truth? How do faith and reason relate? What about truth and myth? Etc. In this chapter, we will look at Lewis's writings on the most basic of all these questions, the first one: What is truth? Then chapter two will examine his perspectives on the related questions that flow from it as they are applied to the pursuit of theological truth.

WHAT IS TRUTH?

"Beauty is truth, truth beauty. That is all / Ye know on earth, and all ye need to know," says Keats' Grecian Urn. If the Romantics tended to conflate Truth and Beauty, the Moderns tended to explain Beauty away as a mere subjective emotional response; and now some Post-Moderns seem to do the same with Truth itself. C. S. Lewis, rooted in the classical Christian world view, sought a more whole vision of the relations among the Transcendentals than any of these other approaches can provide. One way of summarizing that Christian view is to say that truth when we find it in the world is a reflection of God's mind, goodness of His character, and beauty of His glory, impressed into the very fabric of what He has made (see Kreeft 23-5). It was Beauty, coming through Joy, or *sehnsucht* (see *SBJ*), that led Lewis to Truth. But to truth he believed he had been led. What was Lewis's view of Truth? How did he defend it against the Reductionisms prevalent in the middle of the Twentieth Century? Can that defense still help us to withstand the assaults typical of our own times? What does this view of truth say about the pursuit of theology? These are the questions on which we shall attempt to shed some light. In our age of Post-Modernism and Post-Foundationalism, when the very concept of truth is subject to deconstruction, there are hardly any more important questions we could address.

THE NATURE OF TRUTH

Simply put, C. S. Lewis held to the classical "correspondence theory" of truth: Truth is a property of propositions such that their content corresponds to the state of affairs in the real and objective external world which they assert to be, and which in fact is, so. So far Lewis is not original in his concept of truth. His contribution at this point is helping us to a fuller and richer understanding of what it means to hold such a concept. For example, he complains that naturalists who don't believe in truth are being disingenuous. From their books, "in which the behaviour of the remotest nebula, the shyest proton, and the most prehistoric man are described, one would have got the idea that they were claiming to give us a true account of real things" (M 24).

The key words here are "account" and "real things." Truth is propositional; it is an *account*. The person holding to these propositions, i.e., making this account, may not be capable of perfect objectivity. Indeed, if he is a finite human being, he cannot be; but his account is an account of objective reality nonetheless, of *real things*. And he can in theory overcome his subjectivity sufficiently to verify the truth of his account, if indeed the nebulae, protons, and cavemen behave as his propositions claim they do; if the state of affairs they assert "obtains" in the real world.

The theoretical possibility of thus sufficiently overcoming our subjectivity—and knowing when we have done so—is then essential to our ability to perceive, know, and state truth as correspondence. Traditional philosophy and nihilistic Post-Modernism actually agree on this point; they part company on the question of whether that possibility exists. Lewis argues that it has to. One person's mental version of New York City can be closer to the truth than another's only because there is an actual New York to compare them to. If when they said "'New York' each meant merely 'The town I am imagining in my own head,' how could one of us have truer ideas than the other? There would be no question of truth or falsehood at all" (*MC* 25).

Post-Kantian relativism, before we even arrive at Post-Structuralism and Deconstruction, holds that the real objective New York, the New York *an sich* (German: "as it is in itself"), is unreachable, and that therefore only the phenomenal New York, the one that exists as an image constructed in our heads, can be directly known. Common sense would seem to be on the side of Lewis and the older Tradition, though; for there actually is a real New York, and the simple expedient of visiting it can determine which of two accounts of it is closer to the reality, so that the town being imagined in one head can be rejected in favor of that being imagined in the other for good and sufficient reason—to wit, the town existing outside of either head. Is Times Square in Manhattan, Brooklyn, Queens, Staten Island, or the Bronx? Unless the real New York outside our heads both exists and is accessible *to* our heads, the question is unanswerable. But the question is in fact answerable; therefore, truth must be what Lewis conceived it to be, an account of New York that is theoretically capable of getting what we think closer to the real place that exists quite apart from what any of us thinks.

The existence of truth in this sense entails the existence of falsehood. Of contradictory propositions, only one of them can be true, and if that one is true, the other must perforce be false. Lewis thought the Hindus described by his student Dom Bede Griffiths sounded delightful, but wanted to know, "What do they deny? That's always been my trouble with Indians—to find any proposition they would pronounce false. But truth surely must involve exclusions?" (*L* 3:704). A precondition of truth then is the universal validity of the law of non-contradiction. Two contradictory propositions cannot both be true in the same way, in the same place, at the same time. If they could, the claim that either was true would be empty.

In other words, a true thought "reflects," not just the mind of the thinker, but "universal reality" ("*De Futilitate*" 60). "Christianity claims to give you an account of *facts*—to tell you what the real universe is like" ("Man or Rabbit?" 108). One who claims anything less is simply not claiming that Christianity (or any other account of the state of things) is *true*.

The radical nature of this concern for truth was apparent already by the middle of the Twentieth Century, as can be seen by looking at some of the typical academic concerns of late Modernism with which Lewis contrasts it.

> What makes some theological works like sawdust to me is the way the authors can go on discussing how far certain positions are adjustable to contemporary thought, or beneficial in relation to social problems, or "have a future" before them, but never squarely ask what grounds we have for supposing them to be true accounts of any objective reality. (*Malcolm* 104)

Screwtape encourages Wormwood to make good use of such a climate:

> Your man has been accustomed, ever since he was a boy, to have a dozen incompatible philosophies dancing about together inside his head. He doesn't think of doctrines as primarily "true" or "false," but as "academic" or "practical," "outworn" or "contemporary," "conventional" or "ruthless." Jargon, not argument, is your best ally in keeping him from the Church. Don't waste time trying to make him think materialism is *true*! Make him think it is strong or stark or courageous—that it is the philosophy of the future. (*SL* 8)

> In the intellectual climate which we have at last succeeded in producing throughout western Europe, you needn't bother about that [the fact that earlier writers like Boethius had told the truth]. Only the learned read old books, and we have now so dealt with the learned that they are of all men the least likely to acquire wisdom by doing so... When a learned man is presented with any statement in an ancient author, the one question he never asks is whether it is true. He asks who influenced the ancient writer, and how far the statement is consistent with what he said in other books, and what phase in the writer's development, or in the general history of thought it illustrates, and how it affected later writers, and how often it has been misunderstood... and what the course of criticism has been on it for the last ten years, and what is the "present state of the question." (*SL* 128-9)

Now in the Post-Modern world we have added concerns for what racial, class, or gendered interests the ideas in question advance, how they fit into or illustrate the power-broking structures of society, etc. It is not that these questions, or the ones Lewis noticed (which are still with us), are always devoid of interest, legitimacy, or relevance. They become problematic when they are used as a substitute for the search for *truth*, a way of endlessly deferring the question of truth, which is thought to be unattainable anyway. And that is precisely how they often do function, not surprisingly given that Derrida correctly realized that once the very possibility of truth has been banished, the "play of signification" is extended precisely to infinity (1207).

Here is the point: Lewis would want to ask of the claim that, by the very nature of discourse, questions of truth are endlessly deferred: "Is it true? Does it correspond to the way things actually are in the real world?" And this is a question that Derrida, for example, would have had to refuse to answer; it is a question that simply has no meaning in his system. If we accepted the Deconstructive analysis, we would have to limit ourselves to questions of race, gender, class, and power too, for the truth question would be unaskable.

So the question whether a view of truth can itself be true (or false) turns out to be pretty basic. Can we correct the New York in our heads by the one in the American Northeast, or are we rendered unable to do so, trapped inside our heads, whether by Kantian categories or by the specious language games preferred by Post-Modern intellectuals? Putting off for the moment a field trip to the Big Apple, we can realize that there is no question as to which side of that divide Lewis occupied.

Not all people who have held the correspondence theory of truth have been theists. But Christian theism if accepted does provide a solid grounding for such a view of truth. If we believe in a personal and rational God who not only acts but speaks, and who has created our finite minds in His image, then it is easier to conceive of truth as both existing and knowable. There is a stable reality to which our propositions can correspond, and our minds were designed to deal with that reality by the same Mind that designed it. If God exists and has spoken, then He is Himself the ultimate source of truth, and His Word the ultimate criterion of truth. The complaint that there is no "God's eye view of the world" is then simply based on a false premise. There is one; God has it; and He has communicated at least some parts of it to us. All truth then comes from Him, either directly or indirectly. Lewis of course lived comfortably in this world: "Whatever was true in Akhenaton's creed came to him, in some mode or other, as all truth comes to all men, from God" (*RotP* 86).

So far Lewis is solidly in the mainstream of Christian thinking about truth. Augustine and Aquinas, Calvin and Wesley, Cardinal Newman and Carl F. H. Henry would all have affirmed these basic points, though not perhaps with Lewis's characteristically deft use of apt analogy. What Lewis adds to the discussion is some careful thinking about the relations of truth not only to reason but also to imagination. It was his experience and his conviction that, "All things, in their way, reflect heavenly truth, imagination not least" (*SBJ* 167). How exactly does imagination do so?

Some of Lewis's interpreters, influenced perhaps by the surface resemblance in language between Lewis and the English Romantics, have not paid sufficiently careful attention to how Lewis answers that question. One reads vague statements like, "Truth flows into a person through the imagination" (Uszynski 247) and even more inexact summaries like the following: "Lewis, like many Romantics, intuitively trusted the capacity of imagination to be a 'faculty of truth'" (Tixier 141). What Lewis actually said was much more carefully and rigorously thought out:

> We are not talking about truth but meaning: meaning which is the antecedent condition of both truth and falsehood, whose antithesis is not error but nonsense. I am a rationalist. For me, reason is the natural organ of truth; but imagination is the organ of meaning. Imagination, producing new metaphors or revivifying old, is not the cause of truth, but its condition. ("Bluspels" 265).

Imagination is the faculty or organ not of truth (directly) but of *meaning*, which is the "antecedent condition" of truth. What does this mean? Suppose I utter the proposition, "Blepple hloisats kleply flarg krunk bluzzles," and then ask you for a verdict on its truth or falsehood. I suspect you would be somewhat handicapped in trying to render that verdict by the fact that you would have no idea what I had said. Before you could even begin to form a judgment on the truth question, you would need to know what a hloisat is, how a blepple one differs from a regular one, what it is to flarg, what a bluzzle is, what is the quality of krunkness, and how flarging kleply differs from regular flarging. In order to give you that information I would have to render these objects, qualities, and actions in concrete terms that you could visualize. Your Imagination would be the faculty that enabled you to form a picture—an image—of what the proposition is asserting (or whether it is asserting anything). Then your Reason would compare that mental picture to the picture of reality it has already tested and come to trust, in order to see if correspondence or contradiction resulted.

Imagination, in other words, doesn't give us truth, contrary to what Tixier implies. Just because we can imagine something does not make it real. But Imagination combined with Reason can give us *meaningful truth, truth that impacts us on other levels than mere academic intellectual assent.* This is truth that can appeal to head and heart together. Lewis was the master of giving it to us, whether in his expository prose or his fiction. The hall and rooms of a house for the church and its denominations; two books which have always been resting one on the other for the eternal generation of the Son; the keys of a piano and a tune for the relationship between our instincts and the moral law; entrusting oneself to the waves and floating islands of Perelandra rather than sleeping on the fixed land for faith; the Stone Table for the Law and Aslan's death cracking it for the Gospel; Reepicheep the Mouse for valor, chivalry, and honor: The brilliant artistic construction of these images does not prove that they are images of truth. But their presence in the context of the linear arguments and narrative trajectories of which they are a part makes the truths established by those lines of development mean something; it makes their impact, their beauty, and their relevance easier to see *and to feel.*

Mythology for Lewis was one of the most important places where this contribution of imagination to our ability to grasp the meaning of true (or false) propositions is seen. It is well known that for Lewis myth was not the opposite of truth, as it is in popular usage, but rather one way in which truth can be conveyed or embodied. Myth is not necessarily "lies breathed through silver" (as the pre-conversion Lewis once foolishly said to Tolkien), but can be "a real though unfocused gleam of divine truth falling on human imagination" (Tolkien, "Beowulf" 54; Lewis, *M* 139n.). Myth may then convey these truths to the imaginations of readers, who might then independently verify them through reason and hence validly accept them as true. Thus George MacDonald's modern mythic stories helped move Lewis in the direction of Christian faith by giving a meaning to the concept of holiness, even as Lewis's own stories have done for countless readers since. The mythical quality of the story refers in Lewis's usage to its meaningfulness rather than its truth or falsehood as such, which must be established on other grounds. Hence Lewis could without contradiction refer to the New Testament story of Jesus' birth, death, and resurrection as "myth become fact" ("Myth Become Fact" 67).

Lewis is careful to use this language correctly even in his fiction. "Long since on Mars, and more strongly since he came to Perelandra, Ransom had been perceiving that the triple distinction of truth from myth and both from fact was purely terrestrial—was part and parcel of that unhappy division between soul and body that resulted from the Fall" (*Pa* 143-4, cf. "Myth Became Fact" 66). Fact in this passage is the bit of reality that truth is about; truth the account that corresponds to that reality; myth the story that allows us to taste the particular tang of that fact ("Myth Became Fact" 66). Ransom experiences in Perelandra the pre-analytical unity that lies behind the differentiated categories.

When one is inside a myth, in other words—say, on Perelandra with Ransom—one experiences the unified reality from which all three flow. When talking about that experience later, one has perforce to use the differentiated language, and Lewis does so consistently. He was doing so even in his earliest Christian fiction: "Child, if you will, it is mythology. It is but truth, not fact; an image, not the very real" (*PR* 171). A true statement about reality is not reality; not even a mythical statement is reality; but it may be true nonetheless, i.e., it may correspond to that reality in a faithful manner. Because the meaningful creating and sustaining acts of a personal, purposeful, and rational God are the ultimate source of all reality, there is indeed a real unity between fact and truth, and between both and myth, the most meaningful statement of truth. Wolfe captures it well: "Ransom's education has led him to see that it is not merely the idyllic worlds of Malacandra and Perelandra which are 'mythological,' but that reality itself, when perceived truly, is as dense with meaning as myth" (Wolfe 68). And some of this meaning may be stated propositionally, and some of those propositions may be confirmed by Reason as true.

Lewis then embraces the traditional and standard correspondence theory of truth and enriches it by relating truth to imagination and myth. Truth is a property of accounts or propositions such that their assertions correspond with reality. Imagination is the organ of meaning, the antecedent condition of truth or falsehood, i.e., of the meaningfulness of those accounts claiming to be true or false. Reason, which distinguishes and discerns correspondence or non-correspondence (between those propositions and each other, between them and reality) and pursues their implications, is the organ of truth. Myth is a story that enables the imagination to receive and taste ways of seeing the world that reason can then confirm as true or false.

This view of truth, traditional and standard, was already under attack in Lewis's own day, and that attack has only intensified since. How did he defend it?

THE DEFENSE OF TRUTH

Above we raised the question whether a view of truth can itself be true. It is time to see how Lewis answered that question in the case of the correspondence theory of truth. He gives two basic reasons why we should accept the correspondence theory of truth as true. First, it cannot be denied without self-contradiction. Second, it corresponds to the way in which people do in fact come to true knowledge about the world.

Lewis advanced the argument from self-contradiction in many ways and in many contexts. The most well-known and fully developed place is the chapter of *Miracles* originally titled, "The Self Contradiction of the Naturalist." Attempts to answer technical objections raised by Elizabeth Anscombe when the argument was presented at the Oxford Socratic Club caused the water in that chapter to be muddied a bit in later editions, with the title changing to the "Cardinal Difficulty" of Naturalism. Either way, the argument is that Naturalism must itself be false because it participates in the inevitable self-refutation of all views that entail radical skepticism. (See Reppert for a fine history and evaluation of the Anscombe debate, and Williams, "Printing Error," to bring that discussion up to date.)

A good summation of the argument appears in the essay "*De Futilitate:*"

> Can we carry through to the end the view that human thought is *merely* human: that it is simply a zoological fact about *homo sapiens* that he

> thinks in a certain way; that it in no way reflects ... universal reality? The moment we ask this question we receive a check. We are at this very point asking whether a certain view of human thought is true. And the view in question is just the view that human thought is not true, not a reflection of reality ... In other words, we are asking, "Is the thought that no thoughts are true, itself true?" If we answer Yes, we contradict ourselves ... There is therefore no question of a total skepticism about human thought. ("*De Futilitate*" 60-61)

If true statements do not correspond to real states of affairs in the external world, if they are not "reflections of reality," then the very claim that truth is not a reflection of reality does not correspond to the way things actually are either, and thus it self-destructs. This is so whether the reason why we allegedly cannot know that some statements accurately reflect reality is the physical determinism entailed by naturalism (Lewis's opponent in *Miracles*), the cynicism of the Greek sophists, or the linguistic solipsism of Post-Modern Deconstructionists.

Lewis's usual foil was naturalism. If Nature is all that there is, then the laws of physics—not the laws of logic—determine everything. The thoughts I am having are mere chemical reactions taking place in my head, determined solely by the movements of atoms set in random motion by purposeless and unintelligent processes ages ago. But, then, so are the thoughts of the person who disagrees with me. "What we called his thought was essentially a phenomenon of the same sort as his other secretions—the form which the vast irrational process of nature was bound to take at a particular point of space and time" ("Religion without Dogma" 136). Who is to decide between these two chemical reactions? A third chemical reaction produced by the same random, purposeless processes? This takes us nowhere. So Lewis quotes J. B. S. Haldane: "If my mental processes are determined wholly by the motions of atoms in my brain, I have no reason to suppose that my beliefs are true ... and hence I have no reason for supposing my brain to be composed of atoms" (*M* 22). Lewis agreed. If naturalism were true, it would have to be false. For if it is true, then:

> All our present thoughts are mere accidents—the accidental by-product of the movement of atoms. And this holds for the thoughts of the materialists and astronomers as well as for anyone else's. But if their thoughts—i.e., of Materialism and Astronomy—are merely accidental by-products, why should we believe them to be true? I see no reason for believing that one accident should be able to give me a correct account of all the other accidents. ("Answers" 52-3)

It follows then that

> At least one kind of thought—logical thought—cannot be subjective and irrelevant to the real universe: for unless thought is valid we have no reason to believe in the real universe.... I conclude then that logic is a real insight into the way in which real things have to exist. In other words, the laws of thought are the laws of things. ("*De Futilitate*" 63)

That thought be logical is a necessary but not a sufficient condition of truth that is *known* to be truth. A proposition that someone holds may just happen to be true; it may be true by luck. But unless it has a logical basis, we cannot *know* it to be true. And a proposition may be logically consistent or coherent without corresponding to external reality. To maintain a belief in knowable truth, in other words, we must have more than logic but cannot have less. Thus we can be certain that, "No account of the universe can be true unless that account leaves it possible for our thinking to be a real insight" (*M* 20).

The correspondence theory of truth itself then is not only logically consistent; it is logically necessary if there is to be any knowable truth at all. Furthermore, it matches the way people actually come to discover and hold truth. How do we actually come to know truth? The additional element that we have to add to logic is *experience*. There is a real New York that transcends any of our perceptions of New York (the New York "in my own head" that we saw above) and is capable of correcting those perceptions and adjudicating between them. If we do not know which picture of the city is more accurate, we can go and look.

But can we really? Post-Modern theory argues that we cannot step outside of our perceptions to experience the New York *an sich* because the perception we receive through experience is itself mediated through our background, our beliefs, our language, and our situatedness. There is no such thing as uninterpreted experience; any experience to which we might appeal has already been interpreted, so that there is no "God's eye view" from which our perceptions can be evaluated and no final conclusion that can be reached about what reality is in itself outside our perceptions. As Derrida famously put it, "There is nothing outside the text."

Was Lewis then caught in a naïve Modernism so that his appeals to reason and experience are simply passé? He never had the opportunity to respond to thinkers like Derrida, of course. But he was confronted by earlier forms of cultural and epistemological relativism, and so we can easily imagine what his response might have been. Radical skepticism is no less self-refuting when it is based on clever theories about language than when it is based on philosophical or scientific naturalism. It cannot be true without untruthing itself; therefore, it cannot be true. In the case of Post-Modern forms of this sophistry, Lewis might have noted the prevalence of reductionistic thinking. The demonstration that we cannot avoid having our thinking *influenced* by our language, race, gender, class, etc., is mysteriously elevated (while no one is looking) into the conclusion

WHAT IS TRUTH?

that our thinking must perforce be *determined* by those influences. The fact that we normally define language by using other language is extrapolated into the theory that language only refers to other language and has no ability to refer to anything outside of language. But as Smith points out,

> Language . . . is the only means we have of making truth claims. Likewise, it is the only means we have of debating the veracity of such claims. Unless we wish to give over the entire business of making and challenging claims to truth, we must accept the referentiality of language, metaphoricity and all. Otherwise, we must be ready to admit that statements such as "Metaphor is nonreferential" do not refer to anything except themselves. Such would probably be the starting point of any defense Lewis might make of the referentiality of metaphor. (22).

Can the real New York ever, even potentially, break through all these influences to smack us in the face with reality? Our experience tells us that, whatever the dictates of Theory to the contrary may be, in fact it can if we just step out of the ivory tower into the street. Lewis's attitude toward experience, and toward the external world which provides us with those experiences, is therefore quite refreshing compared to the suffocating claustrophobia of much current thinking:

> What I like about experience is that it is such an honest thing. You may take any number of wrong turnings; but keep your eyes open and you will not be allowed to go very far before the warning signs appear. You may have deceived yourself, but experience is not trying to deceive you. The universe rings true wherever you fairly test it. (*SbJ* 177)

Truth then is a property of propositions such that they correspond to real states of affairs in a real world. We hold to this view because to deny it is self-refuting and because reality rewards us in the search for truth in such terms when we approach it fairly. One must assume these truths even to argue against them. And the best response to those theories that seem to compromise or deny them is not just counter-theorizing, but stepping outside of the ivory tower into the street to allow the real New York to do its work.

THE RELEVANCE OF TRUTH

Lewis not only expounds the correspondence theory of truth, enriches it by relating it to imagination as well as reason, and defends it successfully; he also has a lot to say about its implications for life and thought.

First, if we are confident in the existence of truth and the ability of human minds to know it, we are liberated from chronological snobbery. We are freed from the provincialism of the biases of our own age to become citizens of history and receive truth from any mind in any time, not just those who share the perspectives of our own limited "situatedness." "Space does not stink because it has preserved its three dimensions from the beginning. The square of the hypotenuse has not gone mouldy by continuing to equal the square of the other two sides" ("Poison" 76). Truth becomes something we can find *and hold on to*. Only if it is reduced to perspective does it change into something else by the mere passage of time.

Second, it is impossible fully to understand human nature or to seek its fulfillment without a robust understanding of the nature of truth and confidence in its reality. In *The Abolition of Man*, human beings are those creatures who live not by instinct but by *understanding* of the *Tao*. Lewis agreed with Aristotle that all men naturally desire to know: "One of the things that distinguishes man from the other animals is that he wants to know things, wants to find out what reality is like, simply for the sake of knowing. When that desire is completely quenched in anyone, I think he has become something less than human" ("Man or Rabbit?" 108).

A human being divorced from the quest for truth is less than human because human beings were created in the image of the God of truth, for fellowship with the God of truth, which entails not just the knowledge but also the embracing of truth and the rejection of the lie. This fact makes our orientation toward truth a matter not just of fulfillment but of moral obligation.

> When Professor Price defended scientists, speaking of their devotion to truth and their constant following of the best light they knew, it seemed to him that he was choosing an attitude in obedience to an ideal. He did not feel that he was merely suffering a reaction determined by ultimately amoral and irrational sources, and no more capable of rightness or wrongness than a hiccup or a sneeze. ("Religion without Dogma" 137)

Lewis approves of this stance, even though Price may not have realized that his attitude ultimately flows from the relation of the creature to the Creator who is the God of truth. It is the duty of true humanity to feel this way: "Every free man wants truth as well as life: . . . a mere life-addict is no more respectable than a cocaine addict" (*M* 24).

Therefore, to acquiesce in the mere freeplay of perspectives rather than pursuing the search for truth is to betray the purpose for which our minds were created. In a passage that prophetically anticipates a Post-Modern buzz word, the liberal bishop in *The Great Divorce* is warned, "Thirst was made for water; inquiry for truth. What you now call the free play of inquiry has neither more nor less to do with the ends for which intelligence was given you than masturbation has to do with marriage" (44). The choice of metaphor is not only daring but telling. Truth was intended to be experienced not just as an intellectual abstraction but as a participation in reality that has union with the ultimate Reality, the Source of all reality, as its end. The rejection of truth is finally a rejection of that union, a form of spiritual adultery. Every philosophy that reduces truth to merely a subjective mind state dehumanizes us and cuts us off, not only from God, but from all that is good and real. As the George MacDonald character in *The Great Divorce* explains, "Every state of mind, left to itself, every shutting up of the creature within the dungeon of his own mind—is, in the end, Hell. But Heaven is not a state of mind. Heaven is reality itself" (*GD* 69). The Dwarfs in *The Last Battle*, clinging to the stable-litter of their minds, are a graphic picture of this epistemological captivity.

Flowing from all this is a third point: Seeking and finding and embracing the truth is not a matter just of intellectual curiosity but of moral and spiritual life and death. The importance of truth cannot be overstated in this view. And because truth flows from the creative decrees of the spiritual God who created the material world, the true propositions whose embrace is so crucial to us correspond not just to physical reality but to the unseen realities, to morals and values, as well. This means that, as in the argument of *The Abolition of Man*, morals and values *are* objective realities, not just subjective feelings or perspectives. Therefore, "Unless we return to the crude and nursery-like belief in objective values, we perish" ("Poison" 81).

The most critical truth to be embraced or refused is of course the truth about the God from whom the world of reality flows. Every person therefore has a moral obligation to consider the claims of the Christian faith very seriously—whether or not he or she sees any immediate pragmatic benefit in holding those beliefs. This above all is not a merely academic discussion.

> Christianity claims to give you an account of *facts*—to tell you what the real universe is like. Its account of the universe may be true, or it may not, and once the question is really before you, then your natural inquisitiveness must make you want to know the answer. If Christianity is untrue, then no honest man will want to believe it, however helpful it might be; if it is true, every honest man will want to believe it, even if it gives him no help at all. ("Man or Rabbit?" 108-9)

Truth comes before any use we might make of it, and we find it only when we recognize that fact. "If you look for truth, you may find comfort in the end. If you look for comfort, you will not get either comfort or truth—only soft soap and wishful thinking to begin with, and in the end, despair" (*MC* 39). Though the search for truth is a value in itself that supersedes any pragmatic benefit that might come from finding it, there is of course pragmatic benefit to knowing and embracing the truth: comfort, perhaps, and more important things besides.

"If Christianity should happen to be true, then it is quite impossible that those who know this truth and those who don't should be equally well equipped for leading a good life" ("Man or Rabbit?" 109). But there is something even greater at stake than how good a life we might lead. We noticed Lewis's statement of what is at stake in the Introduction, but it is worth quoting again:

> Here is a door, behind which, according to some people, the secret of the universe is waiting for you. Either that's true, or it isn't. And if it isn't, then what the door really conceals is simply the greatest fraud, the most colossal "sell," on record. Isn't it obviously the job of every man (that is a man and not a rabbit) to try to find out which, and then to devote his full energies either to serving this tremendous secret or to exposing and destroying this gigantic humbug? ("Man or Rabbit?" 112)

Lewis devoted his life to "serving this tremendous secret," to living, explaining, and defending the Christian faith. The fourth implication of Lewis's view of truth as he develops it is what it means for living the Christian life. To believe in truth and take it seriously is to make the quest for truth paramount not only in deciding to become a Christian, but also in those decisions one makes because one is a Christian—for example, the choice of a local church or a denomination. Applying his analogy of the church universal as a house with its hall and rooms, Lewis advises, "Above all you should be asking which door is the true one; not which pleases you best by its paint and paneling." The bottom line question should not be whether we liked that kind of service, but rather, "'Are these doctrines true?'" (*MC* 12).

TRUTH AND FAITH

If truth is central to what Christianity is, then we have to understand the central Christian act—belief—in terms of our concept of truth. Faith becomes something oriented to truth, a stance one takes toward the truth. If this is so, it becomes harder to think of faith as a primarily emotional response, or as unrelated to specific propositions about God and the world, or as the inclination to affirm as true propositions that would otherwise not commend themselves as such. Faith is trust in a Person which causes us, not merely to acknowledge, but to embrace as true, those ideas and facts about that Person which we have come to believe (in Lewis's case, on what he thought were good grounds) that He has revealed to us. Faith adds the emotional and personal element of trust and commitment to what would otherwise be a merely notional relationship to those propositions. That is why Lewis can say, "I define Faith as the power of continuing to believe what we once honestly thought to be true until cogent reasons for honestly changing our minds are brought before us" ("Religion: Reality or Substitute?" 42). He devotes an entire essay, "On Obstinacy in Belief," to explaining this relational element as the reason why the Christian's belief, once established, does not waver with "every fluctuation of the apparent evidence" (29). For one who holds Lewis's classical view of truth, then, faith is something that is more than propositional and evidential, but it can never be less.

Faith then is a stance toward a Person, and to certain propositions seen in relation to the Person who is believed to have revealed them, which embraces them as true not as a matter of opinion but of trust and commitment. The lack of evidence is not what constitutes this stance as belief or faith rather than knowledge. Lewis (and many others) have thought the evidence quite good. But the fact that the particular relationship to which these beliefs lead and which they nurture is the rather overwhelming and life-changing one of creature to Creator, sinner to Savior, and servant to absolute Sovereign—a relationship infinitely satisfying to many who embrace it but daunting enough in prospect to have caused Lewis to describe his conversion as being dragged kicking and screaming into the Kingdom—means that there is a lot more going on than the mere disinterested perusal of evidence. There are many more sources for doubt than lack of irrefutable evidence. So Lewis can see faith as the support of reason as much as the other way around:

> Religion may win truths; without Faith she will retain them just so long as Satan pleases.... If we wish to be rational, not now and then, but constantly, we must pray for the gift of Faith, for the power to go on believing not in the teeth of reason but in the teeth of lust and terror and jealousy and boredom and indifference that which reason, authority, or experience, or all three, have once delivered to us for truth. ("Religion: Reality or Substitute" 43)

Truth then for the Christian is a serious intellectual matter that can never be only intellectual. It is at the heart of our created humanity and of its fulfillment in relationship to its Creator. In a healthy and whole human being, truth simultaneously informs the intellect, inspires the emotions, and energizes the will. Lewis would have understood Bacon:

> The inquiry of truth, which is the lovemaking or wooing of it, the knowledge of truth, which is the presence of it, and the belief of truth, which is the enjoying of it, is the sovereign good of human nature.... Certainly it is heaven upon earth to have a man's mind move in charity, rest in providence, and turn upon the poles of truth. (Bacon 40)

It is not just reason and imagination that are unified by Lewis's holistic view of truth; it is head and heart, being and doing, and every other aspect of our humanity as well. That unity is well expressed by Lewis's final bit of advice: "A man can't always be defending the truth; there must be a time to feed on it" (*RotP* 7). In his fiction, his poetry, and his expository writing, Lewis helps us to do just that.

CONCLUSION

C. S. Lewis's exposition of truth, its nature, its grounds, and its implications, is increasingly a voice crying in a wilderness of radical perspectivalism. Various forms of reductionism today conspire to render truth claims nothing more than subjective responses and cynical power plays. Sadly, so pervasive is this way of thinking, so cloaked in the robes of academic sophistication and respectability, that even some Christians have inconsistently acquiesced in such views and helped to perpetuate them. Lewis can help us see what is at stake as well as provide a roadmap back to sanity.

The materialist reductionism Lewis battled is still with us. Reppert, for example, critiques thinkers like Patricia Churchland who think that evolutionary explanations of the nervous system render the concept of truth otiose: "Either truth is our highest epistemic goal and there is a state of the person called 'believing truly,' or else we have no epistemic goal and we can engage in various cognitive projects without being held to an absolute standard by which those projects can be judged" (77). To that materialist reductionism have now been added other forms of cultural and linguistic reductionism with similar or even more deadly effects. Edwards notes,

> Some recent composition theorists have come to view their task as stripping away the illusions that language can capture and bear witness to "truth" or "reality." ... The purpose of writing instruction under the new literacy regimes is to prepare the writer to recognize and inhabit the world of "truths" that he himself creates, as opposed to the world of truths he might discover outside himself.... Lewis would regard these views as a retreat to a Gnosticism that not only does not shield humankind from manipulation or error, but instead guarantees error by undermining the ontological status of knowledge and belief. (103)

Those who still aspire to the wholeness of an examined life and connection to a reality greater than themselves will find in Lewis a stout defender of the legitimacy and necessity of that quest, and an experienced guide to lead us in it. Is truth when we find it in the world a reflection of God's mind, goodness of His character, and beauty of His glory, impressed into the very fabric of what He has made? C. S. Lewis not only explains why we should think so; he lets us taste and see.

CHAPTER 2

Prolegomena B
The Task of Theology

> *Everyone has warned me not to tell you what I am going to tell you in this last book. They all say 'the ordinary reader does not want Theology: give him plain practical religion.' I have rejected their advice. I do not think the ordinary reader is such a fool.* (MC 135)

All right, then: Truth is a property of propositions such that they correspond with what they assert to be so about the real world. Is it possible to generate propositions in finite human languages that correspond with what is so about the infinite God? Can theology, in other words, really claim to be about truth? If so, how? How is it possible, and what must we do to ensure that we can realize that possibility? Those are the questions that have to be answered next.

THE DOCTRINE OF REVELATION

Lewis's definition of theology makes those questions pressing: "By theology, we mean ... the systematic series of statements about God and about man's relation to Him which the believers of a religion make" ("Is Theology Poetry?" 115). This definition requires us to answer the question, "On what basis do they make them?" How can they possibly claim to know such things? For Christians, the answer is that, before we speak about God, He has spoken to us. Put simply, Lewis explains, "Christians think that God Himself has taught us how to speak of Him" ("Priestesses" 237). Finite human beings are capable of doing what they otherwise could not do, speak truly about the infinite God, because He has made statements of His own, statements that instruct us in how to speak truly and profitably about Him. Who else could know better how to tell us just what we need to hear about Him? So we love Him because He first loved us (1 Jn. 4:19), and we speak of Him because He first spoke to us. Other religions may reflect human attempts to answer such questions on their own, but the Christian religion is not something we invented; it is not even something God invented, but rather "His statement to us of certain quite unalterable facts about His own nature" (MC 47).

How does God make these "statements"? The traditional Christian answer is that He makes them in nature, in history, in Scripture, and supremely in Christ. God speaks in nature because the heavens declare His glory (Ps. 19:1) and the things which are visible speak of His invisible attributes (Rom. 1:20). As developed in the classical arguments for God's existence, the universe testifies to His reality and nature by being contingent, intelligently designed, finely tuned, etc. God speaks in history through His mighty acts such as the rescue of Israel from Egypt in the Exodus and the life, death, and resurrection of Christ, the climactic revelation to which everything else points. He speaks in Scripture through the inspired words of the Prophets and the Apostles, anticipating, predicting, narrating, and explaining that supreme revelation in Christ, and interpreting the non-verbal forms of revelation. Because the revelations in Scripture come to us already in propositional form, in other words, they guide us in the task of interpreting what we learn from the other sources and formulating it into propositions of our own which constitute the "systematic series of statements" about God and man which is our theology. To this standard account Lewis would add the "good dreams" that God sent even to the Pagans, and which we access through pagan myths, which spoke to us of such motifs as the dying god before Christ enacted them in history as "myth become fact."

REVELATION IN NATURE

Each of these forms of revelation has its own role to play, complementary to that played by the others. Lewis has some original insights about the role of nature: it is more than just a vaguer, less focused form of what we receive from Scripture or history. One thing we get from nature is "an iconography, a language of images" that gives meaning to the ideas God reveals in other ways (FL 36). Lewis explains, "Nature never taught me that there exists a God of glory and of infinite majesty. I had to learn that in other ways. But nature gave the word glory a meaning for me. I still do not know where else I could have found one" (FL 37). The splendor of the night sky, the vastness and power of the ocean, the sublimity of a mountain landscape, the diversity in unity of the passing seasons, allow our imaginations to form some concept of infinity, majesty, glory, etc., that gives them meaning and keeps them from being mere abstractions when we apply them to the more explicit revelations in history or Scripture.

Nature is part of God's whole program of revelation because He intends His revelation to speak to the whole person. Nature's role is to engage the imagination, for reason is the organ of truth, while imagination is the organ of meaning ("Bluspels" 265). Nature functions this way, not arbitrarily, but because it reflects its Maker: as Lewis explained to Father Peter Milward, SJ, on 10 Dec. 1956, because invisible realities are manifested to us by visible ones, "one might from one point of view call the whole material universe an allegory" (*L* 3:816). Not only does nature give meaning to our ideas, it also impels our response to those truths in worship by making it meaningful too: "Of every created thing I praise, I should say, 'In some way, in its unique way, like Him who made it.' Thus up from the garden to the Gardener, from the sword to the Smith. To the life-giving Life and the Beauty that makes beautiful" (GO 50).

REVELATION IN HISTORY

Even more explicit is God's revelation through His mighty acts in history. As Lewis explains in his treatment of the problem of evil, "Christianity is not the conclusion of a philosophical debate on the origins of the universe. It is a catastrophic *event*." It is not a system into which we have to fit whatever facts confront us; "It is itself one of the awkward facts that have to be fitted into any system we might make" (*PoP* 12, emphasis added). The key phrase here is *catastrophic event*. There was actually a coordinated series of them, leading up to the coming of Christ: Creation itself, the Fall, the Flood, the Call of Abraham, the Exodus—all pretty catastrophic. The one Event, or complex of events, that Lewis no doubt had in mind is the incarnation, birth, life, death, and resurrection of Christ. Christian theology is not first and primarily a series of philosophical reflections (though it generates quite a few of them); it is a response to something that happened in history, something that Christians believe changes everything. "God so loved the world that He gave His only begotten Son" (Jn. 3:16) is not a philosophical speculation or the conclusion to a deductive argument. It is something that happened in first-century Palestine. Christians do not typically believe it as the conclusion of a long chain of abstruse reasoning. They believe it because they think God acted in Christ to reconcile the world to Himself (2 Cor. 5:19). They believe it as a response to that *act*.

It might seem surprising to some that Lewis saw history as a source of revelation, if they remember his skepticism about what he called "historicism," the belief that historians through historical method can discern a meaning or goal to history as a whole. But Lewis did not reject history as a source of revelation outright. He objected to the *extension* of the concept of revelation to events in history on which God had not commented in Scripture. He explains,

> I am not denying all access whatever to the revelation of God in history. On certain great events (those embodied in the creeds) we have what I believe to be divine comment which makes plain so much of their significance as we need, and can bear, to know. On other events ... we have no such comment. ("Historicism" 112)

"Divine comment"? This phrase leads to the importance of Scripture as the lens that brings historical (and natural) revelation into focus. But the doctrine of Scripture is important enough to merit a chapter of its own, so we will say nothing more about it here.

REVELATION IN MYTHOLOGY

Perhaps Lewis's most original contribution to the theology of revelation is the way he sees myth, including pagan myth, as a source of revelation—not of authoritative revelation (like Scripture) but of substantive revelation (like nature and history). This concept is "original," not in the sense that Lewis was the first to think of it (for he got the idea from Tolkien and from Chesterton before him), but because it is mainly through Lewis that most conservative Christians are first introduced to the idea that pagan myth could be anything other than false religion. To understand Lewis's view here, we have to understand something about how he returned from atheism and materialism to the Christian faith.

As a young man Lewis had come to the place where he cared for nothing but the gods and heroes and believed in "nothing but atoms and evolution and military service" (*SbJ* 174). The stab of "joy" or romantic longing (*sehnsucht*) that came to him through the great myths seemed to hint at a larger world of meaning and purpose, but he thought there was no reason to believe in any of the religions, that modern knowledge had exploded them and left only materialism and cynicism in their place. But first G. K. Chesterton's book *The Everlasting Man* and then Christian friends like J. R. R. Tolkien began to challenge his pessimistic assumptions.

The first mention of *The Everlasting Man* in Lewis's autobiography gives it a significant role in preparing the young atheist for that fateful evening on Addison's Walk with J. R. R. Tolkien and Hugo Dyson in 1931 which would lead to Lewis's conversion: "Then I read Chesterton's *Everlasting Man* and for the first time saw the whole Christian outline of history set out in a form that seemed to me to make sense" (*SbJ* 223).

How did *The Everlasting Man* prepare Lewis for the conversation with Tolkien and Dyson on Addison's Walk? The skeptical Lewis had that evening foolishly described myth and fairy tale as "lies breathed through silver," provoking from Tolkien the response that was later summarized in poetic form in the piece that became part of the essay "On Fairie Stories."

> "Dear Sir," I said—"Although now long estranged
> Man is not wholly lost or wholly changed.
> Dis-graced he may be, yet is not dethroned,
> And keeps the rags of lordship once he owned:
> Man, Sub-creator, the refracted Light
> Through whom is splintered from a single white
> To many hues, and endlessly combined
> In living shapes that move from mind to mind.
> Though all the crannies of the world we filled
> With Elves and Goblins, though we dared to build
> Gods and their houses out of dark and light,
> And sowed the seed of dragons—'twas our right
> (Used or misused). That right has not decayed:
> We make still by the law in which we're made. (54)

Tolkien's full response elaborated what he would later in that essay call the doctrine of sub-creation: human beings are creative because we are created in the image of the Creator; we make (stories, among other things) because we are made in the image of the Maker whose creation is the Story we call the history of the universe. In other words, myth and its power can only fully be understood in the light of the Christian doctrine of the *imago Dei*, which explains what myth is, why it is, and why describing it simply as lies is just too simple. "Used or misused, that right has not decayed; / We make still by the law in which we're made" (54).

Well, Lewis had already encountered in *The Everlasting Man* the idea that Christianity is "that pure and original truth that was behind all mythologies like the sky behind the clouds" (258) and Chesterton's connection of "the philosophy of stories" with man's uniqueness: he is "a creator as well as a creature" (18). Thus, "Man is not merely an evolution but a revolution" (8). And this, as Chesterton explained, is why human stories, as reflections of The Human Story, are so unlike the apocryphal "history of cows in twelve volumes" which "would not be very lively reading" (158).

So then, Tolkien and Dyson did not have to start from scratch. They were watering a seed that Chesterton had already planted when they told Lewis that, as he summarized the conversation to his friend Arthur Greeves, "The story of Christ is simply a true myth," affecting us emotionally and aesthetically just like other myths do, "but with this tremendous difference that *it really happened.*" That explained why Lewis loved the great myths and fairy stories even without believing in them and why he loved the idea of sacrifice, especially a god sacrificing himself to himself, when he met it in other myths: they were adumbrations of the truth, "God expressing Himself through the minds of the poets, using such images as He found there, while Christianity is God expressing

Himself through what we call 'real things'" (*L* 1:977; cf. Sayer 225-7, Green and Hooper 116-18). And they were watering another Chestertonian seed when they told Lewis that the significance of myth flows from human nature as made in the image of the Maker. Both ideas were already there in *The Everlasting Man*, which had already shown Lewis the Christian outline of history in a way that made sense. And the connections between the two ideas were there too, waiting for Tolkien and Dyson at the right moment to pull them together.

The truth that lies behind all the great myths like the sky behind the clouds; the true myth that works on us like all the others but unlike them really happened: these ideas came together on Addison's Walk on September 19, 1931, and, as a result, on September 28 Lewis realized that he had finally come to believe that Christ was the Son of God while riding in Warnie's side-car on the way to the Whipsnade Zoo. The conversation with Tolkien had "illuminated what Lewis already knew to be true and pulled all the previously disjointed pieces into a harmonious vision of reality" (Burson and Walls 162). It was the tipping point in his journey to theism and Christian faith, and became central to his thinking from then on. (See for example the essay "Myth Became Fact," which is Lewis's way of saying the things he learned from Chesterton and Tolkien.)

Pagan myths may very well have been simply false religion to the people who actually believed in them. To Lewis they were something God used to point him to Christ. They had awakened in him a sense of the divine and a fascination with the motif of the dying god who sacrifices himself for his people. Thus they pointed to truths, truths which were not strictly true as embodied in the myths, but profoundly true as they were fulfilled in Christ. Much as nature functions to give meaning to theological ideas by speaking to the imagination, so myth can prepare the way in a similar manner:

> To be truly Christian, we must assent to the historical fact and also receive the myth (fact though it has become) with the same imaginative embrace which we accord to all myths.... Perfect Myth and perfect Fact: claiming not only our love and our obedience, but also our wonder and delight, addressed to the savage, the child, and the poet in each one of us no less than to the moralist, the scholar, and the philosopher. ("Myth" 67)

THE IMPLICATIONS OF REVELATION FOR THEOLOGY

We can speak about God because He has taken the initiative to reveal Himself to us in nature, history, myth, and Scripture; and in Christ, who is the Lord of nature, the climax of history, the fulfillment of myth, and the theme of Scripture. For Lewis, God's revelation is directed to the whole person, specifically, to the imagination as much as to the reason. What do these perspectives mean for our understanding of what theology is and how we should pursue it?

REVELATION AND TRUTH

For Lewis, the study of what God has revealed about Himself and His relation to us is the study of the truth about those things. "Religion involves a series of statements about facts, which must either be true or false" (*MC* 72). Christian theology is not just mystical speculation about the Unknown. If God has revealed Himself, that act changes everything, as Lewis understood. It means that theology is about a created world that has a certain form; it is about a history in which certain events took place. Lewis allows no fact-value dichotomy anywhere in his thinking, and he is not going to allow it here. If God really exists, then He is the source of all reality, and therefore reality is what theology is about. God's laws, for example, are not just emotional statements of "values" but descriptions of moral reality: they have "*emeth*, 'truth,' intrinsic validity, rock-bottom reality, being rooted in His own nature" (RotP 61). To say that theology is about truth is simply to say that it is about reality.

> What makes some theological works like sawdust to me is the way the authors can go on discussing how far certain positions are adjustable to contemporary thought, or beneficial in relation to social problems, or "have a future" before them, but never squarely ask what grounds we have to supposing them to be true accounts of any objective reality. (*LtM* 104)

To say that theology is about truth and reality means that its truth is objective. "In coming to understand anything we are rejecting the facts as they are for us in favour of the facts as they are" (*EiC* 138). What revelation says is a reality that is prior to any response we might or might not make to it.

Theological statements may have far-reaching practical consequences. "If Christianity should happen to be true, then it is quite impossible that those who know this truth and those who don't should be equally well equipped for leading a good life" ("Man or Rabbit?" 109). But theological statements have these consequences because, and only because, they are true. "Christianity is a statement which, if false, is of *no* importance, and, if true, of infinite importance" ("Christian Apologetics" 101). To ask first whether an idea is "beneficial in relation to social problems" is to get the cart before the horse. We believe theological statements because they commend themselves to us as true, not because we think they are emotionally satisfying or useful. If the Christian faith has nothing to offer us but a little more good advice, "then Christianity is of no importance" (*MC* 137). The question of truth comes first.

REVELATION AND "CHONOLOGICAL SNOBBERY"

If theology is about truth based on fact, then its content should be basically stable. It is not going to change with every passing generation and its changing prejudices and perspectives. Christianity "is what it is and was what it was long before I was born and whether I like it or not" (*MC* 7). We can develop in our understanding of the truth, but the truth itself does not change. And a search for truth that is revealed in history and in ancient myth, a truth that by its very nature is found by looking into the past, brings with it a respect for the ancient formulations that have stood the test of time. Thus we should emulate theologians like Athanasius, whose glory is "that he did not move with the times; it is his reward that he now remains when those times, as all times do, have moved away" ("Old Books" 206). Chronological snobbery, the prejudice that says the most modern and up-to-date perspectives are always the best, must be resisted, and that resistance must often take the form of the restoration of the tried and true from the past: "Would you think I was joking if I said that you can put a clock back, and that if the clock is wrong it is often a very sensible thing to do?... If you are on the wrong road, progress means doing an about-turn ... and the man who turns back soonest is the most progressive man" (*MC* 36).

> Prejudice against the new would be equally prejudiced; new insights into old truth are certainly possible. But prejudice against the new is not the temptation to which our generation is prone. So the faithful theologian will be one who reminds us that "All that is not eternal is eternally out of date" (*FL* 188).

REVELATION AND REASON

For Lewis, if theology is about reality, then it is related to reason, for reason is the organ of truth. As we saw in chapter one, "Logic is a real insight into the way in which real things have to exist. In other words, the laws of thought are also the laws of things" ("*De Futilitate*" 63). Indeed, both Philosophy and Theology are "younger sisters" of Reason (*PR* 68). This does not mean, as in much modern theology, that human reason limits what revelation can say, but rather that the truths of revelation, once revealed, will obey the laws of reason because the mind of God is the source of both. Reason alone cannot reveal truth; it cannot determine content. (It is not the organ of truth in that sense.) But it tells you what you can do with the content that is delivered to you, whether it is revealed by empirical experience or divine authority. Thus, the truth that God reveals about Himself can be expected to go beyond reason, but it will not ever contradict reason.

Lewis deals with the role of reason in two works that bookend his career, his first and last Christian novels. Lady Reason in *The Pilgrim's Regress* and The Fox in *Till We Have Faces* both represent reason and speak to both its role and its limits. In response to John's questions, Lady Reason answers, "I cannot tell you, because you do not know" (*PR* 67). Reason cannot generate truth; it can only tell us the legitimate implications of truth we get from other sources. It can "bring things out of the dark part of your mind into the light part of it" (*PR* 67).

The Fox, unlike the Lady, is not an allegorical figure for reason. He symbolizes something broader that includes reason, philosophy, and science. His implications for the theological task are similar, though. Not only reason, but human thought (including reason) are indispensable but can only take us so far. They are necessary but not sufficient tools for understanding the divine. Psyche, trying to explain her faith in the god of the mountain to Orual, says that "The Fox hasn't the whole truth. Oh, he has much of it. It'd be dark as a dungeon within me but for his teaching. And yet . . ." (TWHF 70). Trying to explain her knowledge of the gods after she has met them, she says, "There was a lot of the Fox's philosophy in it—things he says about gods or 'the divine nature'—but mixed up with things the Priest said, too, about the blood and the earth and how sacrifice makes the crops grow" (TWHF 109-110). What philosophy and mythology have of truth must somehow be integrated into one vision, because neither alone really lets you understand the gods; for that, you have to *meet* them. Only then can you know what really to make of either philosophy or mythology. God must reveal Himself or there is no real theology. Reason must serve, must wait upon and be dependent on, that act of revelation. But reason *must* serve revelation. Revelation is trans-rational but not irrational.

REASON AND ANTITHESIS

So, then, if reason cannot generate knowledge of God by itself but applies to the knowledge that revelation has delivered, what follows? First, antithesis applies to theological statements. Truly contradictory statements can no more be true about God than of anything else, for He is "above" reason only by virtue of being its Source. Hence, "being a Christian does mean thinking that where Christianity differs from other religions, Christianity is right and they are wrong" (*MC* 43). The self-contradictory is "absolutely impossible" (*PoP* 15). "Meaningless combinations of words do not suddenly acquire meaning simply because we prefix to them the two other words 'God can'" (*PoP* 16). Because God's thoughts are higher than ours, because He is infinite, theology will contain many apparent paradoxes. God is something more superior to us than we can measure or imagine. "Unless you know God as that—and therefore know yourself as nothing in comparison—you do not know God at all. As long as you are proud you cannot know God" (*MC* 111). But because God is rational, there will be no true contradictions.

If antithesis applies to theological propositions, then if one of them is true, its opposite is false. As Bill the Blizzard reminds us, "Eh? Two views? There are a dozen views about everything until you know the answer. Then there's never more than one" (*THS* 72). People have a general reluctance to face this fact, especially when dealing with matters as exalted as theology. We want to have our (il)logical cake and eat it too. Lewis explains that attempts to marry heaven and hell are perennial. They are

> based on the belief that reality never presents us with an absolutely unavoidable "either-or"; that, granted skill and patience and (above all) time enough, some way of embracing both alternatives can always be found; that mere development or adjustment or refinement will somehow turn evil into good without our being called on for a final and total rejection of anything we should like to retain. (*GD* 5)

Lewis rejects such beliefs as dangerous errors.

THEOLOGY AND METAPHOR

God's revelation sometimes comes to us in ready-made propositions—but not often. Nature is an allegory of spiritual reality; history gives us not propositions about God's attributes or intentions but events which show them in action. Mythology captures human yearnings for and glimpses of divine reality perhaps, but one can hardly derive doctrines from them. Even Scripture, though it is revelation propositionalized, as it were, comes to us mostly in the language of history and poetry rather than theology. This situation is not an obstacle; it is a stepping stone, if we understand it. It means that we must pay attention to images, figures, and metaphors, for they are the very substance of revelation, not merely adornments of it. Lewis understood that, because God has chosen to reveal Himself in such terms, the terms are a given that we just have to accept and must not tamper with. Liberal theologians think they are making an advance in understanding by translating revelation into abstract terms, but they are really just obscuring it.

> All language, except about objects of sense, is metaphorical through and through. To call God a 'Force' (that is, something like a wind or a dynamo) is as metaphorical as to call Him a Father or a King. On such matters we can make our language more polysyllabic and duller; we cannot make it more literal. ("Horrid Red Things" 71)

Lewis understood that such attempts are often simply a smokescreen for the rejection of God's actual message to us in favor of a modern secular world view. As he wrote to Mary Van Deusen on 16 Jan. 1959, "'Demythologising' the N.T. always really means *re*-mythologising it: i.e., clothing it in the popular scientific and historical theories of your own period which are in fact transitory and will soon seem as mythological as those of the first century" (3:1012).

The images and metaphors—Father, King, Judge, Savior, etc.—were chosen by God as the way He wants us to think of Him. They are not arbitrary, culturally bound pictures of universal philosophical abstractions that we can safely dispense with. To think so is to misunderstand not only revelation but also language and literature. To change them is to change everything. "We have no authority to take the living and semitive figures which God has painted on the canvas of our nature and shift them about as if they were geometrical figures" ("Priestesses" 239).

THE NECESSITY OF CRITICAL THINKING

If these things are true, then another implication of understanding the role of reason in theology is that good theology, and following from it good Christian living, are not possible without careful thinking. God's revelation is not a random series of unrelated propositions but rather a coherent and unified vision of reality with Him at the center. Understanding this truth requires attention to the implications and relations of the beliefs we proclaim and live by. Our fallen propensity to use our minds for rationalization makes some Christians suspicious of the mind, but the abuse does not overturn the right use. For Lewis, the Enemy of our souls understands this even if we do not. Screwtape warns Wormwood that "the trouble about argument is that it moves the whole struggle onto the Enemy's own ground" (SL 8), and reminds him that "the way must be prepared for your moral assault by darkening his intellect" (SL 95). In her attempt to deceive Puddleglum and the children, the Green Witch throws on the fire a powder that "made it harder to think" (TSC 181). Sound thinking about God and the truths He has revealed does not by itself ensure, but it does foster, obedience and true spirituality, while unsound thinking about these matters has moral consequences as well: "Nonsense draws evil after it" (FL 48). The very essence of Satan's rebellion against God as Milton portrays it is summed up in his call, "Evil be thou my good." This prayer, Lewis notes, "includes 'Nonsense be thou my sense'" (PPL 92).

Positively, all our faculties are engaged in understanding truth about God, and the processes by which we evaluate it are not radically different from those we use with any other set of data. This explanation of Lewis's conclusions about the reality of God and how he came to them is typical:

> Authority, reason, experience; on these three, mixed in varying proportions, all our knowledge depends. The authority of many wise men in many different times and places forbids me to regard the spiritual world as an illusion. My reason, showing me the apparently insoluble difficulties of materialism and proving that the hypothesis of a spiritual world covers far more of the facts with far fewer assumptions, forbids me again. My experience even of such feeble attempts as I have made to live the spiritual life does not lead to the results which the pursuit of an illusion ordinarily leads to, and therefore forbids me yet again. ("Religion: Reality or Substitute" 41)

THE LIMITATIONS OF REASON

Theology presents us with a practical dilemma. If God is true and the Source of reason, then the truth about Him ultimately coheres as unified and consistent; but if God is infinitely above us, we will not always easily be able to discern that unity and consistency. We must never affirm actual contradictions, but we are often presented with truths that we have a hard time holding simultaneously in our finite minds. Lewis wisely realizes that we just have to make up our minds to live with this tension. Mrs. Emily McLay had been troubled about strongly Calvinistic conclusions that seemed to follow from biblical assertions that we did not chose God, but He chose us (Jn. 15:16, Eph. 1:4, etc.). Lewis wrote to her on 3 Aug. 1953 that: "Generalisations are legitimate only when we are dealing with matters to which our faculties are adequate. Here, we are not" (3:355). The MacDonald character in *The Great Divorce* says that our questions about hard issues like predestination versus free will cannot be answered because we are trying to see eternity through the lens of time. In such a case, "All answers deceive" (*GD* 124). We cannot answer such questions. Maybe God could answer them; but they may not be answerable at all.

> Can a mortal ask questions which God finds unanswerable? Quite easily, I should think. All nonsense questions are unanswerable. How many answers are there in a mile? Is yellow square or round? Probably half the questions we ask—half our great theological and metaphysical questions—are like that. (*GO* 55)

Therefore, we should stick to the narrow path of what has been revealed and avoid speculation, or at least carefully distinguish between our speculations and revealed truth. As Lewis wrote to Edward T. Dell, on 4 Feb. 1949, "I have no *doctrine* on such a purely speculative point" (2:914).

The fact that our theology will never achieve a final synthesis in which all questions are answered is owing to our own limitations (e.g., as sinful people and as people who inhabit time rather than eternity), not to any irrationality in God or flaws in reason itself. We must finally stick to what we have been told: "To know what would have happened, child?" said Aslan. "No. Nobody is ever told that" (*PC* 149). This conclusion is consistent with the premise that theology begins with revelation. We must not forget that the purpose of revelation is to make it possible for fallen human beings to know and worship and serve God again through the redemption which is in Christ. It is not primarily to satisfy our curiosity. Thus, The Lord's statements about Hell, like all His statements, "are addressed to the conscience and the will, not to our intellectual curiosity" (*PoP* 107). Therefore a right relationship with God, which includes a profound humility before Him, is a prerequisite to a wholesome pursuit of theological truth.

THEOLOGY AND HUMILITY

Theology requires clear thinking and serious intellectual effort. But these things alone are not sufficient. That stance of humility is required both for the willingness to receive God's revelation as revelation and the ability to process it profitably. Not only Atheism but also much bad theology arises from our lack of willingness to let God be God. "What you see and hear depends a good deal on where you are standing: it also depends on what sort of person you are" (*TMN* 148). Ultimately we must be dead to self and willing to take up our cross daily before we are ready to receive and do theology. Only so is the humility to give up our preconceived notions attainable. Otherwise, we will end up like Uncle Andrew: the more Aslan sings in the creation of Narnia, the more beautiful and articulate the song is, the harder Uncle Andrew tries to convince himself that all he could hear was roaring. "Now the trouble about trying to make yourself stupider than you really are is that you very often succeed" (*TMN* 150). Uncle Andrew's problem is not a lack of evidence or experience, for he is hearing the very same symphony of creation as everyone else. It is a lack of faith. He refuses to receive what he is being offered. He does not have the humility to receive or to trust, and consequently he cannot believe. He does not understand that, while understanding doctrine can lead to obedience, a heart that wants to obey is often the prerequisite to understanding—as Jesus said in John 7:17. So Lewis points out, "The minimal religion in fact cannot, while it remains minimal, be acted on. As soon as you start to *do* anything you have assumed one of the dogmas" ("Religion Without Dogma?" 141).

This humility has practical consequences. It prevents us from putting too high a value on our individual views, and makes us attentive to the wisdom of the great creedal consensus at the core of the Christian tradition. It is highly unlikely that where Augustine, Aquinas, Luther, Calvin, and Wesley all agree against me, I am the one who is right while they are wrong. "The only safety" in dealing with those issues where Christians disagree "is to have a standard of plain, central Christianity ('mere Christianity' as Baxter called it) which puts the controversies of the moment in their proper perspective" ("Old Books" 201). The humility to accept mutual correction is also important, and that correction comes not just from our contemporaries but from all the saints who have gone before us. No single individual mind is adequate to comprehend the rich range of Christian truth. Indeed, "the one really adequate instrument for learning about God is the whole Christian community waiting for Him together" (*MC* 144).

THE ROLE OF FAITH

And so the role of reason in theology (its necessity, its limits, and the humility that flows from the recognition of those limits) leads inevitably to a consideration of the role of faith. Indeed, if our knowledge of God depends on His revelation, then theology begins and ends with faith. We must humbly listen to, trust, and believe what is given to us before we can think about it and understand it. Unlike many moderns, Lewis understands that this does not mean that faith is blind acceptance, a leap in the dark. Revelation may come with or include the reasons why we should accept it, and the questions raised by our existence in the world along with the inadequacy of secular philosophy to answer them may have prepared us to accept those reasons. Yet still the decision to trust or not is set before us, and the pride that insists on our being able to verify everything ourselves and believe only what we can comprehend with our fallen and finite minds weighs against that decision to trust. We face this reality in its starkness at Aslan's table. "'You can't know,' said the girl. 'You can only believe—or not'" (*VDT* 217). Not only the humility to receive grace, but also Reepicheep's courage, is required to accept the invitation to the feast. Reason can take us part way, but not all the way. Only after the decision to trust—which is faith—can the real theological feast begin.

Lewis at this point is in line with the New Testament and the older Christian tradition. Faith is trust, pure and simple. It is not an alternative way of knowing other than reason or some kind of mystical experience that somehow bypasses reason and normal experience. It is personal trust in God as heavenly Father that embraces His promise of salvation in Christ. It is the personal element, not some alternative way of knowing, that makes it more than disinterested calculation. Lewis defines it in practical terms as "the power of continuing to believe what we once honestly thought to be true until cogent reasons for honestly changing our minds are brought before us" ("Religion: Reality or Substitute" 42; cf. "Obstinacy in Belief"). God responds to our faith so that it brings us into a personal relationship with Him that goes beyond what we can specify and enables us to persevere through the changing tides of emotion.

Though Lewis does not use the phrase, we could define faith as he presents it as "openness to revelation." Uncle Andrew hears the music of Narnia's creation as noise because that is all he is willing to hear. The liberal theologian in The Great Divorce refuses answers and can never experience the historic Christian faith as true because he has closed himself to the very possibility: "For me, there is no such thing as a final answer" (*GD* 43). His saved friend from the Mountains asks him, "When in our whole lives did we honestly face, in solitude, the one question on which all turned: whether after all the Supernatural might not in fact occur?" (*GD* 40). The ultimate expression of unbelief is the

Dwarfs in the stable, whose cynicism forces them to experience violets as manure. "'You see,' said Aslan. 'They will not let us help them. They have chosen cunning instead of belief. Their prison is only in their own minds, yet they are in that prison; and are so afraid of being taken in that they cannot be taken out'" (*TLB* 185-6). It brings us full circle to our initial insight. The reason of finite creatures cannot discover the truth about the infinite God on its own. Either He has revealed Himself, and rational theology is possible, or He has not. And we are either open to that possibility, in which case theology is possible for us, or we are not. Lucy or the Dwarfs: that is the choice that lies before us at the beginning of the theological task.

CONCLUSION

And at the end? "But who is Aslan?" asks Eustace. "Do you know him?" "Well, he knows me," Edmund replies (*VDT* 117). We love God because He first loved us (1 Jn. 4:19); we can speak of Him because He first spoke to us. Theology is about knowing God, but knowing God is about more than theology. We cannot know God personally without knowing certain things about Him—otherwise we might be worshipping a false god. But the information is not for its own sake but is to the end of the personal knowing. Christian faith is not in abstract Theism but in the God of Abraham, Isaac, and Jacob, the Father of our Lord Jesus Christ. "We trust not because 'a God' exists, but because *this* God exists" ("Obstinacy" 25).

And that is ultimately why theology and theological truth matter. The liberal theologian in The Great Divorce is told, "You think that [there is no final answer] because hitherto you have experienced truth only with the abstract intellect. I will bring your where you can taste it like honey and be embraced by it as by a bridegroom. Your thirst shall be quenched" (*GD* 43). Lewis himself had experienced at least a few foretastes of that vision. He wrote Sister Penelope, CSMV, on 9 Nov. 1941, "There is so much difference between a doctrine and a realization" (*L* 2:495). You study the doctrines in hopes of receiving the realization.

Theology is not that final vision. We must not confuse the two, but neither should we despise theology, for it can be part of what helps to enable us to come there. Lewis compared theology to a map of the ocean. In this analogy, religious experience, which for the Christian can at best be real personal experience of fellowship with God, would be like walking on the beach and getting wet with the spray. That is reality; the map is only a picture. But even our experiences in this life are only glimpses, and we want to get to the place where we will be able to see much more. So Lewis's advice is good: "As long as you are content with walks on the beach, your glimpses are far more fun than looking at a map. But

THE TASK OF THEOLOGY

the map is going to be more use than walks on the beach if you want to get to America" (*MC* 136). Even here and now we will experience more of the glimpses if we use the map. As long as we stick to the central consensus that had guided the church over the centuries, to mere Christianity as it were, the maps are quite trustworthy. "Maps can be wrong. But the experienced walker knows / That the other explanation is more often true" ("Pilgrim's Problem," *Ps* 120).

Lewis hews to that central path in his most basic explanations of the nature of the theological task. He points us to God's self-revelation in nature, in history, and in Scripture. He helps us see more clearly what nature contributes to that revelation by thinking carefully about the role of imagination in responding to nature. His nuanced defense of the necessary role of reason, despite its limitations, may sound radical to modern and post-modern ears, but faithfully represents the heart of the Christian tradition going back to the Apostles through Augustine. His common-sense view of faith as personal trust cuts through a lot of mystical verbiage to get us back to what the Apostles certainly meant when they told us in the earliest preaching of the Gospel to *believe* on the Lord Jesus Christ (Acts 16:31).

Lewis's most original contribution to theological prolegomena is his most controversial and problematic: adding pagan myth to nature and history as a source of general revelation. When we understand the role that mythology played in Lewis's own conversion and understand in that context what he meant by saying that Christ was the fulfillment of all that was true in even the pagan myths, then Christianity as "myth become fact" is a powerful insight that enhances our appreciation for the depths and the wholeness of God's revelation and of His work for our salvation. But this is also an idea that is perilously susceptible to misunderstanding and needs to be handled with great care.

For most of the earliest Christians, as for Hebrew believers in Yahweh before them, pagan mythology was simply the false religion of their neighbors, more of a stumbling block than an aid to faith. And we are returning to an age when the rise of serious neo-paganism once again makes it more dangerous to say some of these things, harder to say them without being misunderstood. Pagan deities as mere symbols rather than false gods were a luxury that we might have had in the West for a millennium or so, ending with Lewis's own life—but it is one that we may have less and less. Yet even in the midst of the living paganism of the ancient world, the Apostle Paul on Mars Hill was able to appeal to a pagan altar to an unknown god as a pointer to the real One. Therefore, we should be aware of the dangers associated with using Lewis's insight carelessly, but not be frightened away from it completely. Truth, not danger, is the ultimate arbiter of theology, and Paul's example confirms that there is truth in Lewis's insight.

Lewis is revealed as an important theologian, then, not just because he was a writer able to present theological content with winsome clarity to the masses, but because his presentation of the nature and purpose and task of theology shows powerfully how it can and should be made to speak to the whole person. His defense of truth as objective correspondence to reality is one of the most incisive and rich we have ever seen. And his insights into how that truth can be pursued insistently push us toward an openness to it that involves head and heart, mind and imagination, not just both working but working in concert. He wants, he pushes us to want, to "make imagination's dim exploring touch / Ever report the same as intellectual sight." And he shows us how to do it. To the extent that we are able to follow him, we will be able to affirm as he did: "Then could I truly say, and not deceive, / Then wholly say, that I BELIEVE" ("Reason," *Ps* 81).

CHAPTER 3

Bibliology
The Doctrine of Scripture

"Remember the signs. Say them to yourself when you wake in the morning and when you lie down at night, and when you wake in the middle of the night. And whatever strange things may happen to you, let nothing turn your mind from following the signs. . . . Here on the mountain I have spoken to you clearly: I will not often do so down in Narnia." (TSC 25)

Theology begins from the fact that God has revealed Himself in Christ through nature, history, mythology (for Lewis), and Scripture. For historic Christians, Scripture has always had a privileged place in that constellation of sources. Nature is cursed, corrupted by the human fall, and thus no longer reflects her Maker perfectly. History contains no events unrelated to God's interactions with humanity, but many events not directly or obviously connected to the central salvific-historical core of creation, fall, and redemption in Christ. And history uninterpreted by revelation has no rubrics of its own to point us to those mighty acts as especially significant, i.e., as *being* that central salvific core. Mythology, even if Lewis is right, is at best gleams of truth falling on corrupt human imaginations. Those sources of revelation can only speak with full clarity and power if there is a key, a Rosetta Stone, as it were, to focus our attention in them and interpret what they give us. Scripture is admirably fitted to take that role. It contains not only words about God from people who were closest to the central events of salvation history, but also many sections which purport to deliver the words of God Himself. And for even the human reportage of and commentary on those words, there is claimed a kind of "inspiration" that makes the whole Book not just words about God but the Word of God. It is therefore authoritative in a way that the other forms of revelation are not.

All historic Christians would affirm something like this about the Bible. But significant questions remain. What is the precise nature of the "inspiration" claimed for the biblical writers? What are the grounds of that claim? What is the nature and extent of the authority that it grants them? How far does it guarantee the accuracy, even the inerrancy and the infallibility of their words? How does that authority relate to the authority of the church? What does all this mean for how we should read Scripture and use it in our theology? Lewis's perspectives on these questions are among his most insightful—and controversial.

INSPIRATION

The Bible is set apart from other human books by the claim that it is uniquely *inspired*. Where does the concept of "inspiration" come from? The Apostle Paul claimed of the Old-Testament writings that "all Scripture is inspired by God" and hence profitable for teaching, reproof, correction, and training in righteousness" (2 Tim. 3:16). The word translated "inspired" is the Greek word θεοπνευστοσ (*theopneustos*), which literally means "breathed (*pneustos*) or spoken by God (*theos*)." That which is inspired is the γραφη (*graphe*), the writings themselves (not just the thoughts or ideas in them). So the human words written by the Prophets are in some sense also being attributed by Paul to God. Then Peter indicates that the writings of the Apostles also count as Scripture, referring to Paul's writings as belonging with "the rest of the Scriptures" (2 Pet. 3:16), which is generally taken by historic Christians as extending the claim for inspiration to the New Testament as well.

The question is, in what sense can we say that the words of Scripture are the words of God Himself as well as the words of Moses, Isaiah, Paul, etc.? The claim made by the Greek text of 2 Timothy 3:16 is a very strong one, and the earliest of the Church Fathers tended to take it strongly, picturing the human authors as flutes played by the Holy Spirit or as secretaries taking dictation from Him. This is known as the "mechanical dictation" theory of inspiration. However, because the personalities and styles of the individual human authors come through in their individual works so strongly, few Christians (even Fundamentalists) hold it today, except for specific passages such as the Ten Commandments which are actually presented as dictated or written by God directly. The opposite extreme would be to see inspiration as essentially no different from the elevated state of mind in which any literary genius writes. In this sense, we could say that Shakespeare was "inspired." No historic Christian would hold that biblical inspiration as described by Paul was nothing more than that.

THE DOCTRINE OF SCRIPTURE

The historic doctrine as held by both conservative Protestants and traditional Catholics is called "plenary verbal inspiration." As one popular systematic theology text summarizes it very succinctly, "All the words of Scripture are God's words" (Grudem 75). Nineteenth-century Princeton theologian Charles Hodge defined inspiration more fully as "an influence of the Holy Spirit on the minds of certain select men which rendered them the organs of God for the infallible communication of his mind and will" (1:154). Contemporary Evangelical Millard Erickson in a similar vein calls it "that supernatural influence of the Holy Spirit on the Scripture writers which rendered their writings an accurate record of the revelation, or which resulted in what they wrote actually being the Word of God" (225). Or as I have expressed it, inspiration is "that work of the Holy Spirit by which He produced the Word of God using human minds as instruments, so guiding, influencing, and superintending their activity that the words they wrote were the very words of God" (*Person and Work* 25). The standard doctrine is more subtle than mechanical dictation, then. God influenced and guided the minds of the human authors so that the words they wrote fully expressed their own personalities and were their words, generated by their thought processes, but equally were the very words God chose and wanted to express His meaning and convey His revelation to human beings.

C. S. Lewis was not a professional theologian, so we cannot expect the same kind of precision in his concept of inspiration. This is a weakness and also (potentially) a strength; wrestling with the idea without using the traditional language might produce some interesting insights. He wrote to Lee Turner on 19 July 1958 that he thought the main question was not so much *whether* the Bible is inspired as *how* it is. Our forebears thought that

> the Holy Spirit either just replaced the minds of the authors (like the supposed "control" in automatic writing) or at least dictated to them as secretaries.... I myself think of it as analogous to the incarnation—that, as in Christ a human soul and body are taken up and made the vehicle of Deity, so in Scripture a mass of human legend, history, moral teaching, etc. are taken up and made the vehicle of God's word. (*L* 3:960-61)

It is clear that Lewis rejected the mechanical dictation theory. It is not clear who the "ancestors" are to whom he is referring. Much more nuanced views of inspiration existed by the time of the Reformation, but Lewis does not interact with them, and as we shall see, his statements about "Fundamentalists" show no direct knowledge of their actual views, which he presents in a caricatured form typical of those not actually part of their circle. These broad brush strokes make us suspect that Lewis had never encountered a nuanced statement of the classic doctrine that would have allowed him to distinguish it from mechanical dictation.

The analogy with the incarnation is suggestive, but raises the question how far it is to be pushed. In the incarnation, God actually became man. But Lewis stops short of saying that the legend, history, etc. actually become the word of God; they become its "vehicle." What exactly does that mean? Human literature is "taken into the service" of the Word of God (*RotP* 111). Again, this is a small step back from affirming with Paul that the writings are inspired in a sense that makes them actually breathed by God, makes them His words. And this small step may have huge consequences as the doctrine of inspiration is worked out, as we shall see.

Lewis agrees with the classical doctrine that inspiration involves the influence of the Holy Spirit on the minds of the biblical authors, but he is somewhat vague about the nature and extent of that influence. He writes, "On all of these [forms of literature] I suppose a Divine pressure" (*RotP* 111). "Pressure" is an interesting metaphor. The human authors are being pushed, in the direction of truth, we may suppose—but how effectively and how far? Lewis wrote to Janet Wise on 5 Oct. 1955, "I believe the composition, presentation, & selection of all the books to have been guided by the Holy Ghost. But I think He meant us to have sacred myth and sacred fiction as well as sacred history" (*L* 3:653). Given Lewis's explication of "myth become fact," there is not necessarily any departure from classic doctrine here. But we wonder what counts as "fiction"? And other statements open up more definite rifts.

For example, we are told that "all Holy Scripture is in some sense—though not all in the same sense—the word of God" (*RotP* 19). In similar words,

> The whole Old Testament consists of the same sort of material as any other literature—chronicle (some of it obviously pretty accurate), poems, moral and political diatribes, romances, and what not; but all taken into the service of God's word. Not all, I suppose, in the same way. (*RotP* 111)

This raises all sorts of questions: in what sense/way? What are the different senses/ways? How do we know which one we are dealing with in any given passage? Because Lewis is answering *ad hoc* questions and not writing a treatise on how we should receive and use the Bible, he does not answer such questions. But the nebulosity of his concept of inspiration raises them, and does so insistently. For Lewis, the words of Scripture convey the Word of God, they are the vehicle of the Word of God, they are in the service of the Word of God. But he never says they *are* the Word of God. The difference is not trivial. In fact, what we affirm at this point controls how everything else in our doctrine of Scripture will develop.

THE DOCTRINE OF SCRIPTURE

SCRIPTURE, MYTH, AND HISTORY

Almost all Christians recognize that Scripture contains many genres: history, poetry, law, prophecy, biography, epistle, apocalyptic, etc. Each has something to contribute to the overall message, and they make their contributions in different ways, each needing to be read according to its own nature. Lewis as a literary scholar was of course sensitive to this aspect of the biblical text. He is especially good at helping us read the Psalms as what they are, poetry (*RotP*). He also has much to say about the two genres that may be most critical for accurately understanding the Bible, history and myth.

History is crucial because the ultimate form of revelation for Christians is the incarnation, where God actually enters into human history in Christ. Event and word coincide in the biblical text in such a way as to make the Bible the key to understanding God's revelation in history, highlighting and elucidating the central events that show Him to us. But biblical history does not begin with the life of Christ. The birth, life, death, resurrection, and ascension of Christ are the climax of a sequence of God's interventions in history that stretch from the expulsion from the Garden to the call of Abraham, the Exodus, the Davidic/Solomonic kingdom, and the exile and return of Judah from exile, all setting the stage for God's ultimate visitation of our earth in the coming of Christ.

Lewis understood the importance of biblical history but was not willing to commit himself to the accuracy of every detail of it as reported. He wrote to Clyde S. Kilby on 7 May 1959 that the importance of some events, such as the Resurrection, are dependent on their actually having happened, whereas the importance of others, such as Lot's wife being turned into a pillar of salt, are not. "And the ones whose historicity matters are, as God's will, those where it is plain" (*L* 3:1045). Conservative believers will appreciate the emphasis on the reality of the resurrection, and the plainness of that reality. But they might wonder what about the other narrative, other than its greater remoteness, makes it somehow less historical. The fate of Lot's wife is certainly of trivial importance compared to the resurrection; but, then, so is everything. And the text itself does not indicate any hesitancy about its actually having happened. If the New Testament history is not something that just happened to occur, but is the fulfillment and completion of a series of events beginning in the Old Testament, it may not be so easy to dismiss certain events as not needing to have happened. And how do we determine which events needed to have happened and which did not? The small gap that opened up between text and Word in Lewis's view of inspiration opens up space for many questions and creates room for uncertainty. This crack in the door may not be easy to close once it has opened.

Lewis makes some conservative readers bristle when he talks about myth in Scripture because most people who use that language use it to mean that the Bible is not essentially different from other ancient religious writings, and that we can dismiss its historicity much more cavalierly than Lewis does. But if we understand how Lewis used that language, there is nothing inherently problematic about it, nothing inherently contradictory to historicity. Biblical myth is "myth become fact." "Just as God is none the less God by being Man, so the Myth remains Myth even when it becomes Fact. The story of Christ demands from us, and repays, not only a religious and historical, but also an imaginative response" (*M* 139). This is a positive contribution to our appreciation of biblical revelation.

But the gap between text and Word opens up room for problems here as well. Not all that is mythical in Scripture seems to have made the full transition to "fact" in Lewis's mind. He wrote to a Mrs. Johnson on 14 May 1955 that you see in the Bible a process "in which something which in its earliest levels ... was hardly moral at all, and was in some ways not unlike the pagan religions, is gradually purged and enlightened until it becomes the religion of the great prophets and of Our Lord Himself" (*L* 3:608). We need not argue about the process itself as described here. God's people were surrounded by paganism and not unaffected by it. But was this gradual purging completed by the influence of the Spirit in inspiration, or is some of the Old Testament still hardly moral and not unlike paganism? What does this do to our picture of Yahweh before the "great prophets" appeared? The answers are unclear at best.

Lewis has a lot to say about the role of myth in Scripture in his brilliant book *Miracles*. There too we have much intriguing insight but also many unanswered questions. The mythology of the Hebrews was "the mythology chosen by God to be the vehicle of the earliest sacred truths, the first step in that process which ends in the New Testament where truth has become completely historical" (*M* 129). The chosen mythology, chosen to give us the right picture of God, is a wonderful way of putting it. But this time the assumed religious evolution itself raises troubling questions. So Genesis, we presume, is pretty much simply myth? Myth has not completely become fact until the New Testament? What does that say about the Exodus? Where do we draw the line, when Christ is presented as the Passover Lamb and the Lord's Supper is clearly a re-application of the Passover meal? It is all one seamless history to the biblical writers. "Just as, on the factual side, a long preparation culminates in God's becoming incarnate as Man, so, on the documentary side, the truth first appears in mythical form and then by a long process of condensing or focusing becomes incarnate as History." Myth as Lewis understands it here is "at its best, a real though unfocused gleam of divine truth falling on human imagination" (*M* 139).

THE DOCTRINE OF SCRIPTURE 65

How far does inspiration focus it? How far can we trust inspiration to have focused myth for us? If the same God worked in history all along, and inspired the Prophets as well as the Apostles to write about that history, why should myth not be taken as fact all the way along? The gap between text and Word then raises issues of trust, and that leads us to the next topic: the doctrine of inerrancy.

INERRANCY?

The classic doctrine of inspiration, because it follows the Apostle Paul in not positing any distance or distinction between the words of Scripture and the words of God, any gap between text and Word, draws the conclusion that because God is a God of truth, therefore the Bible teaches only truth; its statements when rightly interpreted are true in all that they affirm. The technical term for this doctrine is *inerrancy*. Scripture has no errors; it teaches only the truth; it doesn't get anything wrong.

The doctrine of inerrancy applies of course only to what the text *affirms* or *asserts*. A biblical character, for example, who notes that the sun has risen is not in error because he is not making a statement affirming Ptolemaic cosmology; he might well have believed it, but that is not his topic now; he is simply using a common expression to assert that it is morning. When the trees of the field clap their hands, the Psalmist is using poetic language; he is not making an erroneous scientific statement about oak or cedar anatomy. The Bible speaks truth, and only truth, in all that it *affirms*.

Many modern people assume that the complete factual accuracy of Scripture has long been exploded by research, but in fact the case is very different. The Bible, where it can be checked, proves to be remarkably accurate. Not every individual statement can be independently verified, and there do remain discrepancies that have not been explained; but when one comes to the text without an anti-supernatural bias, they are surprisingly few. The doctrine of inerrancy cannot be established by inductive study of the external evidence because discrepancies will always remain; you cannot prove a negative (no errors). "Remarkably accurate" will always be the most that can be proved by that method. But it is not unreasonable for conservative believers to attribute the remaining problems always to their own ignorance, not to the text. It is a reasonable conclusion, a reasonable and consistent act of faith, for those who accept the Bible as the Word of God on the testimony of Paul and Jesus.

But when there is any distance at all, even a small one, between the words of the Bible and God's words, then all error cannot logically be excluded, and the believer's implicit trust in the text is unavoidably compromised. So we should not be surprised to find that Lewis, who leaves such a gap, does not affirm inerrancy. In fact, he trusted the Bible far more than most liberal scholars who deny inerrancy, sometimes sounding as if he did believe in it. For example, he wrote to Dom Bede Griffiths on 28 May 1952, "Yes, Pascal does directly contradict several passages in Scripture and must be wrong" (*L* 3:195). He wrote to Mrs. Emily McLay on 3 Aug. 1953 that for him it was a first principle that "we must not interpret any one part of Scripture so that it contradicts other parts; and specially we must not use an Apostle's teaching so that it contradicts that of Our Lord" (*L* 3:354).

Both of these statements logically entail inerrancy. If there are errors in the text, then clearly some few passages (those which contain them) at least could contradict other passages (those that don't). To presuppose complete consistency among the biblical writers is to imply that they all share the same truth. If Scripture ever errs, then it is theoretically possible that Pascal could disagree with one of those erring passages and still be right. One is tempted to say that Lewis typically treated the New Testament at least as if it were for all practical purposes inerrant. Indeed, in most of his writings he seems to uphold a high view of Scripture and to encourage his readers to trust the Bible over the conclusions of its modern critics. "I do not wish to reduce the skeptical element in your minds. I am only suggesting that it need not be reserved exclusively for the New Testament and the Creeds. Try doubting something else" ("Modern Theology" 164).

Nevertheless, Lewis could not say that the Bible was inerrant, and indeed does say the opposite: after all that inspiration as he understood it could do, "errors of minor fact are permitted to remain" (*L* 3:961). Which, we wonder, are the minor facts? But it gets worse than that:

> The human qualities of the raw materials show through. Naivety, error, contradiction, even (as in the cursing Psalms) wickedness are not removed. The total result is not "the Word of God" in the sense that every passage, in itself, gives impeccable science or history. It carries the Word of God; and we (under grace, with attention to tradition and to interpreters wiser than ourselves, and with the use of such intelligence and learning as we may have) receive that word from it not by using it as an encyclopedia or an encyclical but by steeping ourselves in its tone or temper and so learning its overall message. (*RotP* 111-12).

Whatever we may conclude about Scripture itself, Lewis was at least on occasion inconsistent. One logically cannot believe that "contradiction" is "not removed" and then also give the advice that we must never interpret Scripture in such a way that it contradicts itself. If any contradiction remains, then there must be at least one set of passages for which "contradiction" is the correct, the only accurate, interpretation.

THE DOCTRINE OF SCRIPTURE

Even more shocking to many of Lewis's fans would be the inclusion of "wickedness." Now, the stoutest inerrantist believes that there is wickedness in the Bible, in the sense that human sin is discussed very frankly and the wickedness of evil people such as King Ahab is reported accurately. But Lewis means something quite different. Commenting on David's statement in Psalm 23, "Thou preparest a table before me in the presence of mine enemies," Lewis explains, "The poet's enjoyment of his present prosperity would not be complete unless those horrid Joneses (who used to look down their noses at him) were watching it all and hating it.... The pettiness and vulgarity of it, especially in the surroundings, are hard to endure" (*RotP* 21). The cursing (or "imprecatory") Psalms contain hate and vindictiveness according to Lewis: "I think that even in the Psalms this evil is already at work" (*RotP* 67). This is not just evil being described, explained, or reported; these are real evil attitudes on the part of biblical writers, part of their "raw material" that inspiration has not completely removed, and which remains in our Bibles as part of the *content* of their writing.

There are other ways of understanding those passages, less unflattering to the writers (see Williams, "An Apologist's Evening Prayer" 247f). Our purpose here is to see that Lewis's doctrine of inspiration allowed him to view them as, not just reporting, but embodying evil. It is little wonder that he had to appeal away from specific passages to the "overall message" in order to find the "word of God" in the Bible. Once again, the inadequacy of this approach to the text is revealed on the level of practical advice. What good is it to "steep ourselves" in the "tone or temper" of Scripture if that tone and temper include jealousy, hate, and vindictiveness? Someone has to choose which passages we are to believe and which we are not, which we are to steep ourselves in and which we are not—and that person, not the Text, becomes the real Authority. Once the text only *conveys* the Word of God, rather than *being* the Word of God, the authority is inevitably transferred from the text to the interpreter, whether the reader or someone else, some "expert" to whom the reader defers.

The inerrancy of Scripture and the authority of Scripture are then inevitably linked because our view of both flows from our understanding of inspiration. Lewis would have been loath to transfer divine authority from the text to the critic because he understood how little the critics deserve our trust ("Modern Theology and Biblical Criticism"). But the gap he posits between text and Word cannot help but have that effect. Biblical imagery has authority because it was written down by people closer to God than we are, and has been accepted by serious and thoughtful Christians down through church history ("Weight of Glory" 33). Well, yes. But you could say the same thing about many of the Christian writers of the patristic era. You could mostly say the same thing about Pascal, who must nevertheless be wrong when he disagrees with

Scripture, while other biblical passages are not to be interpreted as doing so. This statement does nothing to explain the unique authority that all branches of Christendom give the biblical text. Lewis cannot explain it, because words about God, however venerable and profound they may be, cannot have the same authority as God's Word.

LEWIS AND "FUNDAMENTALISM"

In the doctrine of Scripture, particularly with reference to its inspiration, authority, and inerrancy, then, Lewis comes short of teaching the historic doctrine of the church. He does not seem to be aware that this is the case; indeed, it was never his intention so to fall short. As he said in *Problem of Pain*, "If any parts of the book are 'original' in the sense of being novel or unorthodox, they are so against my will and as a result of my ignorance" (*PoP* viii). This is a promise he usually keeps admirably. How then did Lewis manage to be unorthodox on this point? I think it was precisely as a result of his ignorance. His statements about what he called "Fundamentalism" help us to pinpoint exactly where this ignorance lay. Here is what I mean:

> I have been suspected of being what is called a Fundamentalist. That is because I never regard any narrative as unhistorical simply on the ground that it includes the miraculous. Some people find the miraculous so hard to believe that they cannot imagine any reason for its acceptance other than a prior belief that every sentence in the Old Testament has historical or scientific truth. (*RotP* 109)

In a similar vein, Lewis wrote to Janet Wise on 5 Oct. 1955 that he himself was not a Fundamentalist "if Fundamentalism means accepting as a point of faith at the outset the proposition, 'Every statement in the Bible is completely true in the literal, historical sense'" (*L* 3:652). Also relevant is Lewis's assumption about the ubiquity of commitment to the mechanical dictation theory on the part of our "ancestors" (*L* 3:960-61).

Lewis understood that Fundamentalists see the Bible as infallible. "One can respect, and at moments envy, both the Fundamentalist's view of the Bible and the Roman Catholic's view of the Church" (*RotP* 112). But he also equated Fundamentalism with literalism, mechanical dictation, and a naïve approach to genre, reducing every statement in Scripture to history or science. Now, Lewis knew that not all of the Bible is history and that none of it is science, in the modern sense of that word. He knew that mechanical dictation is not a credible theory of inspiration capable of dealing with the full complexity of the biblical text. So "Fundamentalism" did not seem a viable option to him.

THE DOCTRINE OF SCRIPTURE

This is all well and good—except that "Fundamentalists" (and their living heirs, Evangelicals, as well as conservative Roman Catholics) will feel that their position in being rejected has been horribly caricatured, since their more informed teachers have never held any such thing. The notion, for example, that "plenary inspiration" and "the mechanical dictation theory" are synonymous is simply ignorant. The so-called Fundamentalists' actual tradition as summarized in the 1978 "Chicago Statement on Biblical Inerrancy" maintains that "we must pay the most careful attention to [the Bible's] claims and character as a human production." As a result,

> history must be treated as history, poetry as poetry, hyperbole and metaphor as hyperbole and metaphor, generalization and approximation as what they are, and so forth. Differences between literary conventions in Bible times and in ours must also be observed: Since, for instance, nonchronological narration and imprecise citation were conventional and acceptable and violated no expectations in those days, we must not regard these things as faults when we find them in Biblical writers. When total precision of a particular kind was not expected nor aimed at, it is no error not to have achieved it. Scripture is inerrant, not in the sense of being absolutely precise by modern standards, but in the sense of making good its claims and achieving that measure of focused truth at which its authors aimed. (qtd. in Packer and Oden 50)

This passage simply summarizes what "Fundamentalist" theologians had held all along, since Hodge and Warfield at least, and definitely what they were saying in the 1950's. (For an example of a British Evangelical who establishes this point, see J. I. Packer's seminal book *Fundamentalism and the Word of God*, which was published in 1958.)

How did this happen? Lewis was part of an intellectual environment in which "Fundamentalism" was not considered intellectually respectable, one, more importantly, in which real Fundamentalists were just not read. Thus it simply never seems to have crossed his mind that Scriptural inerrancy could be held apart from other positions that he knew to be false. He falsely and mistakenly *equated* it with mechanical dictation and literalism. How Lewis would have responded to a more nuanced version of the doctrine of inerrancy than he was apparently ever exposed to we will never know. The point here is to understand that in rejecting that doctrine he was rejecting a straw man, a caricature of what Fundamentalism (and its modern heir, Evangelicalism) actually taught, or teaches. So in an uncharacteristic logical and informational hastiness, Lewis let the infallible and inerrant baby slip away with the literalist bathwater.

READING SCRIPTURE

Lewis is at his weakest as a theologian in his treatment of inspiration and inerrancy. Yet, unlike many who say superficially similar things, Lewis was basically a man of faith. His failings were motivated by misunderstanding, not unbelief. This, plus his unsurpassed expertise as a student of literature, enabled him often to be an excellent practical guide to the art and skill of reading the Bible. Reading in general was after all something Lewis was very good at! His faith, his rejection of chronological snobbery, and his sheer common sense combined to produce practical advice that is often consistent with a higher view of Scripture theologically than he was able to affirm.

Lewis for example realized that basic to any other kind of reading of the Bible we might do is the grammatico-historical approach. Any passage, in other words, means not what it happens to mean "to me," but what it would have meant to its original audience. Any personal application we make must start with that. In other words, the passage means what the words mean in the light of their literary context, their grammatical constructions, and their historical setting. "Any saying is to be taken in the sense it would naturally have borne in the time and place of utterance" ("Why I am Not a Pacifist" 87). Each individual passage should also be understood in the light of the whole. We have seen that Lewis forbade the interpretation of any passage in such a way as to make it contradict any other (*L* 3:354). In order to follow this rule we must know what the other passages say. It is dangerous to build any doctrine on a single isolated prooftext. Lewis takes that commonplace injunction one step further: each genre needs to be seen in the light of the contributions of the others. History tells John that "the pictures alone are dangerous and the Rules alone are dangerous" (*PR* 152). Here "pictures" refers to myth, and "rules" to Law.

Prooftexting is a common mistake made by people who trust the Bible implicitly without understanding the necessarily prior role of context in understanding those texts. Lewis wrote to a Mrs. Johnson on 8 Nov. 1952, that "it is Christ Himself, not the Bible, who is the true word of God." The Bible read rightly will point us to Him, "but we must not use the Bible (our forefathers often did) as a sort of Encyclopedia out of which texts (isolated from their contexts and not read with attention to the whole nature and purpose of the books in which they occur) can be taken for use as weapons" (*L* 3:246).

An even more pernicious form of prooftexting is bibliomancy, which adds a dangerous subjectivity to the context-free zone which is personal interpretation. Lewis wrote to a Mr. Green on 18 June 1962, warning that "the habit of taking isolated texts from the Bible and treating the effect they have on one in a particular mood at a particular moment as direct messages from God is v. misleading" (*L* 3:1353).

We might quibble with the stark dichotomy Lewis draws between Christ and the Bible as the "true" Word of God. He is trying to make a legitimate point: Christ, not the Bible, is the *ultimate* Word of God. Nevertheless, according to the New Testament authors, both are in their way truly the Word of God. But the advice is sound and foundational. Paul's identification of the very words of Scripture as God-breathed explains why the actual words as they were actually written, including both their literary and historical context, are so important; accepting that identification should commit us to respecting the original text and its form as Lewis urges. His faithful instincts allowed him to point us in the right direction here even without that support.

Lewis wrote to Clyde S. Kilby on 7 May 1959, "That the over-all operation of Scripture is to convey God's Word to the reader (he also needs His inspiration) who reads it in the right spirit, I fully believe. That it also gives true answers to all the questions (often religiously irrelevant) which he might ask, I don't" (*L* 3:1046). Two important points are to be noted here. First is that reading the Bible for a believer is not a purely human enterprise. The same Spirit who inspired the writers also is present to help humble readers who trust Him with a teachable attitude. They are not on their own. Technically, Lewis should have used the word *illumination* here instead of *inspiration* for the aid the Spirit gives the reader. The theological tradition carefully distinguishes the two, and for good reason: illumination, though real, does not carry the same promise of infallibility as inspiration does. Second, illumination does not overturn the importance of sound grammatico-historical hermeneutics. The Spirit will not lead us to a meaning or application that is not consistent with what He inspired in the beginning when He influenced the original writers to choose the words they did. We must be asking the same question as the writer in order to get the right answer. It is another reason why naive prooftexting is such a dangerous practice.

Finally, Lewis would have us resist a premature accommodationism in our reading of the New Testament, especially the words of our Lord. It is a tendency of liberal-leaning theologians to try to evade any teaching that does not fit their modernist paradigms by dismissing it as merely a reflection of First-Century culture. Jesus did not really represent the Father when he taught about Hell, for example—he was just reflecting, or accommodating Himself to, beliefs that were current at the time, because otherwise people would not have understood Him. Lewis's Chronological Snobbery Detector must have gone off at such a ploy. He also realized that in an event so momentous as the Incarnation, nothing could be left to chance. "Do we suppose that the scene of God's earthly life was selected at random?—that some other scene would have served better?" ("World's Last Night" 97)

Though his statements about inspiration are sometimes lacking, Lewis's practice often takes the inspiration of Scripture more seriously than some Evangelicals do. Everything in the text, even the choice of metaphor, is there for a reason, and theology has to reckon with the revelation as God gave it, not brushing any detail of it aside for ideological reasons. These are supremely important points. Lewis's practice at this point is often a better guide than his theorizing.

CONCLUSION

Lewis is at his weakest as a theologian when expounding the doctrine of inspiration and its corollaries such as inerrancy. He has good things to say about genre and interpretation and about trusting the text over its negative critics. But an unfortunate lack of interaction with the actual biblical teaching on this topic, not only of Paul (as outlined above) but also of our Lord (see Wenham), left him vulnerable to some of the prejudices of the educated class and kept him from overcoming them as well as he did in most other areas. He was unable to distinguish the historic doctrine of the church from a caricature of Fundamentalism. Not seeing the biblical identification of the words of Scripture as the Word of God, he left a gap between text and Word that unintentionally compromises the Bible's authority. He had a high view of Scripture but one that stopped short of affirming its inerrancy. Fortunately, his practice in interpretation and obedience was often better than his doctrine.

Why have we taken such a critical look at Lewis's teaching in this area? A better understanding of inspiration and inerrancy can help us see the importance of devoted reading and faithful interpretation leading to loving obedience. If we surpass Lewis in understanding at this point, let us not fall behind him in reading and obedience. For he realized that obedience is the bottom line, even when it is costly. As Puddleglum tells the children, "Aslan didn't tell Pole what would happen. He only told her what to do. That fellow [the prince] will be the death of us once he's up, I shouldn't wonder. But that doesn't let us off following the sign" (*TSC* 175).

What would a person understanding and practicing a fully biblical doctrine of inspiration look like? In the words of the Psalmist, "His delight is in the law of the Lord, and in His law he meditates day and night" (Ps. 1:2). Or as Moses expresses it more fully,

> And these words which I am commanding you today shall be on your heart. And you shall teach them diligently to your sons and shall talk of them when you sit in your house and when you walk by the way and when you lie down and when you rise up. And you shall bind them as a sign on your hand and they shall be as frontals on your forehead and you shall write them on the doorposts of your house and on your gates. (Deut. 6:6-9)

Or, as Lewis puts it, "Remember the signs. Say them to yourself when you wake in the morning and when you lie down at night, and when you wake in the middle of the night. And whatever strange things may happen to you, let nothing turn your mind from following the signs" (*TSC* 25).

Amen.

CHAPTER 4

Theology Proper
The Existence and Nature of God

"We trust not because 'a God' exists, but because this God exists" ("Obstinacy" 25).

"But who is Aslan? Do you know him?"
"Well, he knows me," said Edmund (VDT 117).

If then God has revealed Himself so that theology is possible for us, what kind of God is thereby revealed? Who is He? What is He like? What is His nature? What are His attributes? These questions logically come next. They constitute a topos called "theology proper," or the doctrine of God. For historic Christians like C. S. Lewis, God is the eternal Spirit who created everything else. He is personal on the high order of Trinity, being Father, Son, and Holy Ghost; yet these three Persons are one God, not three gods. Being the self-existent and pre-existent Creator of all else, God is not subject to the same limitations of space and time which govern the existence of finite creatures: He is therefore omnipresent, omniscient, and omnipotent. He is also just, righteous, good, wise, gracious, and loving. He is Creator, Judge, Father, and King. He is most importantly the God of Abraham, Isaac, and Jacob, and the God who is the Father of our Lord Jesus Christ. Lewis's exposition of these ideas is as rich and creative as it is faithful and orthodox.

GOD IS

C. S. Lewis wrote his brother Warnie on 24 Oct. 1931 that "God might be defined as 'a Being who spends his time having his existence proved and disproved'" (L 2:7). The jocular definition reminds us that we could easily get the impression from listening to the interminable debates on the subject that the first question of theology is whether God exists. But if theology begins from God's having revealed Himself to us, which Christians believe is the only way it *can* begin, then that can hardly be the case. God, having spoken the world into existence, and having spoken through it and in it since, would be in a position, were He so inclined, to one-up DesCartes and proclaim, "*Dico; ergo sum*" ("I speak; therefore, I am"). Believers could say, "*Dixit; ergo est*" ("He spoke; therefore, He is"). The Christian theologian therefore does not begin by asking whether God exists but by enquiring into what can be known about the One who has already taken the initiative and revealed Himself as existing.

The "whether" question inevitably comes up anyway, though, for Christian philosophers, especially, but for theologians too. It does so because we need to be clear about the grounds of our faith, for our own sake and for the sake of those who have not yet had the experience of being addressed by the revelation of God in Christ that we believe is objectively out there in nature, history, and Scripture. As an apologist, Lewis had to deal with the "whether" question a lot, and gave in *Surprised by Joy* a detailed account of the experiences and reasonings that moved him over time from unbelief to belief. One might get the impression that the existence of God—as opposed to Lewis's belief in that existence—depended on those experiences and reasonings, rather than their depending, like everything else, on His existence. That would be a false impression.

Lewis understood that the answers to whether God exists depend on His prior reality, rather than the other way around. He shows this in his poem "The Apologist's Evening Prayer," where his "cleverness shot forth" on God's behalf and his proofs of Christ's divinity are portrayed as tokens, coins whose "thin-worn image of Thy head" should not be confused with the Reality they represent (*Ps* 129). He shows it in the essay "On Obstinacy in Belief," where the believer's relationship with God has an existence logically prior to and independent of the reasons he consciously holds for believing in it. Those reasons are important and have a significant role to play, but God does not depend on them. The *whether* of God's existence, in other words, comes after and depends upon the *what* and the *how*.

This relationship becomes clear in what may be the most misunderstood of all the classical arguments for God's existence, Anselm's ontological argument. Anselm began by defining God as that Being greater than which none can be conceived. He then argued that such a Being would have to exist necessarily, because any being we could conceive as not existing would be less than the greatest Being that can be conceived.

A superficial understanding of Anselm has led many to reject his argument as invalid. Just because we can imagine something, however great, does not

THE EXISTENCE AND NATURE OF GOD

mean that it exists. Being the greatest thing I happen to be able to imagine is not evidence of existence. (I can imagine a mountain taller than Everest, but that does not mean there is one on earth.) And existence is not an attribute that can be added or subtracted so that a being is "greater" with it than without it. Thus, the ontological argument has a certain circular feel to it. These objections are sound as far as they go; but I think (and it appears that Lewis thought) that they miss the point.

I would argue that Anselm's ontological argument is best used not so much as an argument about *whether* God exists as a meditation on *how* He exists. (His disciple and biographer Eadmer seems to have thought so too; see pp. 29-30 of *The Life*.) God is not just some random contingent entity like you or me who just happens to exist, or who could exist or not. He is not just *a* being; He is the ground of *all* being. In other words, once you understand what God is, you must see that He *has* to exist. I exist (I assure you), but I don't have to; I could as easily not exist. If I ceased to do so, outside of a very small handful of friends and readers (I fondly hope), the universe would not even notice and would be pretty much unaffected. If, on the other hand, God did not exist, nothing else would exist either.

The point is that as long as you are thinking of God as some random being, a bigger version of you or me, who just happens to exist, or who might exist or might not, i.e., whose existence is open to question, you are not yet thinking of *God*. To truly understand who He is, is to see that He exists *necessarily*, unlike you and me. This of course entails that He exists in fact. But Anselm did not start with the open question of whether God exists in fact or not and come up with a clever way of answering, "Yes." His point was that this is precisely what we cannot do. To understand who God is, is to see that the question never was open in that way; it is to see that either we start with Him or we cannot finish with anything.

The practical application of this reasoning to *"whether"* apologetics is the realization that we do not say that God exists because He is the biggest thing we can imagine. He is in fact greater than anything we can imagine. (After all, Anselm did not define God as the greatest being *we* could conceive, but as the greatest that can *be* conceived.) All our imagined gods—like Zeus—are bigger versions of us who could exist or not. And I have noticed that these are the gods that Atheists typically argue against. I am often tempted to say to them, "Congratulations! You have just refuted the existence of Zeus. Thank you for helping us dispose of that lame possibility. Now, let's get back to the topic of *God.*" All our imagined gods—like Zeus, and the infamous Flying Spaghetti Monster—are bigger versions of us who could exist or not. Yet we have a concept of a God who is bigger even than that. Where did we get it?

The God of the Bible is not the kind of thing we would have made up. When we project ourselves onto the cosmos imaginatively, we get gods who are personal but finite, like Zeus or Odin. When we project our abstract reason onto the cosmos, we get gods that are transcendent but impersonal, like Atman or The Force. Such are the gods—the idols—that we build up from below. But what if God's personal Reality were so strong that it could impinge on our consciousness from above? In a discussion of the ontological argument, Lewis wrote to his brother Warnie on 24 Oct. 1931 that "it is arguable that the 'idea of God' in some minds does contain not a mere abstract definition, but a real imaginative perception of goodness and beauty, *beyond their own resources*" (L 2:7, emphasis added). They are justified in believing in God, not because they imagined Him (on their own), but because they could not have. That is why the very concept of His nature, once clearly seen, carries its own conviction of His reality.

Perhaps the reason the ontological argument seems so problematic is that it is convincing only to people who have already *seen* this—people who have been granted at least a faint apprehension of the Glory of God. Perhaps then its best use is not in trying to convince people abstractly of this reality before they have seen it, but rather in helping them to see it, to see why they need to try to grasp for the first time the concept of *aseity*. (To exist *a se* is to exist "on one's own"—not like we exist, *ab alio*, "from another.") It might be able to do this more effectively if the emphasis in its presentation were shifted from the whether of God's existence to the how. I think C. S. Lewis shows us one way in which this might be done.

Lewis used the ontological argument apologetically only once in his public writings, and it was in a rather surprising place. This most sophisticated of philosophical arguments shows up in a presentation to the least sophisticated audience: the children for whom the Narnia books were written. It is the debate between Puddleglum and the Green Witch in *The Silver Chair*. Describing the scene where Puddleglum stomps out the Witch's mesmerizing fire, Lewis wrote to Nancy Warner on 26 Oct. 1963 that "I have simply put the 'Ontological Proof' in a form suitable for children" (L 3:1472). How is this passage a version of the ontological proof?

To answer that question, we will have to take a careful look at Puddleglum's speech. The Witch has been arguing that Overworld and Aslan are only a projection of the children's imaginations. They have seen a lamp and imagined the sun; they have seen a cat and imagined Aslan. The marshwiggle replies:

> Suppose we have only dreamed, or made up, all those things—trees and grass and sun and moon and stars and Aslan himself. Suppose we have. Then all I can say is that, in that case, the made-up things seem a good deal more important than the real ones. Suppose this black pit

THE EXISTENCE AND NATURE OF GOD

of a kingdom of yours is the only world. Well, it strikes me as a pretty poor one. And that's a funny thing, when you come to think of it. We're just babies making up a game, if you're right. But four babies making up a game can make a play-world that licks your real world hollow. (*TSC* 190-91)

How is this passage a version of the ontological argument? The Witch's reductionism could be taken as a rebuttal aimed in effect at the superficial version of the argument: just because you have imagined Aslan does not mean that he exists. Where did the idea of Aslan come from? You just made it up, based on a projection from cats you have seen. Puddleglum's reply calls into question the plausibility of this explanation in a way that transfers the ground to what I have called the deeper version of the argument. The idea of Aslan, he argues in effect, could not have arisen in that way. It is highly unlikely that four children playing a game could have made up a world with a deeper rootedness in reality than the only real and solid world they had ever experienced. The final answer to a refutation of the superficial version of the ontological argument is to remember the experience on which the deeper version is based.

In other words, we have to get past the Witch's reductionistic empiricist epistemology (explanation of knowing) to an ontology (explanation of being) capable of giving us something to know in the first place. How can Aslan be based on the existence of cats when cats cannot even account for their own existence? Is Aslan derived from cats, or are cats derived from Aslan? Something has to be capable of giving reality to everything else, and in Narnia, that is not cats. It is Aslan or nothing. And because Narnia is something, nothing is not a viable alternative.

This is a version of the ontological argument "suitable for children." Therefore, Eustace and Jill will not be basing their faith in Aslan on the rather dense unpacking of the logic of Puddleglum's argument that I have just attempted, but on an intuition of its rightness that comes from something even more basic: the fact that Aslan exists so strongly that His revelatory Reality is able to impinge on their consciousness with self-attesting power.

Aslan is of course a picture of Yahweh, whose name means basically, "I just am" (Ex. 3:14). The children have known Him, and because they have truly known Him they know that to do so is to realize the inadequacy of even saying that they have known Him. "Well he knows me" (*VDT* 117) is a more accurate representation of the situation: it speaks of Aslan's ontological priority to everything, which is felt and shown in (and known by) the epistemological priority expressed in Edmund's reply. If you are thinking of Aslan as just a bigger cat, however much bigger you please, you are not yet thinking of *Aslan*. If you are thinking of Aslan as a cat of any kind whose existence is open to question, you are not yet thinking of *Aslan*.

The children, who have actually met Aslan, know this instinctively, and Puddleglum's speech reminds them of what they know. Thus the ontological argument, even if it be ambiguous as a deductive proof, can serve to bring to a level of insightful articulation the inklings of God's uncreated glory intuited from the majesty-in-contingency of Nature or granted in personal revelation.

GOD IS TRANSCENDENT

We learn from this discussion that Aslan in Narnia and Yahweh in the primary world don't just happen to exist; they exist *necessarily*. It is their very nature to do so. That is what it means to say that they are God. Lewis's perspective here is consistent with the Bible's, in which everything flows from and leads back to the divine name: "I AM" (Ex. 3:14). It does so because the first thing that is revealed about this God is that He is the Creator of all else: in the beginning He created the heavens and the earth (Gen. 1:1). Before Abraham was—before the earth was—"I AM" (cf. Jesus' claim in John 8:58). He is not an object contained in the space-time continuum; He was there before it was. It is His creature. Thus eternity and all the omnis—omnipotence, omniscience, omnipresence—are contained in the action of Genesis 1:1. Because He is the source of all created energy, no created being can possibly be stronger than He is. Because He created and designed everything, He knows all about everything. Because space is His creature, every point of it is always immediately accessible to His operations; and because the space-time continuum is His creature, we can make the same statement about every moment of time. Lewis's way of using the ontological argument shows that he understood this well.

To be the one uncreated Being who just is makes God absolute and transcendent in a way that is hard to communicate to modern people. Lewis had some creative and helpful ways of expressing that transcendence. For example, he wrote to Arthur Greeves on 12 Sept. 1933, defining God as "that which has no opposite." He explains, "We live in a world of clashes, good and evil, true and false, pleasant and painful, body and spirit, time and eternity, etc., but God is not simply (so to speak) *one* of the two clashes but the ultimate thing beyond them all" (*L* 2:121). This was an early statement with a poor choice of examples which might be taken to imply that God is beyond good and evil. Lewis did not intend that, however, but rather a rejection of dualism: Satan, for example, is not God's "opposite" but his rebellious creature, existing on a lower level, as all creatures do.

More accurate is this description of God's transcendent existence:

> The cosmic mind will only help us if we put it at the beginning, if we suppose it to be, not the product of the total system, but the basic,

original, self-existent Fact which exists in its own right. But to admit that sort of cosmic mind is to admit a God outside of Nature, a transcendent and supernatural God. (*M* 30-31)

Transcendence means "standing above;" it does not mean vague or abstract. This is a God who "has purposes and performs particular actions, who does one thing and not another, a concrete, choosing, commanding, prohibiting God with a determinate character" (*M* 83). "If God is the ultimate source of all concrete, individual things, then God Himself must be concrete, and individual in the highest degree" (*M* 89).

Lewis wants to combat the modern tendency to associate transcendent being with abstraction so badly that he boldly calls God "concrete." If God is a spirit, this word cannot be meant literally in its normal meaning of tangible. But Lewis wants us to think of God as something *more* solid than physical reality, as something at the opposite pole from nebulous. He conveys this idea effectively in his portrait of heaven in *The Great Divorce*, where the grass pierces the feet of the spirits from the gray town. So if we take "concrete" metaphorically, it is one of Lewis's more brilliant descriptions of God as the One who is ultimately *real*. There is nothing nebulous about Him; He has a definite what-ness. "He is 'absolute being'—or rather *the* Absolute Being—in the sense that He alone exists in His own right. But there are things which God is not. In that sense He has a determinate character. Thus He is righteous, not a-moral; creative, not inert" (*M* 90). One of the clearest statements is this one:

> God is basic Fact or Actuality, the source of all other facthood. At all costs therefore He must not be thought of as a featureless generality. If He exists at all, He is the most concrete thing there is, the most individual, "organized and minutely articulated." He is unspeakable not by being indefinite but by being too definite for the unavoidable vagueness of language. (*M* 93)

To combine the solidity of a Being who exists necessarily and eternally and is the Source of all other existence with the definiteness of a God who is personal and holy and active taxes our imaginations and our understanding; but this is the God the Bible presents to us. This God has all the absoluteness a philosopher could desire, but He is not the god of the philosophers but of Abraham, Isaac, and Jacob. He is the God of creation and Sinai, of the Cross and the Resurrection. His is what He is, and we must adjust to that uncompromising Reality. "And as Jill gazed at [Aslan's] motionless bulk, she realized that she might as well have asked the whole mountain to move aside for her convenience" (*TSC* 20). Not absolute *or* personal, not infinite *or* individual, not transcendent *or* dynamic: this is not the god we might have imagined but the unconditioned Reality that just is, and who is serenely and supremely both.

> He is Bacchus, Venus, Ceres all rolled into one.... On the other hand, Yahweh is clearly *not* a nature-god. He does not die and come to life each year.... He may give wine and fertility, but must not be worshipped with bacchanalian or aphrodisiac rites. He is not the soul of Nature nor of any part of Nature. He inhabits eternity; He dwells in the high and holy place; heaven is His throne, not his vehicle; earth is His footstool, not His vesture. (*M* 119)

And all this is why we can say that "we trust not because 'a God' exists, but because *this* God exists" ("Obstinacy" 25).

GOD IS SPIRIT

Lewis's metaphor of *concreteness*, as we have seen, is not intended to deny the orthodox doctrine that God is spirit, but rather to head us off from the misunderstandings of the spiritual world to which we are prone. Lewis affirms that God is a spirit in many ways. The very word *Maleldil*, the name of God in the Space Trilogy, means etymologically "Great Spirit" in Old Solar, the language of Deep Heaven.

To say that God is a Spirit is to say that He is not a physical object within the natural universe. He is not made of matter, because matter is one of His inventions. He is not in fact "made" of anything in the way that a physical object is composed of elements and parts; He just is, as we have seen above. But Lewis was well aware that the words *spirit* and *spiritual* do not readily communicate this content to modern people. They have connotations of something less tangible, therefore less real; of being more mysterious only in the sense of being more vague than the everyday physical realities we see around us. Lewis also recognized that synonyms of those words suffer from the same handicap. Words like *incorporeal* mislead us because they imply that God lacks something (a body) that we possess. "It would be safer to call Him *trans-corporeal*" (*M* 93-4). God is not less than us by not having a body; He is different. But even *different* is an inadequate description. God is "trans-corporeal"; He is *beyond* the mundane reality that, for us, is always bodied.

Being a spirit is no more incompatible with being a person than being uncreated is. But it does make a difference in how we conceive of that personality—though not the difference many people assume. At issue here is the traditional explication of "spirit" as meaning "without body, parts, or *passions*." Lewis did not make the common mistake of assuming that God is unemotional. As He is personal, so there is something in Him that corresponds to our emotions.

When Scripture speaks of Him as having love, anger, compassion, etc., it is not merely being metaphorical. These responses are in us, created in His image, because first they were in Him. But our emotions are disordered by the Fall and affected by our bodies. How I feel about something will, apart from grace, be affected by my rebellion; it may also affected by my lusts, by my weariness, or by my hormones. Thus my emotional responses are not always either appropriate or proportional to their objects. Another way of saying the same thing is that we are driven by our passions. God is not.

Lewis explains that we correctly say that God has no passions even though we might misunderstand this assertion because in our case a love that is not passionate is *lacking* something (intensity). But God's love lacks nothing. God does not have passions because "passions imply passivity and intermission" (*M* 95). *Passivity* means here that we do not necessarily choose our passions. *Intermission* means that they are not constant or consistent. God then is both similar to us and different from us: he has personal responses that include love and hate, righteous anger and compassion. But they are always perfectly harmonious, perfectly controlled, and perfectly appropriate. Our bodies (not as such, but as disordered by the Fall) make it impossible for us to be that way. Once again, being a spirit is not for Lewis simply a negation—no body—but also something positive: freedom from unruly passions. (Evil spirits may also have disordered emotions, but theirs are also different from ours in not being complicated by the body. When we are resurrected to life, we will experience freedom from passion *in* the body—but that awaits a different chapter.)

Lewis's exposition of God as Spirit then is consistent with traditional orthodoxy but explains its implications in ways that go beyond most standard treatments.

GOD IS TRI-PERSONAL

One of the most difficult concepts of Christian theology is the doctrine of the Trinity. The word *trinity* blends the roots *tri*, three, and *unity*, one, to express the belief that God is one Being who exists in three Persons, the Father, the Son, and the Holy Spirit. Historic Christians do not confess God as triune out of love of either paradox or perversity, but to try to be faithful to the data of Scripture. For Scripture presents as true the following set of propositions: the Father is God; the Son is God; the Spirit is God; Father, Son, and Spirit are not just different names for the same person but rather three discrete Persons; yet there is only one God, not three.

The doctrine is not contradictory. It would be if it maintained simultaneously that there is one God and that there are three Gods, but that is not what it says. There is one God who is tri-personal. It is difficult for us to imagine a singular tri-personal Being because in our experience we normally find a correspondence between one being and one person. When we do not, there is something very wrong: Multiple Personality Disorder. Diversity of person in finite human beings compromises their integration, their unity. But for God, this is not so: His richness of being demands something more: "Christian theology does not believe God to be a person. It believes Him to be such that in Him a trinity of persons is consistent with a unity of deity" ("Poison" 79). What the doctrine of the Trinity tries to do then is to capture the richness of God's existence: He is a singular unity of being containing a plurality of personhood.

We ourselves are personal beings—the only fully personal ones we know by direct experience. Some of the higher animals approach the borders of personality, but we *are* persons. Well, God is something more personal than we are, not less. Lewis tried to capture that idea by calling the section of *Mere Christianity* that deals with the Trinity "Beyond Personality." This was a good move on his part. He understood that the doctrine of the Trinity is not about abstruseness for its own sake but is meaningful for us because it is about the *way* in which God is personal: He is *more* personal than we are, not less, and in the manner specified as Father, Son, and Spirit by the way He is revealed to us in Scripture. All that we saw above about God's dynamic individuality and concreteness comes into play here, focused in God as the spring from which personality flows as fulfilled in love and community, which all have their source in His very inmost nature. Lewis points out that implication in a connection noted by many. People like to quote the statement that "God is love." But they don't realize that "the words 'God is love' have no real meaning unless God contains at least two Persons. Love is something that one person has for another person. If God was a single person, then before the world was made, He was not love" (*MC* 151).

Christians have found many analogies to the Trinity in nature, and none of them are perfect. Mind, emotion, and will, for example, are aspects of human personality, not actually distinct persons. Lewis makes good use of an analogy from geometry: "In God's dimension, so to speak, you find a being who is three Persons while remaining one Being, just as a cube is six squares while remaining one cube" (*MC* 142). He develops the geometrical analogy in terms provided by Edwin Abbott's brilliant little allegory *Flatland*. In that book the inhabitants of a two-dimensional world try to understand three dimensions, with limited success that reminds us of our own limitations in understanding the spiritual world. So Lewis notes that God is three persons while being one God the way a cube has six squares while staying one body. "We cannot comprehend such a structure any more than the Flatlanders could comprehend a cube. But we can at least comprehend our incomprehension, and see that if there is something beyond personality it ought to be incomprehensible in that sort of way." (*M* 87)

Lewis elaborates: "Flatlanders, attempting to imagine a cube, would either imagine the six squares coinciding, and thus destroy their distinctness, or imagine them set out side by side, and thus destroy the unity. Our difficulties about the Trinity are of much the same kind" ("Poison" 79-80). Thus the Trinity is beyond reason but not contrary to reason, because it is beyond it in just the way we would expect if God encompasses higher dimensions of personality than we do.

Lewis's exposition of the Trinity has two strengths. First, it helps us see how something that initially looks contradictory can on further reflection be seen simply as hard to imagine but still intelligible. Second, it helps us see that the Trinity is about the profound way in which God is personal and relational: relationality is actually at the heart of His nature. By contemplating this mystery, we can more easily believe that, in spite of being infinitely higher than we are, this God actually wants to relate to us. Trinitarian theology reminds us that God is higher than we are not be being more abstract but by being *personal* on a higher level. "'Wouldn't [Aslan] know without being asked?'" said Polly, tempted to make God's omniscience compromise His ability to relate. "'I've no doubt he would,' said the Horse (still with his mouth full). 'But I've a sort of idea he likes to be asked'" (*TMN* 178). Relationship is the point. This is the kind of God of whom such a thing would be true. So the doctrine of the Trinity rightly understood is a powerful antidote to the temptation to construct an abstract Absolute to protect ourselves against the God who is really there, a process Lewis described so well:

> An "impersonal" God?—well and good. A subjective God of beauty, truth, and goodness, inside our own heads—better still. A formless life force surging through us, a vast power which we can tap—best of all. But God Himself, alive, . . . perhaps approaching at an infinite speed, the hunter, king, husband—that is quite another matter. (*M* 96)

Yes. Father, Son, and Holy Spirit is quite a different matter indeed.

GOD IS FATHER

God then is more personal than we are as Father, Son, and Spirit. The unity of the three Persons is traditionally understood to mean that they are all unequivocally God, equal in power, glory, and honor; the relationships, however, are not interchangeable, but rather the tripersonal unity of the Deity is articulated hierarchically. The relationships are not abstractly equivalent but personal and individual. The Father generates and sends the Son; the Father and the Son send the Spirit; the Son does what He sees the Father doing, and comes to reveal the Father. The Spirit comes to reveal the Son. But the reverse language does not appear in Scripture: The Son is not ever said to send the Father, nor does the Spirit send the Father or the Son. So amongst the divine Persons the Father is something like a first among equals. This fact, plus the paradigmatic nature for His followers of Jesus' way of relating to God, means that if we are looking for just one word to describe what God is to His people, the word that Christians have traditionally used is that He is our heavenly *Father*.

This is the traditional view, which Lewis held. But he was aware that challenges to it were already in the wind. He wondered about those already advocating female priests in the Church of England in his own day. "Suppose the reformer stops saying that a good woman may be like God and begins saying that God is like a good woman. Suppose he says that we might just as well pray to 'Our Mother which art in heaven' as to 'Our Father'" ("Priestesses" 237). We no longer have to suppose such a thing. But radical feminist theologians today do not stop with saying that we *might as well* pray to God as mother; some of them think that any male imagery about God is so tainted by what they see as the evils of patriarchy that it can only contribute to the ongoing oppression of women and amount to blasphemy. And they have prevailed so far that large segments of the church are so uncomfortable with the traditional language that they refer to God as our Parent in heaven and resort to barbaric neologisms like *Godself* to avoid using *Himself* as the reflexive pronoun in referring to God. Lewis would have thought this a tragic and misguided mistake.

Jettisoning the traditional Christian understanding of God as Father is a mistake first of all because it undermines the very understanding of biblical revelation that makes theology possible in the first place. Lewis reminds us that Christians can only speak meaningfully about God at all because they "think that God Himself has taught us how to speak of Him" ("Priestesses" 237). In an event so central to salvation history and so revelatory of God's relationship to us as the incarnation, it will not do to say that Jesus just happened to be a son and could just as well have called God his Mother in Heaven, there being a fifty-percent chance either way. Nothing in that event, so close to God's heart and so carefully and prophetically planned, could have been accidental. That is one reason why Lewis insists that "we have no authority to take the living and semitive figures which God has painted on the canvas of our nature and shift them about as if they were geometrical figures" ("Priestesses" 239). Perhaps theologians, more oriented to philosophy than philology in the modern world, do not sufficiently appreciate the crucial role played by imagery in literary texts. But the Bible is more a literary than a philosophical text, and the God it reveals in Christ is the God it reveals. Lewis was right to emphasize that the issue at stake is one of authority. If we can shift and replace the biblical imagery whenever it makes us uncomfortable or does not fit with our own ideologies, then the authority has indeed passed from the Text to us. Once that has happened, all we can have left is not God's revelation of Himself, but only our speculations about Him.

The second reason Lewis gives for keeping the masculine imagery is that changing it changes much more than just language. "A child who had been taught to pray to a Mother in heaven," he claims, "would have a religious life radically different from that of a Christian child" ("Priestesses" 237). Lewis does not elaborate what the difference would be. But he would certainly have known that goddess worship is usually associated with mystery religions and fertility cults, and that the masculine imagery for God in the Old Testament served to separate ancient Israel from such conceptions. Remember the passage from Miracles quoted earlier:

> He is Bacchus, Venus, Ceres all rolled into one.... On the other hand, Yahweh is clearly *not* a nature-god. He does not die and come to life each year.... He may give wine and fertility, but must not be worshipped with bacchanalian or aphrodisiac rites. He is not the soul of Nature nor of any part of Nature. He inhabits eternity; He dwells in the high and holy place; heaven is His throne, not his vehicle; earth is His footstool, not His vesture. (M 119)

Creating the world out of nothing is very different from giving birth to it. Nurturing imagery is given to the Spirit (brooding over the waters), but the imagery of God as Father reminds us that God has a different and more radical kind of transcendent sovereignty over creation than a fertility god can have, yet in a way that paradoxically also affirms His personal intimacy with us, as Simon Chan has pointed out (50). And the Fatherhood of God affects the way we relate to Him in a way that actually challenges the male ego rather than affirming it. The bottom line for Lewis is that "what is above and beyond all things is so masculine that we are all feminine in relation to it" (THS 316).

Lewis then defends the traditional understanding of God as our heavenly Father in terms that have proved prophetic. Whatever conclusions we may reach about gender roles in ministry, Lewis's warnings here are astute. We cannot say we believe that God has revealed Himself in Christ and then alter the details of that revelation whenever they do not comfortably fit with the spirit of the age. Scripture uses both masculine and feminine imagery, but some images are foundational in ways that others are not. To be Christians is to learn what it means to have God as our heavenly Father, and Jesus is the perfect one to teach us that.

GOD IS CREATOR

That God is the Creator of everything else that exists is the very first affirmation that Scripture makes about Him. Every pagan creation myth begins with some version of "In the beginning was the world." For the Baylonians, it was Apsu and Tiamat, the primordial fresh- and salt-water seas; for the Greeks, Zeus is the son of Chronos, time. The world is eternal, and the gods came from it—we could say "evolved" from it—like us, only earlier and with more power. They are therefore immortal but not eternal, powerful but not omnipotent, far-seeing but not omniscient. They are finite and limited, less than the cosmos which gave birth to them. Genesis turns all that on its head with the most profound words ever uttered by human lips up to that time: "In the beginning, God created the heavens and the earth" (Gen. 1:1).

A true creation story makes possible a very different kind of God. We have already seen its implications for God's transcendence above. Indeed, all his unique attributes flow from that affirmation. Omnipotence: if He made everything else that exists, what could possibly overcome Him? Omniscience: if He designed everything else that exists and has overseen its whole history from the beginning, what could He not know? Omnipresence: if the very space-time continuum itself came out of his workshop, as it were, then every point of space is immediately accessible to his operations at all times. Eternality: if the very space-time continuum came out of His workshop, then every moment of time is also always immediately accessible to His operations as well.

All this Lewis understood and affirmed. His primary contribution to the doctrine of creation was that of giving us a compelling picture of it that the imagination can grasp in *The Magician's Nephew*. Nothingness is invaded by music that brings forth stars, earth, plants, and animals. The glory of God is seen in the way that the act of creation combines power and intelligence into something that seems more than either. "With an unspeakable thrill, [Polly] felt quite certain that all the things were coming (as she said) 'out of the Lion's head'" (*TMN* 126).

GOD IS ETERNAL

We have seen that God's essential attributes flow logically from the fact that He is the Creator of everything else that exists. Lewis has things to say about each of them that are consistent with that basic insight while fleshing it out. If God created time, then He must be eternal. But how do we understand what eternity is or how it relates to time? The best we can do is probably an analogy, and the best analogy is one that is rooted in the very concept of creation. So Lewis profitably pursues the idea that God relates to our time the way a novelist or playwright relates to the fictional time of his work. "God is not hurried along in the Time-stream of this universe any more than an author is hurried along in the imaginary time of his own novel" (*MC* 147). Between two moments of a character's experience in a novel, no time passes at all for that character. But the author can spend all the time he likes thinking about that character before writing the next sentence, and that time does not appear in the time of the novel at all (*MC* 146). Something like this must be what God's relation to our time is like. It does not explain but helps us to imagine how He can attend to (and answer) millions of prayers at once. Lewis knows that this is not a "perfect illustration," but thinks it gives us a "glimpse" of the truth (147). It is hard to imagine a better glimpse. It avoids a purely negative view of eternity as "timelessness" in favor of a dynamic relationship with creation and with time that preserves our ability to imagine God as fully personal.

The same analogy also helps us understand the relationship between God and what we call "chance." Lewis wrote to Mrs. D. Jessup on 3 Feb. 1955:

> Suppose that in a novel a character gets killed in a railway accident. Is his death due to chance (e. g. the signals being wrong) or to the novelist? Well of course, both. The chance is the way the novelist removes the character at the exact moment his story requires. There's a good line in Spenser to quote to oneself: "It chanced (almighty God that chance did guide)." (*L* 3:574-5)

God's eternity, His not being trapped in our time flow but relating to it like an Author to the time flow of a novel or play, makes it easier to grasp and accept the mystery of how He exercises His sovereignty, how it can be absolute without compromising the integrity of the characters' choices or the reality of intervening causes. In even a well-written human story, a faint reflection of God's creative process, a good character takes on a life of his own and his choices flow organically from his personality, so that his deeds are truly both his own work and that of the author. How much more would this be true on the divine level?

Finally, seeing God as the Creator of the timeline who stands above it like Shakespeare above *Hamlet* makes it easier for us to grasp our existential situation as creatures of time who ultimately have to do with something higher than time. The biblical expression is that to God a thousand years is as a day and a day as a thousand years (2 Pet. 3:8). The experiential result is that for we who live in an insistently linear time, the life of faith seems to involve an awful lot of waiting. It is helpful to see that this experience is an effect of our position; it is not ultimate reality. The God in whom we trust is neither hurried nor impatient nor late. "I call all times soon," said Aslan (*VDT* 174).

GOD IS OMNIPRESENT

If God is the Creator of the space-time continuum, then what is true of His relationship to time is equally true of His relationship to space. Since we have already covered the one in some detail, we need not say too much about the other, for they are quite parallel.

Omnipresence means that God is not a "thing" inside of space like you and I are; space is a thing outside of Him, as it were. Rather, as His creature, just as every moment of time is immediately available to His operations, so is every point of space. In that sense He is present everywhere. In classical theology, He is not extended through all of space like some giant gas or pudding, but all of Him is present at every individual point. Maybe it is better to say that every point is present to Him. But He is not doing the same thing everywhere, nor relating to every point of space in the same way. Always He is sustaining and overseeing, for nothing would exist without Him. But He relates to His creation *personally*. He is not present in a believer in the same way He is in a rock; He is not present in anything in the same way as He is in Christ. Lewis understood this well. "God is present in each thing but not necessarily in the same mode; not in a man as in the consecrated bread and wine, not in a bad man as in a good one, not in a beast as in a man nor in a tree as in a beast, not in inanimate matter as in a tree" (*LtM* 74).

In a world understood post-Einstein as a space-time continuum, eternality and omnipresence are two sides of the same coin—omnipresence applied equally to space and time. It is not then surprising that Lewis used a very similar analogy to explain divine omnipresence:

> Looking for God—or Heaven—by exploring space is like reading or seeing all of Shakespeare's plays in the hope that you will find Shakespeare as one of the characters or Stratford as one of the places. Shakespeare is in one sense present at every moment in every play. But he is never present in the same way as Falstaff or Lady MacBeth. Nor is he diffused through the play like a gas. ("The Seeing Eye" 168)

Lewis here is in line with the historic theology of the church, but he does a better job of helping us imagine what these propositions mean than most theologians have been able to do.

GOD IS OMNIPOTENT

From God's position as the Creator of all else that exists follows not only His eternality and omnipresence, but also His omnipotence. He is all powerful. Lewis, like most classical theologians, but unlike many Christians and their critics, had thought carefully about what that means. It means that God has unlimited power. Because nothing exists that was not created by Him, nothing exists that is not derivative in its being and power from Him. Therefore, nothing exists that could overcome Him or thwart His will. The greatest power in the Universe other than God is by definition weaker than He is, for it depends for its own power and its very existence on His sustaining will.

Omnipotence then means all-powerful; but it does not mean that God can do "anything." He cannot draw a square circle, for example, because if the resulting figure had four right angles and four equal sides it would not be a circle; and if it were perfectly round it would not be square. This is not a sign of weakness on God's part, because no amount of power will help in the attempt to draw such a figure. What prevents it is not lack of power but the law of non-contradiction; in other words, as we shall see later, what prevents it is not God's lack of power but His positive character as a logical and truthful Person. By the same token, the allegedly unanswerable question whether God can make a stone so big He can't lift it has a very simple answer, and that answer is "no."

Lewis, following Aquinas and most of the Christian theological tradition, was quite clear about such things. "Omnipotence means power to do all that is intrinsically possible." Contradictions like square circles and stones so big that omnipotence cannot lift them are intrinsically impossible; it is God Himself who makes them so. Thus, "You may attribute miracles to Him, but not nonsense.... Meaningless combinations of words do not suddenly acquire meaning simply because we prefix to them the two other words 'God can'" (*PoP* 16). Lewis reiterates, "It is no more possible for God than for the weakest of His creatures to carry out both of two mutually exclusive alternatives; not because His power meets an obstacle, but because nonsense remains nonsense even when we talk it about God" (*PoP* 16).

Omnipotence does not mean that God can contradict Himself. It does mean that He can do things that would be impossible for us. Christians believe as an essential part of the content of their faith that God is able to make Nature do things it would not otherwise have done, and has sometimes done so, albeit rarely, so that the basic stability and order of the natural world is not compromised (*PoP* 21-22). Miracles are not contradictions of the laws of logic. They might not even break the laws of nature. In his extended discussion in *Miracles*, Lewis raises the possibility that miracles might simply result from an application of power or force that our understanding of those laws could not have anticipated. Once asserted, that force would alter the outcome our equations would have predicted. But a ball on a billiards table shoved by an invisible hand would not disobey the laws of physics in any way while going into a different pocket than the one we had expected. Lewis raises this possibility not to advance a doctrine about how miracles occur, but because Hume's famous argument against the rationality of belief in miracles had begun by defining them as violations of natural law. If that definition is not necessarily so, then the rest of Hume's argument is rendered moot. The bottom line is that God can certainly heal the sick, multiply loaves and fishes, still the storm, or raise the dead, and can be expected to do so on rare occasions in order, for example, to point out the validity of the claims of His Messenger.

All of this flows from belief in creation. We human beings are caught in a causal nexus that limits our freedom significantly. We are often thwarted not just by our own natures but by the nature of external reality. God, on the other hand, as Creator, stands above that nexus of cause and effect, so that He is limited only by His own nature and His own choices. So, Lewis explains, "The freedom of God consists in the fact that no cause other than Himself produces His acts and no external obstacle impedes them" (*PoP* 23). What external obstacle could? He is omnipotent, being the Creator. He is limited by no lack of power, but only by His own nature and His own choices. Lewis's exposition of these ideas is richly biblical and apologetically astute.

GOD IS OMNISCIENT

God's omniscience is another attribute that logically flows from His role as Creator. If there is nothing He did not design and bring into being, nothing He does not sustain in being, then there is nothing whose existence He has not accounted for. If every point of space and time is accessible to His operations, then He is also aware of what is transpiring at every point of space and time. He believes all true propositions and no false ones. He is the author and wellspring of truth and knowledge as well as of existence and life; and none of those streams by definition can rise above its source.

Lewis does not have a lot to say about omniscience directly. His treatment of God's eternity is relevant here, though. The picture of God as an author relating to the timeline of his characters also helps us to understand that there is nothing about their world that God is unaware of or cannot spend an eternity (of their time) contemplating. One of Lewis's virtues is his ability to take the most abstract and abstruse theological ideas and not only make them clear but do it in a way that shows their practical significance. God's eternity, His transcendence of our timeline and its implications for His knowledge of it, helps us to pray, as we saw above. And in a similar way, His infinite knowledge and foreknowledge is not seen simply as a limitless catalog of facts, but as related to God's heart and His costly way of relating to us: "God saw the crucifixion in the act of creating the first nebula" (*PoP* 72). God's knowledge is not just a catalog of facts but involves a stance toward them that relates them to His character as a God of truth and of love.

GOD IS TRUE

The God of the Bible is not just a Being who happens to be truthful and trustworthy (fortunately for us). He is the Being whose essential nature is the source of the very concepts of truth and faithfulness and the reason why they apply in the world that He designed. In other words, the very reason why the law of non-contradiction is universally valid is that we live in a world made by the God who keeps his covenant and who cannot lie. That is why Lewis can say that "Logic is a real insight into the way in which real things have to exist. In other words, the laws of thought are also the laws of things" ("*De Futilitate*" 63).

As we saw in the chapter on Lewis's exposition of the nature of truth, this has implications for how we think about God. His thoughts are above our thoughts, but not by using a different logic than ours. The rules of thought are not just ideas we made up, but are real insights into the way things have to be in a universe made by a rational God who made us in His image. The laws of thought are the laws of things. Thus, in Christian theology, there are many mysteries but no real contradictions. In other words, we might affirm one God existing in three persons, but we will not simultaneously affirm one God only and three Gods.

Because God is a God of truth and covenant faithfulness, His character is the criterion of truth for us not only ethically but also epistemologically. This is why Lewis could speak with such confidence of real contradiction as an automatic disqualifier for religious truth claims. God "cannot do what is contradictory: or, in other words, a meaningless sentence will not gain meaning simply because someone chooses to prefix to it the words 'The Landlord can'" (*PR* 181). In a similar vein, "Omnipotence means power to do all that is intrinsically possible.... You may attribute miracles to Him, but not nonsense.... Meaningless combinations of words do not suddenly acquire meaning simply because we prefix to them the two other words 'God can'" (*PoP* 16). So, as we saw in our discussion of omnipotence above, God cannot make a stone so big He cannot lift it, not because He is weak but because, unlike us, His logic does not fail Him. "It is no more possible for God than for the weakest of His creatures to carry out both of two mutually exclusive alternatives; not because His power meets an obstacle, but because nonsense remains nonsense even when we talk it about God" (*PoP* 16).

God is a God of truth. He cannot lie; He cannot contradict Himself; He will not fail to keep His word. You can depend on these truths as much when living your life as when constructing your theology. Lewis did so with confidence because he understood that what to us are "rules" of logic and truthfulness are simply the practical articulation of who God is. He "owns" those rules in a far more profound sense than just having arbitrarily made them up and imposed them. And that is why Aslan can ask the searching rhetorical question, "Do you think I wouldn't obey my own rules?" (*VDT* 170).

GOD IS GOOD

When God created the universe He obviously gave it being and form; He also gave it value by calling it "good" (Gen. 1:4, etc.). Goodness flows from God as much as being or design does. It is therefore also one of His essential attributes. As Lewis summarizes it, "God's will is determined by His wisdom which always perceives, and his goodness which always embraces, the intrinsically good" (*PoP* 88).

But what does this mean? Is it simply circular to say that the good comes from God because God is good? It is hard to talk about goodness and God without Plato's "Euthyphro Dilemma" coming up: is something good because God says it is, or does God say something is good because it is good?

Lewis understood that the dilemma is of course a false dilemma. The correct answer is "neither." God's attribution of goodness is not an arbitrary decision, nor is it based on some standard external to Himself. Rather, his own character is the standard for goodness, and we can see that this standard is not arbitrary but necessary once we ponder His identity as the Creator alongside Augustine's analysis of the nature of evil as a privation or perversion of the good. For creation is a constructive, not a destructive, act. And evil is always a perversion of some prior good; otherwise it could not exist at all. So Lewis asks, "Is it rational to believe in a bad God?" No, he concludes: such a God "couldn't invent or create or govern anything" (GO 27). We often ask why a good God would create such an imperfect and often painful world. The answer is that He didn't. He permitted the Fall of His world. But if He had been destructive rather than creative, harmful rather than beneficent, chaotic rather than intelligent and purposeful, there would and could have been no world to fall. Creation is of necessity an act of superabounding goodness. A world that continues to exist and to be redeemable cannot have Satan as its source.

Lewis confirms the biblical teaching that God is good—or, perhaps more accurately, perceives its necessary truth—by performing two different thought experiments. The first was trying to imagine an evil god and finding that the idea just won't work, as we saw above. The second involves the difficulty of *knowing* God as evil. If He were, how would we ever know it? Lewis reasons,

> If a Brute and Blackguard made the world, then he also made our minds.
> If he made our minds, he also made that very standard in them whereby

we judge him to be a Brute and Blackguard. And how can we trust a standard which comes from such a brutal and blackguardly source? ("*De Futilitate*" 66)

An evil god by definition then is not a knowable god; but we do know something about God. And so, once again, Lewis helps us see that to affirm His goodness is not to spin a logical circle but to bow to the necessity of who He is and must be.

If God is the source of goodness as well as of being, then He is also the source of the *Tao*, the moral law whose objective existence Lewis established in *The Abolition of Man* and traced back to God in *Mere Christianity*. It is a Law which elucidates as well as commands goodness. The existence, form, and design of the universe witness to God's existence, His power, and His intelligence, but the moral law reveals Him even more profoundly, "just as you find out more about a man by listening to his conversation than by looking at a house he has built" (MC 37).

Lewis was well aware that our experience of living in a fallen world often tempts us to doubt the goodness of God. Reminding himself that the Creator could not logically be ultimately evil was part of the process of pulling himself back from despair after the death of his wife from cancer. He knew that in such times it is easy to see only the evil in the world, and that belief in a good God is then an act of faith—faith that needs to be supported by an understanding of logical necessity and by being reminded of historical reality. "What reason have we," Lewis asks again in *A Grief Observed*, "except our own desperate wishes, to believe that God is, by any standard we can conceive, 'good'? Doesn't all the *prima facie* evidence we have suggest the opposite? What have we to set against it?" The ultimate answer foreshadows the atonement: "We set Christ against it" (*GO* 26).

So we learn about goodness by looking at God, as He is revealed as Creator and Lawgiver, and especially as He is revealed as Redeemer in Christ. And when we do, we come to understand that God is wholly and purely good, and we are not. As Lewis realized, "We want not so much a Father in Heaven as a grandfather in heaven—a senile benevolence who, as they say, 'liked to see the young people enjoying themselves'" (*PoP* 28). To find that this grandfatherly God is not the One who exists is rather a shock; we thought that goodness would not be so disturbing of our comfort zones! "People who have not been in Narnia sometimes think that a thing cannot be good and terrible at the same time" (*LWW* 140). Our concept of the good has, at many points, to be corrected by our knowledge of God. But our corruption is such that it is refined and corrected, if we are willing to accept redemption—not simply overturned. A God who is wiser than we must have different ideas than we do on many subjects including good and evil. But if His moral judgments differ from ours in such a way "that our 'black' may be His 'white,' we can mean nothing by calling Him good" (*PoP* 25). In other words, God's goodness is superior to ours but is not of a completely different kind; it "differs from ours not as white from black but as a perfect circle from a child's first attempt to draw a wheel" (*PoP* 27).

All the attributes of God, when rightly seen theologically, lead us to a vision of God that inspires worship. Lewis wrote to Arthur Greeves on 12 Sept. 1933, echoing 1 John 1:5, that "there is no evil whatever in God. He is pure light. All the heat that in us is lust or anger in Him is cool light—eternal morning, eternal freshness, eternal springtime: never disturbed, never strained" (2:122). Theology when it is most doxological is also at its most practical. We fall into evil when we pursue the good in wrong ways—but usually it is a good that we are pursuing. In the same letter, Lewis continues, "God not only understands but shares the desire which is at the root of all my evil—the desire for complete and ecstatic happiness. He made me for no other purpose than to enjoy it. But He knows, and I do not, how it can be really and permanently obtained" (2:123).

There is only one way happiness can be finally and eternally obtained: by seeing God as the greatest good so that we make Him *our* greatest good. In what may be his most profound statement on the goodness of God, Lewis explains,

> If you want joy, power, peace, eternal life, you must get close to . . . the thing that has them. They are not a sort of prize that God could, if He chose, just hand out to anyone. They are a great fountain of energy and beauty spurting up at the very centre of reality. If you are close to it, the spray will wet you: if you are not, you will remain dry. Once a man is united to God, how could he not live forever? Once a man is separated from God, what can he do but wither and die? (MC 153)

God is good. Therefore, the whole Christian life is about getting into the spray. (For more on Lewis's concept of goodness, see the chapter on goodness in Williams, *Reflections from Plato's Cave*.)

GOD IS JUST

Surely it is a comforting thought that God is good. But we saw that God's goodness is so high, so pure, and so severe that, when it reminds us of how far short we fall of it, it is not entirely comforting. That discrepancy introduces an attribute of God that fallen sinners must find positively threatening: the divine justice, or, to put it even more starkly, His wrath.

In classical theology God's justice is His propensity always to do what is right seen from the standpoint of His role as the upholder of the Moral Law of the universe. One practical outcome of such considerations is the absolute necessity that sin be punished. Because all human beings are sinners, we think we have a vested interest in versions of God's goodness that reduce to Lewis's grandfather in heaven, and we tend to see justice or wrath as incompatible with such reduced versions of goodness. But Lewis understood that it is precisely God's goodness that demands a high view of His justice: "When we merely say that we are bad, the 'wrath' of God seems a barbarous doctrine; as soon as we perceive our badness, it appears inevitable, a mere corollary from God's goodness" (*PoP* 46). And surely he was right. What would we think of a goodness that had a high tolerance for evil, that did not implacably oppose it? That would be a very superficial kind of goodness indeed.

Lewis's most extended treatment of justice is not directly focused on divine justice, but on human justice—but it shows that even on an earthly level, the more "enlightened" view of justice that confuses it with mercy ends up being horribly cruel and not really just at all. In "The Humanitarian Theory of Punishment," Lewis looks at well-meaning attempts to reform penal justice with a wary eye. In pursuit of a more compassionate way, they may be giving up an essential concept that will come back to bite them:

> According to the Humanitarian theory, to punish a man because he deserves it, and as much as he deserves, is mere revenge, and therefore, barbarous and immoral. It is maintained that the only legitimate motives for punishing are the desire to deter others by example or to mend the criminal. ("Humanitarian Theory" 287)

What is the missing concept? "The Humanitarian theory removes from Punishment the concept of Desert. But the concept of Desert is the only connecting link between punishment and justice" ("Humanitarian Theory" 288). Remember Lewis's doctrine of objective value from *Abolition of Man*. There are certain qualities in the universe that deserve a specific response from us, whether we give it or not: reverence, contemplation, approval, condemnation, etc. Likewise, there are certain actions on our part that truly merit a response from society—or from God. Though punishing a criminal because he deserves it might seem more cruel than trying to reform him, it may not work out that way. The theory of desert treats him as a person with dignity who is free once the punishment has been meted out. But if society is trying to "cure" him, it is treating him as less than a moral agent and subjecting him to a "treatment" that may have no ending place short of the Gulag. Thus, "Mercy, detached from Justice, grows unmerciful" ("Humanitarian Theory" 294).

What people deserve as punishment from society may be debatable. But Lewis has simply applied to societal justice the conceptual framework that the Bible and the Christian tradition have always taught about the situation between human beings and God. As sinners—as rebels against the high King of the universe—we deserve eternal punishment, and God, being just, must give it to us. How God's love and mercy may be exercised in the light of this situation sets up the crucial theological problem to which the atonement is the solution. That is the topic of a later chapter. What we face as we contemplate the doctrine of God's justice and wrath is the profound difficulty of that problem. To downplay justice in favor of goodness is to cheapen the brilliance of the solution Christian theology will present to it by misunderstanding the terms of the problem itself.

Such cheap solutions Lewis was wise enough to disallow. Thus, when we reach the atonement—when we experience it—we will find that "anger—no peevish fit of temper, but just, generous, scalding indignation—passes (not necessarily at once) into embracing, exultant, re-welcoming love." To try to salvage a view of God's love by downplaying His justice and even wrath is to miss the full impact of that redemptive moment. "Turn God's wrath into mere enlightened disapproval, and you also turn His love into mere humanitarianism" (*LtM* 97). Thus it is because of God's goodness *and* His love that we insist on His justice.

GOD IS HOLY

The root meaning of the biblical words for holy, Heb. *qadosh* and Greek *hagios*, is separation. When applied to God, it refers to His exalted separation from all that is evil or corrupting. It makes Him "high and lifted up," as when Isaiah saw Him on His throne with the seraphim calling out, "Holy, holy, holy!" (Is. 6:1-3) and Isaiah felt himself to be a man of unclean lips by contrast. The result is reminiscent of that moment Lewis described in the history of religion "when the Numinous Power to which [people] feel awe is made the guardian of the morality to which they feel obligation" (*PoP* 10). One could say it is God's goodness and righteousness seen from the perspective of His transcendence. Holiness thus functions as a kind of summation of all of God's attributes, both moral and metaphysical.

Lewis does not speak much of God's holiness under that term. He does not analyze it, but he evokes it, often when he is speaking of transcendence or of the numinous. One gets a sense of it when recalling that Aslan is not a tame lion. Rat and Mole meeting Pan in *The Wind and the Willows* is used as a prime example of the numinous: "'Afraid?' murmured the Rat, his eyes shining with unutterable love. 'Afraid? of Him? O, never, never. And yet—O Mole, I am afraid'" (*PoP* 6). Lewis notes that a human response to it is depicted in Mallory: "Galahad 'began to tremble right hard when the deadly (= mortal) flesh began to behold the spiritual things'" (*PoP* 6).

Because people come to resemble what they worship, God's holiness gets transmitted to His people as part of the moral transformation that takes place as a result of regeneration. Their relationship to God makes them holy, i.e., distinct from the world, separated from its corrupting influence and set apart from it for His service. One might expect this to make the saints as threatening as God Himself is in His holiness. But He gives them something of His goodness without giving them His corresponding role as Judge so that this setting apart actually makes them surprisingly attractive—they are examples of restored humanity. This quality was what drew Lewis to MacDonald: "I did not yet know (and I was long in learning the name of the new quality, the bright shadow, that rested on the travels of Anodos. I do now. It was *holiness*" (*SbJ* 197). "How little people know who think that holiness is dull," he wrote to his American correspondent. "When one meets the real thing... it is irresistible" (*LAL* 19). And because participating in it is an aspect of getting into the spray of God's goodness, Lewis concludes that "to become holy... must be great *fun*" (*MC* 188). That goodness, that restoration, and that fun are reflections then of who God is in His essential nature.

GOD IS LOVE

And so we come to what may be the most profound statement of all: God is love. Christians who have grown used to this claim may not realize how radical it is. But try to see how foreign it would be to any other faith. "Zeus is lust" might make sense, but "Zeus is love" would be ludicrous. One might say that Aphrodite is love, but it would be in a very different sense than what Christians mean. Allah is merciful, but "Allah is love" does not appear in the Koran. Some of the gods of Hinduism could be spoken of as compassionate—but they are ultimately too impersonal to fully inhabit the Christian claim.

There is a reason for the uniqueness of the Christian claim, and it goes back to the very core of the mystery of the Christian God's inner nature. No other god has relationship as essential to its being. The statement that God is love flows from and leads back to the doctrine of the Trinity. Lewis understood this well: "The words 'God is love' have no real meaning unless God contains at least two Persons. Love is something that one person has for another person. If God was a single person, then before the world was made, He was not love" (*MC* 151).

Before the world was made, the Father loved the Son and the Spirit, the Son, the Father and the Spirit, and the Spirit, the Father and the Son. That love just is the life of God, and into that love He invites His creatures. God then is not the unmoved mover of Greek philosophy but the dynamic moving Mover of the Trinity and Creation: "Nothing marks off Pagan theism from Christianity so sharply as Aristotle's doctrine that God moves the universe, Himself unmoving, as the Beloved moves a lover. But for Christendom, 'Herein is love, not that we loved God but that He loved us'" (*PoP* 40, quoting 1 John 4:10). We have already seen creation as the overflow of God's superabundant goodness, but it is more dynamic and personal even than that: "The living, dynamic activity of love has been going on in God for ever and has created everything else" (*MC* 151). We saw that Lewis described God's goodness as a fountain springing up at the heart of reality. What energizes that fountain is love.

> We begin at the real beginning, with love as the Divine energy. This primal love is Gift-love. In God there is no hunger that needs to be filled, only plenteousness that desires to give. The doctrine that God was under no necessity to create is not a piece of dry scholastic speculation. It is essential. . . . God, who needs nothing, loves into existence wholly superfluous creatures in order that He may love and perfect them. (*FL* 175-6)

The depths of that love are shown most profoundly at the Cross; but that is another chapter. Nevertheless, we see already that only this kind of God, only a God who is love, could generate a faith that centers in such a place.

CONCLUSION

In theology proper, the doctrine of God, Lewis shows that he has richly and profitably absorbed the best thinking of the Christian tradition. He resists the temptation to try to make God more acceptable to modern audiences; he knows that Aslan is not a tame lion. "Many of those who say they dislike Milton's God," he noted, "only mean that they dislike God: infinite sovereignty de jure combined with infinite power de facto, and love which, by its very nature, includes wrath also—it is not only in poetry that these things offend" (*PPL* 130). Lewis knew that without facing the challenging and, to modern sensibilities, off-putting parts of theology, we could never get to the sweetness of its marrow.

His formulations of the doctrine of God are orthodox in content but often daring in expression, in ways that make what often appears only as very abstruse doctrine suddenly appear both understandable and meaningful. Lewis's emphasis on the concreteness of the reality of God as opposed to the abstraction of much academic theological language about Him helps on both of those scores. Few theologians have so well explained the difference it makes to the Christian life that we believe in the Trinity, for example, which opens up to us the mysteries of relationality and love. Lewis was not a pastor, but there is often a pastoral slant to his expositions of doctrine. He explains God's relationship to time in ways that help us past stumbling blocks to prayer.

To do this successfully, a theologian needs to be able to think in pictures *and* to be logically rigorous about the implications of those pictures. Few are as skilled in both sets of those tools as Lewis was; indeed, few academic theologians know how to think in pictures at all. But Lewis had pondered not just the ideas but also the imagery, and done so wisely. For example, rather than simply dismissing as naïve and childish the picture of God as "a grave old king with a long beard," Lewis knew how to access the wisdom of childhood without being led astray by it.

> That image is a Jungian archetype. It links God with all the wise old kings in the fairy-tales, with prophets, sages, magicians. Though it is (formally) the picture of a man, it suggests something more than humanity. At the very least it gets in the idea of something older than yourself, something that knows more, something you can't fathom. (*GO* 27)

Theology for Lewis is not just about abstract ideas academically debated; it is about a Person with whom we have to do. Aslan, God incarnate as He might have been if He had gone to a world like Narnia, is good, I tell you—but he is not tame. And "he seems to be at the back of all the stories" (*TH&HB* 223).

Yes.

CHAPTER 5

Anthropology and Hamartiology
The Nature of Man and His Fall

"I do indeed, Sir," said Caspian. "I was wishing that I came of a more honorable lineage."
"You come of the Lord Adam and the Lady Eve," said Aslan. "And that is both honor enough to erect the head of the poorest beggar, and shame enough to bow the shoulders of the greatest emperor on earth. Be content." (PC 232-3)

The Christian account of the world is a dynamic and dramatic one. Post-modernists are suspicious of grand metanarratives, but Christianity unashamedly offers the grandest one of all, the Story of creation, fall, redemption, and restoration, which Christians insist is the only way of understanding the ultimate truth of things. One cannot be a real Christian without overcoming those suspicions, however justified they may be in general, to accept *this* metanarrative as simply and objectively true.

Therefore theology, the systematic exposition of that body of truth, must begin, like a Russian novel, by introducing the characters. The central character, the great Protagonist who drives the drama, is God Himself, whom we introduced in the previous chapter. But second in importance only to Him—astoundingly so, given that in the hierarchy of reality we are placed a little lower than the angels—is Man. For we as human beings are the ones who were created, who fell, and who have been redeemed and are being restored. So the next topics in theology are anthropology and hamartiology, the doctrines of man and of sin. Who are we; what were we meant to be; what have we become; and what is the precise nature of the fall from which we are redeemed by the coming of Christ: these are the questions that must occupy us next. C. S. Lewis has a great deal of insight to offer on them, along with some places where his understanding may fall short of the full biblical picture.

ANTHROPOLOGY: THE DOCTRINE OF MAN

Let us begin with two popular and widely quoted statements by Lewis that sound bizarre and outlandish if you are thinking of human beings as simply another animal a bit higher in the scale of random evolution. They raise the question, "What could justify talking about human beings this way?" That is exactly the question we should be asking. (For a book-length treatment of that question as answered by Chesterton and Tolkien as well as Lewis, see my book *Mere Humanity*.) Here are the statements:

> If individuals live only seventy years, then a state or a nation or a civilization, which may last for a thousand years, is more important than an individual. But if Christianity is true, then the individual is not only more important but incomparably more important, for he is everlasting, and the life of a state or a civilization, compared with his, is only a moment. (*MC* 73)

> It is a serious thing to live in a society of possible gods and goddesses, to remember that the dullest and most uninteresting person you can talk to may one day be a creature which, if you saw it now, you would be strongly tempted to worship, or else a horror and a corruption such as you now meet, if at all, only in a nightmare. ("The Weight of Glory" 45)

If naturalism is true, if human beings are randomly evolved biological organisms and no more, then they only last seven or eight decades and subsequently just cease to exist. They might be remembered for another generation or two, and then, for most of them considered as individuals, it will be as if they had never existed. Even the few who are remembered for the life of a civilization will not be around to take any satisfaction in their lasting achievements or their fame (or infamy as the case may be). Once their life is extinguished it will be, for them, as if they had never been.

Christianity teaches that men and women did not evolve by chance but were purposefully created, and created in the image of God. Historic Christians differ on the question of how much God used evolution in the process of creating human beings, from very little to a lot; they are unanimous in saying that naturalistic evolution cannot be the whole story. Rather than evolving by chance, we were created deliberately for a high purpose. "Man is not the centre. God does not exist for the sake of man. Man does not exist for his own sake" (*PoP* 36). Man exists for the sake of the purpose for which he was created: to serve the living God.

We share a physical nature with the animals but also have immortal souls that distinguish us from them and unite us to the spiritual world, to God and angels. "We are now as we ought to be—between the angels who are our elder brothers and the beasts who are our jesters, servants, and playfellows" says

Ransom of a moment when St. Anne's anticipates the final restoration (*THS* 378). How can we believe such a thing in a world dominated by reductionistic philosophies? If God exists and has revealed Himself, then in that revelation He reveals us as well, created in His image. Thus Christian theology gives us permission to believe what our hearts already tell us:

> Atoms dead could never thus
> Move the human heart of us,
> Unless the beauty that we see
> Part of endless beauty be. (*L* 1:373)

What exactly does it mean to have been created "in God's image"? Lewis gives insight into his answer to that question in a passage which he offers as a "myth," i.e., "an account of what *may have been* historical fact:"

> For long centuries God perfected the animal form which was to become the vehicle of humanity. . . . But it was only an animal because all its physical and psychical processes were directed to purely material and natural ends. Then, in the fullness of time, God caused to descend upon this organism . . . a new kind of consciousness which could say "I" and "me," which could look upon itself as an object, which knew God, which could make judgments of truth, beauty, and goodness, and which was so far above time that it could perceive time flowing past. (*PoP* 64-5)

Many conservative Christians will think Lewis conceded too much to the theory of evolution here and did not hew faithfully enough to a literal reading of Genesis. We have already dealt with the weaknesses in Lewis's doctrine of inspiration in chapter three, and raised the question, "Why couldn't the Old Testament as well as the New be 'myth become fact'?" So let us not be distracted by that issue here. Lewis does affirm the necessity of a miraculous act to make human beings different from the rest of the animal creation, and gives an interesting account of the difference it made, an account consistent with both biblical teaching and observation.

Animals are described as creatures whose bodies and minds (in so far as they have them) are "directed to purely material and natural ends." Higher animals are certainly possessed of intelligence. Chimps for example will arrange boxes into a pile that lets them retrieve a banana suspended from the ceiling, or sharpen sticks to dig termites out of their nests. But their intelligence seems to be wholly pragmatic in its orientation. They will not arrange the boxes or the sticks into complex symmetrical patterns just so they can sit back and contemplate their handiwork. Man is the only creature who finds it natural to engage in that kind of behavior.

Man is thus not only aware but self-aware, aware of himself as a self: he has an ego. Mrs. Frank L. Jones had written to Lewis asking, "What is a soul?" Lewis wrote back on 7 Feb. 1950, "I am. This is the only possible answer: or expanded, A soul is that which can say 'I am'" (*L* 3:10). This expansion of awareness that results from having a soul happens on multiple levels. We are aware of ourselves, of the world as having uses other than pragmatic ones, of truth, goodness, and beauty as transcendental values (transcending, that is, their pragmatic usefulness to us), of time, and ultimately of God. Interestingly, the evil Witches of Narnia do not seem to have an appreciation for the non-utilitarian: they "are not interested in things or people unless they can use them. They are terribly practical" (*TMN* 86). Human "rational souls" by contrast include "not merely the faculty to abstract and calculate, but the apprehension of values, the power to mean by 'good' something more than 'good for me,' or even 'good for my species'" ("Religion and Rocketry" 85). The soul includes, in other words, the ability to participate in the *Tao* of *The Abolition of Man*.

These levels are all related, and related spiritually: that is, they all flow from an ability to stand above the realm of mere physics and see beyond it to realities that cannot be reduced to, or deduced from, atoms in motion. This fact is consistent with the idea that the soul is not simply functional in nature but involves a non-physical, i.e., spiritual, component. Not being physical, the human soul is not subject to dissolution, but survives the death of the body to await the resurrection.

Lewis thinks such transcendence of the physical, and its consequent survival, essential to the full concept of personhood. In the argument from reason in *Miracles*, physical determinism is seen as incompatible with intentional rationality. And as Lewis reasons about the death of his wife, Joy, "If H. is 'not,' then she never was. I mistook a cloud of atoms for a person" (*GO* 25). Obviously the biological organism known as Joy Davidman would had existed; but the immortal soul, the *person* Lewis knew, something—some*one*—who was more than just a chemically determined biological machine, would not have.

Why did God create mankind with such endowments? For relationship, for fellowship with Himself, is a true but incomplete answer. God already had the angels for spiritual fellowship, so why grant the kind of soul we have been discussing to a physical creature? Man participates in both the physical and the spiritual worlds because he was designed to be the bridge between those two worlds, to rule the physical creation for God as His subregent. The verbs from Genesis giving Adam his agenda in the Garden include *subdue, rule, dress,* and *keep* (Gen. 1:28, 2:15). Even after the Fall, we have not lost our position as the stewards of creation, though now ruling it in rebellion and stewarding it often rather badly. Redemption is about restoring the right relations not only between man and God and man and his fellow man but also between man and nature, the disruption of each being entailed by the other.

Lewis pictures this strategic relationship of man upward to God and downward to nature by the special role that sons of Adam and daughters of Eve are given in Narnia. Even in the land of Talking Beasts, a different world from the one Adam was created to rule, things are not right unless they are rightly related to human beings. "We beasts remember, even if Dwarfs forget, that Narnia was never right except when a son of Adam was King" (*PC* 71), says the Badger Trufflehunter. And the prophecy about the end of the Long Winter is equally pregnant with meaning:

> When Adam's flesh and Adam's bone
> Sits at Cair Paravel in throne,
> The evil time will be over and done. (*LWW* 87)

It is hard fully to appreciate the wonder of what humanity was intended to be, but without an inkling of it, we cannot begin fully to appreciate the depths to which we have fallen or the glory to which the Gospel promises to restore us. Many readers are no doubt thinking of the famous passage in "the Weight of Glory" where Lewis talks about the non-existence of "ordinary" human beings: we are all going to be either gods and goddesses that we would be tempted to worship if we met them now or unimaginable horrors out of a nightmare (*WoG* 45). To give physical creatures eternal souls, to breathe into them the breath of life, is to give them a high destiny, the frustration of which is an evil of cosmic proportions. The sinfulness of sin is therefore seen both in the majesty and goodness of the God against whom it is committed, and also in that of the original state of the creature that it perverts and damns. As Hyoi points out, "No, *Hman*, it is not a few deaths roving the world around him that make a *hnau* miserable. It is a bent *hnau* that would blacken the world" (*OOTSP* 75). So Lewis muses,

> Indeed the only way in which I can make real to myself what theology teaches about the heinousness of sin is to remember that every sin is the distortion of an energy breathed into us—an energy which, if not thus distorted, would have blossomed into one of those holy acts whereof "God did it" and "I did it" are both true descriptions. (*LtM* 69).

Perhaps the most profound expression of this theme is the fact that perfect humanity in the person of Tor on Perelandra is a perfect likeness of Christ (*Pa* 205). It does not get any higher than that! Lewis, as the narrator trying to convey Ransom's description, wonders how idolatry was avoidable in looking at him, and concludes that the better the portrait the less the likelihood of mistaking it for the reality—for the great portrait is more than just a xeroxed copy. Christ is the template for humanity as it is meant to be. Thus we have to understand the height of our creation before we are ready to look at the sobering reality of our fall.

HAMARTIOLOGY: THE DOCTRINE OF SIN

Sadly, of course, human beings as they currently exist are not rightly related to God, to each other, or to the natural world. How did this happen? What does it mean? At their very creation the Talking Beasts of Narnia are given an ominous warning:

> "Creatures, I give you yourselves," said the strong, happy voice of Aslan. "I give to you forever this land of Narnia... The Dumb Beasts whom I have not chosen are yours also. Treat them gently and cherish them but do not go back to their ways lest you cease to be Talking Beasts. For out of them you were taken and into them you can return. Do not so." (*TMN* 140)

It is not a perfect parallel. Man by falling did not cease to be a Talking Beast or even a spiritual one, though he did become, in biblical language, spiritually dead. And Narnian Talking Beasts do not seem to have fallen corporately as a single race ("in Adam") as humans did. But like us, the Narnians faced the possibility of falling to a lower status or position than the one they had been given. How might they do so? How did we do the equivalent in our own story?

THE FALL

It is not in Narnia but on Perelandra that we find the clearest answers to this question. For on Perelandra we have a new couple who recapitulate the fall story from Genesis, though with a different outcome. Like Adam and Eve, Tor and Tinidril are the lord and lady of their world; if the parallel with Adam and Eve is followed through completely, they are empowered to act representatively for all their offspring. They face the same kind of temptation with the same kinds of issues at stake. Ransom, on Perelandra to observe the temptation of the Green Lady by the Unman, realizes that "her purity and peace were not, as they had seemed, things settled and inevitable like the purity and peace of an animal—that they were alive and therefore breakable, a balance maintained by a mind and therefore, at least in theory, able to be lost" (*Pa* 68).

This was the staggering experiment that Maleldil had dared to try: creating real persons who were not automata but who could choose to love and obey Him freely—or not. Note the positive words in the description of Tinidril's condition, along with the chilling alternatives they entail. Her purity and peace are "alive and therefore breakable." They are "maintained by a mind" in a conscious, deliberate, and continued act which does not have to be chosen or continued. If it is chosen, all is well. "It is I, I myself, who turn from the good expected to the given good. Out of my own heart I do it," Tinidril exclaims (*Pa* 69). The temptation on Perelandra is our own, being played out before our eyes, with (at this point in the narrative) the outcome still in the balance. And this makes the human heart the most wondrous and potentially terrible thing that God has created.

The word *alive*, in contrast to the dead automata which would be the alternative to it, conveys the glory that is possible if the experiment succeeds—or can be salvaged. It also conveys what is at stake in making persons who are truly alive, persons who can truly choose and not just respond mechanically. As Ransom realizes, "Either something or nothing must depend on individual choices. And if something, who could set bounds to it?" (*Pa* 142). For that which is alive and not immutable can die. These then are the choices: to live close to the spray of all that is good and wholesome in the exuberant joy of the life of God which is the Great Dance at the end of Perelandra, or to share in the living death which is the "life" of the Unman, sunk beneath the rind.

What then exactly is the set of choices that sends us to one or the other of those destinies? Most simply it is obedience versus disobedience. But it is obedience or disobedience not to a set of rules considered as such so much as obedience or disobedience that flow from one's relationship to a Person, a relationship either of love and trust or of resentment and rebellion. Ransom thinks that Maleldil made one law without any obvious point "in order that there might be obedience.... Where can you taste the joy of obeying unless He bids you do something for which His bidding is the *only* reason?" (*Pa* 118). Obedience becomes an end in itself if we know and love the goodness of the One who asks it of us. Lewis portrays well the fact that, while disobedience involves breaking a rule, the really significant thing about it is the breaking of a relationship.

That relationship involves a recognition of the reality of who the Creator is and who we are, and the breaking of it involves lying to ourselves about that reality. As Lewis explains in *The Problem of Pain*, "The proper good of a creature is to surrender itself to its Creator—to enact intellectually, volitionally, and emotionally, that relationship which is given in the mere fact of its being a creature. When it does so, it is good and happy" (*PoP* 78). Such intellectual, volitional, and emotional enactment would be worship, trust (or faith), devotion, and obedience. But what if a creature could be deceived into pursuing a kind of role reversal? Then it must be evil and miserable. This was the horrible mistake of our first parents:

> They wanted ... to "'call their souls their own." But that means to live a lie.... They wanted some corner in the universe of which they could say to God, "This is our business, not yours." But there is no such corner ... This act of self will on the part of the creature, which constitutes an utter falseness to its true creaturely position, is the only sin that can be conceived as the Fall. (*PoP* 68)

Ransom, for whom Adam's choice in those terms has become habitual, keeps finding the presence of Maleldil on Perelandra less than congenial. It "was intolerable only at certain moments—at just those moments in fact (symbolized by his impulse to smoke and to put his hands in his pockets) when a man asserts his independence and feels that now at last he's on his own" (*Pa* 72). Or as Orual puts it in her controversy with the gods, "There's no room for you and us in the same world. You're a tree in whose shade we can't thrive. We want to be on our own" (*TWHF* 291). Hence the question that reverberates throughout *Perelandra*: Will The Green Lady try to exist on her own and come to have the same conflict that Ransom and Orual experience? Or can she somehow avoid the fate of the human race on earth?

This horribly tragic decision that our parents made and Tinidril might make is not adequately described as a mere mistake. It was, as Lewis says, a lie—and a lie that for our first parents could not have been completely innocent because they knew personally the God whom they had chosen to disobey with their act of self will. Lewis never lets us forget for long the personal aspect of these choices. To disobey this God is not simply an expression of the desire for a little more autonomy. It is an act of rebellion, of treason against one's good and gracious Lord. Aslan is the Son of the Great Emperor over the Sea, to remind us that God is not just God but also King. So Lewis wrote his friend Ruth Pitter on 4 Jan. 1947 that in our fall we were "joining the wrong side in a battle which had already begun" (*L* 2:754). To rebel against God is not just to go off on our own (though that would be living a lie and therefore bad enough); it is joining sides with His Enemy. It is throwing our support behind The White Witch or The Bent One. Hence, human beings are not just creatures who are imperfect and need a little moral improvement. Instead, "We are, as Newman said, rebels who must lay down our arms" (*PoP* 79). Rebellion is the inescapable essence of our new relationship to God. Trying to explain the bentness of the human race, the Seroni come to this conclusion. "'It is because they have no Oyarsa,' said one of the pupils." Oyarsa was the spirit ruling Malacandra under Maleldil (God) whom the Malacandrans were supposed to obey. "It is because every one of them wants to be a little Oyarsa himself," said Augray (*OOTSP* 102). And that is indeed the bottom line. The meaning of sin is not just that we have broken a few arbitrary rules. It is that we ultimately want, like Satan, to overthrow God and put ourselves in His place.

This rebellion has consequences beyond our own personal spiritual destiny. Speaking of Milton's portrait of Satan in a way that reflects the reality of the actual Enemy, Lewis notes that "to admire Satan then is to give one's vote not only for a world of misery, but also for a world of lies and propaganda, of wishful thinking, of incessant autobiography. Yet the choice is possible. Hardly a day passes without some slight movement towards it in each one of us" (*PPL* 102). Sometimes the movement is more than slight.

So then this is our fall. We were created to have bodies like the animals but immortal souls like the angels so that we might rule over earth as God's lieutenants. We were given gifts of reason and self-consciousness and language so that we might fulfill that role. God might have used evolution to create our bodies, but there was a superadded miracle required to give us our souls with those attendant gifts. Tragically, at some point, our ancestors disobeyed God and broke their relationship with Him, joining the rebellion of Satan that had already begun. This is a "myth" in the sense that it is a story that explains the world, but that does not mean it did not happen—though Lewis does not commit himself to all the literal details of the Genesis account. But neither does he dismiss them: "For all I can see," he says, "it might have concerned the literal eating of a fruit" (*PoP* 68). The resulting alteration in our relationship with God and in our situation persists to the present day.

THE RESULTS OF THE FALL

Two facts about Adam and Eve put them in a position to have a profound impact on the subsequent history of their race. First, they were our first parents, from whom all of us are descended. Second, if, like Tor and Tinidril, Adam and Eve were not just private individuals but in fact the king and queen of the infant human race and the world over which it was to rule, then their rebellion would have consequences of a different kind for their decisions, including the decision to rebel, were made, not just for themselves, but in a sense on our behalf, and made with consequences, not just for us, but for the whole physical creation. The biblical idiom for this relationship is to say that we are "in Adam." Lewis thought the meaning of that cryptic phrase possibly inaccessible to modern people, but was sure it was not "a mere 'idiom'" (*PoP* 58). In other words, it meant something, and something real: an interconnectedness that went beyond just being members of the same family and which explains the fact that all human beings are born into the world as sinners.

The Fall did not destroy us utterly. We still retain a capacity for reason, a moral sense, creativity, and language, which still distinguish us from even the higher animals. But all these things have been marred, disordered, severed from the purpose they were meant to serve. When our parents became alienated from God, from the world, and from themselves, so did we. The change was profound and perpetual. As Lewis explains it, the new condition was transferred hereditarily to all of Adam and Eve's descendants, "for it was not simply what biologists call an acquired variation; it was the emergence of a new kind of man—a new species, never made by God, had sinned itself into existence" (*PoP* 71).

Lewis explained what this means in practical terms for modern humans in a letter written to Elsie Snickers on 18 May 1953. Sin is not just a matter of poor thinking and hence it cannot be completely cured by education.

> This view was put forward: by Socrates.... But I think it overlooked the (to me) obviously central fact that our *will* is not necessarily determined by our *reason*. If it were, then ... "sins" wd. not be sins at all but only mistakes, and would not require repentance but only correction. But surely daily experience shows that it is just not so. (*L* 3:329-30)

A simple thought experiment confirms the accuracy of Lewis's description. When discussing this issue in class, I ask the students to remember (without sharing) the last thing they did that they are truly ashamed of. Then I ask, "How many of you knew better before you did it?" So far the response has been unanimous; they all knew better. Knowing what is right is not sufficient for choosing it. There is something wrong with us, something very precisely *perverse* about us, that cannot be fully accounted for by ignorance or confusion. Our wills are not determined by our reason. The biblical story of the Fall turns out to be the only adequate account of who we actually are. By joining the rebellion of what Lewis calls "The Bent One," Adam and Eve bent or twisted their own natures, and they transmitted that "bent" toward rebellion to their descendants. And, most horribly of all, they put themselves and their offspring in the position of being actually hostile to the God who is the only source of life, goodness, and love. As Lewis observes, "If there does exist an absolute goodness it must hate most of what we do. That is the terrible fix we are in" (*MC* 38). This is the problem to which the atonement is the only possible solution: We have placed ourselves under God's curse and rendered ourselves ineligible for His blessing.

Because of Adam's relationship not only to God but also to Nature, his curse affected the whole earth. The biblical language is that the ground was cursed for his sake. This perspective on Nature—it is not as we know it simply good or evil but a good thing cursed—makes sense of the strange mixture of good and evil which we find not only in our humanity but in the natural world as well. Lewis expressed this view in a letter to Joyce Pearce on 20 July 1943. He thought it inconceivable that nature as we know and experience it could be adequately explained either as the simple good that God intended it to be or as simply evil: "It looks like a good thing spoiled" (*L* 2:584). The young Lewis had become an atheist because of his reaction to the evil in Nature. As he matured he realized that such a view was too simple, leaving the naturalist with the "problem of good." "A good thing spoiled" rings true to what we experience, and the biblical doctrine of the Fall explains why this is so.

THE FALL AND THE GOSPEL

The Gospel is the good news, the story of what God has done in Christ to reverse and undo the damage done by the Fall. (Exactly how it proposes to accomplish this feat will be our subject in the chapter on the Atonement.) Thus, there is no Gospel without the Fall. And this presents a problem for modern Christians, who live in a world where naturalistic evolution (as the default account of origins) and relativism (as the default account of morals) renders their audience—and sometimes themselves—more unaware of the problem to which Christianity would offer a solution than any other generation in history. Lewis noticed the beginnings of this situation over sixty years ago, and the problem has only gotten worse since he wrote. "When the apostles preached, they could assume even in their Pagan hearers a real consciousness of deserving the Divine anger ... Christianity now has to preach the diagnosis—in itself very bad news—before it can win a hearing for the cure" (*PoP* 43). He elaborates, "Christ takes it for granted that men are bad. Until we really feel this assumption of His to be true, though we are part of the world He came to save, we are not part of the audience to whom His words are addressed" (*PoP* 45).

Why is it so hard for us to become part of that audience? One of the effects of the Fall was coming to know good and evil. In a sense, Adam and Eve had been ignorant of evil, and could not therefore have had a full understanding of good with no point of comparison. But because they learned about evil by becoming enmeshed in it, the clarity about that contrast that they might have gained through obedience was sacrificed. Tor and Tinidril came to know about good and evil in a different way, by resisting the temptation that was offered them:

> We have learned of evil, but not as the Evil One wished us to learn. We have learned better than that, and know it more, for it is waking that understands sleep and not sleep that understands waking. There is an ignorance of evil that comes from being young: there is a darker ignorance that comes from doing it. (*Pa* 209)

It is that second kind of darker ignorance that Christian evangelists and apologists now have to deal with. As Aslan laments, "Oh Adam's sons, how cleverly you defend yourselves against all that might do you good!" (*TMN* 203). Only by the aid of the Holy Spirit can these defenses be overcome. Indeed, we fight against ourselves and our own interests, so perverse is the understanding of good and evil we fell into by our disobedience. Lewis wrote to Arthur Greeves on 12 Sept. 1933 that God understands and even shares the desire that motivates us to choose sin: the desire for intense and unending happiness. "He made me for no other purpose than to enjoy it. But He knows, and I do not, how it can be really and permanently obtained" (*L* 2:123).

Modern ideologies aid and abet the endarkenment that is inherent in our fallen and sinful estate. We started with the picture of man created in the image of God as a living soul whose life meant the power of making choices that were profoundly significant for good or ill. We contrasted this picture with that of the automaton, the programmed robot, which was the alternative way of understanding humanity. As the Christian world view recedes in influence, it is replaced by reductionistic philosophies that can only see human beings as animals or as biological machines—as robots. Machines can only malfunction. They cannot be responsible, they cannot sin, and hence they cannot be redeemed. Thus by masking our problem, the Enemy keeps us blind to the solution offered by the Christian faith.

These reductionist philosophies are taken to their logical conclusion by the National Institute for Coordinated Experiments, the N.I.C.E., of *That Hideous Strength*. Frost, for example, has spent his whole life telling himself that thoughts, no less than emotions or moral impulses, are really just chemical reactions taking place in his body with no transcendent significance. The brain is just a biological computer; the mind is an illusion. Ironically the macrobes, demonic powers in the service of The Bent One, have used this radically materialist philosophy to manipulate Frost into serving their diabolical interests—for what cruel or unhuman or disgusting thing can be resisted once guilt and revulsion have been reduced to mere chemical phenomena? In the end, having used him up, they destroy him.

> Like the clockwork figure he had chosen to be, his stiff body, now terribly cold, walked back into the Objective Room, poured out the petrol and threw a lighted match onto the pile. Not till then did his controllers allow him to suspect that death itself might not after all cure the illusion of being a soul. (*THS* 358)

Fortunately, characters like Frost are balanced by Mark Studdock, a typical modern who has started down the same philosophic path but is given by God the grace (and humanity) to turn back from it.

According to St. Paul, "The natural man does not receive the things of the Spirit of God" (1 Cor. 2:14). Lewis helps us to understand why this is so and to see how modern ideologies make the blindness inherent in our sinful rebellion against the truth even darker. This understanding can help us resist the temptation to depend on our own brilliance and remind us to look for hope to the only place it can be found: the fact that "the light shines in the darkness, and the darkness cannot overcome it" (John 1:5).

TOTAL DEPRAVITY?

Lewis's description of human nature as created in the image of God and fallen into sin shows a good grasp of the Christian story and its implications. Unfortunately, his lack of training in formal theology caused him to make one statement that could foster serious misunderstanding. After his discussion of the Fall in *Problem of Pain*, he says, "I disbelieve [the doctrine of total depravity] partly on the ground that if our depravity were total we should not know ourselves to be depraved, and partly because experience shows us much goodness in human nature" (*PoP* 54-5).

It is clear that Lewis rejected the doctrine of total depravity. It is also clear from his reasons for rejecting it that he did not understand it. He objects that "if our depravity were total we should not know ourselves to be depraved" and that experience observes much good in human nature. And he notes elsewhere, correctly, that "the general tenor of Scripture does not encourage us to believe that our knowledge of the Law has been depraved in the same degree as our power to fulfill it" ("Poison" 79). But these objections are completely beside the point. For, of course, as Lewis himself had repeatedly shown, we do in fact underestimate the extent of our depravity and often deny it altogether. And the doctrine of total depravity as classically presented does not claim that there is no good in man.

This common misunderstanding arises from confusing *total* depravity with *utter* depravity. According to one standard summary, total depravity does not imply that every sinner is "as thoroughly depraved as he can possibly become" or that there is no good in man; indeed, classical reformed thought affirms that there is much good in fallen human beings by common grace. Rather, the "total" means that the pollution of our nature by sin is totally "pervasive": "the inherent corruption extends to every part of man's nature, to all the faculties and powers of both soul and body" (Berkhof 246-7; cf. Grudem 497). As a result, though much natural good may remain by common grace (Kantzer 313-95), we are totally unable (apart from special grace) to do anything that is spiritually good or worthy of salvation. One must pay attention to the specific ways in which the adjective *total* and the adverb *totally* are used in such expositions, which are not the ways that Lewis supposed.

It is not so clear that Lewis would actually have disagreed with the classical formulation of total depravity had he known it, nor that any of his human characters are an exception to it. Even believers are not unaffected by the effects of the Fall, as Lewis knew: "The main thing we learn from a serious attempt to practice the Christian virtues is that we fail" (*MC* 125). That failure is not "total" in the sense that no whiff of virtue can be discovered in our practice, but it is "total" in the sense that not one thought, intention, or act can be found untainted by sin, when measured against the standard of God's holiness. And that is why the goodness we have is "totally" unable to merit salvation. Lewis does not deny any of this, but his ignorance of the context for the word *total* in the classic doctrinal formulations of total depravity makes him seem to. Therefore, his statement about total depravity is a glitch in what is otherwise a pretty good grasp of the Creation/Fall story and its implications.

CONCLUSION

The Christian faith involves a number of doctrines about the human race and the sinful state into which it has fallen. But those doctrines are fully understood and appreciated only in so far as they flow from and accurately explicate the *story* of our creation, purpose, fall, and redemption. Lewis's spotty knowledge of formal theology led him into some inaccuracies about the doctrines (e.g., his misunderstanding and rejection of the doctrine of total depravity), but he got the main outlines of the story right. His retelling of it in *Perelandra* is possibly the most insightful commentary on it since Milton's *Paradise Lost*, a poem Lewis had profitably studied.

That retelling brings out well the exalted calling involved in our creation, the high stakes of the responsibility we were given, and the horrible consequences of our rebellion. It sets the stage for the dramatic possibilities in our redemption and restoration. The best understanding of these issues will come from studying the standard theologians in the light of the story as fleshed out by Lewis. Then we may get the full import both of Caspian's wish and Aslan's response:

> "I do indeed, Sir," said Caspian. "I was wishing that I came of a more honorable lineage."
>
> "You come of the Lord Adam and the Lady Eve," said Aslan. "And that is both honor enough to erect the head of the poorest beggar, and shame enough to bow the shoulders of the greatest emperor on earth. Be content." (*PC* 232-3)

CHAPTER 6

Christology
The Person of Christ

"Yes," said Queen Lucy. "In our world too, a stable once had something inside it that was bigger than our whole world" (TLB 177).

The fall of the human race presents a key theological problem, to which the Incarnation and the atonement are the solution. It is a problem of course only for theologians; God foresaw the perfect solution to it all along and had counted the cost, as it were, before the foundations of the world. But for us finite people trying to understand, the Fall seems to have created a conflict between God's very attributes: His justice, demanding the death penalty for sin, and His love, wishing to show mercy to His creatures. God's attributes of course cannot really conflict, but in this case only His wisdom could keep them in harmony, allowing Him to be, in biblical terms, simultaneously "just and the justifier of the one who has faith in Jesus" (Rom. 3:26). The sacrificial death of Christ is what makes that harmony possible, in ways that will be explored in chapter seven; and in order to die, the Second Person of the Trinity had to be born and live as a human being. So nothing is more central to the Christian faith than the Incarnation of the Son.

Christology is the doctrine of how we understand that incarnation. Who and what was Christ? A mere man? The divine Son of God in human flesh? Or something else, the Incarnation of something more than human but less than God Himself? And if Christ was truly God incarnate, how do we understand the relationship between His divine and human natures? The standard answer of the Creeds is that Jesus was one Person with two natures, fully God and fully man, without mixture or confusion. Helping us grasp the meaning and the grounding of those formulae is the theologian's job. Lewis's contributions to that task are, as you would expect, always interesting and often helpful.

THE CENTRALITY OF THE INCARNATION

In its historic sense, a Christian just is a person who worships the man Jesus as God. Without this strange phenomenon there is no Christian faith. If his followers had thought of Jesus as nothing more than a lay rabbi whose teaching they happened to like, they would have remained simply Jews. People are not generally willing to die for their favorite preacher. But the early Christians proclaimed that Jesus Christ is Lord (κυριοσ Χριστοσ) in a way that made it inconsistent for them to bow to Caesar, who was worshipped by Romans as a deity. And they would rather have died than to admit any other "Lord" (in that sense) than Jesus.

C. S. Lewis saw no reason why that old definition should not apply to modern Christians as well. He wrote to Dom Bede Griffiths on 21 Dec. 1941: "The Divinity of our Lord has to be believed whether you find it a help or a 'scandal' (otherwise you are not a Xtian at all)" (L 2:502). Other doctrines, even "the Anselmic theory of the atonement," were not on that level of essential importance. And while Lewis did not elevate any theory of how the atonement works to the same level, he saw that there were theological as well as historic reasons for clinging to the deity of Christ, reasons related to the atonement. He wrote to Arthur Greeves on 11 Dec. 1944 that the deity of Christ

> seems to me not something stuck on which you can unstick but something that peeps out at every point so that you'd have to unravel the whole web to get rid of it.... He became man precisely to do and suffer what as God He cd. not do and suffer. And if you take away the Godhead of Christ, what is Xtianity all *about*? How can the death of one *man* have this effect for all men? (L 3:1555)

These were good questions. By asking them, Lewis showed good insight into the way the Incarnation permeates every facet of Christian teaching. God is the God and Father of our Lord Jesus Christ, who is the exact image of that Father. It is the act of that God in Christ which takes away the sin of the world. So close is the identification between Jesus and God in the New Testament writings that to ignore it precisely unravels the whole web. So while in the modern world we find the oxymoronic phenomenon of the person who thinks of himself as Christian without affirming the deity of Christ, Lewis understood the contradiction inherent in such unbelief. Without the confession of the Incarnation of God in the man Jesus, there would have been no Christianity and there are no true Christians.

THE PERSON OF CHRIST

THE CASE FOR THE INCARNATION

But why would anybody have come to believe such an outlandish thing? The fierce monotheism and horror of idolatry in First-Century Judaism would seem to make such an affirmation inconceivable, even if it didn't present the theoretical problem of how the infinite God could be fully present in a finite human being. Indeed, it took Jesus' first followers some time to get their heads around the idea. Their first reaction was not, "Jesus Christ is Lord," but rather, "What manner of man *is* this?" They lived with Him; His humanity was inescapable. But He also spoke like no man ever spoke (with authority, not as the Scribes) and did things no man had ever done. And then, while they were experiencing all of that, they were confronted with the really staggering difficulty of His claims. Jesus is too obviously *good* to be dismissed as a blasphemous heretic (though His enemies the Pharisees are quite willing to do so), and yet one cannot escape "the quite appalling nature of this Man's theological remarks" ("What are We to Make" 156). What were they? As Lewis puts it, the claims of Christ are truly shocking: "Among these Jews there suddenly turns up a man who goes about talking as if He was God. He claims to forgive sins. He says He has always existed. He says He is coming to judge the world at the end of time" (*MC* 54).

None of the normal categories the disciples were familiar with would work with the Son of Man. There had been miracle-working prophets before, but no prophet of Yahweh would ever have made the claims that Jesus made. You just cannot imagine Elijah saying, "I and the Father are one," or "Before Abraham was, I Am." But if Jesus is a lying fraud, why is God working in and through Him so powerfully? The one thing none of His contemporaries was willing to say was that He was a good man and great moral teacher who was just innocently mistaken about those, er, ill-advised personal claims. "You can't really be very well 'adjusted' to your world if it says you 'have a devil' and ends by nailing you up naked to a stake of wood" (*FL* 81).

Lewis analyzed the options open to Jesus' contemporaries and came up with his famous "Trilemma" argument. Other apologists have similarly listed those options as "Mad, Bad, or God" or "Lunatic, Liar, or Lord." Here is Lewis's version:

> A man who was merely a man and said the sort of things Jesus said would not be a great moral teacher. He would either be a lunatic—on the level with the man who says he is a poached egg—or he would be the Devil of Hell. You must make your choice. Either this man was, and is, the Son of God: or else a madman or something worse. You can shut Him up for a fool, you can spit at Him and kill Him as a demon; or you can fall at His feet and call Him Lord and God. But let us not come with any patronizing nonsense about His being a great human teacher. He has not left that open to us. He did not intend to. (*MC* 56)

Jesus claimed to be God. There are only a few logical possibilities of how to deal with that fact. Either He was lying, or He was insane, or He was telling the truth. The disciples were eventually forced to realize that they could not believe He was lying or insane, so He must have been telling the truth: the Person they encountered in the man Jesus of Nazareth was somehow the same Being as the living God, however hard that might be to understand. (The full Trinitarian explanation of this phenomenon would of course come later.) People who fully ponder the disicples' testimony in the Gospels should arrive at the same conclusion today, Lewis implies; or at least they cannot take the easy way out and say He was a good moral teacher but not God.

There is a lively ongoing debate about whether Lewis's Trilemma is a valid argument. I think it is, and I make my full case for that conclusion in a special section which follows this chapter. The objections boil down to different versions of the claim that Lewis committed the fallacy of false dilemma; i.e., there are other possibilities that his Trilemma does not consider. Maybe Jesus did not really make the claims or did not mean them the way we have taken them; maybe he could simply have been sincerely mistaken about His deity without being insane. I will try to show that all these additional possibilities on careful consideration are not real possibilities after all, so the Trilemma stands. But here we are trying to understand its implications for Lewis's Christology. They are two: first, Lewis was fully committed to the deity of Christ as a historical fact central and essential to the Christian faith. Second, Lewis by pursuing the line of argument in the Trilemma came to a good understanding of the uniqueness of Jesus among the religious leaders of mankind.

> If you had gone to Buddha and asked him, "Are you the son of Bramah?" he would have said, "My son, you are still in the vale of illusion." If you had gone to Socrates and asked, "Are you Zeus?" he would have laughed at you. If you had gone to Mohammed and asked, "Are you Allah?" he would first have rent his clothes and then cut your head off. If you had asked Confucius, "Are you Heaven?" I think he would have probably replied, "Remarks which are not in accordance with nature are in bad taste." ("What are We to Make" 157-8)

But when Peter said, "Thou art the Christ, the Son of the living God," Jesus said, "Flesh and blood has not revealed this to you, but my Father who is in heaven" (Mat. 16:13-17). The contrast is certainly worth some thought.

THE REALITY OF THE INCARNATION

Familiarity may have blinded many modern Christians to what a radical and difficult concept the whole idea of incarnation is. It is not hard to think of Jesus as a man; it is possible to think of Him as God. To think of Him as both at the same time is not so simple. The early Christians were so impressed by Jesus' deity that they were susceptible to forgetting His humanity and veering off into Gnostic heresies such as Docetism (the idea that Jesus' physical body was only an appearance). They had to be reminded by John that Jesus had come *in the flesh* (1 Jn. 4:2-3). Some modern conservative Christians suffer from the same tendency. I've seen them stumble over His admission of ignorance about the date of the Second Coming (Mat. 24:36) and get offended by a discussion of whether He would have had acne as a teenager. Another type of modern finds His deity embarrassing and wants to spiritualize it away so that Christ is the Son of God only in a sense that is available to all men. Bree had a bit of that tendency. Until he was corrected, his theology of Aslan would have made him something of a Narnian liberal. "'No doubt,' continued Bree, 'when they speak of him as a lion they only mean he's as strong as a lion or... as fierce as a lion. Or something of that kind. Even a little girl like you, Aravis, must see that it would be quite absurd to suppose he is a real lion'" (*TH&HB* 214). His first meeting with Aslan very quickly disabused him of those notions. "'Now Bree,' he said, 'you poor, proud, frightened Horse, draw near. Nearer still, my son. Do not dare not to dare. Touch me. Smell me. Here are my paws, here is my tail, there are my whiskers. I am a true Beast'" (*TH&HB* 215).

One of the first places where people who are squeamish about the supernatural aspects of Christian belief in Jesus as the God-man start squirming is with the virgin birth, or more accurately, the virginal conception of Christ. Lewis wrote to a Mr. Young on 31 Oct. 1963: "I believe in the Virgin Birth in the fullest and most literal sense: that is, I deny that copulation with a man was the cause of the Virgin's pregnancy" (*L* 3:1476). Lewis then will have nothing to do with either way of escaping the full reality of the Incarnation. We must take the Incarnation with full seriousness as something in which God got His hands dirty, as it were.

Lewis's full commitment to the deity of Christ makes impressive his efforts to reckon fully with His full humanity as well, and is the context in which those efforts should be understood. Such a passage is this one:

> I certainly think that Christ in the flesh was not omniscient—if only because a human brain could not, presumably, be the vehicle of omniscient consciousness, and to say that Our Lord's thinking was not really conditioned by the size and shape of His brain might be to deny the real incarnation.... Thus, if Our Lord had committed Himself to any

scientific or historical statement which we knew to be untrue, this would not disturb my faith in His deity. (*PoP 122*)

Lewis goes too far in the last sentence. Up to that point I think his reasoning is flawless, and is a good explanation of Christ's professing, for example, not to know the day or hour of His return (Mat. 24:36). But it is one thing to say that an infinite number of truths could hardly be registered at any given moment in a finite brain; it is quite another to have the Lord "commit" to something erroneous and *teach* it with divine authority. The fully orthodox position is to believe that His perfect relationship with the Father and His perfect dependence on the Holy Spirit would have protected Him, even in human form, from such error. His human nature as such could not have experienced omniscience, but if the orthodox understanding is true, He was *personally* still in touch with it through His relationship to the Father, and hence able to access it whenever He needed it. If even the merely human authors of Scripture could be protected from error by the Holy Spirit, surely the Son of God would be also. Lewis's blind spot concerning the doctrine of inspiration then shows up here as well. But if Lewis was mistaken about one of the implications of the Incarnation, he was absolutely right to insist that Jesus' humanity was a fully real humanity. Otherwise, how could He have been "in every point tempted like as we are, yet without sin"? (Heb. 4:15).

What is true of omniscience counts for the other attributes as well. Jesus as a man was not omnipotent—He got tired and had to eat and sleep—but He had access to the omnipotence that belonged to Him as God and so was able to feed the multitudes and calm the storm. Jesus as a man was not omnipresent—if He was in Galilee, He was not in Jerusalem. But He was personally in contact with the Father and the Spirit who are everywhere. This may be hard to grasp, but Lewis reminds us that we are surrounded by (and contain) phenomena equally mysterious. "The God-Man was omniscient as God but ignorant as Man. This, no doubt, is true, though it cannot be imagined.... But the physical sciences, no less than theology, propose for our belief much that cannot be imagined" (*WLN* 99).

One of those mysteries is too close perhaps for most of us to observe: the mystery of our own rationality as Lewis had explained it in the Argument from Reason in *Miracles*. Trying to conceive how in the one person of Christ the divine and human could coexist "would be a fatal stumbling-block if we had not already discovered that in every human being a wholly supernatural entity is thus united with a part of Nature" (*M* 114). Reason cannot just be a chemical reaction taking place amongst the atoms in our heads, or we would have no reason to suppose our heads made of atoms. There is therefore in every one of us something that transcends the merely physical but somehow interacts with it. In other words, "The discrepancy between a movement of atoms in an astronomer's cortex, and his understanding that there must be a still unobserved planet beyond Uranus, is already so immense that the Incarnation of God Himself is, in one sense, scarcely more startling" (M 115).

Lewis understood that while we have to insist on the reality of the Incarnation, we are probably not in a position to understand the mechanism of it, to understand *how* the divine and human natures could both belong to one Person. One reason for that difficulty is our inability to step outside of time. It would be a mistake to ask "how Christ could be *at the same moment* ignorant and omniscient, or how he could be the God who neither slumbers nor sleeps *while* he slept. The italicized words conceal an attempt to establish a temporal relation between his timeless life as God and the days, months, and years of his life as man" (*WLN* 100). Because our own understanding is necessarily time-bound in a way that God's is not, this kind of explanation is simply not something we are in a position to give. But we can see that we are not in that position, and that it makes sense that we are not. So our lack of answers to the "how" questions should not be an impediment to our faith.

Lewis was a great one for trying to get people past their stereotyped romantic assumptions so they could meet the iconoclastic reality of the Person revealed in the biblical text.

He wrote to Edward Lofstrom on 16 Jan. 1959, scoffing at the standard portrait of a "gentle Jesus meek and mild":

> The most striking thing about Our Lord is the union of great ferocity with extreme tenderness.... He is also a supreme ironist, dialectician, and (occasionally) humourist.... You are on the right track now, getting to the real Man behind all the plaster dolls that have been substituted for Him. This is the appearance in Human form of the God who made the Tiger *and* the Lamb, the avalanche *and* the rose. He'll frighten and puzzle you: but the real Christ *can* be loved and admired as the doll can't. (*L* 3:1011)

A real God incarnate in a real man with a real and definite personality: the Narnian way of conveying this idea is through the motif that Aslan is not a tame lion. As Mr. Beaver insists, "'Course he isn't safe. But he's good. He's the King, I tell you" (*LWW* 86).

Lewis's emphasis on the reality of the Incarnation is a needed one. It is easy to let distance and familiarity blur the shocking and sharp edges of the reality which the Christian story claims invaded our everyday world at the height of the Roman Empire. Lewis helps blow away the cobwebs by reminding us that "The heart of Christianity is a myth which is also a fact" ("Myth" 66). Indeed. For the one who was incarnated was the Son of the One that Lewis calls the Father of all Facthood—God and man; myth and fact; one Person with two natures, without mixture or confusion.

THE THEOLOGY OF THE INCARNATION

Alright, then: we must accept the full divine and human reality of the Incarnation without trying to explain how it could have happened. But we still have to state what happened in the Incarnation carefully because of the tendency people have to soften the difficulty of the concept by compromising one or the other of the two sides of it. Theological formulations of the doctrine of the Incarnation then have the function of preserving the mystery more than that of explaining it. Lewis tries to capture that mystery by asking the question this way: "What can be meant by 'God becoming Man?' In what sense is it conceivable that eternal self-existent Spirit, basic Fact-hood, should be so combined with a natural human organism as to make one person?" (*M* 114). The question does a good job of capturing the difficulty, but may not be phrased in the best possible way. The divine and human natures of Christ are not "combined" so as to "make" one person; rather, the one divine Person who already existed took on a real human nature without compromising His divinity.

Lewis followed the classic Creeds in such matters; as he said, his own beliefs are "written in the common Prayer Book" (*MC* 8). Here is the way the Thirty-Nine Articles of the Church of England handles the theology of the Incarnation, reflecting the language of the Nicene Creed and the definitions of the Council of Chalcedon, accepted by all major branches of Christianity:

> The Sonne, which is the Worde of the Father, begotten from euerlastyng of the Father, the very and eternall GOD, of one substaunce with the Father, toke man's nature in the wombe of the blessed Virgin, of her substaunce: so that two whole and perfect natures, which is to say, the Godhead and manhood, were ioyned together in one person, neuer to be diuided, whereof is one Christe, very GOD and very man, who truly suffered, was crucified, dead, and buried, to reconcile his father to vs, and to be a sacrifice, not only for original gylt, but also for all actual sinnes of men. (Schaff 488)

Not just God; not just man; fully God and fully human, with no mixture or confusion between those two natures (i.e., He was not some kind of divine-human hybrid): this the church has been careful to affirm in order to be faithful to the Scriptural testimony to Christ and also to preserve the unique significance of His death. For nothing less than a human death could be relevant to human sin, and nothing less than the death of God could suffice to atone for all the sins of the whole world.

Lewis helps us grasp a couple of elements of this classic Christology in interesting ways. First, if it was truly God ("very God of very God") who was incarnated in Christ, and yet in doing so the Father has not vacated Heaven nor abdicated his throne, then the Incarnation of Christ presupposes the doctrine of the Trinity. The One incarnated must be fully God, yet not the Father. So the Father, the First Person of the Trinity, begets a Son, the Second. In the language of the Nicene Creed, the Son was "begotten, not made." As Lewis explains, you make something different from yourself, but you beget something that is the same species as yourself (*MC* 138). Therefore the Son, being the "only begotten" (or more accurately, "uniquely begotten" Son, Jn. 3:16), is "of one substance with the Father." But the Son must not have come into existence in time; He cannot have *begun* to exist, or He would be less than God, like the Son as Arius understood him. So the Father could not have begotten the Son in time, but must have been doing so for all of eternity. Lewis tries to help us imagine such a thing with one of his characteristic analogies: imagine that there are two books lying on a table, one on top of the other, and that they have always been in that position (*MC* 149-50). Lewis tries again: think of the Son as always "streaming forth from the Father, like light from a lamp, or heat from a fire, or thoughts from a mind" (*MC* 151). So there was never a time when the Father had not begotten the Son and when the Holy Spirit was not proceeding from their love. Analogies can be dangerous, but these seem well chosen to illustrate the doctrine of the eternal generation of the Son.

Second, Lewis's concept of "transposition" may help us to understand certain aspects of the Incarnation. He notices that if one tries to attend to the physical manifestations accompanying various emotional states, they tend to be identical. If you think of an intense aesthetic experience and the shock of very bad news, both may be accompanied physically by, say, a fluttering in the diaphragm. The same physical sensation then may be pleasurable in one context and painful in another. But it would be absurd to conclude reductionistically that pleasure and pain—or beauty and anguish, or lust and love—are really the same thing simply because they share the same physiology. This phenomenon permeates all of reality once we notice it. Life uses the same chemical elements as inorganic matter; emotion uses the same physical movements as sensation; the mind uses the same synapses as the brain. So pervasive are these relationships that the skeptic can always make a convincing case for reductionism (life is just chemistry, love is just lust, thought is just neurology), and that case will always miss the point. In all such transpositions, the lower can only be understood from the standpoint of the higher: the mind can study the brain, but the brain by itself can never understand the mind.

How does this relate to Christology? Well, Lewis explains, the creeds say that the Incarnation worked "not by conversion of the Godhead into flesh, but by taking of the Manhood into God." What can that mean? Well, just as chemistry uses atoms, biology uses chemistry, emotion uses physiology, and the mind uses the brain, yet none of these things can thereby be reduced to the level beneath it, so maybe that is how the spiritual Person of God related to the humanity of Jesus. In other words, perhaps "humanity, still remaining itself, is not merely counted as, but inevitably drawn into, Deity" ("Transposition" 113). A physical sensation, without becoming anything less than a sensation, becomes more when it is "drawn into" an emotional experience of joy. This may not explain how the human nature of Jesus could relate to the divine; after all, we cannot really explain how the mind relates to our own brain. But it does show that the relation is not a strange or unexpected one, for it recapitulates a pattern imprinted deeply on every level of the creation from the bottom to the top. It appears to be the way the Creator works. If so, the Incarnation is simply the highest instance of it.

THE RATIONALE OF THE INCARNATION

The Incarnation of the Second Person of the Trinity as a human being was not just some arbitrary thing that God randomly decided to do. Christians receive it as the ultimate revelation of God's inmost nature, of His love and justice as they respond to the fall of the beloved creature made in His own image. Thus, the Incarnation of the Son is the most profound stooping of Godhead to identify with His creature in its utmost wretchedness that can be imagined. Pagans might well ask with Bardia, "I wonder do the gods know what it feels like to be a man?" (*TWHF* 66). Christians who have pondered the Person of the Christ know the answer to that question.

The Incarnation is foreshadowed from the very first pages of Scripture by the uniqueness of man as the one creature made in God's image and likeness. There is then an appropriateness in the Incarnation that would not have been obtained with any other creature, for there is already a profound kinship between the infinite Person and the finite persons who were designed for fellowship with Him. In Narnia, the land of Talking Beasts, God appears as the King of Beasts, just as in our world He appears as that creature who was given the kingship over the beasts. "'Aslan a man!' said Mr. Beaver sternly. 'Certainly not. I tell you he is the King of the wood and the son of the great Emperor-beyond-the-Sea. Don't you know who is the King of Beasts? Aslan is a lion—the Lion, the great Lion'" (*LWW* 86).

The identification and the stooping implied in the Incarnation are staggering—but as so often in Christian theology, staggering in a way that makes sense, in so far as we are capable of receiving that sense. The MacDonald character in *The Great Divorce* explains, "Only the Greatest of all can make Himself small enough to enter Hell. For the higher a thing is, the lower it can descend—a man can sympathize with a horse, but a horse cannot sympathize with a rat" (*GD* 123-4). Thus the very Highest, precisely because He is highest, can fully sympathize with a man and express that sympathy by an identification with him in his plight that goes beyond metaphor and becomes the ultimate Reality around which the entire Christian faith revolves. Digory, preparing to go in search of the apple which can save Narnia for years from the Witch, and which could save his mother from her fatal illness, begins to find out what that means as portrayed in Aslan:

> Up till then he had been looking at the Lion's great feet . . . ; now, in his despair, he looked up at its face. What he saw surprised him as much as anything in his whole life. For the tawny face was bent down near his own and (wonder of wonders) great shining tears stood in the Lion's eyes. They were such big, bright tears compared with Digory's own that for a moment he felt as if the Lion must really be sorrier about his Mother than he was himself. (*TMN* 168)

Digory's subsequent experience will confirm the truth of this feeling, as in response to his faith and obedience in yielding up the apple to Aslan, he is allowed to pick one for his mother as well. But first he hears what may be one of the most poignant speeches in the whole Narniad: "'My son, my son,' said Aslan, 'Grief is great. Only you and I in this land know that yet. Let us be good to one another'" (*TMN* 168). He will need this promise to sustain him during the trial and temptation to come, when he is tempted to steal the apple for his dying mother. Had he done so, it would have cured her, but not to his joy or hers. For "length of days with an evil heart is only length of misery" (*TMN* 208). Nevertheless, because Aslan has entered the world, all will be well. "That is what would have happened, child, with a stolen apple. It is not what will happen now. What I give you now will bring joy. It will not, in your world, give endless life, but it will heal. Go. Pluck her an apple from the Tree" (*TMN* 209).

It is then no exaggeration to say that the Incarnation of Christ is the ultimate Reality around which the entire Christian faith revolves. And so, in thinking about how it fits into the larger story, we come back full circle to our original emphasis on its centrality. More will be said about the rationale for the Incarnation in the chapter on the atonement. But we have seen enough to be reminded how profoundly true it is to define a Christian as a person who worships the man Jesus as God.

CONCLUSION

Lewis's Christology is orthodox, solid in its adherence to and understanding of the central core of historic orthodoxy. Though he sometimes draws an unwarranted conclusion (as when he said that he would not be troubled by the discovery that Jesus had said something incorrect about history or science), his great strength is his insistence on the reality of the Incarnation and his principled refusal to compromise either strand of it, the divine or the human. He understood its centrality and explains well some of the reasons for it. He resists the temptation to try to explain the traditional orthodox formulations in a way that would strip their mystery rather than preserving it, but he helps us understand how such things could be, even if we cannot fully grasp them. All of this puts him in a position to answer the most pressing question with the most powerful rejoinder. "What reason have we, except our own desperate wishes, to believe that God is, by any standard we can conceive, 'good'? Doesn't all the prima facie evidence we have suggest the opposite? What have we to set against it?" Everything we have seen here justifies the simplicity of the answer: "We set Christ against it" (*GO* 26).

Amen.

INTERLUDE

Lacking, Ludicrous, or Logical? The Validity Of Lewis's "Trilemma"

"Then comes the real shock. Among these Jews there suddenly turns up a man who goes about talking as if He was God. He claims to forgive sins. He says He has always existed. He says He is coming to judge the world at the end of time" (MC 54).

No philosophical argument that C. S. Lewis ever made is more well-known—or more controversial—than his famous "Trilemma" (not his word), or "Lord/Liar/Lunatic" (not his phrase) argument for the deity of Christ. N. T. Wright observes accurately that "this argument has worn well in some circles and extremely badly in others" (32). And some of the sharpest critiques have come from within the believing community.

It is curious that an argument that has become a staple of popular Christian apologetics should be rejected as fallacious by many who presumably accept its conclusion. With not only the validity of a much used argument but also the competence of the greatest apologist of the Twentieth Century at stake, it is time to take a fresh look at Lewis's argument and its critics. Can we still use the Trilemma? If so, how should we approach it? At the end of the day, how does Lewis come off as an apologist and an example to other apologists? We will try to shed some light on such questions before we are done.

First, let's remind ourselves of the argument itself as it is presented in *Mere Christianity*. (See Brazier 91-102 for a survey of other works in which Lewis gives a version of the argument.) Lewis is addressing a person who says, "I'm ready to accept Jesus as a great moral teacher, but I don't accept his claim to be God." We note first of all that the Trilemma is presented not so much as an argument for the deity of Christ *per se*, as a refutation, a heading off at the pass, of one popular way of evading the claims of Christ. This, Lewis argues, is the one thing we cannot say:

A man who was merely a man and said the sort of things Jesus said would not be a great moral teacher. He would either be a lunatic—on the level with the man who says he is a poached egg—or else he would be the Devil of Hell. You must make your choice. Either this man was, and is, the Son of God: or else a madman or something worse. You can shut Him up for a fool, you can spit at Him and kill Him as a demon; or you can fall at His feet and call Him Lord and God. But let us not come with any patronizing nonsense about His being a great human teacher. He has not left that open to us. He did not intend to. (56)

Many critics treat Lewis's Trilemma as original. But it is actually a refinement of a much older argument, the *aut Deus aut malus homo* ("either God or a bad man") which goes back at least to the Patristic period. (See Brazier 103-26 for a survey of its use before and after Lewis.) Lewis makes the dilemma a trilemma by subdividing the *malus homo* option into two types of badness—mendacity and insanity—which are potentially relevant to the case of the claims of Christ to be God. Later thinkers have expanded it again to a Quadrilemma: Lord, Liar, Lunatic, Legend, or alternatively, Lord, Liar, Lunatic, Innocently Mistaken. In this chapter I will use the familiar term Trilemma to refer to the *aut Deus aut malus homo* (or "Mad, Bad, or God") argument in whatever iteration we find it, because it was Lewis's tripartite form that gave it classic expression for most of us.

Lewis's version of the argument involves the following steps.

1. Jesus claimed to be God. (This is assumed in *Mere Christianity*.)
2. There are three logical possibilities in the case of such a claim:
    2A. He was telling the truth.
    2B. He was lying.
    2C. He was mistaken (and hence insane, given the nature of the claim).
3. A liar or a megalomaniac (the relevant form of insanity) could not be a Great Moral Teacher.
4. Therefore, we must either accept Jesus' claim or reject him as immoral or insane. The merely mortal Great Moral Teacher option is logically eliminated.

Note that one could go on to argue that (5) Jesus was not a liar, (6) Jesus was not insane, therefore (7) Jesus was God. One could; many have; I might; in the next chapter of *Mere Christianity* Lewis does—but in the original passage from *Mere Christianity* itself, Lewis leaves it at (4). Lewis is explicit about his purpose: "I am trying here to prevent anyone saying the really foolish thing that people often say" (55). Lewis does not claim to have *proved* the deity of Christ beyond a shadow of doubt, but only to have clarified our choices. Jesus was (A) telling the truth and is the Son of God; he was (B) lying; or he was (C) mistaken—and one cannot be mistaken about the particular claim being made (deity) and be fully sane. The only choice Lewis claims to have eliminated absolutely is that Jesus was simply a great, but merely human, moral teacher—for a person who is a liar or a megalomaniac hardly qualifies as a great moral teacher.

Now, the argument is surely presented as *support* for the deity of Christ in that Lewis thinks that the other two choices will be hard choices for most people to make, as well as choices that give inferior explanations for the full data of the phenomenon of Christ. But people could still make them. "You can shut him up for a fool...." The easy choice—that Jesus was a great moral teacher but not God—is the only one Lewis actually purports to have eliminated completely. How well did he succeed?

The basic problem Lewis's critics have had with this argument, even in this limited understanding of it, is their contention that it commits the fallacy of False Dilemma, the premature closure of options. Marvin D. Hinten uses it as an example of one of Lewis's alleged weaknesses: he "overlimits choices" (8). If it can be shown that there are other legitimate possibilities for how to understand the claims of Christ, it is urged, the argument fails.

The other possibilities suggested fall into basically two categories: first, the possibility that Jesus did not actually make the claims attributed to him, or that if he did, he did not mean them as the bald claims to deity for which conservative Christians have taken them; and, second, the possibility that someone could indeed be sincerely mistaken about his identity without being truly insane in a way that would necessarily compromise his views of ethics or his status and authority as a moral teacher. We will examine each of these categories in turn, and then look at an additional objection: that, even if the propositions of the Trilemma are probably true individually, their combined probabilities fall below the threshold of persuasiveness (the "diminishing probability argument," or DPA).

THE CRITIQUE: BIBLICAL CRITICISM

First, it is argued, modern biblical criticism does not allow us to make the naïve assumption either that Jesus said everything that the New Testament attributes to him or that what he did say has the meaning conservative Christians have always attached to it. Few believers are ready to sign up for the Jesus Seminar and question wholesale whether the words of Jesus as reported in the canonical Gospels are authentic. But believers do need to concern themselves with the fact that many secular people today will not begin with a presumption of their authenticity. Thus, Wright thinks that Lewis's argument "backfires dangerously when historical critics question his reading of the Gospels" (33).

It is equally common to question whether Jesus' statements really add up to a clear and unequivocal claim to deity. All that is needed to deprive Lewis's argument of its logical force is the probability that Jesus' words should be taken in some other sense. For some, Lewis's failure to consider such a possibility robs him of all credibility. "Lewis' view that Jesus' claims were so clear as to admit of one and only one interpretation reveals that he is a textually careless and theologically unreliable guide" (Beversluis 1985, 54).

What are these other possible readings? Here things get a bit murky. It is apparently easier to suggest that a greater knowledge of, say, First-Century Jewish background would make such readings possible than it is to come up with specific examples. Thus, Beversluis: "Lewis's discussion suggests that all individuals of all times and places who say the kinds of things Jesus said must be dismissed as lunatics. But this overlooks the theological and historical background that alone makes the idea of a messianic claim intelligible in the first place" (1985, 56). How exactly a knowledge of that background would alter the nature of Jesus' claims is not made clear. The best Beversluis can manage is, "When they did dispose of him, it was not on the ground that he was a lunatic but on the ground that he was an imposter" (Beversluis 1985, 56).

N. T. Wright takes a different tack, appealing to the "strong incarnational principle" (32) which was the Jewish Temple, the sign of God's presence among his people. Lewis doesn't so much get Jesus' deity wrong as "drastically short circuits" the original Jewish way of getting there: "When Jesus says, 'Your sins are forgiven,' he is not claiming straightforwardly to be God, but to give the people, out on the street, what they would normally get *by going to the Temple*" (33; emphasis in the original). By not taking us deeply enough into First-Century Jewish culture (at least as understood by Wright), Lewis fails to give us "sufficient grounding in who Jesus really was" (33).

Readers willing to brave the technicalities of biblical criticism can easily get the impression that there is a solid scholarly consensus to the effect that we can't really assume that Jesus said everything the Gospels present him as saying. Representative is Frances Young's contribution to John Hick's symposium *The Myth of God Incarnate*, "A Cloud of Witnesses." Young takes it for granted that the New-Testament writings were produced by people trying to come to grips with the meaning of Christ and doing it in terms of their own developing situations in their churches. Few would question that picture of things; I do not. But Young draws from it the conclusion that the picture we get of Jesus is "the result of believers searching for categories in which to express their response to Jesus, rather than Jesus claiming to be those particular figures" (15). Thus, "The titles were attributed to Jesus by the early Christians and were not claimed by Jesus himself" (17). Only in John's Gospel are claims actually put into Jesus' own mouth as opposed to the mouths of his disciples, and John according to Young is not a historical account at all but a later meditation on the meaning of Jesus' life. If this conclusion is true—or is even as solidly supported by a real scholarly consensus as is implied—then the Trilemma would have great difficulty getting off the ground, with its initial premise (that Jesus claimed deity) being not only moot but incapable of ever being established.

BIBLICAL CRITICISM: A RESPONSE

Lewis's argument as presented in *Mere Christianity* simply presupposes that Jesus said and meant the things he is traditionally taken to have said and meant: it treats "a man who was merely a man and said the sort of things Jesus said." The argument is presented in the form, "Given that Jesus said and meant these things, this is what follows." To note that the initial premise is controversial in some circles is not a refutation; a refutation would require establishing that the initial premise is false, or at least probably not true. And this, as I will argue, has simply not been done.

Why does Lewis, though, make an initial assumption that does not appear to be one that we can actually afford safely to make? It was not because he was unaware of biblical criticism. It seems to me that most critics of Lewis have simply ignored the original audience for the Broadcast Talks that eventually became *Mere Christianity*: not college educated people but simple British laypersons during World War II. To bring up the technical issues of biblical criticism with that audience would have been a foolish introduction of questions they were not asking, unnecessary complications they did not need to deal with. With a more sophisticated audience, one would of course have to be prepared to make a case for the authenticity of the Gospel accounts and deal with alternative interpretations, because the truth of the initial premise is indeed essential to the argument. That Lewis knew of this challenge and was prepared to meet it when appropriate is proved by essays such as "Modern Theology and Biblical Criticism." Kreeft and Tacelli also recognize the necessity of having a response to the critical argument; they expand the Trilemma to a Quadrilemma: Lunatic, Liar, Lord, or Legend (161-74). Their divinity-claiming Jesus is not a legend because the documents are too early to have allowed for a long period of gradual magnification of Jesus' reputation by later followers.

Beversluis in 1985 rejected this defense: "When Lewis ... justifies the popular approach on the ground that 'if you are allowed to talk for only ten minutes, pretty well everything else has to be sacrificed to brevity,' he presents not a justification but an excuse.... Why not write a longer book in which 'everything else' *can* be fully and fairly discussed?" (1985,57). But here Beversluis falls prey to that regrettable tendency of reviewers to criticize the book they would have preferred the author to have written rather than the book he actually wrote. Would Beversluis have an audience of simple laypersons remain unaddressed? Does he really think it makes sense to confuse them with technicalities that do not concern them? As for the "longer book," one could say that it exists in *Miracles* or can be reconstructed from various essays that do address different, more sophisticated audiences. In *C. S. Lewis's Case for the Christian Faith*, Richard L. Purtill has a fine discussion of that larger argument gleaned from a more generous sampling of the Lewis corpus, in chapters 4-5 (45-71). Most of Lewis's critics simply ignore that context.

In his second edition of *C. S. Lewis and the Search for Rational Religion*, Beversluis tries to respond to the arguments of Lewis and others that support a traditional reading of the Gospels as giving an accurate and reliable report of Jesus' claims. He says that all such arguments "uncritically assume that the synoptic Gospels are historically reliable sources" (2007, 116). Instead of scholarship, apologists like Peter Kreeft and Ronald Tacelli offer "a flurry of unscholarly pseudo-questions" (2007, 118), such as why the apostles would be willing to die for what they knew was a lie. "Real" New Testament scholars don't ask such questions because they "know" that none of the original apostles had anything to do with the Gospels. "All mainstream New Testament Scholars agree that the synoptic Gospels are fragmentary, episodic, internally inconsistent, and written by people who were not eyewitnesses" (2007, 123).

For someone who claims to find fallacious motes in the eyes of others, Beversluis has a curious blindness to the beams in his own eyes. His whole argument here depends on the fallacies of *Ad Verecundiam* and *Dicto Simpliciter*. Even if all serious biblical scholars did agree with Beversluis, that fact in itself would not make them right. But they can only be said to agree by the sleight of hand of simply (and arbitrarily) defining a "mainstream" scholar as a skeptical one. Beversluis's unqualified generalization—*all?*—has never in fact been true, and is less true now than it has been at any time in the modern age. Richard Bauckham's magisterial *Jesus and the Eyewitnesses* is just one recent counter-example. A basic source like Stephen Neil's classic *The Interpretation of the New Testament* could have provided Beversluis with many more.

Beversluis in his revised edition also responds specifically to Lewis's own arguments in "Modern Theology and Biblical Criticism." He simply dismisses Lewis's point that people who claim to find myths and legends in the Gospels need to know something about myths and legends and his observation that source criticism, when applied to modern authors where it can be checked, is almost always wrong. Beversluis patronizes these concerns as "The Argument from Personal Incredulity" (2007, 123). Nevertheless, Lewis's incredulity is not just a rhetorical ploy but has very good and specific grounds in his claim that the whole enterprise of skeptical criticism is methodologically flawed—an issue that Beversluis just fails to address. But that claim is central to the case against this alleged "consensus." We will have more to say about this below. So far, we have to conclude that the authenticity of the sources simply has not been overturned by this argument.

The alternative interpretations of Jesus' claims are not impressive either. How is the statement "When they did dispose of him, it was not on the ground that he was a lunatic but on the ground that he was an imposter" (Beversluis 1985, 56) a problem? "Liar" is one of the implied horns of the Trilemma. Isn't an imposter just one form of liar? Isn't Liar at least as incompatible with Great Moral Teacher as Lunatic? And N. T. Wright seems to expect of his readers a sophistication in modern interpretations of Jewish culture that even the Pharisees of Jesus' day did not manifest. After Jesus' declaration that the sins of the paralytic were forgiven prior to his healing, they were not saying, "Who is this who speaks blasphemies? Where can sins be forgiven but *in the Temple* alone?" They were saying, "Who is this who speaks blasphemies? Who can forgive sins but *God* alone?" (Luke 5:21; emphasis added). In other words, Lewis's argument deals with the reactions Jesus' contemporaries actually made to him—not the one Wright thinks they should have made! Wright thus tempts one to apply to him Lewis's verdict from "Modern Theology and Biblical Criticism": these critics are so adept at reading between the lines that they have forgotten how to read the lines themselves.

Beversluis fares no better when he claims that all that is needed is to suppose that Jesus had been "*authorized* to forgive sins by God" (2007, 124, emphasis added). This again simply ignores the actual reaction by Jesus' contemporaries. *They* took Jesus' words as a claim to deity, and he did nothing to allay their concerns. In order to understand their reaction, as well as the significance of Jesus' allowing it to take place, modern readers might be helped by imagining the reaction of a radical Muslim Fundamentalist to a mere human being who claimed to be Allah. It is ironic that Lewis is accused of ignoring the cultural context of the Gospels' claims for Jesus by people who have obviously failed to make the effort to imagine the fierce monotheism of First-Century Judaism—a basic and essential prerequisite to any audience analysis of the words of Jesus! Far from Lewis's views of the Gospels revealing him as "a textually careless and theologically unreliable guide" to them, it would seem that the accusation would better fit Lewis's critics. Chesterton asked a pertinent question in his version of the argument: "Mahomedans did not misunderstand Mahomet and suppose he was Allah. Jews did not misunderstand Moses and identify him with Jehovah. Why was this claim alone exaggerated unless this alone was made?" (246).

Young commits the same kind of fallacious band-wagon appeal to scholarly consensus as Beversluis, and adds to it a brazen *non sequitur*. Surely the New-Testament writers were indeed struggling to understand Jesus in terms of their own problems. This is simply to say that they were human beings. It does not follow that they put their own ideas into Jesus' mouth, or into the mouths of his close associates (like Peter in his famous confession), or that they manufactured incidents like Jesus forgiving sins, along with the reactions of those present. These are conclusions that would have to be reached independently, needing more grounds than the assumption that things just must have happened that way because that is how "real scholars" understand the evolution of the New Testament.

That Young is imposing a concept of evolution on the New-Testament documents rather than reading it out of them is suggested by the strange statement that their "dates of origin span approximately three quarters of a century" (14). First, that is very unlikely. The earliest documents are the first epistles of Paul, which are probably from the fifties. But practically the whole New Testament, including all four canonical Gospels, was already being quoted *as Scripture* by the Apostolic Fathers by the end of the First Century—meaning it had to be in circulation some time before that (Bruce 18-19, Holmes, Richardson). The actual period of composition then may be as little as half what Young suggests, and his suggestion is hardly indisputable—but it is needed to give time for the evolution of the early Christians' understanding of Jesus that is assumed to have happened. And that is precisely the point. Included in the collection accepted by the end of the First Century are all four canonical Gospels and the undisputed Pauline epistles—all the major documents on which the traditional account of the claims of and for Christ are based. Even if later dates for a few of the disputed epistles be granted, the earlier dates we must accept for the rest make it harder to posit the kind of evolution critics like Young assume.

Young is very honest about the source of the presuppositions that drive such an understanding. "The Christians of the early church lived in a world in which supernatural causation was accepted without question." But such a world view is "unthinkable now." "There is no room for God as a causal factor" in the modern mind, and Christian scholars according to Young must simply bow to that situation (31). *But if we want honestly to examine the question whether Jesus could have claimed to be—and been—the Son of God, that is precisely the point on which we have to keep an open mind!*

Young's closed mind, and that of his cohorts in the mainstream critical "consensus," renders what looks like textual scholarship an exercise in philosophy determining in advance what texts are to be allowed to say. In this, he is typical of the whole enterprise of negative biblical criticism. That is precisely why that critical consensus is unimpressive to conservative believers. It is philosophically prejudiced and methodologically flawed, not to mention actually balanced by a significant body of criticism that, without the predisposing naturalistic bias, reaches very different conclusions. Recall Lewis's observation that the kind of reconstructive techniques practiced by skeptical scholars have an accuracy record near zero when applied to contemporary documents where the results can be checked ("Modern Theology" 159-61). I would argue, much as Lewis did, that Jesus' contemporaries, who were or had access to eye witnesses, are in a better position to know what he said than modern experts trying to reconstruct the documents according to their own preconceived modernist philosophies. For anyone who looks at the critical issues in that light, the initial premise of the Trilemma remains strong.

In summary, Lewis's Trilemma did not, in fact, "backfire" with the audience for whom it was intended, even if it doesn't work with negative historical critics, a "failure" that Lewis himself would have expected. Even a more sophisticated audience that objectively examined the data would have to admit that the complications raised by modern biblical criticism do not overturn the initial premise of the Trilemma. According to the *documents* (as opposed to tendentious theoretical interpretations and reconstructions of them), Jesus in fact claimed deity: he made the statements and performed the actions, and he meant what he said. This is confirmed by the reactions his contemporaries actually had to those words and deeds.

Anyone using the Trilemma today should be prepared to make the case that Jesus actually made the claims whenever it is needed. The wise apologist will not simply repeat Lewis's paragraph from *Mere Christianity*, but rather adapt it to his own audience. This will involve notations such as "Here be prepared to insert 'Modern Theology and Biblical Criticism,'" along with further updated arguments." Unlike his critics, we should look to Lewis's other books and essays as evidence for how he himself would have used the argument from *Mere Christianity* in different contexts, and then follow suit ourselves.

THE CRITIQUE: MISTAKEN IDENTITIES?

The second major attempt to show that Lewis failed to cover his bases involves, amazingly, the denial that only an insane person could sincerely but mistakenly believe himself to be God, or that such a mistake would automatically disqualify him as a great moral teacher. McGrath thinks that "the option that Jesus was someone who was not mad or bad, but was nevertheless *wrong* about his identity, needs to be considered as a serious alternative" (227). Along that line, Beversluis originally asserted that "we could simply suppose that although [Jesus] sincerely believed he was God, he was mistaken" (1985, 55): not lying or insane, just mistaken. He elaborates, "If we deny that Jesus was God, we are not logically compelled to say that he was a lunatic; all we have to say is that his claim to be God was false. The term lunatic simply clouds the issue with emotional rhetoric" (1985, 55). In his second edition, he adds documentation from psychological studies of insanity to the effect that "delusional people are deluded about something . . . but they are rarely, if ever, deluded about everything" (2007, 126). Just because a person is deluded about who he is does not necessarily mean that he is deluded about the content of his moral teachings. Beversluis concludes, "The sober answer to the question is No, this is not the kind of blunder that only a lunatic would make" (1985, 55).

Well, this assertion is generally correct; but surely its application to the specific case of Jesus would take some supporting. No doubt people may be sincerely mistaken about a lot of things, even having to do with their own identity, without being necessarily insane; and they can be insane without being wrong about morals. But make no mistake: we are being asked here to believe that a person could be mistaken about the claim that "before Abraham was, *I Am*," a person who was in a position to be familiar with the standard translation of the Tetragrammaton, the Old Testament name of God, and still be considered a sound thinker about morals (or anything else). Is this really credible? Marvin D. Hinten shows how such support might look. When he teaches *Mere Christianity*, he asks his class

> if they believe angels really did appear to Joan of Arc to say she was God's chosen instrument to save France. Half the class shake their heads no; the other (quicker-thinking) half simply sit and think it over, because they already see where it is going. None of them see Joan as insane or demonic, so if they apply Lewis's line of reasoning they will have to admit God really did send angels to Joan, which they have no intention of admitting. I then bring Mohammed into the mix, a man who genuinely seems to have felt Gabriel appeared to him with teaching from God. We discuss ways in which a goodhearted person could be genuinely mistaken about their [sic] role in life: an *idée fixe*, a hallucination, etc. (8)

Daniel Howard-Snyder has the most sustained and rigorous argument for the idea that Jesus could have been merely mistaken about being God. He admits that believing one is divine when one is not is believing something "importantly false," but then claims that "merely being wrong about something important, even something as important as whether one is divine, neither implies nor makes it likely that one is a lunatic, insane, deranged, or otherwise fit to be institutionalized" (463). To support this audacious claim, he tries to imagine scenarios in which Jesus could have had what seemed to him adequate grounds for believing he was God, grounds that, while seemingly adequate, turned out to be fallible—grounds that could be accepted by someone who was not insane. Perhaps Satan could have given him the ability to perform miracles and duplicated in his mind the subjective experience of being divinity incarnate. Perhaps Jesus, convinced that he was the Messiah, found exegetical grounds in the Old Testament for believing that the Messiah was in some sense divine. (This would be plausible because in fact the early Christians did find such textual arguments for Christ's divinity after the fact). For Howard-Snyder, these are "good but fallible grounds" that a person might have for believing in his own divinity (474). Jesus might have made such deductions in error, or applied them to himself in error, without being insane. Howard-Snyder does not claim that either scenario actually obtains, but simply that their possibility makes it impossible to dismiss the "sincerely mistaken but still sane" option; therefore the Mad, Bad, or God argument fails.

O. K., so the argument goes, you can be mistaken about your identity without being insane. Likewise, you can be mistaken about your identity without undermining your views of ethics. Lewis "apparently thought that if certain factual claims Jesus made about himself were false, a disastrous conclusion would follow about the truth, sanity, and reliability of his moral teachings. But why say that?" (Beversluis 1985, 55). Beversluis goes on to ask, "Did Lewis think that if Jesus were not God, there would no longer be any reason for believing that love is preferable to hate, humility to arrogance, charity to vindictiveness, meekness to oppressiveness, fidelity to adultery, or truthfulness to deception?" (1985, 55). For Howard-Snyder, we are not in a position to say that the diabolic deception or exegetical misapplication scenarios "are significantly less likely or plausible than the God option" (478).

So the Trilemma fails at every point by this view. You can, in theory, be mistaken about your identity without being insane *and* without having false views of ethics; therefore, Lewis has failed to eliminate the "Great Moral Teacher but not God" view of Jesus and has hung his apologetic on a fallacious hook. "Contrary to what Lewis claims, we *can* deny that Jesus was God and say that he was a great moral teacher" (Beversluis 2007, 135).

MISTAKEN IDENTITIES? A RESPONSE

Let us begin by remembering the conclusion of Lewis's Trilemma: that Jesus could not have been a great moral teacher but not God. The response of the critics is, well, why could he not have been just sincerely mistaken about God without being insane, or have been mentally imbalanced in some sense and still be a great moral teacher? So we need to be clear about what it would take to be a great moral teacher. I would suggest the following criteria: first, you have moral teachings that both resonate with humankind's most basic instincts about right and wrong but also state them in ways both profound and challenging. Second, you have and live with admirable consistency before your followers a life that is in accordance with your own version of those teachings. Third, you must be sufficiently in touch with reality that your teachings have general credibility. Clearly, if Jesus had been lying about his claims, he would be disqualified by the second test; but few accuse him of that. More importantly for this discussion, a person who failed the third test would also have problems with the trustworthiness needed to fully inhabit the role, even if he were not morally culpable for them. This is where the rubber meets the road in evaluating the claim that Jesus could have been simply mistaken about his deity.

Most of Lewis's critics succeed in undermining his argument only by use of a clever sleight of hand known as the fallacy of Equivocation. The argument most of them are critiquing is simply not the one that Lewis made. Most of the criticisms deal with the *general concept* of mistaken identity, whereas Lewis is dealing with a very *specific case* of it, the false claim *to be God*. As Horner rightly puts it, Beversluis's representation of the case (if "certain factual claims Jesus made about himself were false") is hardly adequate. "The factual claims in question are of cosmic, as well as supremely personal and existential, consequence" (77). Treating such vastly different cases of mistaken identity as equivalent is illogical at best and dishonest at worst. But Lewis's critics have to do it in order to make their criticisms sound plausible. (Howard-Snyder does deal more directly with the specific claim to divinity, but does not take it with sufficient seriousness, as I will try to show.)

This weakness becomes very clear when we examine the examples Hinten uses to support the claim that mistaken identity does not necessarily entail insanity. Joan of Arc and Mohammed thought they had seen angels and had a special role in history as a result. One can just imagine that they could have been victims of some kind of hallucination or had some kind of experience that they misinterpreted, and that this could all have happened without compromising their general soundness of mind, or their views of ethics. But the problem is that such examples are simply not relevant to Lewis's argument. Joan and Muhammed did not claim to be *God*. That is, they did not claim to have existed from eternity in a special relationship with God the Father that made them Lord and gave them the authority to command the elements and forgive sins. They did not claim that they had a prior existence that was omniscient, omnipotent, and omnipresent—all of which is implied in and entailed by the specific nature of Jesus' claims. They did not claim that he who had seen them had seen the Father. *They did not claim to be the Yahweh of the Patriarchs and Moses incarnate in human flesh*!

How is it possible to miss the profound difference between all other mistakes about one's own identity and this one? One who wrongly believes that he is Napoleon has only confused himself with another finite human being. (Even this would present problems for the claim to be a great moral teacher. As Horner correctly observes [77], having correct views on ethics is necessary, but hardly a sufficient condition for being a great moral teacher.) As Kreeft notes, "A measure of your insanity is the size of the gap between what you think you are and what you really are" (see his discussion 59-63). Indeed. Chesterton makes a similar point: "Normally speaking, the greater a man is, the less likely he is to make the very greatest claim. Outside the unique case we are considering, the only kind of man who ever does make that kind of claim is a very small man: a secretive or self-centered monomaniac" (247).

Kreeft and Chesterton are right: to believe that one is Yahweh differs from all other such mistaken claims by an order of magnitude that is ... well, infinite. It compounds a mistake of fact ("I am this finite created being, not that one") with an error in metaphysics ("I am not *a* finite being at all, but the Ground of all Being"). This is not, as Lewis's critics want to believe, merely a matter of degree. The gap between any creature and the Creator is a difference of kind.

One might object that while the difference between the Creator and the creature is a difference of kind, the *claim* itself does not so differ from other claims, since all delusions are ontologically false to the same degree, that is, completely. But even if we accept this analysis and agree that all false claims are equally incorrect, it does not follow that all such errors are equally serious, much less morally equivalent. Falsely claiming to be Napoleon, for example, does not make one guilty of blasphemy. Mistaking one creature for another is an error, conceivably innocent; mistaking a creature for the Creator is idolatry. The error attributed to Jesus would be of the latter variety, and surely not irrelevant to his status as a Great Moral Teacher—especially among First-Century Jews! Anyone sincerely mistaken about being God would miss our third criterion for great moral teacher, being clearly out of touch with reality. Any First-Century Jew so mistaken would run afoul of the second as well, being guilty of two of the most serious sins recognized by that society: blasphemy and idolatry.

To put it bluntly, therefore, Lewis's critics' ability to rebut his argument depends on their ability to substitute a different and inferior argument while no one is looking and get away with it. When, like Lewis, we remember the radical nature of what Jesus actually claimed, and compare it with the ridiculously inadequate examples urged against the Trilemma, the attempts to evade its force become laughably absurd.

An equal lack of attention to what Lewis actually said appears in the attempt to evade his claims about the implications of the relationship between Christ's person and his teaching. Beversluis asks, "Did Lewis think that if Jesus were not God, there would no longer be any reason for believing that love is preferable to hate, humility to arrogance, charity to vindictiveness, meekness to oppressiveness, fidelity to adultery, or truthfulness to deception?" (1985, 55). But Lewis was not evaluating the moral truth of Jesus' teaching; he was examining the claims of the *Teacher*. His whole argument presupposes the self-evident truth of the teachings (cf. *MC* 137), which is part of the evidence to be considered in evaluating the sanity of the Teacher. What is under scrutiny is the claims of the Teacher. Lewis is not saying that, if he were insane enough to wrongly think he was the omnipotent God, Jesus' moral teaching would be refuted. He is saying that the self-evident truth of those teachings and their widely acknowledged superiority to all other attempts to state the same ideals refutes, i.e., is incompatible with, the notion that their source was a blatant liar or a megalomaniac. Nothing that his critics have said makes those propositions any more consistent than they ever were before. Beversluis's question is simply beside the point.

Howard-Snyder is an exception to my dismissal of the attempts above to show that mistaken identity does not entail insanity because he does try to deal with the specific case of mistakenly believing that one is God. Yet in reading his argument I cannot escape the impression that, having used the word "God" in one sentence, he immediately forgets in the next sentence what that word means. How else could anyone write with a straight face a sentence like this? "Merely being wrong about something important, even something as important as whether one is divine, neither implies nor makes it likely that one is a lunatic, insane, deranged, or otherwise fit to be institutionalized" (463). It is not so much the "importance" as the *nature* of the claim to divinity that calls into question the sanity of any mere mortal who makes it, and guarantees the insanity of anyone who makes it falsely. Indeed, some of Jesus' opponents, and for a while even members of his own family, questioned his sanity—not surprisingly. They had not evacuated the word *God* of its meaning, or the concept of God of its transcendence. Howard-Snyder rhetorically softens the nature of the claim even with his diction: the abstraction to be "divine" rather than what is at issue, the concrete and personal claim to be *God*. I repeat: it is the claim to have existed from eternity in a special relationship with God the Father that made a person Lord and gave him the authority to command the elements and forgive sins. It is the claim that he had a prior existence that was omniscient, omnipotent, and omnipresent. It is the claim that he who had seen this one had seen the Father. It was, particularly for Jesus, the claim to be *the Yahweh of the Patriarchs and Moses incarnate in human flesh*.

Howard-Snyder also confuses the issue by introducing the word *institutionalized*. The Trilemma does not require that a Jesus falsely claiming divinity would qualify for any specific modern diagnosis of a pathology justifying institutionalization; it only requires that he be unbalanced enough to be out of touch with reality and thus disqualified as a great moral teacher. Surely megalomania would suffice as such a disqualification? And surely the false claim to be God, made sincerely, would count as megalomania? If not, perhaps our requirements for "great moral teacher" have receded as far as our concept of what it takes to be God!

If we remember what it means to be God, then we must agree with Stephen T. Davis that we are "not prepared to allow that anybody other than God ever has sufficient reason to consider himself divine" (491). Howard-Snyder's attempts to imagine scenarios in which a sane person could be falsely persuaded that he is God fail at two points. First, they again have forgotten the full meaning of what it would have meant for a devout First-Century Jew to think he was God. Howard-Snyder realizes correctly that it would not be enough for Satan to grant the power to do miracles, because prophets were believed to have performed miracles. So he has to have Satan reconstruct for Jesus the subjective experience of being God incarnate. The problem with this is that no one who has not been God incarnate could possibly know what that experience is. Hence, we have to ask, how would falsely assuming that one is having it not be megalomania? Having Jesus conclude his divinity through faulty exegesis of the Hebrew Bible runs up against the same problem. Surely a *sane* person who understands the concept of God would conclude of any text that persuaded him that he was, contrary to all his experience, eternal, immortal, omnipresent, omniscient, and omnipotent, that there was a problem either with the text or with his reading of it.

The second problem with Howard-Snyder's scenarios is that, to establish the reasonableness of the sincerely-mistaken option, they would have to establish it, not for just any imaginable abstract figure, but for *Jesus*. Howard-Snyder lays down two ground rules at the outset: we must not treat the historical accounts as inspired Scripture, and we must not import into the discussion any independent evidence for Jesus' divinity, such as his miracles, teaching, or resurrection, etc. (458). Many apologists are prepared to accept the first condition for the sake of argument; few are prepared to accept the second. There is a good reason for this refusal. The purpose of the Trilemma is not just to establish some abstract truth but to facilitate an encounter with Christ by clarifying the options of how we can understand *him*. And so the question is, for example, not whether Satan could persuade some abstract random person that he was divine, but whether it makes sense to say that he could so have persuaded *Jesus*. Does *Jesus* strike us as a person who had been so deluded, as a person under Satanic influence? Interestingly, Jesus had his own answer to that scenario: if he did his great works by the power of Satan, then that would mean that Satan was fighting against his own kingdom, since Jesus' works were clearly works of mercy and goodness (Mat. 12:25-28).

In summary, the attempts to show that the Trilemma omits valid but unconsidered options all fail. In order to reject Lewis's argument, you have to be prepared to affirm that a person in his right mind can sincerely but mistakenly believe, not simply that he has been visited by an angel, but that he is Almighty God, the Creator of the Universe, and still retain any credibility on anything else he might say. Since very few people in their right minds are prepared to accept that conclusion, most of Lewis's critics are forced to try to undermine his argument by sneakily substituting a straw man for it. Refuting that weak substitution, they then pretend to have refuted the Trilemma. But no reader who is actually paying attention should fall for this shell game—for that is what it essentially is. Howard-Snyder's attempt to support the sincerely mistaken option must be taken more seriously, for it does attempt to deal with the claim to be God rather than merely with the concept of mistaken identity in general. But it also fails by omitting to keep the full concept of deity in the forefront of our minds throughout the discussion.

DIMINISHING PROBABILITIES?

Another attempt to find problems with the Trilemma does not attack its individual propositions but accepts for the sake of argument that they are each probably true. The problem is that when there are many such propositions, even if each is probably true, when the probabilities are multiplied together, the probability of the whole is significantly weakened. For example, if you have four propositions that are each probably true with a probability of .85, the probability of all four being true together is only .522—even odds, hardly a compelling case.

In the case of the Trilemma as Howard-Snyder analyzes it, you have to affirm that Jesus claimed to be God, that he was not lying, that he was not insane, and that he was not merely mistaken without being insane. If all four of these propositions are true, then it follows with deductive validity that he was telling the truth and was God. But all four are historical propositions, therefore only probably true because historical investigation cannot yield mathematical certainty. And all four, especially the first, are contested. Howard-Snyder gives what he considers charitable and generous ranges of probability to each proposition, ranging from .7-.9 for the claim to divinity to .85-.95 for the others, and ends with a range of only .43-.77 for the whole. Therefore, he concludes, we should "profess ignorance and suspend judgment about the matter" rather than claiming that the Trilemma shows it to be rational to believe in Jesus' divinity (462).

There are a number of ways in which we could respond to this case. We could argue for higher values for the probabilities; but skeptics would have their own arguments for why they should be lower, and we would really be arguing the case for the truth of each proposition, which we are going to have to do anyway. Nevertheless, we have already argued that it is not necessary to follow Howard-Snyder's rule about excluding evidence for the deity of Christ from outside the Trilemma itself. A person who looked at these four propositions in the light of the evidence for the resurrection set forth in a book like Morison's *Who Moved the Stone?* and in the light of the fulfillment of prophecy, etc., might well come up with high enough values that the final result would still be quite believable. Howard-Snyder's "range" (.43-.77) is simply a recognition that people come to different conclusions. One who thought with good reason that the actual probability was .77 (or higher) would hardly be required to suspend judgment simply because people who think it is .43 exist. Still, whatever values we assign must be less than absolute certainty. So far, therefore, the diminishing probabilities argument at worst can only qualify our confidence in the conclusion of the Trilemma; it does not overturn it.

I think the analysis I just gave is correct; but I also think that there is a deeper problem with the probability argument. It is easy to forget that in the Trilemma we are not simply debating various abstract propositions but ultimately dealing with our response to a person. The purpose of the argument is to enable us more intelligently to answer the basic question Jesus puts to us: "Who do you say that I, the Son of Man, am?" (Mat. 16:13-18; see Brazier 103-6). Even Howard-Snyder admits that the Trilemma is deductively valid; his problem is the extent to which we can have confidence in the individual propositions (457). But the bottom-line question is whether I trust this Person that the historical accounts and the preaching of the Gospel present to me—even when He makes the most audacious claims. And one does not decide to trust another person simply by juggling a probabilistic calculus, but by responding to the gestalt of his total personality. Of course, one is justified in doing so only as long as the propositions of the formal argument are believable both individually and together. If they were not, the gestalt would not matter; if they were not, it would be a sign that the gestalt was leading you astray. But one does not decide to trust a person on the basis of propositions and their logical relationships alone.

In making this judgment in Jesus' case, we gain clarity by using the Trilemma: by asking, "Is he lying? Is he crazy? Could he be just simply mistaken about *this* claim?" The Christian hopes that the response will be, "In *his* case—no, I don't think so," and that the Trilemma will then help to guide the seeker toward the logical response of faith: "He is telling the truth." It will not be the Trilemma alone which generates this response, but rather the totality of Christ's person as revealed by the Gospel (aided and brought into focus by the Trilemma and its validity) and brought home to the seeker by the Holy Spirit. Nothing less has ever produced that response or ever will. I think Lewis understood this truth, for at the end of his presentation in *Mere Christianity* he hopes that his elimination of the great moral teacher copout will push us back to Christ himself: "*He* has not left that open to us. *He* did not intend to" (56, emphasis added).

The diminishing probability argument then is not as impressive as it first seems, and is ultimately irrelevant to the way the Trilemma actually works.

EXTRAORDINARY CLAIMS?

A similar attempt to weaken the apparent force of the Trilemma is the "Extraordinary Claims" argument: according to this argument, an extraordinary claim (like the resurrection or deity of the man Jesus) requires extraordinary support. Historical arguments, by their nature never more than probabilistic, are inherently incapable of providing such support. Therefore such claims cannot be supported by apologetic argument and must be believed if at all by sheer blind faith.

The problem with the argument from extraordinary claims is that it cuts both ways. Is the notion that this vast, intricate, mathematically rational and fine-tuned universe just randomly popped into existence out of nothing and then proceeded to organize itself by pure chance into DNA, etc., not an extraordinary claim? Is the notion that the Disciples were all transformed from clueless cowards to men who turned the world upside down by a contention they knew to be false not an extraordinary claim? Is the notion that a merely human person can believe himself to be the omnipotent, eternal Creator of the universe and not be insane not an extraordinary claim? Surely they are. So if, when you think it through, you can avoid one extraordinary claim only by affirming another set of them, equally extraordinary, we must realize that the argument from extraordinary claims takes us nowhere and should therefore be abandoned. We simply have to make the best judgment we can on the evidence we have, however "extraordinary" the conclusion may seem to some to be.

CONCLUSION

How then do we evaluate the Trilemma as an apologetic argument? Brazier asks whether it is a failure and concludes, "No, because it generated speculation, got people talking" (186). It has certainly done at least that! And it has done much more as well.

In conclusion, Lewis's Trilemma is still a strong argument and can be used with confidence if we allow it to be nuanced and strengthened by its context in Lewis's body of writings as a whole and if we understand its proper role in clarifying the options. It is unfair to take a paragraph aimed at a lay audience and complain that it is inadequate to deal with people who have a more sophisticated set of issues. Of course the classic passage from *Mere Christianity* needs to be supplemented when used with more sophisticated audiences, by Lewis's other writings and by information and arguments that have come to light since he wrote. But the basic argument is sound. It is one thing to claim that it commits the fallacy of False Dilemma; it is quite another to show that other credible and valid options actually exist. Lewis's critics have simply failed to do that. The argument as presented by Lewis does not purport to prove the deity of Christ by itself, but it supports it by analyzing the logical options available and pointing out the difficulty of seeing Jesus as a liar or a lunatic. Attempts to see him as a liar or a lunatic are tendentious and ignore the actual facts of his life, and attempts to find other options, such as a sane person sincerely mistaken about his deity, fail in the same way and fail doubly when we understand the real magnitude of the claim being made.

Second, Lewis's position as the dean of Christian apologists remains unchallenged. He was not infallible, but neither was he guilty of writing something in the Trilemma that was "not top-flight thinking" (Hinten 8). His unique combination of wide learning, no-nonsense clarity, elegant language, and apt analogy remains as the standard to which we should all aspire and the example we should seek to emulate. When examined carefully, the Trilemma supports that conclusion; it is not an exception to it.

Liar, Lunatic, or Lord? Lacking, Ludicrous, or Logical? Plunk for Liar or Lunatic if you must. But let's not come with any patronizing nonsense about how Lewis gave us a fallacious argument. He has not left that open to us. He did not intend to.

CHAPTER 7

Soteriology
The Atonement and Salvation

"Though the Witch knew the Deep Magic, there is a magic deeper still which she did not know. Her knowledge goes back only to the dawn of time. But if she could have looked a little further back into the stillness and the darkness before Time dawned, she would have read a different incantation. She would have known that when a willing victim who had committed no treachery was killed in a traitor's stead, the Table would crack and Death itself would start working backward." (LWW 178-179)

C. S. Lewis was not an exegetical theologian. That is, his first move in answering any theological question was not to try to discover inductively what Scripture teaches on the topic. I am not saying that he ignored the teaching of Scripture, but one does not often find him directly expounding it as the basis of his theological positions. Rather, having concluded that historic Christianity was true, he tried to discern the consensus about its content among others across the denominations and periods of history who had come to the same conclusion and then think through the implications of those ideas and find intelligent ways to illustrate and apply them.

This approach served Lewis well in those doctrines for which that consensus is unified and does in fact faithfully represent the teaching of Scripture. Thus, in theology proper or in Christology, there are few points at which any faithful historic Christian would feel compelled to dissent from Lewis, few points at which such people would not be positively edified by Lewis's writings. But in the chapter on bibliology, the doctrine of Scripture and its inspiration, we found that inattention to what the Apostle Paul had actually *said* about inspiration (that it applies to the *graphe*, the actual text of Scripture, 2 Tim. 3:16) led to

Lewis positing a distinction between Word and Text that unintentionally undermines the authority of Scripture and creates numerous points of disagreement between Lewis and the traditional theology to which he had tried to be faithful. Soteriology, the doctrine of the atonement and of salvation, is the other major place in which this weakness, the failure to approach theological questions exegetically, shows up. It is not that Lewis does not have many good things to say about salvation; but this is the area in which his version of things, even as it often inspires and edifies them, most fails to satisfy all of his historic Christian readers, especially conservative Evangelical Protestants. Let's see if we can read Lewis with some discernment in this area.

THE NECESSITY OF THE ATONEMENT

The first question about an atonement involving the death of Christ is why any such drastic act on the part of God should be needed. The answer must begin with the recognition that Satan's rebellion against God, and Adam's joining him in that rebellion, have consequences that God is not willing simply to ignore or to cancel out by arbitrary fiat as if the moral choices which led to them had no significance. God may bring good out of evil, but not simply by pretending (or letting anyone else pretend) that the evil did not happen. As Ransom tells the Green Lady about the fall of his own race, "Of course good came of it. Is Maleldil a beast that we can stop His path or a leaf that we can twist His shape? Whatever you do, He will make good of it. But not the good He had prepared for you if you had obeyed Him. That is lost forever" (*Pa* 121).

Fortunately, God does respond to evil, and He does so redemptively. Oyarsa tells Ransom that, "We think that Maleldil would not give [Thulcandra] up utterly to the Bent One, and there are stories among us that He has taken strange counsel and dared terrible things, wrestling with the Bent One in Thulcandra. But of this we know less than you; it is a thing we desire to look into" (*OOTSP* 121).

Man's relationship to God, and consequently to himself and to the world, has been disrupted by his rebellion against his Creator. Lewis understood this well. "Fallen man is not simply an imperfect creature who needs improvement: he is a rebel who must lay down his arms" (*MC* 59). Adam and Eve did not simply break an arbitrary rule; by their disobedience they joined Satan's rebellion against God, and their race has been oriented to rebellion ever since. The original disobedience and all the others which have followed it, as acts of rebellion flowing from rebellious hearts, incur what Frances Schaeffer called "true moral guilt." This guilt is a basic fact to which God's justice must respond, and it cannot simply be wished away. As Lewis put it, the mere passage of time does nothing to solve the problem of the fact or of the guilt of sin. "The guilt is washed out not by time but by repentance and the blood of Christ" (*PoP* 49). The human race must therefore be lost unless God intervenes in some way. That intervention is what we call the atonement.

God must intervene because one of the things human beings lost as a result of the Fall was the ability to extricate themselves from the situation they had created. This inability has two dimensions: first, the guilt itself is intractable, and second, the very instrument that would be trying to reform itself, the soul or the heart, has been corrupted. Orual admits, "I could mend my soul no more than I could mend my face. Unless the gods helped" (*TWHF* 282). But with that help (and "help" is only one aspect of it), we can reach the point that Edmund did. "It is very true," said Edmund. "But even a traitor may mend. I have known one that did" (*TH&HB* 230).

One of the things that was corrupted is our very notion of what acceptability before God would look like. We think of ourselves as pretty good people if we are just less obviously selfish or corrupt than our neighbors. But one can be a relatively nice person and still be a sinner—still a rebel against God's just rule. Therefore, Lewis wisely reminds us that making people nicer would not necessarily save their souls. "A world of nice people, content in their own niceness, turned away from God, would be just as desperately in need of salvation as a miserable world—and might even be more difficult to save" (*MC* 182).

What makes an atonement necessary is not just man's defection but also the nature of the God from whom we have defected. There might be some wiggle room with the pagan gods. Orual asks, for example, "Are the gods not just?" The Fox replies, "Oh no, child. What would become of us if they were?" (*TWHF* 297). But the God against whom we have really sinned *is* just, and absolutely so. He is as absolute in justice as He is in power or knowledge or any other attribute. If that were the whole story, there would be no atonement; man would just be lost. But God is also love, and mercy, and grace. Therefore, there will be an atonement, and one that will fully accord with all of God's attributes. None of them will be swept under the rug.

Because the atonement will be the unified response of God's full Personality, His whole being and character, to the situation created by sin, it will have to take a very definite shape. And because this shape is not an arbitrary waving away of guilt but is dictated by the rock-hard realities of what sin is and who God is, that shape will be non-negotiable. Sinners must either take it for what it is, or leave it, because it could no more have been on other terms than God could be a different Person. So the human race finds itself in the position that Jill was in when she first met Aslan:

"I daren't come and drink," said Jill.
"Then you will die of thirst," said the Lion.
"Oh dear!" said Jill, coming another step nearer. "I suppose I must go and look for another stream then."
"There is no other stream," said the Lion. (*TSC* 21)

We can speak of the necessity of the atonement then in two ways. First, atonement is absolutely needed if a just God is to show mercy to sinful man. Second, in that atonement, there cannot be an arbitrary overlooking of the evil that has occurred, but rather a necessary satisfaction of all the attributes of God, particularly both His justice and His love. The atonement is not a random act of mercy but rather the most profound expression of who God is. Lewis does not lay out that necessity and analyze it as I have done here. If he had, I think there would have been less ambiguity in his treatments of the nature of the atonement in the next section. But his statement in *Problem of Pain* about the guilt of sin not being erased by time but only by the blood of Christ is consistent with the first necessity, and the portrayals of these issues in his fiction are consistent with the second, as can be seen above. Often Lewis's portrayals of soteriology are more biblically focused than his expositions of it.

THE NATURE OF THE ATONEMENT

Essential to any version of historic Christianity is the belief that God has done something about human sin, and that this something was the death of Christ. How exactly the death of Christ relates to sin and to sinful human beings, how it solves the problem created by sin, has not been so easy to understand. A number of theories have been advanced to answer that question: vicarious penal substitution, the ransom theory, the *Christus Victor* theory, the moral influence theory, and the example theory among them.

Penal substitution holds that Christ received in our place the just punishment that sin deserved. In the ransom theory, sin made human beings lawfully subject to Satan, and they had to be redeemed or bought back from that servitude. In the *Christus Victor* theory, Christ conquers Satan by His death and the redeemed are spoils of war. For the moral influence theory, the death of Christ is a powerful object lesson of God's love that overcomes our rebellious spirits. The example theory has the death of Christ setting us a radical example of obedience which will save us if we follow it. There is Scriptural language suggesting all of these ideas, though clearly some of them cut closer to the heart of salvation than others. No one would deny, for example, that Christ is our moral example—but is that how He *saves* us? Only a superficial understanding of the Fall would be satisfied by a positive answer to that question.

Lewis's first concern with the atonement is that we understand that it is the fact of Christ's death, that is, God's act in Christ's death, that saves us, not a particular theory about how it works. In this emphasis he was clearly correct, but his way of putting it might sometimes have implied too much. He explains that Christians have stated it in many ways: that Christ died for our sins; that He did for us what we should have done for ourselves; that we are washed in the blood of the Lamb; that Christ defeated or conquered death. "They are all true. If any of them does not appeal to you, leave it alone and get on with the formula that does. And, whatever you do, do not start quarreling with other people because they use a different formula from yours" (MC 157).

Lewis is not concerned to reject any of the theories; he thinks they are "all true"; but he does not want us to become fixed on one to the exclusion of the others. He wrote to a Mr. Young on 31 Oct. 1963 that he thought the different ideas such as sacrifice, ransom, conquest, substitution, etc. "are all images to *suggest* the reality (not otherwise comprehensible to us) of the Atonement. To fix on any *one* of them as if it contained and limited the truth like a scientific definition wd. in my opinion be a mistake" (L 3:1476). The deity of Christ is a defining doctrine that determines whether one is a Christian or not; the theories of the atonement are not. As we saw in the chapter on Christology, Lewis suggested to Dom Bede Griffiths on 21 Dec. 1941, that "the Divinity of our Lord has to be believed whether you find it a help or a 'scandal' (otherwise you are not a Xtian at all) but the Anselmic theory of Atonement is not in that position" (L 2:502).

Lewis's distinction between the fact of the atonement and the theories about it is sound and important. We are saved by the death of Christ, and by putting our faith in it, not by having a perfect understanding of it. But if Scripture indeed teaches some of those theories, it might behoove us to try to understand why, rather than just simply dropping those that don't "appeal" to us. Lewis indeed seems to have been moving in the direction of recognizing this truth as he matured in the faith. Apparently the original language of the Broadcast Talks had been even more dismissive than what appeared in the published form of *Mere Christianity*. Lewis wrote Griffiths on 21 Dec. 1941 that he thought he had gone too far in implying that the various theories of the atonement "were 'to be rejected if we don't find them helpful.' What I meant was 'need not be used'—a very different thing" (L 2:502). I would like to have seen even more movement. Even "need not be used" is less than the response required of us for something Scripture actually teaches. But we can agree with the point Lewis was trying to make: none of the theories is itself the Christian faith. "The central Christian belief is that Christ's death has somehow put us right with God and given us a fresh start. Theories as to how it did so are another matter" (MC 57).

There are two theories in particular that we have to be concerned with here. First is vicarious penal substitution, which Evangelical faith has seen as central and essential to any biblical understanding since the Reformation, but which Lewis includes in the optional ideas that can be dropped if we don't find them helpful. Then there is Lewis's suggested alternative theory of "vicarious repentance," laid out in Mere Christianity.

Lewis gives the following characterization of vicarious substitution: "God wanted to punish men for having deserted and joined the Great Rebel, but Christ volunteered to be punished instead so God let us off" (MC 57). The language here hardly presents that doctrine in the most positive (or accurate) light. It implies a just Father negotiating with a gracious Son rather than a God who is wholly both just and all loving, with the Father and the Son cooperating in a plan that would satisfy both of those attributes. There is also an air of arbitrariness in the phrase "let us off" that does not accurately represent what the doctrine says. Lewis may have been coming as he matured spiritually to realize that he had been less than completely fair to the theory. He remarks, vicarious substitution "does not seem to me quite so immoral and so silly as it used to" (MC 57). But the representation of it remains in Mere Christianity: to the extent that "let us off" is indeed arbitrary, the theory would in fact be immoral. Is it unfair for God to punish Christ in our place? To answer that question, we will have to look at the Scriptural basis for the doctrine.

The biblical teaching on the atonement begins with the idea of substitution. Lewis recognized the importance of this concept. He rightly called it "a principle very deeply rooted in Christianity: . . . *Vicariousness*" (M 123). Vicariousness is a literary phenomenon: we experience through a character vicariously events which have not happened to ourselves directly. I have not personally participated in an ill-fated cavalry charge, but Tennyson's "Charge of the Light Brigade" lets me have that experience *vicariously*. So in theology, something similar happens. Christ dies instead of us. *Christ dies and we don't*; He dies and we live. In His death, Jesus, in other words, acted on our behalf.

The implications of this vicarious, substitutionary acting may have been more specific than Lewis recognized. Jesus applied to himself the language of Isaiah 53:12, "And he was numbered with the transgressors." He who knew no sin was, in other words, counted as a sinner. The good Shepherd "lays down his life for the sheep" (John 10:11). He lays down his life "for his friends" (John 15:13). God demonstrates His love for us in that "while we were yet sinners, Christ died for us" (Romans 5:8). "*For* sheep/friends/us" means on our behalf, in our place. And perhaps the most radical statement of this substitution is that God "made Him who knew no sin to be sin on our behalf" (2 Cor. 5:21). Jesus is taking our

THE ATONEMENT AND SALVATION

place, standing in for us—but how? Specifically he is standing in for us *as sinners*, as people standing before the bar of God's judgment. And what does He do for us there? He becomes our *propitiation* through His blood.

Propitiation means an offering that turns away God's wrath against sin, and against us as sinners. Many moderns have been reluctant to embrace propitiation because they are hesitant to accept the idea that God could be wrathful, seeing God's implacable opposition to sin as a primitive or barbaric notion unworthy of a God of pure love. But the New Testament is fully committed to both justice/wrath and love. According to Jesus Himself, "He who has the Son has eternal life, but he who does not obey the Son will not see life, but the wrath of God abides on him" (John 3:36). In Romans 5:9 Jesus' blood saves us quite explicitly from the wrath of God. Jesus "rescues us from the wrath to come" (1 Thes. 1:10). When Christ returns He will deal out "retribution" and "penalty" to those who do not know God (2 Thes. 1:8). This is because "the wrath of God is revealed from heaven against all ungodliness and unrighteousness of men" (Rom. 1:18). Sin *deserves* and *demands* punishment, and God as a God of justice is as fully committed to meting it out as He is committed as a God of love to providing a way out for us, even at great personal sacrifice.

And that is where propitiation comes in. In His death, Christ took our place and received in full the wrath that sin deserves, allowing us to be spared. We are justified by grace, God's unmerited favor; that is, God is able to count us as righteous only because Christ has been "displayed publicly as a propitiation in His blood" (Rom. 3:25). You see the same idea expressed in other words when "Christ redeemed us from the curse of the Law, having become a curse for us" when He died on the tree (Gal. 3:13). But it isn't just Paul. John says that Christ is "the propitiation for our sins" (1 John 2:2). John makes propitiation the expression of God's love in 1 John 4:10. And Peter says that Christ "bore our sins in His body on the cross" (1 Peter 2:24). In the incarnation, Christ took on our nature so that He could take Adam's place as the head of our race and thus have the right to represent us (Rom. 5). Thus, the substitution which has him dying for us in our place is not arbitrary. As the Son of Man, He *does* represent us.

The conclusion is inescapable. Christ dying in our place, specifically to take for us the penalty that our sin deserved, is central to the New Testament's way of presenting the atoning significance of His death. The building blocks of this understanding come not just from Paul but from the Lord Himself and the disciples John and Peter as well. Lewis was right to say that no one theory of how the atonement works exhausts its meaning; he was right to say that no one theory of how it works *is* the atonement. But he was less than fully biblical in saying that vicarious penal substitution was just one theory among many and could be dropped if we don't find it helpful.

What does it matter if we just drop the idea of vicarious penal substitution? Rejecting it might seem at first to increase the emphasis on God's love; but in fact it compromises our sense of the seriousness of sin and of the rightness of God's just opposition to it, and hence undercuts our full appreciation of the profundity of (ironically) His love and His grace. They can only be fully apprehended in the light of the difficulties they had to overcome so that God could be at the same time "just and the justifier of the one who has faith in Jesus" (Rom. 3:26). Modern people may not feel the urgency or the necessity that God must forgive sinners in a way that fully upholds His justice. But it was important to the biblical writers, and therefore presumably to God, and the penal substitution theory is the church's recognition of that importance. Therefore, it ought to be important to us as well.

Lewis may have been on the way to an acceptance of the truths I've tried to convey here. He hints at it by saying that penal substitution did not seem as silly to him as it used to, and he shows it more strongly by the way in which Aslan dies in Edmund's place on the Stone Table. But when he was writing *Mere Christianity*, he was still casting about for a way of understanding the atonement that made sense to him then. The result was the doctrine of vicarious repentance. As Lewis explains,

> Fallen man is not simply an imperfect creature who needs improvement: he is a rebel who must lay down his arms.... This process of surrender —this movement full speed astern—is what Christians call repentance .... It needs a good man to repent. And here comes the catch. Only a bad person needs to repent: only a good person can repent perfectly. (*MC* 59)

What does this dilemma have to do with the death of Christ? Repentance is a kind of death. Indeed, one biblical metaphor for it is "dying to self" (Rom. 6:2, 11, etc.). Repentance

> is not something God demands of you before He will take you back and which He could let you off if He chose: it is simply a description of what going back to Him is like. If you ask God to take you back without it, you are really asking Him to let you go back without going back. It cannot happen. (*MC* 59-60)

The end result is that "we now need God's help to do something which God, in His own nature, never does at all—to surrender, to suffer, so submit, to die" (*MC* 60). So Christ becomes a man and experiences death so that He can come alongside us and, in and through us, help us to do what we otherwise could not do: repent and believe. "He is the representative 'Die-er' of the universe" (*M* 135). Lewis is at least consistent; he does not hold up this idea as a substitute for the other theories, but as one subject to the same limitations as the others. "Remember this is only one more picture...: and if it does not help you, drop it" (*MC* 61).

How should we evaluate the notion of vicarious repentance? I see nothing in it contrary to Scripture. Indeed, the New Testament stresses that we need God's help even to repent and believe. The natural man does not receive the things of the Spirit (1 Cor. 2:14) and even faith is a gift of God, not something we work up in ourselves (Eph. 2:8-9). While the provision of this help is usually attributed to the Holy Spirit, Christ in His mediatorial office can certainly be conceived as participating in it. Remember that I have not argued that vicarious penal substitution exhausts the meaning of the atonement, but rather simply that it is essential to it. The New Testament has language that also speaks of ransom and of Christ as conqueror as well. We can agree with Lewis that each theory is an attempt to express a whole that is greater than the sum of its parts, but we must refrain from implying with him that those parts actually stressed by the New Testament are optional or dispensable in our understanding. We must rather—and here I think Lewis would agree—trust our Lord and His Apostles to know their jobs (instructing us in the truths of the Faith) and let them do them.

Lewis was often better at portraying the atonement than explaining it. Even the rational Greek Fox of *Till We Have Faces* comes in the next life to understand that rationalism cannot be the whole truth, and that blood sacrifice must be more than just a symbol. "The Priest knew at least that there must be sacrifices. They will have sacrifice—will have man. Yes, and the very heart, center, ground, roots of a man; dark and strong and costly as blood" (*TWHF* 295). After Narnia's creation and fall, Aslan implies something like substitution in making the promise which is a kind of Narnian *protevangelium*: "Evil will come of that evil, but it is still a long way off, and I will see to it that the worst falls upon myself" (*TMN* 161).

The Stone Table of Narnia is the place where Lewis tries the hardest to give us a mythic picture of the atonement—perhaps the more biblical because it is mythic. We must not look for one-to-one allegorical correspondences. The Stone Table differs from our atonement, for example, in that Aslan dies for Edmund as an individual, not for any of the Narnian races. But the scene is resonant with biblical and doctrinal motifs. We see echoes of the ransom theory in the Witch's claims of a right to Edmund's blood:

> "Fool," said the Witch with a savage smile that was almost a snarl. "Do you think your master can rob me of my rights by mere force? He knows the Deep Magic better than that. He knows that unless I have blood as the Law says all Narnia will be overturned and perish in fire and water." (*LWW* 156)

The penal substitution theory runs through Aslan's explanation of his resurrection:

> Though the Witch knew the Deep Magic, there is a magic deeper still which she did not know. Her knowledge goes back only to the dawn of time. But if she could have looked a little further back into the stillness and the darkness before Time dawned, she would have read a different incantation. She would have known that when a willing victim who had committed no treachery was killed in a traitor's stead, the Table would crack and Death itself would start working backward. (*LWW* 178-9)

Calling it the deeper magic maintains the sense of mystery, while the phrase "killed in the traitor's stead" captures the essence of penal substitution in a way that here seems anything but silly or immoral. Whether from greater maturity as a theological thinker or as a happy effect of his sound mythopoeic instincts, Lewis gets much closer to an accurate portrayal of the atonement here than he does in the dithering about it in *Mere Christianity*.

THE APPLICATION OF THE ATONEMENT

So far we have been discussing what God did in the death of Christ to provide salvation, that is, to make our forgiveness for sin possible without compromise to His justice. The next question is how that work is applied to the individual believer, and the simple answer is that it is applied by faith: "Sirs, what must I do to be saved?" asks the Philippian jailer, and the answer was, "*Believe* on the Lord Jesus Christ" (Acts 16:30-31). Confessing Christ as Lord and *believing* that God raised Him from the dead is the path to salvation in Rom. 10:9-10, and we are saved by grace through *faith* in Eph. 2:8. We receive the salvation which Christ's death provided when we *believe* that He died for us and rose again and *trust* Him as our Savior—the italicized words both being synonyms of faith. But of course, the simple answer never escapes complications. How do we come to have this faith? Why is faith granted to one person who hears the Gospel, the good news of what Christ has done for us, and not to another? And how does it relate to good works, which also seem to have some role to play? What insights did Lewis have on these questions, and how consistent are they with the biblical account? These are the questions which must occupy us next.

CALLING AND CONVERSION

One cannot pry very deeply into the psychology of conversion without running into seeming paradoxes that have bedeviled Christian theology since its beginnings. If we are dead in our trespasses and sins (Eph. 2:1) and if the natural man does not accept the things of the Spirit nor can he know them (1 Cor. 2:14), then asking people to put their faith in Christ is asking the impossible. The conclusion is inescapable: they can only respond if God has already changed their hearts. But how then *do* we ask them to respond in repentance and faith? For we are commanded to do so. If we go too far down this road in one direction, we make faith possible only by making it meaningless. It may end up sounding like a mechanical response predestined into the cards rather than a meaningful human act. If we aren't careful, in other words, we risk reducing human persons to mere automata and turning God into a cosmic puppeteer. But Scripture will not allow for that conclusion. Yet neither can we give to human beings an ability to accept and believe spiritual truths which Scripture denies them. It will not allow for that conclusion either.

As far as I can see, Scripture gives us no relief from this tension. It just asks us to live with the mystery of how the divine and human wills interact in conversion. As Francis Schaeffer once said in a taped lecture I heard, when it comes to what he called divine sovereignty and human significance, "The Bible simply states both and walks away." Theologians have a hard time resisting the temptation to find a neater solution than the biblical data allows for. To Lewis's credit, he shows a full appreciation of both sides of the dilemma and an unwillingness to sweep either under the rug to arrive at a cheap solution.

Conversion, the process of coming to faith in Christ, begins with calling. "No one can come to me unless the Father who sent me draws him," said Jesus (Jn. 6:44). Lewis reflects that language very closely: "You would not have been calling to me unless I had been calling to you," said the Lion (TSC 23). This calling is understood as happening as the Holy Spirit works in our hearts, applying to them the testimony of our own conscience, the Word of God, the preaching of both Law and Gospel, and the witness of Christians, to bring conviction of sin and enable faith in Christ as the One who saves us from our sins. Most historic Christians would accept what we have said so far. But they understand differently the question of what is determinative in those who respond: the calling of God or the will of the individual. Calvinists stress the former with their doctrine of "irresistible grace" (or better, "effectual calling"); Arminians emphasize the latter in their denial of that doctrine. Each side feels it is affirming something essential: the primacy of grace and God's initiative for the former, the significance of human personality and choice for the latter. Most will conclude that one of those theologies formulates the mystery better than the other (while some on either side foolishly try to eliminate the mystery altogether), but it is hard to deny that both views are simply right in what they consider essential.

Lewis would not have self-identified as a Calvinist, but he understood where Calvinists were coming from and realized that the side of the mystery they represent is at least part of the truth. His explanation of the Calvinist mentality of the Sixteenth Century is a masterpiece of sympathetic portraiture:

> The experience is that of catastrophic conversion. The man who has passed through it feels like one who has waked from a nightmare into ecstasy. Like an accepted lover, he feels that he has done nothing, and could never have done anything, to deserve such astonishing happiness. Never again can he 'crow from the dunghill of desert.' All the initiative has been on God's side; all has been free, unbounded grace. And all will continue to be free, unbounded grace. His own puny and ridiculous efforts would be as helpless to retain the joy as they would have been to achieve it in the first place. Fortunately, they need not. Bliss is not for sale, cannot be earned. 'Works' have no merit, though of course faith inevitably, even unconsciously, flows out into works at once. He is not saved because he does works of love; he does works of love because he is saved. It is faith alone that has saved him: faith bestowed by sheer gift. From this buoyant humility, this farewell to the self with all its good resolutions, anxiety, scruples, and motive-scratchings, all the Protestant doctrines originally sprang. (*OHEL* 33)

Such a Christian affirms the Divine initiative not because he despises human free will but because he has experienced with the Apostle Paul the impossibility of his own will's being a sufficient explanation for his own turn toward such a great salvation. Lewis knew this from his own conversion. He describes himself as being given a choice: he could "open the door or keep it shut." But then he immediately admits, "I say, 'I chose,' yet it did not really seem possible to do the opposite" (*SBJ* 224). He did not decide to seek for God; rather, he pictures himself as the object of "the steady unrelenting approach of Him whom I so earnestly desired not to meet" (*SBJ* 228). It was only after "giving in" that he discovered that this One who had tracked him down and cornered him was the Source of all joy.

Perhaps this is why Lewis was able to portray the Calvinist understanding of effectual calling more clearly and sharply than any Calvinist I know of. Polly experiences that call in the voice of Aslan:

THE ATONEMENT AND SALVATION

> Aslan threw up his shaggy head, opened his mouth, and uttered a long, single note; not very loud, but full of power. Polly's heart jumped in her body when she heard it. She felt sure that it was a call, and that anyone who heard that call would want to obey it and (what's more) would be able to obey it, however many worlds and ages lay between. (*TMN* 163).

Effectual calling does not make us turn to Christ whether we want to or not; rather it gives us the desire for repentance even as it confers the ability to repent and believe. Aslan's call, like God's, "works in us both to will and to do His good pleasure" (Phil. 2:13).

Another passage which well captures the mystery of the divine-human interface in conversion is the un-dragoning of Eustace. Having been transformed into an actual dragon as the objectification of his dragonish nature, Eustace cannot un-dragon himself simply by wanting to or deciding to, much less trying to. As he recounts the story, "'And I thought to myself, oh dear, how many skins have I got to take off?'... Then the lion said—but I don't know if it spoke—'You will have to let me undress you... The very first tear he made was so deep that I thought it had gone right into my heart'" (*VDT* 115). Only Aslan can "undress" the dragon Eustace. Eustace's part is to "let" him. How far is even this "letting" an assertion of Eustace's own will? That turns out to be a strangely difficult question.

It is a difficult question because even though our will does truly act in conversion, it does not do so entirely of its own accord, or without help. Where does God's call, His "help," leave off and our own act begin? The exact location of that spot has not been successfully plotted by our most profound insights of psychology or theology. Lewis struggles to express it as any honest person must. This radical step from being mere creatures to being sons is in a sense voluntary—we must choose it. But "It is not voluntary in the sense that we, of ourselves, could have chosen to take it...; but it is voluntary in the sense that when it is offered to us we can refuse it" (*MC* 186). God does not simply override our wills, but "He is prepared to do a little overriding at the beginning" (*SL* 38). A *little* overriding? What does that mean? The mystery, to Lewis's credit, remains. Unlike too many theologians, he captures it without trying completely to resolve it.

We cannot dissolve the mystery that surrounds conversion, but we can capture the urgency that is the practical response to its reality. Lewis does that well. We can refuse salvation, and we can refuse it finally without even realizing that we have done so.

> Therefore I sometimes fear...
> I may have stepped one hair's
> Breadth past the hair-breadth bourn
> Which, being once crossed, forever unawares,
> Forbids return. ("Nearly They Stood," *Ps* 103)

Therefore we had better accept the offer of the Gospel and accept it wholeheartedly before we even come close to crossing that "bourn." We should realize that

> the last scene of Dr. Faustus where the man raves and implores on the edge of Hell is, perhaps, stage fire. The last moments before damnation are not often so dramatic. Often the man knows with perfect clarity that some still possible action of his own will could yet save him. But he cannot make this knowledge real to himself. (*THS* 353)

Then there are those like Mark Studdock who cross the line in the other direction without fully realizing (at first) what they are doing. The crisis for Mark comes when in the "objective room" of the N.I.C.E. he is asked to trample on a crucifix. He replies, "It's all bloody nonsense, and I'm damned if I do any such thing" (*THS* 337). Little did he know that he was speaking literal truth and not just being profane. He would indeed have been damned if he had obeyed, and his rebellion is the step that sets him on the road to repentance and faith. Why do some of us do such things while others do not? The only answer we can finally give is the grace of God.

Conversion is the beginning of the Christian life. It is the beginning indeed of a whole new kind of life. From being spiritually dead, we become alive to God. Theologians call this change *regeneration*. Lewis expressed it by using two different Greek words for life: *Bios* and *Zoe* (from which we get the English words biology and zoology). *Bios* represents biological life; *Zoe* stands for the spiritual life that begins with conversion. A person going from the one to the other would undergo a change as radical as that of a statue being "changed from being a carved stone to being a real man" (*MC* 140). The Christian life is not just an ethical way, a new leaf we turn over, but quite literally a *life* which sets us on that new ethical way. Thus, Jesus was incarnated "in order to spread to other men the kind of life He has—by what I call 'good infection.' Every Christian is to become a little Christ. The whole purpose of becoming a Christian is simply nothing else" (*MC* 153).

This new life begun with conversion is lived, and grows stronger, in a process theologians call *sanctification*. In it, one absorbs *Zoe* from practices that keep us in touch with its source, Christ. Lewis explains that there are three things that communicate the life of Christ to us: "baptism, belief, and that mysterious action which different Christians call by different names—Holy Communion, the

THE ATONEMENT AND SALVATION

Mass, the Lord's Supper" (*MC* 62). These are what traditional theologians call "the means of grace." To them some would add prayer and Christian fellowship. Lewis anticipated that different branches of Christendom would disagree on where the emphasis lies among them. Evangelicals would have liked him to say more about faith as being the key to the true spiritual operation of the others, though they usually agree that all three have a role to play. (We will have more to say of such things in the chapter on the Christian life.) Lewis refuses to say more, though later he agrees that the change is not so much something the Christian does as something God does in him through faith. "The sense in which a Christian leaves it to God is that he puts all his trust in Christ" (*MC* 128). However mysterious the process of getting there may be, Jack Lewis and many other believers have discovered that putting one's trust in Christ is nothing less than the difference between death and life.

PREDESTINATION AND FREE WILL

Another way of stating the dilemma of understanding God's enabling versus man's response in calling and conversion is in terms of God's predestination versus human free will. In one sense it is the same problem, but this manifestation of it requires its own discussion. Here when recalling his own experience Lewis is as good at capturing the biblical mystery as he was in his treatment of calling. But when it comes to offering theological explanations, he seems more one-sided.

When describing his own conversion, Lewis can sound like a good Calvinist. "I was the object rather than the subject in this affair. I was decided upon" ("Cross Examination" 261). He elaborates on that experience in his description of Ransom on Perelandra:

> You might say, if you liked, that the power of choice had been simply set aside and an inflexible destiny substituted for it. On the other hand, you might say that he had been delivered from the rhetoric of his passions and had emerged into unassailable freedom. Ransom could not, for the life of him, see any difference between these two statements. Predestination and freedom were apparently identical. He could no longer see any meaning in the many arguments he had heard upon the subject. (*Pa* 149)

In a passage which acknowledges this experience but moves beyond description to an attempt to understand its significance, Lewis explains to a Mrs. Emily McLay on 3 Aug. 1953 that everyone must truly feel about his own conversion that he has done nothing toward it. Christ has done everything, even to the point that we did not choose Him, but He chose us. This is what Lewis calls the Pauline account of conversion, and he does not doubt that it is a true picture of what conversion looks like from within. But then, he adds, "It then seems to us logical and natural to turn this personal experience into a general rule 'All conversion depends on God's choice.' But this I believe is exactly what we must not do" (*L* 3:354-5).

Lewis thinks we should refrain from drawing that conclusion because we are not competent to generalize on such a subject. Why not? As we noted above, the George MacDonald character in *The Great Divorce* thinks that questions about predestination cannot be answered because we are trying to see eternity through the lens of time. In such a case, "All answers deceive" (*GD* 124). In his own voice, Lewis wrote to Stuart Robertson on 6 May 1962 that Scripture represents salvation both as God sees it timelessly and as a process worked out in time. "It is beyond our capacity to envision both together" (*L* 3:1336).

The practical outcome of this inability is expressed in the advice Lewis gave to Mary Van Deusen on 20 Oct. 1952. The problem of how to relate free will and predestination is not solvable: "After all, when we are most free, it is only with a freedom God has given us: and when our will is most influenced by Grace, it is still *our will*. And if what *our will* does is not "voluntary," and if "voluntary" does not mean "free," what are we talking about? I'd leave it alone" (*L* 3:237-8).

But Lewis does not quite "leave it alone"—perhaps because of the results he sees in some Calvinists who do not, which he feels need countering. "Propositions framed with the sole purpose of praising the Divine compassion as boundless, hardly credible, and utterly gratuitous, build up, when extrapolated and systematized, into something that sounds not unlike devil worship" (*OHEL* 33). Presumably this devil is the kind of God Burns satirizes in "Holy Willy's Prayer," who arbitrarily picks "ane for heaven and ten for Hell, / a' for thy glory." But is this really the result of taking the Pauline account of conversion to its logical conclusion, or is it a caricature of those like Calvin who try to do so? Lewis does not say, but the vehemence of his reaction risks perpetrating the caricature, even though he has shown at other moments his ability to see beyond it.

Positively, we can say that the MacDonald character's description of the difficulty is insightful and that Lewis's warnings are well taken. Trying to map time on to eternity is no doubt beyond the capacity of creatures who only know time, and some have indeed systematized the insights of the Reformation further than Scripture warrants. But is it possible to stress the truth of "the Pauline account" as something authoritative and try to follow it consistently without compromising the mystery? In so far as he implies that it is not, Lewis overstates his case here.

THE ATONEMENT AND SALVATION

FAITH AND WORKS

Another important question in understanding the application of the atonement is that of the relationship of faith and works in salvation. This is another area in which Lewis creates unnecessary confusion as a result of his procedure of trying to synthesize the received Christian tradition rather than starting from exegesis of what Scripture teaches. The Tradition has had different ways of understanding the apparent tension between Paul and James on the topic.

What does Scripture teach? It teaches that salvation is a free gift of God's grace, not something that can be earned through our works (Rom. 3:22-28); that indeed works and grace are incompatible (Rom. 4:4, Gal. 5:4); that we are saved by grace through faith, apart from works (Eph. 2:1-9), but that good works, though in no way the ground or cause of that salvation, are the necessary fruits of it (Eph. 2:10). This would be plain sailing were it not for the argument of James that we are in some sense justified by works (James 2:14-26). If a person says he has faith but has no works, James asks, can *that* faith save him? No, James replies, which in itself is not problematic; but then he argues that, from this standpoint, Abraham was *justified by works*. His conclusion: "Faith without works is dead."

Is there a conflict or even an abiding tension between Paul and James? Evangelical faith has concluded that there is not. Paul also argues for the necessity of works, and would agree that a faith producing no works is not true faith. Paul is more careful than James to distinguish faith as the *means* of receiving grace, and works as the *fruit* of that reception, because he needed to refute the attempts of the Judaizers to impose the Jewish ceremonial law on his Gentile converts; but there is no essential difference between him and James at that point. The difficulty comes from James's statement that Abraham was *justified by works*, where James uses a key technical term very differently from the way Paul would have used it. The best way of understanding that crux is to realize that the word justify can mean three things depending on context and how it is used: to make righteous, to declare righteous, or to show one's righteousness. Paul normally uses it in the second of those senses ("declare"), while James uses it in the third ("show"). An examination of the contexts of their uses will bear this distinction out. For James, Abraham's works show he was righteous, presumably made so, as Paul would have said, by faith (cf. James 2:18, 2:21). Thus the apparent disagreement between them is only verbal, not substantive. Both see salvation as God's work and our good works as its fruit; they simply use language differently in expressing this common truth.

Lewis sometimes expresses this unified biblical view admirably, and sometimes reflects the confusion of the larger tradition as it struggles to reconcile Paul and James. He admirably captures the common ground between them when he says, "If what you call your 'faith' in Christ does not involve taking the slightest notice of what He says, then it is not Faith at all—not faith or trust in Him, but only intellectual acceptance of some theory about Him" (*MC* 130). He is wonderfully Pauline when he says that the Christian "does not think God will love us because we are good, but that God will make us good because He loves us" (*MC* 64). The forgiven Murderer in *The Great Divorce* has an accurate grasp of what grace means. Replying to his friend's demand that his "rights" be granted, he exclaims, "Oh no. It's not so bad as that. I haven't got my rights or I shouldn't be here. You will not get yours either. You'll get something far better" (*GD* 33-4). And Ransom on Perelandra experiences the freedom that liberation from the necessity of earning salvation brings: "Be comforted, small one, in your smallness. He lays no merit on you. Receive and be glad" (*Pa* 197).

A central passage in *Mere Christianity* begins in what might seem like confusion but rights itself in the end. What finally saves us, good works or faith in Christ? To Lewis it is like asking which of the two blades in a pair of scissors is the one that actually does the cutting. "A serious moral effort is the only thing that will get you to the point where you throw up the sponge. Faith in Christ is the only thing that will save you from despair at that point: and out of that faith in Him good actions must inevitably come" (*MC* 128).

Lewis begins by implying that the answer is more complicated and difficult than it actually is. His usual skill at apt analogy misfires a bit. Faith and works might both be as essential as the two blades of a pair of scissors, but they do not function in the same way. Both blades cut, but only one of the pair of faith and works actually saves. But then the dynamic interplay of the two is worked out well at the end. Works ("serious moral effort") have the effect only of getting us to the point to where we despair in the ability of works to merit salvation so that we turn to faith. And out of that faith, real good works come as its inevitable fruit. Lewis basically gets it right here, but he makes it seem like less clear sailing than it really is.

More troubling in terms of Lewis's understanding of grace, faith, and works is his tendency to portray salvation as the outcome of a series of cumulative moral choices that we make in ourselves: those choices are turning the central you slowly into something else that it was not before: "All your life long you are slowly turning this central thing into a heavenly creature or into a hellish creature.... Each of us, at each moment, is progressing to the one state or the other" (*MC* 87).

We are turning this central thing (the heart, in biblical terms) into something heavenly or hellish by the accumulating effects of *our* choices? Salvation or damnation here seems to be the inevitable product of what *we* have *made of ourselves* by those choices. This might be a perfectly accurate description of the process of damnation, but as a picture of salvation it falls far short of any biblical account. *God*'s work, Christ's work, grace and its effects, are all disastrously absent. While other passages thankfully forbid us from thinking that Lewis held any such thing, this passage taken alone would be completely compatible with the moral therapeutic Deism that blights contemporary Christendom or with older forms of the theology of works. A more biblically grounded Lewis would have avoided the possibility of giving such impressions.

Lewis then can help us appreciate the dynamic relations between grace, faith, and works if we are already grounded in the Biblical teaching about them; otherwise, he may perpetuate some of the confusions on that topic that exist in the larger tradition of the church.

PERSEVERANCE

Alright, then: we are saved by grace, the undeserved work of Christ on our behalf in the atonement, which we receive by faith, and which has good works as its fruit. God's saving work includes the enabling of the very response of faith itself, which is nonetheless somehow mysteriously a real response on our part. The next question in the theology of salvation is whether God's saving work includes a confirmation of and preservation of that faith such that all those who truly believe in Christ will persevere in faith for final salvation, or whether it is possible for a truly saved person to fall away from grace, turn his back on the faith, and be finally lost. The first of those understandings is known as the doctrine of the Perseverance of the Saints (or, less accurately, as the doctrine of Eternal Security). Even faithful and conservative Evangelical Protestants are divided over whether they affirm that doctrine or not. What was Lewis's perspective?

Believers have been divided over this doctrine because Scripture itself seems to say both things. That is, it speaks of salvation as if it were something that could not be lost, but also warns us against losing it as if it could be. Christ's work is spoken of as *saving* people, as accomplishing their salvation, not as merely offering them a probationary trial period. And John says that those who seem to have been believers but who subsequently "go out" from the church show by that going out that they were "never really of us" (1 Jn. 2:19). John clearly supports Perseverance here because if falling from grace were possible, the going out would only show that the apostates had gone out; no further conclusion could be drawn from it. On the other hand we have warnings such as those in Galatians 5:4 and Hebrews 6:4-6, which are not easy to reconcile with the other passages. I think I can reconcile them in a way that affirms Perseverance rightly understood—but doing so would take us too far afield from our topic, which is what Lewis thought on the question.

My purpose here then is not to solve this theological crux but to point out that, whatever Lewis's views might have been on the matter, the Narnia books preserve exactly the same tension and ambiguity on the question that Scripture has. Just as in the New Testament, we have in Narnia a theological principle that seems to say one thing and an individual whose experience seems to say the other. It is early laid down that "once a king or queen in Narnia, always a king or queen" (*LWW* 199). That statement is consistent with Perseverance. But at the end of the story, we have a case that seems to call that understanding into question: "My sister Susan," answered Peter shortly and gravely, "is no longer a friend of Narnia" (*TLB* 169).

Lewis does nothing to resolve the apparent contradiction between these two passages other than to hold out hope that Susan may yet repent of her obsession with being too grown up. Ford thinks it is a mistake to think that Susan died in the railway accident in *The Last Battle* and is "forever fallen from grace." He thinks Lewis allows the other Friends of Narnia to imply an uncharacteristic "harsh and final judgment" about Susan's fate (402). He is certainly right that her fate is still open, for Lewis holds out hope in a letter that the Narnia series is silent about Susan's *final* fate: "She is left alive in this world at the end, having by then turned into a rather silly, conceited young woman. But there's plenty of time for her to mend and perhaps she will get to Aslan's country in the end" (*L* 3:826; cf. 3:1135). "Perhaps." Surely Ford is right about the open-endedness of Susan's fate, but wrong about its implications. This passage is simply inconsistent with the thesis of Lewis being "uncharacteristically judgmental." It is however, consistent with seeing Susan as an example of his respect for the mystery of perseverance as the Bible presents it.

As to whether Susan ever repents and returns to faith in Aslan, then, we have hope but no sure intelligence. But we can note that the Narniad contains a tension on the question that exactly mirrors that of Scripture on the larger one of the perseverance of the saints. This is a form of faithfulness that, whichever side we take on the theological issue, we can only admire.

THE EXTENT OF THE ATONEMENT

One critical question about the atonement remains: To whom does it apply? Three basic answers have historically been given. *Exclusivism*, which is the traditional Evangelical position, holds that the atonement applies efficaciously (i.e., achieves its goal, salvation) only to those who come to put explicit faith in Christ as Lord and Savior. Biblical statements of the Gospel are often put in these terms. Paul's answer to the Philippian Jailer's question, "What must I do to be saved?" is "Believe on the Lord Jesus" (Acts 16:31). His most definitive statement is, "that if you confess with your mouth Jesus as Lord and believe in your heart that God has raised him from the dead you shall be saved" (Rom. 10:9). Exclusivism simply takes such statements at face value. At the opposite extreme would be *Universalism*, which holds that all people will eventually be saved. Universalists appeal to passages which seem to apply salvation to the human race or to "all men," such as Romans 5:18. In between is a position known as *Inclusivism*, which holds that not all men are saved, that those who are saved are saved by the death of Christ, but that it is possible for some who have never heard the name of Jesus to be saved by that death through "implicit faith" by following the light that they had.

I have heard people carelessly classify Lewis as a universalist, but it is clear that he believed that there is a Hell and that there will be people in it. Rather, he was an inclusivist, or at least speculated that inclusivism might be possible. He wrote to a Mrs. Johnson on 8 Nov. 1952, "I think that every prayer which is sincerely made even to a false god or to a v. imperfectly conceived true God, is accepted by the true God and that Christ saves many who do not think they know Him" (*L* 3:245). He explained in *Mere Christianity*, "There are people in other religions who are being led by God's secret influence to concentrate on those parts of their religion which are in agreement with Christianity, and who thus belong to Christ without knowing it" (*MC* 176). Normally people are saved by hearing the Gospel and responding to it, but Lewis holds out the theoretical possibility at least of some pagans being saved by following God's "secret influence" without ever having heard the Gospel or even explicitly knowing the name of Jesus.

This possibility is incarnated in the Calormene character Emeth in *The Last Battle*, who thinks of himself as a loyal worshiper of Tash but who has been, unbeknownst even to himself, really following Aslan all along. He arrives in Aslan's country after his death to hear, to his own surprise, this speech from the Lion:

> Son, thou art welcome.... Not because [Tash] and I are one but because we are opposites, I take to me the services thou hast done to him. For I and he are of such different kinds that no service which is vile can be done to me, and none which is not vile can be done to him. Therefore, if any man swear by Tash and keep his oath for the oath's sake, it is by me he has truly sworn, though he know it not.... And if any man do a cruelty in my name, then, though he say the name of Aslan, it is Tash whom he serves and by Tash his deed is accepted.... Unless thy desire had been for me thou wouldst not have sought so long and so truly. For all find what they truly seek. (*TLB* 205-6)

Traditional Evangelicals are disturbed by Lewis's line of reasoning because they think it unbiblical and fear that, if accepted, it might blunt the urgency of the task of world evangelization if we think that people can be saved without hearing the Gospel. An increasing number of younger Evangelicals find it attractive because they think it makes God seem more loving if the masses of the unreached are not automatically excluded from salvation. In evaluating Lewis's perspective here we must try to see it in the light of Scripture.

The New Testament Apostles make a very specific and explicit promise of salvation on the basis of repentance and faith in Christ as Lord and Savior, as we saw above. Christ Himself authorizes His followers to make that offer to all men on His behalf in what is called the Great Commission (Mat. 28:18-20). There is no other promise made and no other offer recorded, and we do not have the authority to make any such promise or offer. So if you ask me, "What must I do to be saved," I must respond, "Believe on the Lord Jesus Christ." And if you ask me what the pagan overseas must do, I have only the same answer. Then comes the hard question: "What about the person who has never heard the Gospel?" There is only one answer I have been authorized to give. He too must believe on the Lord Jesus Christ. I have no authority to *promise* him salvation on any other basis. There is no Scriptural *assurance* of any such salvation.

Scripture never explicitly answers the hard question with hope for the unreached. Some have tried to find such an answer in the early chapters of Romans when Paul talks about natural revelation (Rom. 1:20), but this will not do because it is part of an argument the conclusion of which is, not that some might follow that revelation, but that it renders all without excuse (Rom. 1:21-2:1). The closest the Apostle comes to dealing with those who have never heard is in Romans 10, where his conclusion offers no definitive hope of any salvation apart from the Gospel. "For the Scripture says, 'Whoever *believes* in Him will not be disappointed'" (emphasis added). This applies to both Jew and Gentile: "Whoever will call upon the name of the Lord will be saved" (quoting Joel 2:32). Then we get the only answer to the hard question that Scripture gives: "How then shall they call upon Him in whom they have not believed? And how shall they believe in Him of whom they have not heard? And how shall they hear without a preacher?" (Rom. 10:11-14). In effect, the only answer Scripture gives to the question of those who have not heard is, "We'd better go and tell them."

Does this mean that we must dogmatically maintain that God could not find a way to save such people through extraordinary means? Not quite, I think. If there are Emeths in heaven I will be very happy (and not terribly surprised), and I will not here and now categorically deny the possibility. But I have no *promise* or *assurance* that there will be Emeths there, and *I am not authorized to extend any such promise*, even by implication. As a theologian, that is, as a teacher of

Christian doctrine, I must be careful not to exceed my authority by holding out such a promise which Scripture does not make. I'm afraid Lewis does do so. As a fictional guess or "supposal," Emeth might not be too problematic. But Emeth incarnates explicit teaching in other expository passages speculating about "secret influence" which make him more than that. This is then another one of those places where, by simply thinking about general Christian ideas rather than attending to the actual teaching of Scripture, Lewis goes beyond what Scripture teaches. Here I think we may legitimately *hope* that Lewis may be right, but we must not *conclude* that he is right. He goes beyond what Scripture authorizes us to say about the fate of the unreached.

CONCLUSION

Lewis has many good things to say about the atonement and salvation. At his best he deftly depicts the dynamics of how calling, faith, and works interact, and he often admirably captures the mystery of divine initiative and human response, divine predestination and human freedom, just as Scripture presents it. He wisely warns us not to substitute our theories about the atonement for the atonement itself. But he fails to give adequate weight to those explanations of the atonement actually taught by Scripture, and he is sometimes less clear than he might have been about the relation of faith and works. He often portrays the atonement more biblically in his fiction than he explains it in his expositions. But in the case of Emeth, he goes beyond what Scripture authorizes us to say about the fate of the unreached. Christians already grounded in Biblical teaching on these matters will find much in Lewis from which they can benefit. Those not so well grounded may at certain points be in danger of being led astray.

Let us then ponder those explanations with discernment so that we may find ourselves at rest before a cracked Stone Table, enchanted to the depths of our souls by the deeper magic from before the dawn of time.

CHAPTER 8

Ecclesiology
The Doctrine of the Church

> *Enemy occupied territory—that is what this world is. Christianity is the story of how the rightful king has landed, you might say landed in disguise, and is calling us all to take part in a great campaign of sabotage. When you go to church you are really listening in to the secret wireless from our friends; that is why the enemy is so anxious to prevent us from going. (MC 51)*

In our discussion of the atonement above we spoke of it mainly as it applies to individuals. But while that was a necessary perspective, it is an incomplete one, for Christ did not come simply to save a random collection of individuals but to save, and by saving to create, a *people*. Peter calls believers "a chosen race, a royal priesthood, a holy nation, a people for God's own possession.... For you were once not a people, but now you are the people of God. You had not received mercy, but now you have received mercy" (1 Pet. 2:9-10). Therefore, inextricably tied to soteriology, the doctrine of salvation, is ecclesiology, the doctrine of the church. What is the nature of this people, how is it organized, and what is its purpose as it awaits the return of its Lord?

Ecclesiology is a surprisingly contentious area of theology because many of the disputes that have divided churches from each other find their home here. Members of a given communion can agree to disagree about, say, Calvinism versus Arminianism more easily than they can agree to disagree about whether church government should be congregational, presbyterian, or episcopal, because the church has to be organized one way or another. You might be able to argue all day long about whether salvation history is organized dispensationally or covenantally without its having much effect on your actual practice of the faith, but children of believers must either be baptized as infants or not. You might care more about other issues, but ecclesiology has a way of forcing your hand.

The divisions that have resulted have been a stumbling block to faith for many. Lewis wrote to Phyllis Elinor Sandeman on 31 Dec. 1953, "I really believe I wd. have come to Christianity much less reluctantly if it had not involved the Church" (L 3:399). His stance of limiting himself to mere Christianity kept him from dealing with many of these more controversial aspects of ecclesiology in his public writings. The closest we come to getting Lewis's views on church government, for example, may be a letter he wrote to his brother Warnie on 25 Dec. 1931: "We should be glad that the early Christians expected the second coming and the end of the world quite soon; for if they had known they were founding an organization for centuries they would certainly have organised it to death" (L 2:30).

Sticking to mere Christianity was a conscious decision to focus on what unites Christians rather than what divides them. It was a good and beneficial decision, but it means that Lewis will not be able to help us much when it comes to choosing between two of the Rooms off the Hall. He does not claim to do so, and indeed refuses that role. Nevertheless, he has much to say about the true basis for Christian unity and what it means for the church to be a community of faith. In private letters he responded to friends who kept pestering him to join them in the Church of Rome by explaining why he could not do so, and these explanations provide some insight into issues on which he remained publicly silent.

THE NATURE OF THE CHURCH

What exactly is the church? Lewis nowhere gives a definition; indeed it is not easy to define the mystical Body of Christ which somehow encompasses the saints who have gone before us, the charwoman in gum boots in the next pew, and the motley crew of squabbling organizations that constitute the congregations and denominations of current Christendom. Since Lewis said that his beliefs were written in the common Prayer Book, we can turn to the Thirty-Nine Articles of the Church of England as a place to start: "The visible Church of Christe, is a congregation of faythfull men in the which the pure worde of God is preached, and the Sacramentes be duely ministered, according to Christes ordinaunce in all those thynges that of necessite are requisite to the same" (Schaaf 499). Or we could say it is the company of believers in Christ, united to Him by faith throughout time and eternity, and gathered into organized local congregations in the present for worship, teaching, evangelism, and service. All such definitions are idealistic. In reality one can never see all true believers gathered, and those who are gathered usually include some tares among the wheat. That is why it is customary to distinguish the invisible church, seen only by God, from the visible church, the imperfect instantiation of the invisible church that we join and see around us.

That Lewis understood these things is shown by the fact that he has Screwtape distinguish the church as human beings encounter it, which is often as much an ally of Our Father Below as it is an instrument of God, from "the Church as we see her spread out through all time and space and rooted in eternity, terrible as an army with banners" (SL 12). We must simply deal with the fact that in the here and now God works through weak and imperfect human vessels who are the only members the church in this life will have. The individual members are weak and imperfect, and so are the congregations and denominations made up of them. Perhaps Lewis's clearest picture of the role the church is supposed to have in the world and in the lives of believers is in a description, not of the church, but of the world:

> Enemy occupied territory—that is what this world is. Christianity is the story of how the rightful king has landed, you might say landed in disguise, and is calling us all to take part in a great campaign of sabotage. When you go to church you are really listening in to the secret wireless from our friends; that is why the enemy is so anxious to prevent us from going. (MC 51)

The church then does not exist because Christ thought it would be nice if individual believers in Him had a kind of optional club as a support group if they wanted it. It is an organism before it is an organization, the family of God's children joined to each other whether they like it or not and organized into an army for the conquest of Satan's kingdom. If this is so, it makes understanding and participating in the church in order to fulfill its purpose a matter of extreme importance.

THE BASIS AND PRACTICE OF CHRISTIAN UNITY

This army has sadly been divided by history into a congeries of factions and denominations, sometimes cooperating but often competing. Dealing with that scandalous but intractable situation is one of the first practical problems that confront us in trying to find our right relationship to the church. Lewis, as we shall see, did not believe that any one of them could claim to be the One True Church in exclusion of all the others. The true church is not Roman Catholic or Episcopal or Presbyterian or Methodist or Baptist. It is not coterminous with any one of them, but is something larger that they all participate in with greater or lesser degrees of faithfulness. One must be faithful to a particular incarnation of the church, but one often finds true fellowship across denominational lines that can sometimes transcend what one finds within one's own flock, which will probably be a confusing mixture of faithfulness and unfaithfulness to Christ and to the Faith. How do we discern that larger reality and rightly relate ourselves both to it and to our own particular congregation and tradition? Lewis had some very helpful things to say in answer to that question.

"High church" versus "low church" refers to an ongoing discussion within Anglicanism between those who put more emphasis on the liturgy and those who put more emphasis on preaching. Lewis thought that was not where the real issue lies. He wrote Sister Penelope, CSMV, on 8 Nov. 1939 that to him the real division was not between the "high" and the "low" church so much as that "between religion with a real supernaturalism and salvationism on the one hand, and watered-down and modernist versions on the other" (*L* 2:285). Real Christianity is a religion about a real supernatural God who has wrought a real salvation for us, so the true church must be one that believes in that God and has embraced that salvation. Theological liberalism, having forsaken real Christianity and the real Christ, has forsaken with it Christ's church, though it continues to meet in steeple-crowned buildings and mouth the old formulae. Lewis could not understand "how a man can appear in print claiming to disbelieve everything he presupposes when he puts on the surplice. I feel it is a form of prostitution" ("Cross Examination" 260). The false church may exist within and alongside the true. The true church exists wherever commitment to the incarnate Christ and the God who is His Father is shared, within and across denominational lines. Lewis was not the first to experience this reality, and he will not be the last; but he articulated it with special clarity. Each denomination is closest to the others at its spiritual center where their truest and most faithful members live, though this closeness might be seen more in spirit than in doctrine. "And this suggests at the centre of each there is something, or a Someone, who against all divergences of belief, all differences of temperament, all memories of mutual persecution, speaks with the same voice" (*MC* 9).

This experience of real Christian communion transcending denominational differences is part of the explanation for Lewis's commitment to mere Christianity. He wrote to the editor of *The Church Times* on 8 Feb. 1952 of his concern that supernaturalists in the church of England lacked a common identity, unlike the low and high church parties. They were the real Christians, and they needed a name. "May I suggest 'Deep Church'; or, if that fails in humility, Baxter's 'mere Christians'?" (*L* 3:164). Surely Lewis's work has been a major force in helping them to find each other, in the Anglican Communion and elsewhere.

The "deep church" is not quite the same thing as the invisible church. It is a subset of the visible church that helps us perhaps to locate the places where the invisible church touches the visible. Thus it is not a substitute for the visible church. Many Christians, frustrated with the inconsistencies of the visible church, see something like the deep church as an excuse to avoid serious commitment to a concrete communion and a particular local congregation. Lewis will have none of that. In his most well-known exposition of the idea, he insists that Mere Christianity is not a substitute for a particular church but is "like a hall out of which doors open into several rooms" (MC 12). It is only in the rooms that there are fires and food and real habitation. It is good to know of the hall, but we have to choose a definite door to one of the rooms. Lewis will not tell us which one to choose, but he does offer this advice: "Above all you should be asking which door is the true one; not which pleases you best by its paint and paneling" (MC 12).

The hall, the deep church common to all mere Christians, is all about the truth common to each of the rooms; so the rooms are about truth too. We should pick the one that best embodies and teaches and serves that common truth as God has given us the light to see it. That is the positive criterion. Though he does not discuss it in *Mere Christianity*, Lewis also had a negative criterion: obsession with legalistic matters not part of that common core of truth is a big red flag. He wrote to a Mrs. Johnson on 16 March 1955 that he strongly objected to "the tyrranic and unscriptural insolence of anything that calls itself a Church and makes tee-totalism a condition of membership" (L 3:580). Positively, commitment to Nicene orthodoxy and supernatural salvation is a requirement; negatively, petty legalism that goes beyond what Scripture itself requires of all Christians is a deal breaker.

This then is the proper basis for Christian unity according to Lewis: a common commitment to a common faith that is unashamedly both supernatural and salvific. This commitment is not a substitute for loyalty to a particular tradition and a particular congregation, but it is rather the context which gives that loyalty its meaning and fosters right relationships with true believers who differ with us on those matters less central to the Faith once delivered to the saints.

There are some practical applications of seeing the church this way. It keeps our focus on the great truths that we have in common and makes us sensitive to the ways in which an opposite focus has so often hindered the cause of Christ. So Lewis wisely lays it down that we should never discuss the issues that divide us "except in the presence of those who have already come to believe that there is one God and that Jesus Christ is His only Son" (MC 6). And because the common supernatural and salvific core matters so much more than the things over which we differ, we should practice great humility and courtesy with our fellow believers, especially those with whom we disagree on those lesser matters. Paraphrasing Paul's exhortations to the early Christians about meat offered to idols (1 Cor. 8), Screwtape imagines the horror to the demonic kingdom of a church that actually acted this way:

You would expect to find the "low" churchman genuflecting and crossing himself lest the weak conscience of his "high" brother be moved to irreverence, and the "high" one refraining from these exercises lest he should betray his "low" brother into idolatry. And so it would have been but for our ceaseless labor. (*SL* 75).

One of the fruits of our study of Lewis's theology and his fine treatment of this point should be that the labors of Screwtape and his colleagues be increasingly frustrated.

CHURCH AS COMMUNITY

What Lewis says about the basis and practice of Christian unity leads logically to the consideration of the church as a community of faith. The word *community* is a blend of the words *common* and *unity*: a unity based on something that is held in common. The greater the importance given to that common factor, the deeper the bond will be. And for the church, the common factor is nothing less than Christ Himself. At the heart of each communion "there is something, or a Someone, who against all divergences of belief, all differences of temperament, all memories of mutual persecution, speaks with the same voice" (*MC* 9).

What kind of community does this common unity with Christ create? The central biblical metaphor that describes it is that of the Body of Christ. Believers are to relate to each other in the church as members of a common body or organism of which Christ is the head (Rom. 12:4-8, 1 Cor. 12:12-27, Eph. 4:4-16, etc.). So Lewis says that in our Christian life "we are not homogenous units but different and complementary organs of a mystical body" ("Priestesses" 238). Here he does not respond to, but anticipates, the "homogenous unit principle" of the Church Growth Movement, which argued that churches containing individuals of similar backgrounds would be able to grow most efficiently. Before the phrase ever became the popular buzz word it became in the 1970's, Lewis had raised the very pertinent question of what might be sacrificed in such growth. There was a very real danger of compromising the very nature of what it was that was supposed to be growing.

Lewis elaborates on the meaning of the body metaphor in the essay "Membership." "The Christian is not called to individualism but to membership in the mystical body.... By *members* [St. Paul] meant what we should call *organs*, things essentially different from, and complementary to, one another" ("Membership" 163-4). He continues to explain what this means. The difference between membership in a body and being part of a collective is shown by the structure of the family. "The grandfather, the parents, the grown-up son, the child, the dog, and the cat are true members (in the organic sense), precisely because they are not members or units of a homogeneous class. They are not interchangeable" ("Membership" 164).

Here Lewis uses his gift for apt analogy to put Paul's essential points in the biblical passages cited above into effective modern language. There is one body, but many differing gifts and offices, all contributing under the one Head to a common purpose, the building up of the body in love so that it can effectively glorify God and proclaim His Gospel. "Not interchangeable" is a particularly accurate summary. Lewis's explanation of these ideas makes them not only easy to understand but eminently practical as well. He wrote Mary Van Deusen on 7 Dec. 1950 that the church is not a voluntary society of people brought together by their common interests or natural affinities, but rather it is "the Body of Christ in which all members, however different (and He rejoices in their differences & by no means wishes to iron them out) must share the common life, complementing and helping and receiving one another precisely by their differences" (*L* 3:68). How do we share our common life in Christ? By complementing, helping, and receiving one another. The end result should be people saying, "Behold, how they love one another!"

The other essay we should think of in connection with the church as a community is "The Inner Ring." Here, unlike in "Membership," Lewis does not talk about the church directly, but rather about group dynamics in general; but what he says about those group dynamics certainly applies to the church. In any group there tends to develop an "inner ring" with the real power and influence, which may or may not correspond to the official leadership. Sometimes there are rings within rings. The desire to be accepted by that group is the source of much human folly and even wickedness. "Of all passions the passion for the Inner Ring is most skillful in making a man who is not yet a very bad man do very bad things" ("The Inner Ring" 154). This certainly applies to churches, which are often the middling Ponds in which very small people can aspire to be Big Fish. This dynamic helps to explain why people so often feel they have been treated so very badly in a group which is supposed to be the Body of Christ building itself up in love. Sometimes they are the victims of the Inner Ring, and sometimes they resent their failure to penetrate it. This is what will naturally happen in an organization with such a high purpose if it does not humble itself and live a life of continual penitence in the power of the Holy Spirit. Lewis's essay can help us understand the terribly practical importance of doing so.

THE CHURCH IN WORSHIP

One of the more obvious and prominent functions of the church is worship; it could indeed be defined as the worshipping community. Lewis never stops to define worship, and he studiously avoided getting roped into controversies about styles of worship ("high" versus "low"). One can only imagine what he would have thought of our own contemporary "worship wars." But he served on a Lambeth commission to revise the Prayer Book, so he did have some occasion to think about worship, and some of those thoughts do emerge in his writings.

He makes an interesting comment while analyzing the different kinds of love in *The Four Loves*. There are some things we love only when we need them, like cold water when we are thirsty. There are people or causes that inspire us with the desire to do good to them. And then there are things whose goodness or beauty inspires contemplation and admiration just because of their inherent worthiness. We relate to God in all these ways: "Need love cries to God from our poverty; Gift-love longs to serve, or even to suffer for, God; Appreciative Love says: 'We give thanks to thee for thy great glory'" (*FL* 33). Worship involves all these modes and can thus be seen as an expression of our multifold love for God. Corporate worship in the church then is designed to foster, inform, nurture, and provide an avenue for such expression.

How might it best achieve such goals? Lewis gives no general treatment of that question, but we know that he appreciated the Anglican liturgy and basically wanted it left alone. He was suspicious of the urge constantly to tinker with it, wishing that the leaders of the Church of England would "remember that the charge to Peter was Feed my sheep; not Try experiments on my rats, or even, Teach my performing dogs new tricks" (*LtM* 5). This feeling did not flow from a knee-jerk conservatism, but from an understanding of what forms of worship are for: they structure, inform, and encourage an encounter with God by focusing our attention in terms of received truth. In order to do so, they need not to call undue attention to themselves. But too much innovation forces them to do just that. Novelty "fixes our attention on the service itself; and thinking about worship is a different thing from worshipping" (*LtM* 4-5). Worship in other words is not a performance; if it has an audience, it is not the congregation but God. Whatever kind of form or structure we use, whether we agree with him that a strongly formal liturgy is helpful or not, we would do well to remember Lewis's theocentric orientation in our own worship traditions.

On questions such as the time and mode of Baptism, Lewis has nothing to say. Should the infants of believing parents receive baptism (paedobaptism), or should it be deferred until they have come to self-conscious, personal faith (believers' baptism or credobaptism)? Should the water be administered by immersion (dunking), effusion (pouring), or spargation (sprinkling)? Likewise, he will not help us define precisely the way in which Christ is present in the bread and wine of The Lord's Supper. However important these questions may be, they are not part of "mere" Christianity, and so we must look for guidance on them elsewhere. Lewis does tell us that the sacraments are one of the important ways in which "the Christ life" is communicated to us (*MC* 62). Evangelicals will agree with this, though they might wish Lewis had added that this only happens when they are received in faith. Nevertheless, Lewis does imply that the sacraments best communicate Christ to us when received in childlike faith rather than pursued as points of controversy implying that we can somehow eliminate the mystery that surrounds them. "The command, after all, was Take, eat: not Take, understand" (*LtM* 104).

IS THERE ONE TRUE CHURCH?

A question that inevitably comes up in ecclesiology is whether there is one true church. On one level the answer is, "Of course!" But the question then boils down to whether any existing communion of Christians can legitimately claim to be that church to the exclusion of all the others, as opposed to its being a spiritual organism that exists within and across the competing organizational structures (denominations) we have created for it. For most of us in the West, then, it takes the form of what we make of the claims of the Church of Rome.

The fact that Lewis avoided dealing publicly with the question in that form actually implies his answer. In terms of his famous analogy from *Mere Christianity*, he wanted to strengthen all the Rooms by strengthening the Hall. This implies that no one Room can claim simply to be the Hall, or the One True Room. And that would apply most pointedly to the one Room that actually advances that claim: The Roman Catholic Church.

Lewis's friend J. R. R. Tolkien was one of the key influences leading to his conversion. Tolkien was a devout Roman Catholic. So naturally Tolkien wondered why Lewis did not come, from his perspective, "all the way" to the Church of Rome. Many other Roman Catholics have wondered the same thing, and some have argued that Lewis should have, or would have, if he had lived long enough. Not wishing to set one denomination against the other but rather to serve the "Deep Church," Lewis consistently refused to address the claims of Rome directly in his public writings. But in his private correspondence he allowed himself to answer the questions of those wondering why he would not cross the Tiber to Rome. Those answers show Lewis to have been a more principled Protestant than some have realized.

Roman Catholics believe that their church is the one founded by Jesus, with Peter and his successors as its earthly heads. Those successors (the Popes) are infallible when speaking *ex cathedra* (i.e., from the papal throne). The authority of the Church and its Tradition is equal to that of Scripture, and in some ways (in effect) above it. Because the Church gave the Scriptures to the world, the Church is the only infallible interpreter of Scripture. All other differences between Protestant and Catholic theology flow from their differing conceptions of the Church's authority in relation to that of Scripture. Is Scripture the only final and infallible authority, or does the Church have independent revelation from God that was not written down and without which readers lack the full context for understanding what *was* written? The New Testament reads very differently from one set of those assumptions than it does from the other. So the first thing that has to be determined is the credibility of the Roman claim to be the only infallible interpreter of Scripture.

Lewis responded to this claim with his characteristically skillful use of analogy. He wrote to H. Lyman Stebbins on 8 May 1945,

> If there were an ancient Platonic Society still existing at Athens and claiming to be the exclusive trustees of Plato's meaning, I shd. approach them with great respect. But if I found their teaching in many ways curiously unlike his actual text and unlike what ancient interpreters said, and in some cases cd. not be traced back to within 1,000 years of his time, I shd. reject those exclusive claims. (*L* 2:646)

The analogy explains admirably the Protestant response to the claims of Rome and their basis. You cannot start with the assumption that the Roman interpretation is correct; this has first to be established textually and independently of the claim itself. And the text will not support it apart from the assumptions the Roman Catholic reader brings to it. Lewis wrote to his Catholic student Dom Bede Griffiths on 26 Dec. 1934 that if they were going to discuss the matters that divided their churches, "it is obvious that you must argue *to* the truth of your own position, not *from* it" (*L* 2:150). If one does not actually find certain Romanist positions plausible as interpretations of the text of Scripture, one has no reason to simply suspend one's intellect and accept that they are on blind faith.

One need not read the Scripture by itself in order to give it a singular place of authority; one can read it, as Lewis did, in the light of the earliest Church Fathers and the consensual tradition that is common to all historic Christians. As he says quite explicitly, "The one really adequate instrument for learning about God is the whole Christian community waiting for Him together" (*MC* 144). *Sola Scriptura,* "Scripture Alone," the formal principle of the Reformation, does not mean that one reads Scripture by oneself, or that one only reads Scripture; it means that Scripture is "alone" at the top of the hierarchy of authority; its pronouncements alone are infallible and final. Lewis's statement should give the lie to the propaganda that claims the Protestant principle means anything else. Lewis's letter to Stebbins continues to describe the results of reading the Bible as the final authority: He rejects Rome where he thinks it differs from universal tradition and apostolic Christianity. These points would include the Roman view of Mary, which he considers "utterly foreign to the New Testament," papalism, and the doctrine of Transubstantiation, which "insists on defining" in a way not reflected by the New Testament. "In a word, the whole set-up of modern Romanism seems to me to be as much a provincial or local variation from the central ancient tradition as any particular Protestant sect" (L 2:646-7).

Lewis, like other Protestants, found circular the Catholic argument that Scripture cannot be a higher authority than the Church because the Church gave us the Scriptures. He wrote to Mary Van Deusen on 28 Dec. 1961:

> Beware of the argument "the Church gave us the Bible (and therefore the Bible can never give us grounds for criticizing the Church)." It is perfectly possible to accept B on the authority of A and yet regard B as a higher authority than A. It happens when I recommend a book to a pupil. I first send him to the book, but having gone to it, he knows (for I have told him) that the author knows more about the subject than I. (L 3:1309)

Therefore, it is the duty of the church, when pointing people to the Bible, to tell them that its Author knows more about the truth than the church does. Both the church and the individual are dependent on God's self-revelation in the written Word for their knowledge of Christian truth and their personal knowledge of the Father and His Son. The church has more resources and a greater depth of collective experience than the individual, but both must remain correctable by the Scriptures for the church to be and remain the best context in which the individual can read the Scriptures. Lewis clearly understood that only Protestant churches could take such a stance toward both the Bible and its readers with full consistency.

Lewis's own practice of the faith was serious but probably would not have satisfied either Anglo-Catholics or extreme Protestants. On the one hand he went to confession, which would seem to some a very un-Protestant thing to do. On the other hand, not every "high" church practice recommended itself to him. He was more cautious than some might have expected when it came to honoring the Virgin Mary, for example. He wrote to Mary Van Deusen on 26 June 1952:

Hail Marys raise a *doctrinal* question: whether it is lawful to address devotions to any *creature*, however holy. My own view would be that a *salute* to any saint (or angel) cannot in itself be wrong any more than taking off one's hat to a friend: but that there is always some danger lest such practices start one on the road to a state (sometimes found in R. C.'s) where the B. V. M. is treated really as a deity and even becomes the centre of the religion. I therefore think such salutes are best avoided. And if the Blessed Virgin is as good as the best mothers I have known, she does not *want* any of the attention which might have gone to her Son diverted to herself. (*L* 3:209).

Lewis here goes farther in being sure to avoid Mariolatry than I was expecting. Most Protestants will think his caution justified. They will also do well to emulate him as well in giving the greatest respect allowable to this impressive woman who stands as an example of faith and obedience to us all.

Lewis was not *anti*-Catholic. He accepted the Church of Rome as one of the Rooms of the House, which some more radical Protestants would not do. But he rejected its claims to have a unique authority as Christ's one true Church. Even when he agreed with Rome on substance, he was careful to maintain a consistent approach to the issue of authority. Lewis is notorious among Protestants for holding the opinion that Purgatory probably exists. But he did not agree with making it a dogma. He wrote to a Mr. Allcock on 24 March 1955 that he considered the existence of Purgatory "intrinsically probable" but, as it is not clearly taught in Scripture or by the earliest creeds, he objected to its being enforced as official dogma. He repudiated what he considered the Roman tendency to be constantly "defining and systematizing and continually enumerating the list of things that *must* be accepted" (*L* 3:588).

Evangelical Protestants should appreciate Lewis's take on the crucial issue of authority. He shows that Romanist claims to unique authority are not grounded in Scripture and are circular in nature. He also shows, importantly, that one need not rush out of the arms of Rome into an irresponsible individualism (or into Rome's arms to avoid irresponsible individualism either). He reads Scripture, not in the vacuum that Roman apologetics thinks is the inevitable result of *Sola Scriptura*, but in the light of the earliest Church Fathers, the Ecumenical Creeds, and the ongoing traditions of the church—just as Luther and Calvin would have wanted. But he does not allow those traditions to take on an authority which rivals that of Scripture itself. Thus he models a balance that deserves wider practice.

Evangelicals will find missing any critique of the Roman theology of salvation. Of the great principles of the Reformation they will find *Sola Scriptura* well defended, but *Sola Gratia* ("Grace Alone") and *Sola Fide* ("Faith Alone") missing. While Lewis by no means denies those doctrines and often writes as if they are true, we saw in the chapter on Soteriology that his understanding of them was not as clear and biblically sharp as was his theology in many other places. Nevertheless, despite the wishful thinking of some Catholics, a principled Protestant Lewis was and remained, combining those principles with an admirably ecumenical spirit. His Evangelical Protestant readers should go and do likewise.

CONCLUSION

The doctrine of the church has been sadly neglected in much modern Evangelical theology. Lewis does not deal with the whole range of it, but his focus on those parts of it that apply to the "Deep Church" provide a needed reminder of why the church is important.

> Enemy occupied territory—that is what this world is. Christianity is the story of how the rightful king has landed, you might say landed in disguise, and is calling us all to take part in a great campaign of sabotage. When you go to church you are really listening in to the secret wireless from our friends; that is why the enemy is so anxious to prevent us from going. (MC 51)

The Father gave to the Son a people, and a people with a purpose: to follow their Master into all the world with the Gospel while living it out individually and corporately; to make disciples and enable those disciples to grow together in love. Lewis has good things to say about the basis and practice of Christian unity, the nature of the church as a community, the church as a worshiping community, and the ways in which the Rooms in the great House of Christendom should relate to the Hall. For many issues relating to the church and its life we will have to look elsewhere for guidance. But Lewis gives us a good start.

CHAPTER 9

Sanctification
The Doctrine of the Christian Life

"Aslan," said Lucy, "You're bigger."
"That is because you are older, little one" (PC 148).

When our sinful indisposition to the truth and our unwillingness to obey it has been overcome by conviction and calling—when, in Lewis's words, we as rebels lay down our arms—we are given by regeneration a new kind of spiritual life. In Lewis's terms, we now have *zoe* in addition to mere *bios*. That new life is nurtured and lived out in the context of the church, the Family of God or Body of Christ. (See chapters seven and eight.) We thus embark on the journey called "the Christian life." How is this new life nurtured? How does it grow and come to be the dominant factor in our experience? How does it transform the life we were living before? How, in other words, does the identity we were given at conversion as sons and daughters of God, forgiven and justified and accepted as righteous, clothed with the righteousness of Christ—how does that identity get worked out in our practical living so that it comes increasingly to be who we really are in our present experience and not just in anticipatory eschatological promise? The answers to those questions are what in theology is called the doctrine of sanctification. We can think of it as the doctrine of the Christian life. C. S. Lewis made a serious attempt to live that life with some integrity. The lessons he learned in the process are the subject of this chapter.

We cannot look to Lewis for answers to some of the questions that come up in the discussion of sanctification. He has no evaluation of Wesley's doctrine of "entire sanctification" or "Christian perfection." He does not deal with the question of what can or should be expected from a "definitive second crisis experience of grace." These are questions that a fully systematic theology would need to deal with because of the sometimes defining way they, or their denial, have functioned in the history of Evangelical faith and practice. But they were not on Lewis's radar. Nevertheless, he made a sincere attempt to live the Christian life in the light of Scripture and Christian tradition, and from that attempt he learned things from which we also can learn.

TRANSFORMATION

When we come to faith in Christ, God forgives our sins and accepts us as we are—but He does not leave us as we are. Those who are truly saved are not only accepted and forgiven (justification) but also brought from death to life (regeneration) and progressively transformed into new people (sanctification). Lewis wrote to Edward T. Dell on 26 May 1949, "Sanctification is the process of 'Christ being formed in us,' the process of becoming like Christ.... *The Imitation of Christ* is a formula for the Christian life" (*L* 2:940). Lewis did not of course mean to imply that we could achieve this transformation by simply mechanically imitating Jesus. It is the Christ life inside us, the *zoe* in addition to *bios*, that works this change from within. How does it get within? "There are three things that spread the Christ life to us," Lewis explains: "baptism, belief, and that mysterious action which different Christians call by different names—Holy Communion, the Mass, the Lord's Supper" (*MC* 62). These are what older theologians called "the means of grace." They are, in other words, appointed means that God uses to help us grow in grace.

Our contribution to the process is to receive the means of grace in faith and to try to follow Christ, but it is the inner dynamic of His presence in our lives through the Holy Spirit that keeps this effort from the futility we would otherwise experience. Without that inner dynamic, "the main thing we learn from a serious attempt to practice the Christian virtues is that we fail" (*MC* 125). With it, we begin, stumblingly at first and never (in this life) perfectly, to succeed. What of those professing Christians in which progress along this path is not very evident? No progress at all raises questions about whether their profession involves any real faith. But because none of us makes continuous and uninterrupted progress, we must be slow to judge. "When a man who accepts the Christian doctrine lives unworthily of it, it is much clearer to say he is a bad Christian than to say he is not a Christian" (*MC* 11).

We get to watch the transformation happening perhaps most directly in Eustace. After his un-dragoning by Aslan, it is recorded by the narrator that "to be strictly accurate, [Eustace] began to be a different boy. He had relapses. There were still many days when he could be very tiresome. But most of those I shall not notice. The cure had begun" (*VDT* 119-20). Progress, though real, can be slow because "it is not easy to throw off in an hour an enchantment which has made one a slave for ten years" (*TSC* 180). Lewis wrote to a Mrs. Jessup on 15 Oct. 1951, that "our regeneration is a slow process. As Charles Williams says there are three stages: (1.) The Old Self on the Old Way. (2.) The Old Self on the New Way. (3.) the New Self on the New Way" (*L* 3:141). Williams's stage one is the description of people before conversion. At conversion they enter stage two, and the rest of their earthly lives are a slow journey toward stage three.

What one learns on that journey is to reorient one's life so that it matches the reality of who we properly are in relationship to God. "The proper good of a creature is to surrender itself to its Creator—to enact intellectually, volitionally, and emotionally, that relationship which is given in the mere fact of its being a creature. When it does so, it is good and happy" (*PoP* 78). When it does not, by implication, it is bad and miserable. While this reorientation is accepted in principle at conversion, what it means has to be worked out in the practical details of living, involving the breaking of many habits of thought, feeling, and action which had accumulated during the "enchantment" under which the "Old Self" had labored in its fallen and rebellious condition. Our beliefs may have changed when we came to faith in Christ, but our instincts have to be retrained. At first we may not fully understand the need, much less the process. Lewis explains what that confusion is like in one of his classic analogies. A puppy theologian would think the whole process of house training raised serious questions about the goodness of man.

> But the full-grown and full-trained dog, larger, healthier, and longer-lived than the wild dog, and admitted, as it were by Grace, to a whole world of affections, loyalties, interests, and comforts entirely beyond its animal destiny, would have no such doubts (*PoP* 32).

The mature Christian, like the full-grown dog, experiences what are indeed intimations of a higher life. For a Christian it is nothing less than a foretaste of that final transformation in the next life which theologians call glorification. Lewis portrays it wonderfully in the death of the sensuous lizard previously oppressing the sinner and its resurrection as the magnificent stallion that the man now freed from it rides off into the mountains of heaven in *The Great Divorce* (*GD* 102). In an equally compelling passage from the Chronicles of Narnia we realize that the goal of this growth, which is also the means of it, is an increasingly expanding vision of the glory of God in the face of Jesus Christ. Or, in Lewis's words, "'Aslan,' said Lucy, 'You're bigger.' The Lion replies, 'That is because you are older, little one'" (*PC* 148). The greater Christ is to us, the greater we ourselves become, blessedly free of any concern with our own greatness because our eyes are full only of Him.

OBEDIENCE

Much of the transformation consists of an increasing desire to obey Christ and an increasing ability to do so. Obedience is thus important enough to be a topic in its own right. The first thing to be said about it is that it is subject to much misunderstanding. A mechanical obedience to a set of rules as rules can take us away from Christlikeness rather than toward it, as the Pharisees of the New Testament illustrate. Lewis, therefore, reminds us that "we might think that God wanted simply obedience to a set of rules: whereas He really wants people of a particular sort" (*MC* 77). Christian obedience is not obedience for its own sake but for the sake of the One we have come to love and trust. After all, "if what you call your 'faith' in Christ does not involve taking the slightest notice of what He says, then it is not Faith at all—not faith or trust in Him, but only intellectual acceptance of some theory about Him" (*MC* 130). So obedience is valuable as an expression of the faith or trust we have in Christ which makes that faith more than just an intellectual theory. The "sort" of people God wants is the sort who obey Christ in a Christlike spirit for the sake of Christ as a result of the process of "Christ being formed" in them. Such obedience is an act of love, not the pursuit of some abstract righteousness for its own sake.

The character Vertue in *Pilgrim's Regress* shows what can happen when we do not understand the Christocentric and relational nature of Christian obedience. He tries to walk a path of Kantian disinterestedness in which the Right or the Good is compromised if it is not done purely for its own sake. He discovers that trying to be above "ulterior" motives puts him in a contradictory position. "I believe that I am mad," said Vertue presently. "The world cannot be as it seems to me. If there is something to go to, it is a bribe, and I cannot go to it; if I can go, then there is nothing to go to" (*PR* 113). Motivation is undermined when there is no personal element to such obedience. Any reward for one's obedience—even so innocent a reward as the knowledge that one has pleased one's Master—seems like a "bribe" which compromises one's devotion to virtue itself. But that is the problem. Our devotion is not to virtue but to the all-virtuous *Person* with whom we have to do—the Person we love. John, the pilgrim of *Pilgrim's Regress*, has not yet risen to a full appreciation of the role of love in obedience, but he anticipates it with the correct realization that *desire* has to have something to do with the quest. "Vertue," said John, "give in. For once yield to desire. Have done with your choosing. *Want* something." Vertue, who sees not even as far as John at this point, finds that, in the absence of love, motivation is ultimately destroyed. "I cannot," said Vertue. "I must choose because I must choose because I must choose; and it goes on forever, and in the whole world I cannot find a reason for rising from this stone" (*PR* 113).

Elwin Ransom in *Perelandra*, by contrast, understands that Christianity is a very different proposition from Stoicism or Kantianism, precisely because the personal element is central in it. "I think He made one law of that kind in order that there might be obedience," Ransom tells Tinidril, speaking of the seemingly arbitrary prohibition of sleeping on the fixed land. "Where can you taste the joy of obeying unless He bids you do something for which His bidding is the *only* reason?" (*Pa* 118). Maleldil's (God's) bidding is a sufficient reason for obedience not because it is a bidding (which is all that Vertue knows) but because it is *His* bidding. The Green Lady gets Ransom's point because she understands her relationship to Maleldil as parallel to her relationship to the beasts who delight to please her. "Oh brave Piebald!" she says, "This is the best thing you have said yet" (118). Obedience that flows from love and finds pleasing the beloved as its reward is a very different thing from obedience for its own sake. Vertue's dutiful choice of natural good is better than choosing natural evil—but it is sub-Christian. And the differing dynamic affects not only obedience but also the very quality of how the good acts are going to be performed. If obedience does not flow from love to love, it is not flowing from the righteousness that is found in Jesus Christ. In these passages Lewis has an accurate understanding of the *raison d'etre* of Christian obedience, and his characters' wrestling with it shows forth that understanding profoundly.

While our primary motive for obedience is love for Christ and desire to please Him, because of God's wisdom and goodness, obedience has many practical benefits for living a good life in general. As Lewis points out, "If Christianity should happen to be true, then it is quite impossible that those who know this truth and those who don't should be equally well equipped for leading a good life" ("Man or Rabbit?" 109). If Christianity is true at all, it is true not just about religion but about the world and life in the world as well. In *Mere Christianity*, following the Moral Law means three things: enabling a harmonic life inside the individual ("directions for running the human machine"), establishing fair play and thus harmony between individuals, and enabling the pursuit of "the general purpose of life as a whole." Lewis pictures obedience as keeping life ship-shape: keeping your own ship in working order, avoiding crashes with other ships, and keeping the whole fleet sailing toward its port (*MC* 69-71). To see this is to realize that, all things being equal, obedience to the moral law will make life go better for all people, whether they are Christians or not. But the Christian has four advantages: a clearer understanding of why this is so, a higher motivation for obedience in the love of God, a perfect example of it to follow in Christ, and "help towards obeying," in the transformation discussed above, to which the non-Christian does not have access (*MC* 93).

In learning to obey God out of love for Him, it helps to realize that the "rules" are expressions of His love for us. We could say that they are the expression of His character, but that amounts to the same thing, for God is love. That is to say that they are not just rules but are descriptions of what a fulfilled life looks like when followed, not in a forced or self-righteous way, but out of love. They are not just arbitrary prohibitions but descriptions of moral reality, and therefore of reality. Disobedience or self-righteous obedience puts us at odds, not just with God, but with the reality He created. Lewis understood this well. He noted, for example, that

> every preference of a small good to a great, or a partial good to a total good, involves the loss of the small or partial good for which the sacrifice was made.... You can't get second things by putting them first; you can get second things only by putting first things first" ("First and Second Things" 280).

When we choose evil over good, or even lesser goods over greater goods, we are fighting against the objective hierarchy of goodness built into the world by God, and thus our pursuit of what we think is good is frustrated. God's law is not a set of arbitrary prohibitions, but rather a description of the way He has made the world in accordance with His own character. He created this moral hierarchy, this order of goodness, and revealed it to us in the *Tao* perceived by conscience and the Law written in Scripture, because He loves us. It is there to promote our true happiness, not to frustrate it. Thus Lewis wrote to Arthur Greeves on 12 Sept. 1933 that in the worst of the passions he had pursued in his past sins, he was wanting something good and approved by God, something he was right to desire. But of course he was pursuing it in a wrong way. Therefore, "When we are tempted, we must remember that just because God wants for us what we really want and knows the only way to get it, therefore He must, in a sense, be quite ruthless toward sin" (*L* 2:123).

There are laws such as the prohibition of sleeping on the fixed land in Perelandra whose only purpose is obedience as an expression of love for and trust in Maleldil. They exist to teach us that in a loving relationship with our God and King, obedience is its own reward. But most of God's laws are also there to help us navigate His world for our good. All are expressions of His love. Seeing this helps us not only to practice obedience but to practice the right kind of obedience: obedience from the heart. This is the path to the fulfillment of what we were created to be. That is why Lewis wrote to Bede Griffiths on 28 July 1936 that the redeemed person will be different from what he was before not just by being different but "by being that of which we should say—Ah—he is himself at last" (*L* 2:202). We are our true selves only when we are rightly related to our Creator.

Law as much as grace is an expression of God's love, but the Law seems rather to be oppressive and a "ministry of death" (2 Cor. 3:7) because in the Fall we put ourselves in opposition to it, both in deed and inclination. We cannot now be saved by keeping it, and our efforts to do so lead either to frustration and despair or to self-righteousness. We cannot be saved by our obedience; we obey because we are being saved. Lewis is not always clear about this distinction, as when he describes salvation as the result of our decisions making little changes to our core selves (*MC* 87), rather than the changes being ultimately the result of God's transforming grace in our lives through faith. But sometimes he captures it quite well. The main thing we learn from trying to keep the law before our conversion is that we fail. Similarly, "No man knows how bad he is till he has tried very hard to be good.... Only those who try to resist temptation know how strong it is" (*MC* 124). But then things change. After conversion, we discover that while we still do not succeed perfectly, the dynamic has altered. Trusting Christ does not mean we stop trying to do good or cease our efforts to do what He says, but it does mean doing these things in a different way. To say that you trusted Jesus but had no intention of doing what He says would be self-contradictory. Therefore, "if you have really handed yourself over to Him, it must follow that you are trying to obey Him. But trying in a new way, a less worried way. Not doing these things in order to be saved but because He has begun to save you already" (*MC* 129).

The "less worried" obedience that Lewis captures in this passage is one of the most helpful descriptions of the Christian life I have ever seen. Many Christians stumble over the difficulty of how to conceptualize our own efforts to follow Christ if the crucial work is actually His rather than ours. Do we become passive and just "let go and let God," as one formula has it? No, our efforts continue, but in a "new, less worried way" based on an understanding that grace is what makes our efforts meaningful. Similarly, only Aslan can save Narnia. But as Peter observes, "We don't know when he will act. In his time, no doubt, not ours. In the meantime he would like us to do what we can on our own" (*PC* 187). Understanding this not only enables obedience, it makes our continuing failures no longer threatening. Thus Lewis reminds us, "A live body is not one that never gets hurt, but one that can to some extent repair itself. In the same way a Christian is not a man who never goes wrong, but a man who is enabled to repent and pick himself up and begin over again after each stumble" (*MC* 64). "Enabled": that is the key. And the practical result of this less worried obedience is that it reinforces the transformation that is already happening from the inside. "Very often," says Lewis, "the only way to get a quality in reality is to start behaving as if you had it already" (*MC* 161).

Everything Lewis has understood about the dynamic of obedience in the

Christian life—the way it allows us to live in accordance with reality, the way it enables not just a mechanical conformity but a joyous dance—is incarnated in one wonderful picture of a Narnian custom. This is what Christian obedience in love and in Christian community looks like: The Narnian Snow Dance. As Jill climbs out from the underground realm in *The Silver Chair*, she emerges into a ring of dancers surrounded by brightly dressed Dwarfs throwing snowballs.

> They weren't throwing them *at* the dancers as silly boys might have been doing in England. They were throwing them through the dance in such perfect time with the music and with such perfect aim that if all the dancers were in exactly the right places at exactly the right moments, no one would be hit. This is called the Great Snow Dance, and it is done every year in Narnia on the first moonlit night when there is snow on the ground. (*TSC* 231)

If everyone is doing what he should where he should and when he should, nobody gets hit. Not only does nobody get hit, but the resulting spectacle is a wonderful and beautiful thing to behold: a great Dance. But if you get out of step with the dance, there are consequences. You follow the steps, not just to say you have kept the rules, but for the sake of the Dance.

DEVOTION

The Christian life, as we have seen, is ultimately about loving God. But even the most devout believer does not love God as he ought, nor does he feel even the love of which he is capable at all times or always at the same level. Therefore, the word *devotion* has become not only a synonym for love but also the designation for a set of practices designed to give expression to, reinforce, cultivate, and increase the love for God already in our hearts. Thus, in addition to public worship, a private regimen, formal or informal, of personal Bible study, prayer, meditation, and perhaps fasting has become for most believers a part of the Christian life. The spiritual life seldom thrives without a reasonably regular attention to such practices. What does Lewis have to teach us about this aspect of Christian living?

First, to understand what it means to love God, Lewis examines what love is, what we mean when we say the word *love*. In *The Four Loves* he looks at the four Greek words for love, which denote affection, friendship, romantic love, and divine love. He notes that even human loves cannot operate truly without grace. We try to make love itself a kind of god, but "the loves prove that they are not worthy to take the place of God by the fact that they cannot even remain themselves and do what they promise to do without God's help" (*FL* 166). Only the

God who is love can enable us to love each other, much less Himself. Devotion is then not just something we do; it too must be a response to God's work within us.

Lewis also analyzes love in terms of how we relate to the loved object. We love some things because we need them (a cold drink because we are thirsty), others because they inspire us to serve them (a cause or a person), and others still because we appreciate them whether we need them or not (the smell of a field of sweet peas, a work of art). We relate to God in all these ways. "Need love cries to God from our poverty; Gift-love longs to serve, or even to suffer for, God; Appreciative Love says: "We give thanks to thee for thy great glory" (*FL* 33).

Appreciative love is the highest of these, and the one that most draws us closer to the Father. Using different terminology, Lewis writes to Malcolm, "Gratitude exclaims, very properly, 'How good of God to give me this.' Adoration says, 'What must be the quality of that Being whose far-off and momentary coruscations are like this!' One's mind runs back up the sunbeam to the sun" (*LtM* 90). Christian devotion is about putting our minds and hearts in such a position that the journey back up the sunbeam becomes possible for them. And it is about loving God more, and hence our fellow creatures more for his sake, not about loving other things less. "It is probably impossible to love any human being simply 'too much.' We may easily love him too much in proportion to our love for God; but it is the smallness of our love for God, not the greatness of our love for the man, that constitutes the inordinacy" (*FL* 170).

How then is such love to be cultivated? The experience of the saints through the ages suggests that we need both public worship and private devotional meditation on a regular basis. We must pursue both. Lewis wrote Mary Van Deusen on 7 Dec. 1950, that some people (here Lewis includes himself) find it more natural to seek God in solitude, but they need to attend church as well. And others whose natural approach is through a public worship service also need to have private devotions consistently. However we feel about it, all of us need both (*L* 3:68). We must be humble enough to realize that practices which do not come as second nature to us may be necessary in our drawing near to One who is so high above us and so much greater than we are.

Public worship, private Bible reading, prayer, and meditation: it is important to be faithful in these practices, but not to misunderstand what we are doing. The focus is not on us and on how we are feeling. Emotional responses naturally accompany devotion, but they are not the thing itself. We are not being "religious" for the sake of religion, nor for the sake of our feelings, but for the sake of God. Lewis explains, "To be religious is to have one's attention fixed on God and on one's neighbor in relation to God. Therefore, almost by definition, a religious man ... is not thinking about religion; he hasn't the time" ("Lilies" 32). Religion is what we call what he is doing when looking at it from the outside. Lewis here is a healthy corrective to much subjectivist Evangelical piety. We are often too focused on whether we are "passionate," when we would be far more so if we were more focused on what we should be passionate about: the living God.

Many find Lewis's emphasis here to be quite practical. Emotion is properly a byproduct of devotion, not the thing itself. It is liberating to realize that, as Lewis wrote to Dom Bede Griffiths on 14 April 1934, at least in his experience, genuine devotion is most easily achieved when we are thinking about something else. "Sit down to meditate devotionally on a single verse, and nothing happens. Hammer your way through a continued argument, just as you would in a profane writer, and the heart will sometimes sing unbidden" (*L* 2:136). It is most likely to do so when we are not concerned about whether it is singing at all. This theocentric rather than egocentric focus transforms not only our relationship to God but our receptivity to His gifts as well. "Say your prayers in a garden early, ignoring steadfastly the dew, the birds and the flowers, and you will come away overwhelmed by its freshness and joy; go there in order to be overwhelmed and, after a certain age, nine times out of ten nothing will happen to you" (*FL* 39). Lewis's advice about devotions is then summed up in two pieces of very practical advice. First, have them. Second, as you are having them, remember that they are about God, and not about you.

THE INNER LIFE

An aspect of the Christian life that has received much attention over the years is what we might call "the inner life": what is going on inside us, in our hearts and minds, as we pursue the life of faith. It makes sense that this should be so, since the new life that Lewis called *Zoe* is a transformative dynamic that works outward from the heart to the hands and feet. Also, a number of emotional responses to the Gospel and to God's work in our lives are mentioned in the New Testament as being a natural and expected part of Christian experience: godly sorrow leading to repentance (1 Cor. 7:10), the joy of salvation (1 Pet. 1:8), the peace that passes understanding (Phil. 4:7). The inner life then is related to our discussion of devotion above. How do we know when what we are feeling is the real thing, and what do we do when those emotions ebb and flow and do not seem very consistent?

Lewis has a couple of perspectives that can help people deal with such questions. First is what Screwtape calls "the law of undulation" (*SL* 36). Our emotions are affected by many factors, including the state of our bodies, and our religious emotions are no exception. They are naturally going to go up and down, to fluctuate, for reasons that have very little to do with their object. Therefore, it is dangerous to assume that their presence guarantees very much in the way of sanctification, nor that their temporary absence necessarily signals a problem. This is why Lewis wrote to Genia Goelz on 13 June 1951 telling her not to bother too much about her emotions. "When they are humble, loving, brave, give thanks for them: when they are conceited, selfish, cowardly, ask to have them altered. In neither case are they *you*, but only a thing that happens to you" (*L* 3:127). He further explained to her on 15 May 1952 that feelings are not the real spiritual experience—only a sign of it. "The real thing is the gift of the Holy Spirit which can't usually be—perhaps not ever—experienced as a sensation or emotion. The sensations are merely the response of your nervous system. Don't depend on them" (*L* 3:191). The emotional reaction is the byproduct of the Spirit's work, not the thing itself.

If this view of our feelings is true, then it follows that, while emotions are important, they are not crucial; far more important are attitudes, inner stances that we adopt toward spiritual realities, stances that are more permanent and less variable than emotions. For example, the believer discovers that once he has committed himself to Christ, "what would, a moment before, have been variations in opinion, now become variations in your personal *attitude* to a Person. You are no longer faced [simply] with an argument which demands your assent, but with a Person who demands your confidence" ("Obstinacy" 26; emphasis added). Feelings about that Person may come and go. What matters in the long run is the attitude we have toward Him, for it is the basis and source of whatever appropriate emotional responses we may be enabled to have to Him. This understanding allows for greater stability in our spiritual lives. We realize that our faith does not necessarily wax and wane with our feelings of subjective confidence. Thus Lewis can "define faith as the power of continuing to believe what we once honestly thought to be true until cogent reasons for honestly changing our minds are brought before us" ("Religion: Reality or Substitute" 42). Feelings of subjective confidence are much more fickle than the stance of commitment that underlies them. We are better able to enjoy the feelings when we do not confuse the two.

Failure to understand the difference can be devastating, as in the case of the many believers who, while *believing* in the forgiveness of sins, cannot bring themselves to *feel* personally forgiven—perhaps because they have a hard time forgiving themselves. Lewis rightly wrote to a Miss Breckenridge on 19 April 1951, "I think that if God forgives us, we must forgive ourselves. Otherwise it is almost like setting up ourselves as a higher tribunal than Him" (*L* 3:109). His argument was sound, but probably did not directly address the root of Breckenridge's problem. Meanwhile, he himself was about to enter a new experience of the very reality of which he spoke. Lewis wrote to Sister Penelope CSMV, 5 June 1951,

> I realize that until about a month ago I never really believed (tho' I thought I did) in God's forgiveness. What an ass I have been for not knowing it and for thinking I knew. I now feel that one must never say one believes or understands anything: any morning a doctrine I thought I already possessed may blossom into this new reality. (*L* 3:123).

The dates on the two letters are interesting. In April of 1951, Lewis wrote to Breckenridge with correct advice about dealing with the issue of feeling forgiven. In May, apparently, he experienced the doctrine of forgiveness blossoming into a "new reality," which he wrote about to Sister Penelope in June. His own experience illustrates the fact that a deeper realization of the truth and reality of Christian teaching, a more fully integrated whole-person response to that doctrine involving the emotions, sometimes comes simply as a gift. That gift moreover is easier to receive when we do not make our feelings central. We often act as if the Christian life were about our feelings, rather than realizing that the feelings themselves are about the central truths and realities that the Christian life is really about. Lewis can help us see that the advice not to bother too much about subjective feelings of joy and peace may actually be the path to enjoying more of those feelings.

The Christian life is finally not about maintaining a particular mix of religious emotions; it is about serving the Lord, and we most often serve Him by serving our fellow man. Lewis wrote to Arthur Greeves on 20 Dec. 1943, "The great thing, if one can, is to stop regarding all the unpleasant things as interruptions of one's 'own' or 'real' life. The truth is of course that what one calls the interruptions are precisely one's real life, the life that God is sending one day by day" (*L* 2:595). They are the adventure Aslan sends us, the blessings brought by the next wave of Perelandra to our floating island. Love God and love your neighbor, Lewis would say to us, and your emotional life will take care of itself.

PRAYER

If the Christian life is about living in a personal relationship with God through Jesus Christ—about having "one's attention fixed on God and on one's neighbor in relation to God" ("Lilies" 32)—then nothing is more central to it than prayer. There or nowhere are we in personal contact with God. Lewis knew how it must look to the unbeliever:

> Master, they say that when I seem
> To be in speech with you,
> Since you make no replies, it's all a dream
> —One talker aping two. (*Ps* 122)

Nevertheless, if the reasons Lewis gives for believing that God is real are valid, then the reverse is actually closer to reality: "Thou art One forever, and I / No dreamer, but thy dream" (123). Or, in other words,

> Prayer is either a sheer illusion or a personal contact between embryonic, incomplete persons (ourselves) and the utterly concrete Person. Prayer in the sense of petition . . . is a small part of it; confession and penitence are its threshold, adoration its sanctuary, the presence and vision and enjoyment of God its bread and wine. ("The Efficacy of Prayer" 8)

If God is real, if revelation is real (that is, if He has spoken to us), if the incarnation is real (that is, if He has reached down to us), then and not otherwise would it follow that prayer can indeed be such a personal contact. And if it is contact with such a great God, then the rest of Lewis's statement would follow from that fact. Petition is a part of it, but a small part. And as for the rest, since I cannot improve on Lewis's words, I will repeat them: "Confession and penitence are its threshold, adoration its sanctuary, the presence and vision and enjoyment of God its bread and wine." It is no accident that Lewis develops the analogy of a church and a worship service to explain prayer, for prayer is indeed the essence of both public and private worship.

Prayer is an act, not an experience; and it is an act of faith. Emotions may well accompany it, but they are not its essence. The attempt to make prayer into an emotional experience, to "realize" it, had driven the young Lewis at Belsen to the point almost of insanity. "My nightly task was to produce by sheer will power a phenomenon which will power could never produce" (*SbJ* 61). The sheer frustration of the experience was a factor in the loss of his childhood faith. To prayer, then, applies the principle that Lewis later learned to apply to the emotional side of religion in general: emotion is a by-product of devotion, not the thing itself. In prayer one deliberately opens oneself up to God, waits silently before Him, and pours out to Him one's very self in communion. This will include petition, but more importantly confession and repentance, and most importantly, adoration. One does this not to have an "experience" (which may or may not happen), but because it needs doing, because God is God and we are we. It is one of the major ways in which the relationship with Him, the friendship with Him that His grace in Christ makes possible, is enacted. There is blessing that comes from it, but the blessing happens when we seek, not blessing, but God.

Lewis dealt with some of the theoretical problems raised by prayer, such as how our petitions could possibly have any effect on a God understood as both omniscient, omnipotent, and infinitely wise. How could such a Being be influenced to act, or to act differently, by our requests? Yet we are invited to ask, even for such mundane things as our daily bread, in the model prayer Jesus gave His disciples. When Polly wonders whether Aslan wouldn't know what the children needed without needing to be asked, Fledge replies with a simple wisdom that can hardly be bettered: "'I've no doubt he would ... but I've a sort of idea he likes to be asked'" (*TMN* 178). Prayer is part of our *relationship* with God.

Lewis hints at perspectives that can help with the more theoretical problems too: God probably does not experience time in successive moments like we do, but relates to our time the way Shakespeare related to Hamlet's, so that He can give all the attention He wants to the millions of prayers clamoring for His awareness at any moment (*MC* 146-7). But ultimately Lewis realized that such questions are beyond our full understanding and have no definitive answers except the realization that we must respond in faith to the fact that God Himself asks us to ask and would not do so if our response was meaningless. Lewis wrote to his brother Warnie on 21 Feb. 1932, "The efficacy of prayer is, at any rate *no more* of a problem than the efficacy of all human acts" (*L* 2:49). Our inability to explain definitively how our free will relates to God's sovereignty and predestination does not stop us from choosing or acting; neither should similar difficulties stop us from praying. God has chosen to relate to us personally. The best response to that invitation is not puzzlement but confession, repentance, and adoration—and, yes, petition. The God who stoops to us in grace does not stoop half way.

CONCLUSION

Christian faith puts the believer on a path of transformation that leads to a less worried obedience and to a communion with the heavenly Father that is emotionally satisfying when we do not make our emotional satisfaction the focus of our faith journey. Lewis lived this life well, and he describes it well. He does not deal with all the questions which a full theology of sanctification would need to address, but what he does have to say is often both wise and practical. His writings thus complement the traditional theologies in ways that can promote practical faith and real sanctification. What could be better than that?

CHAPTER 10

Theological Aesthetics
Christianity and Culture

"The work of a Beethoven and the work of a charwoman become spiritual on precisely the same condition, that of being offered to God" (*"Learning in Wartime,"* 55).

I have lamented the fact that typically Evangelical systematic theologies lack a section on art, beauty, or aesthetics, while Roman Catholic theologians like Von Balthazar have made theological aesthetics the organizing principle of their dogmatics ("Writers Cramped"). The older Protestant theologians gave some attention to these things through the Calvinistic doctrine of Common Grace, but it has not been a great emphasis for contemporary Evangelicals. Francis Schaeffer was a lonely exception to the rule. Here C. S. Lewis was most fortunately not a typical Evangelical, for he has much to say about the relationship between Christianity and culture. Behind Lewis's view of the relationship between Christianity and culture lay Tolkien's doctrine of subcreation, expounded in the essay "On Fairie Stories" and the poem "Mythopoeia," which gives a poetic account of the conversation with Lewis on Addison's Walk that led to his conversion (Carpenter, *Tolkien*, 147). Put simply, human beings are creative because they are made in the image of the Creator. This makes their creations, including their culture, the sum total of that creative activity, theologically significant. In Lewis's thinking, this truth is balanced by a profound recognition of the value to God of the individual human soul, with its eternal destiny hanging in the balance in a way that would seem to relativize all merely temporal things, including human cultures and civilizations. Lewis's thinking mostly moved between those two poles with his characteristic good sense.

THE VALUE OF CULTURE

The Christian's relationship to culture is one area in which the development of Lewis's thinking cannot be ignored. In a cluster of essays from 1939-40 he seems to question his own level of involvement in cultural activity as a writer and a tutor in English literature. In later writings he would come to speak more freely and less defensively about the value of human culture. But at the beginning of World War II he seems strangely negative. He says "the Christian knows from the outset that the salvation of a single soul is more important than the production or preservation of all the epics and tragedies in the world" ("Christianity and Literature" 10). Indeed, it is. But we also read that "The glory of God, and, as our only means to glorifying Him, the salvation of human souls, is the real business of life" ("Christianity and Culture" 14). No one can doubt the supreme value of the salvation of a human soul, nor that for people living under the Great Commission it is "the real business of life." But to say that this is our *only* means of glorifying God seems excessive and extreme, especially for Lewis. Then when we read that "I think we can still believe culture to be innocent after we have read the New Testament; I cannot see that we are encouraged to think it important" ("Christianity and Culture" 15), we must wonder what is going on.

To understand what Lewis is saying here, we must understand the error against which he was reacting—perhaps over-reacting. He rejects, quite rightly, the modern idea that "cultural activities are in their own right spiritual and meritorious—as though scholars and poets were intrinsically more pleasing to God than scavengers and bootblacks" ("Learning in Wartime" 55). The substitution of culture for religion that descends from Matthew Arnold was strong in Oxford at the time, and Lewis rightly stood against it. Lewis would still be opposing it, though in a more mature and balanced manner, fifteen years later in the essay "Lilies that Fester" (1955). In 1940 he felt a need to deflate the spiritual pretensions of the learned and the cultured, and did it so strongly that he used unadvised phrases (saving souls our "only means to glorifying" God, culture not "important") that he would not have used later.

Meanwhile, we should not lose Lewis's point in the excesses of his rhetoric. Never one to shirk the hard questions, he demands that scholars like himself ask how it is right or even conceivable "for creatures who are every moment advancing either to Heaven or to hell to spend any fraction of the little time allowed them in this world on such comparative trivialities as literature or art, mathematics or biology." We must not miss why he is asking this question. As a scholar serious about his Christian faith, he needs to be able to answer it. And if he asks it so starkly, it is because if our human culture can withstand that enquiry, "it can stand up to anything" ("Learning in Wartime" 48-9). Lewis wants to be able to affirm the spiritual value of human culture in a way that will not be confused with Arnold's turning it into an idol, and he wants to be sure that he does not do it cheaply.

How then does it stand up? We certainly want people on the way to Heaven or Hell to have clean streets and polished shoes, even as we want them to have good epics and symphonies and scholars who can help them more fully understand and appreciate those epics and symphonies. The Christian view is that providing such services is a way of loving our neighbors, and hence a way of glorifying God. Lewis affirmed this, even though his saying that the salvation of souls was the *only* way we have of glorifying God does not make that affirmation easy to see. You can see that he does affirm it when you realize what is the point he was trying to make: "The work of a Beethoven and the work of a charwoman become spiritual on precisely the same condition, that of being offered to God" ("Learning in Wartime" 55).

In other words, love of our neighbor and faithfulness to our calling that flow from our love of God are what make us spiritual, not being learned or cultured. The scavenger, bootblack, and charwoman are accepted by God and pleasing to God (and glorify God) by virtue of that love and that faithfulness, no less than the composer of the symphony, the poem, or the lecture. This principle is universal: It applies to all natural and earthly functions that are not forbidden and hence inherently sinful. "All our merely natural activities will be accepted, if they are offered to God, even the humblest, and all of them, even the noblest, will be sinful if they are not" ("Learning in Wartime" 54). This is the classic Christian understanding, in its Reformation form which emphasizes the equal spiritual value of the humble and the "secular" callings when pursued as unto the Lord. In this cluster of essays from the beginning of the forties, Lewis arrives at that understanding, though he makes a bit of an uncharacteristic muddle of the process of getting there.

Though Lewis does not explicitly make the connection (Tolkien did), this Christian view of culture flows from the Christian doctrine of creation. God created the world and put Adam and Eve into it to keep and dress the Garden. We were made to be stewards of God's world; after our Fall we continue to rule it, but selfishly and in rebellion rather than as His servants. Therefore, salvation is not a matter primarily of removing us from the world but of restoring us to our proper role in it, to care for it and to develop it as we care for each other under God.

Lewis did understand well the nature of the relationship God wants us to have to the world on that basis. He says, "Christianity does not simply replace our natural life and substitute a new one; it is rather a new organization which exploits, to its own supernatural ends, these natural materials" ("Learning in

Wartime" 54). The word *supernatural* is perhaps not the best choice in that sentence; "spiritual ends" might be more accurate. Miracles are not in view here, but rather a redirection of the natural life to spiritual (i.e., godly) ends. More clearly, Lewis says that Christianity "was never intended to replace or supersede the ordinary human arts and sciences: it is rather a director which will set them all to the right jobs, and a source of energy which will give them all new life, if only they will put themselves at its disposal" (*MC* 79). What does this mean in practical terms? "Christianity does not replace the technical. When it tells you to feed the hungry, it doesn't give you lessons in cookery" ("Answers" 48; cf. *MC* 79). If we are to feed the hungry, there must be agriculture and commerce and transportation and culinary arts, things which human beings develop out of their own God-given creativity and capacity for labor. We learn to cook because we are human; we use that skill to feed the hungry rather than just ourselves and our family, and we do it as a conscious service to God out of love, because we are Christians.

THE LIFE OF THE MIND

This pattern we have been seeing then applies to all of human culture. The Christian properly may pursue all the practical and fine arts on this basis. This includes the cultivation of the mind. Thus, God "wants a child's heart but a grown-up's head" in His followers (*MC* 75). Lewis is careful to avoid the two opposite errors of anti-intellectualism on the one hand, or of worshiping the intellect on the other. Christian intellectuals are always tempted to think that their capacity to think well makes them better Christians, but it is not necessarily so, intellectual and spiritual pride being a particular danger for them. And that pride in its ugliness often tempts Christians who are not intellectuals to despise the life of the mind as being inherently unspiritual. Lewis's good sense cuts a plain and safe road through that minefield. God does not love less, or have less use for, people born with inferior brains. "He has room for people with very little sense, but He wants everyone to use what sense they have" (*MC* 75). Lewis gives us the pointed reminder that "God is no fonder of intellectual slackers than of any other slackers" (*MC* 75).

Christianity is not a religion only for eggheads, and, rightly understood, it constantly deflates their intellectual pride. But it is a religion whose natural tendency should be to elevate the level of thinking of its adherents. God is the God of truth and His mind is the source of Reason. Therefore the rampant anti-intellectualism that characterizes so much of American conservative Christianity is nothing less than a form of false teaching, of heresy, especially when one considers that it was Jesus Himself who told us that the Great Commandment involved loving the Lord your God with, among other things, all your mind (Mat. 22:37). The Lord even went out of His way to do so, adding the mind on His own authority to an Old-Testament quotation that had not explicitly mentioned it (Deut. 6:5). That is one reason why Lewis is so refreshing to many American Evangelicals trying to escape the anti-intellectualism of their upbringing. Intelligence without arrogance, and without the defensiveness that comes from the feeling of having barely escaped a narrow subculture of anti-intellectualism, is a sadly rare experience for many of us. It allowed Lewis to say with a natural clarity that we find hard to achieve what ought to be true for all believers. Living a full Christian life in itself tends to sharpen one's intelligence. No special education is required to become a Christian because "Christianity is an education in itself. That is why an uneducated believer like Bunyan was able to write a book that has astonished the whole world" (MC 75).

ART AND ARTISTRY

An important part of human culture is art, including literature, the art about which Lewis knew most. His approach to art is characterized by his conviction that there is a legitimate distinction between first and second things, and that confusing them destroys both. Lewis took it as a universal law: "Every preference of a small good to a great, or a partial good to a total good, involves the loss of the small or partial good for which the sacrifice was made. . . . You can't get second things by putting them first; you can get second things only by putting first things first" ("First and Second Things" 280). Turning a good thing into an idol ironically destroys the very goodness of the thing we thus overvalue.

Christian faith provides a basis for distinguishing first and second things. If God exists and created the world, then there is an objective hierarchy of goodness that begins with and proceeds from the basic distinction between the Creator and the creation (Williams, "The Mind is its own Place"). This distinction gives us a basis for avoiding what Meilander calls "the sweet poison of the false infinite." He sees it as one of Lewis's most central themes that "to be fully human involves a certain stance toward the things of creation: delighting in things without seeking our security in them" (8). If, on the other hand, the world just exists on its own or evolved by chance, then there is no basis for such a distinction, for everything just is, and all hierarchical rankings are, arbitrary.

Lewis wrote a lot about this insight as related specifically to the experience of beauty, not only in his autobiography but also in expository works like *The Four Loves*, where he makes the first and second things even more explicit in Christian terms. "We can't get through; not that way. We must make a detour—leave the hills and the woods and go back to our studies, to the church, to our

Bibles, to our knees. Otherwise the love of nature is beginning to turn into a nature religion" (38). The reason why turning Nature into a religion is a mistake is that "Nature cannot satisfy the desires she arouses nor answer theological questions nor sanctify us. . . . But the love of her has been a valuable and, for some people, an indispensable initiation" (39). If God is God and Nature his creature, this is just what we should expect.

Applied to the beauty we seek to capture in art, as opposed to that which we find in nature, this distinction leads to a rejection of Aestheticism, the theory of "art for art's sake." Art exists not for its own sake but for the sake of the beauty or truth it expresses: that is the first thing to which art is the second. So Lewis notes wryly that "all the greatest poems have been made by men who valued something else more than poetry—even if that something else were only cutting down enemies in a cattle-raid or tumbling a girl in a bed" ("Christianity and Literature" 10). Art that is completely self-referential is, not to put too fine a point on it, boring. The law of first and second things is inexorable, and it applies not only to individual works of art but also to the culture or civilization of which they are a part: "We shall never save civilization as long as civilization is our main object. We must learn to want something else even more" (*MC* 119).

The law of first and second things applies equally to both the creation and the reception of art. The artist should remember that "no man who values originality will ever be original. But try to tell the truth as you see it, try to do any bit of work as well as it can be done for the work's sake, and what men call originality will come unsought" ("Membership" 175). And the reader should remember that "those who read poetry to improve their minds will never improve their minds by reading poetry" ("Lilies" 35). Originality is a byproduct of faithfulness, and mental improvement is a byproduct of the love of the truth or beauty that the art is about. This perspective protects the artist's ego as well as his work. "Always, of every idea and of every method, he will ask not 'Is it mine?', but 'Is it good?'" ("Christianity and Literature" 9). Because God is God, first things are first things, horses are horses, and carts are carts—and it is possible to get them in the right order rather than have the cart before the horse. Therefore, "An author should never conceive himself as bringing into existence beauty or wisdom which did not exist before, but simply and solely as trying to embody in terms of his own art some reflection of eternal Beauty and Wisdom" ("Christianity and Literature" 7). To forget this, as either writers or readers, is to condemn ourselves to the ennui of false sophistication and the obscurity of irrelevance.

Because great art can embody eternal truth and beauty rather than merely temporal perspectives, because it exists as a second thing to serve eternal truth and beauty, it can have a significance and importance that are denied it when it tries to be a first thing itself. It can embody eternal values because they exist due to God's existence, and because human beings are made in His image (remember Tolkien's doctrine of sub-creation). Because of what theologians call the doctrine of Common Grace, even non-Christian artists can do this by virtue of their humanity—though they may not know or understand that they are doing so. As the Painter Spirit tries to tell the Painter Ghost in *The Great Divorce*, "When you painted on earth—at least in your earlier days—it was because you caught glimpses of Heaven in the earthly landscape. The success of your painting was that it enabled others to see the glimpses too" (*GD* 80).

If human beings are to live lives of virtue and fulfillment, they must live them in accordance with eternal truth and in sympathy with eternal beauty. Therefore, if art can help us to have a vision of those realities (or obscure that vision), it can have a powerful impact for good or evil far beyond what Lewis seemed to allow it in those essays with which we began this chapter, where he was more concerned with deflating cultural pride. He was right there to insist that the Poet is not spiritually superior to the Bootblack, as he is right here to insist on the vital importance of the role of the faithful Poet, for both points are rooted in the prior reality of God as Creator. But it seems the more mature Lewis would have to drop the implication that the right kind of approach to culture is not *important*. And he did.

Its importance is seen in Lewis's controversy with critics like I. A. Richards over "stock responses." Richards thought the purpose of poetry was to express original, sophisticated, and interesting refinements of sensibility, and denigrated much traditional verse as dealing only in crude "stock responses." Lewis thought this emphasis completely wrong-headed. What mattered in the sentiments expressed in literature was not that they were original or sophisticated but that they be good, true, beautiful, and right. And this mattered because one of art's functions was to preserve and transmit the central values, hard won from the barbarism which is our natural condition, that made civilization possible.

> That elementary rectitude of human response at which we are so ready to fling the unkind epithets of 'stock,' 'crude,' 'bourgeois,' and 'conventional,' so far from being 'given,' is a delicate balance of trained habits, laboriously acquired and easily lost, on the maintenance of which depend both our virtues and our pleasures and even, perhaps, the survival of our species. (*PPL* 56-7)

It is not that originality as such is despised; rather, one should be trying to capture in new and arresting ways the values, the ways of seeing the world, that have been validated by time and experience.

The older poetry, by continually insisting on certain Stock themes—as that love is sweet, death bitter, virtue lovely, and children or gardens delightful—was performing a service not only of moral and civil, but even of biological, importance.... Poetry was formerly one of the chief means by which each generation learned, not to copy, but by copying to make, the good Stock responses. (*PPL* 57)

Providing this service does not of itself make the Poet more spiritual, but it certainly does make him important.

EDUCATION

If poetry is one way of transmitting the wisdom of the ages across the generations, education is another. Both are important aspects of human culture. As a professional educator, Lewis fought a long battle against the modern tendency to lose the distinction between liberal education and merely vocational training. His aspirations for university life went even beyond that in ways that our contemporaries may find astonishing. He actually distinguishes three goals: "Schoolmasters in our time are fighting hard in defence of education against vocational training; universities, on the other hand, are fighting against education on behalf of learning" ("Our English Syllabus" 21).

Training, as Lewis uses the term here, is gaining the ability to perform a job, to make a living. Education is preparation for more than that—for life as a free citizen, not just as a cog in an economic machine. Or we could say that training is preparation for work, and education for leisure, all the things outside of work as mere breadwinning—family, art, religion, politics, etc.—which justify the labor required to win our bread and keep life going. As Lewis explains, "Human life means to me the life of beings for whom the leisured activities of thought, art, literature, conversation are the end, and the preservation and propagation of life merely the means" ("Our English Syllabus" 23). Training makes one a good physician, lawyer, salesman, or factory worker; education makes one a good citizen and a full human being. And then comes learning, the pursuit of knowledge for its own sake, which Lewis takes to be the purpose of the university. The university exists for those who have already been both trained and educated and who wish to make the sacrifices required to pursue knowledge for its own sake.

This all means that the standards Lewis thought within reach only seventy years ago would be incomprehensible today. "There is an intrinsic absurdity in making current literature a subject of academic study, and the student who wants a tutor's assistance in reading the works of his own contemporaries might as well ask for a nurse's assistance in blowing his own nose" ("Our English

Syllabus" 30). The battles he referred to, for education and for learning, have all been lost. Today most undergraduates come to university neither trained for anything practical nor in any sense really educated, possessing not even the grammar of their own tongue, no logic, and precious little rhetoric. Even the PhD degree hardly rises to the pursuit of "learning" in Lewis's sense, having become essentially the union card for college instructors.

Many of us are concerned about this plunge in educational standards, but few understand as well as Lewis did what is really at stake. Our laudable desire to extend education to more and more people entails a lowering of standards, as Lewis feared. "Our danger is that equality may mean training for all and education for none" ("Our English Syllabus" 22). (It has actually gotten worse than that, for many now complain that even training has suffered.)

If indeed we value the life for which "the leisured activities of thought, art, literature, conversation are the end, and the preservation and propagation of life merely the means" ("Our English Syllabus" 23), then the loss of education in its true sense is frightening. "If education is beaten by training, civilization dies" ("Our English Syllabus" 22). It dies because leisure becomes a pointless quest for experience or stimulation rather than for higher values—we become in that sense less civilized. But it may also die because neither leaders nor voters are critical thinkers with a rootedness in the lessons of history or in the philosophical and religious foundations of their culture and its values. When people are no longer educated, no longer grounded in the classics or skilled in grammar, logic, and rhetoric, how shall they understand the challenges that confront them? How shall they preserve the hard-won civilization that they can no longer understand or appreciate? "Civilization is a rarity, attained with difficulty and easily lost. The normal state of humanity is barbarism" ("Our English Syllabus" 23).

Lewis then wanted to protect learning against education, which he thought should have occurred before the student reached university. But he understood that protecting real education from the encroachments of mere vocational training was just as important. That is the crisis that faces us today. And of it, Lewis said, in defense of classical education, "I do not know where the last ditch in our educational war may be at the moment; but point it out to me on the trench-map, and I will go to it" ("Idea" 8).

Increasingly the Christian classical school movement and the homeschool movement find themselves in that ditch with Lewis today. For education is rightly the concern of the individual Christian, the Christian family, and the church. One cannot love the Lord with all one's mind if the mind has never been developed, and the church has along with the task of winning the world the task of handing on the Christian tradition to the next generation. That task is as difficult as it is inescapable. Lewis wrote Dom Bede Griffiths on 8 May

1939 that living is a process of "coming to realize truths so ancient and simple that, if stated, they sound like barren platitudes. They cannot sound otherwise to those who have not had the relevant experience: that is why there is no real teaching of such truths possible and every generation starts from scratch" (*L* 2:258). Every generation starts from scratch, and cannot learn the most important truths until it has had the hard experiences that make them meaningful. Lewis is not saying that teaching is pointless, but that it cannot be done once and for all or without the aid of experience. If the "platitudes" are not present when the requisite experiences take place, they can be lost forever.

What will be handed on to the next generation then? Only that which we managed to gather ourselves from the last one.

> No generation can bequeath to its successor what it has not got. You may frame the syllabus as you please. But when you have planned and reported *ad nauseam*, if we are skeptical we shall teach only skepticism to our pupils, if fools only folly, if vulgar only vulgarity, if saints sanctity, if heroes heroism. ("Transmission" 116)

The church and the Christian family should be in the business of developing those saints and heroes, and they can no longer look to the larger culture to instill a commitment to even secular excellence. Lewis reminds us, "I do not think it can be the business of the Church greatly to cooperate with the modern State in appeasing inferiority complexes and encouraging the natural man's instinctive hatred of excellence" ("On Church Music" 97-8).

Lewis does not address the topic of homeschooling directly in his writings, as it was not a controversial issue in his time. But he was himself homeschooled by his mother until her death and then sent to a series of miserable boarding schools until finally getting his real education from a private tutor, W. T. Kirkpatrick. So we can find support for homeschooling in his life. One place where he agreed with conservative Christians of today was on the importance of education and the fact that it did not have to take place in formal institutions—indeed, might in some cases take place better outside of them. In communities where the public schools fail to educate or where they offer secularist indoctrination as a substitute for education, Lewis would have thought that our course was clear. "If any man, in some little corner out of the reach of the omnicompetent, can make or preserve a really Christian school ... his duty is plain" ("Transmission" 119). Whether in homeschool or a classical Christian school or in public schools that are still tolerable, Lewis gives us a philosophy of education rooted in a well thought out view of the relationship between Christianity and culture that can help us chart our course in the challenging times in which we live.

GOVERNMENT

As long as evil needs to be restrained, government will be a prominent feature of human culture. Lewis was what we would call a conservative politically. That is, he believed in the necessity of government but also in the virtue of limited government. One sees a picture of this ideal in the reigns of the Four Kings and Queens of Narnia: they made good laws, stamped out evil, and "generally stopped busybodies and interferers and encouraged ordinary people who wanted to live and let live" (*LWW* 201). By contrast, bad government is depicted in the unlimited tyrannies of the White Witch and Miraz and the bloated bureaucracy that produced the tyranny of the National Institute for Coordinated Experiments (*THS*). Lewis believed in limited government and he did so for sound theological reasons.

First, individual human beings are more important than nations or states. Why? Because individuals live forever and states do not. Lewis made this point at least twice:

> To the Materialist things like nations, classes, civilizations must be more important than individuals, because the individuals live only seventy-odd years each and the group may last for centuries. But to the Christian individuals are more important, for they live eternally; and races, civilizations and the like are in comparison the creatures of a day. ("Man or Rabbit?" 109-10.)

> If individuals live only seventy years, then a state or a nation or a civilization, which may last for a thousand years, is more important than an individual. But if Christianity is true, then the individual is not only more important but incomparably more important, for he is everlasting, and the life of a state or a civilization, compared with his, is only a moment. (*MC* 73)

If therefore you are a Christian theist, not a materialist, the state should have been relativized for you already by your basic beliefs about reality in general and mankind in particular. Any claims to absolute power it might advance in theory or practice are automatically suspect. It follows that government can only be good government by being limited government, not only in its power but also in its aspirations. The Christian, Lewis explains, should not believe any of those politicians who "promise that only if some reform in our economic, political, or hygienic system were made, a heaven on earth would follow" (*PoP* 102).

It is perhaps easier to see that government needs to be limited in power, for as Lord Acton said, power tends to corrupt and absolute power corrupts absolutely. Lewis perceived the deeper truth that the *aspirations* of government, ironically, its very aspirations to do good, help to drive its hunger for power. A government with limited power and reach must also be one with limited ambitions: one that exists to defend its people from foreign aggression and local crime and to protect their rights. Replacing this negative agenda with a more positive one might seem a charitable thing to do, but it can backfire. Lewis notes, "Classical political theory, with its Social, Christian, and juristic key-conceptions (natural law, the value of the individual, the rights of man) has died. The modern State exists not to protect our rights but to do us good" ("Progress" 314).

The problem is that the older concept had built-in limitations which the newer one lacks. Natural law defines a limited set of rights. But once the government, rather than protecting the space in which the individual or the family can pursue its own good, starts trying to provide and ensure that good itself, where does its interference end? There is always more good that can be done for more people—or at least attempted. Thus Lewis feared that "the higher the pretensions of our rulers are, the more meddlesome and impertinent their rule is likely to be, and the more the thing in whose name they rule will be defiled" ("Lilies" 48). This is consistent with the biblical perspective that the primary purpose of government is the restraint of evil. It is true that Paul says it is a minister ordained by God for good, but in context, the primary good it performs is the restraint of evil (Rom. 13:1-7).

For Lewis, then, the good things in life do not come from the government but from the labor of the individual, from his circle of friends, and from the family. One could add the church, the business, and the school for a more complete picture. The point is that government cannot provide these goods. It can only inhibit others from stealing them, destroying them, or preventing their growth and enjoyment, and it exists for no other purpose than to safeguard them.

> To be happy at home, said Johnson, is the end of all human endeavor. As long as we are thinking only of natural values we must say that the sun looks down on nothing half so good as a household laughing together over a meal, or two friends talking over a pint of beer, or a man alone reading a book that interests him; and that all economies, politics, laws, armies, and institutions save insofar as they prolong and multiply such scenes, are a mere ploughing the sand and sowing the ocean, a meaningless vanity and vexation of spirit. ("Membership" 161-2)

Limiting the aspirations, pretensions, and ambitions of the state then is the best way to ensure that it does perform its rightful (and necessary) function and does not become tyrannical.

As for the form government should take, Lewis's views remind one of Churchill's crack that democracy is the worst form of government in the world except for all the others. The Bible does not mandate one particular form of government, but democracy has the advantage of being compatible with biblical teaching on the fall of humanity. That is, there are two different motives for supporting democracy, and they tend to produce very different results. Should we let people rule themselves because they are worthy and capable of doing so, or should we limit the amount of power any one person can have because people cannot be trusted with too much of it? It is clear which side of that divide Lewis fell on. He said, "I am a democrat because I believe that no man or group of men is good enough to be trusted with uncontrolled power over others" ("Reply" 81). He explains that he believes in the equality of citizens before the law. But there are two very different reasons why one might do so:

> You may think all men so good that they deserve a share in the government.... That is, in my opinion, the false, romantic doctrine of democracy. On the other hand, you may believe fallen men to be so wicked that not one of them can be trusted with any irresponsible power over his fellows. ("Membership" 168)

If democracy is the best form of government, theocracy is the worst. This is so because in reality it is not (until Christ returns) actually the rule of God but rather the rule of men over other men in God's name. This pretense of ruling for God not only gives them the kind of power Lewis would not have trusted them with in any case, but tempts them to the various ways of exceeding the government's healthy and legitimate aims discussed above. So why is theocracy the worst form of government?

> All political power is at best a necessary evil: but it is least evil when its sanctions are modest and commonplace, when it claims no more than to be useful or convenient and sets itself strictly limited objectives. Anything transcendental or spiritual, or even anything strongly ethical, in its pretensions is dangerous and encourages it to meddle with our private lives. ("Lilies" 40)

This rejection of theocracy, then, sums up much of what Lewis had to say about the role of government. It is a necessary evil in a fallen world; it governs best when governing least; its proper role is to restrain evil and thereby create a safe space in which individuals and families can pursue those goods which make life worth living; its pretensions to do more than that are a problem. Like everything else in Lewis's view of first and second things, when government tries to become a god, it becomes a demon.

Contemporary Christians concerned about the intrusions of an increasingly secular state hostile to traditional values in their lives should find encouragement in Lewis's perspectives.

> It is the man who needs, and asks, nothing of Government who can criticize its acts and snap his fingers at its ideology. Read Montaigne: that's the voice of a man with his legs under his own table, eating the mutton and turnips raised on his own land. Who will talk like that when the State is everyone's schoolmaster and employer? ("Progress" 314).

Christian homeschoolers may find themselves in a unique position to answer such a question.

CONCLUSION

C. S. Lewis understood that culture as a human creation was a complex mix of good and evil. If we are to maximize the good and minimize the evil, we need Christians, the church, the arts, education, and government pursuing the good under God in their proper roles. Christianity and culture must be distinguished but cannot be separated. They are going to influence each other for good or evil. Christians acting as salt and light can make a profound difference. Lewis wrote to Warnie on 8 April 1932 that even after accounting for the possibility of prejudice, he could not

> help thinking the Christian world is (partially) "saved" in a sense in which the East is not. We may be hypocrites, but there is a sort of unashamed and reigning iniquity of temple prostitution and infanticide and torture and political corruption and obscene imagination in the East, which really does suggest that they are off the rails—that some necessary part of the human machine, restored to us, is still missing with them. (*L* 2:70)

It may be politically incorrect to say so, but I cannot see how we can say that he was wrong. But if he was right, we must recognize that the West is also much further "off the rails" today than it was when Lewis wrote, with abortion on demand making the infanticide Lewis spoke of pale in comparison.

What can we do about this change? Cultural and political ills should be addressed directly, of course. But if Lewis was right that the West had escaped certain evils because of the influence of Christianity on it, then the ultimate solution to getting back on the rails is for the church to do its job of evangelism and discipleship. And that is the subject of the next chapter.

CHAPTER 11

Poimenics
Evangelism and Apologetics

"You are yourself the answer. Before your face questions die away" (TWHF, 308).

Poimenics is from the Greek word for "shepherd." It is that branch of theology that has to do with the care of the flock, with how to take the content of the rest of theology and build it into the lives of Christians in the church. It is about how evangelists and pastor-teachers can best perform the function Paul gives them in Eph. 4:12, "equipping the saints for the work of service." It is often called "pastoral theology." Lewis was not a pastor, though Providence gave him an informal pastoral role in many lives which is often on display in his letters. He was an evangelist of sorts as well as perhaps the most effective apologist the church has known. So in this chapter we will see what we can learn from him about evangelism and about the role apologetics can play in that ministry.

EVANGELISM

C. S. Lewis did not talk a lot about evangelism. He just did it. He often did it indirectly, but it got done. There is no direct appeal for conversion in the Broadcast Talks that became *Mere Christianity*, for example, but there is an exposition of the Christian faith designed to elucidate its attractiveness as an answer to the problems of fallen man as well as to underscore its truth. And conversion was often the result, as famously with Charles Colson. But while Lewis's approach to evangelism may have been indirect, it was not unintentional. When Sherwood Eliot Wirt of the Billy Graham Evangelistic Association asked Lewis whether he would say that the aim of his writing was "to bring about an encounter of the reader with Jesus Christ," Lewis replied, "That is not my language, yet it is the purpose I have in view" ("Cross-Examination" 262). He said elsewhere that "Most of my books are evangelistic, addressed to *tous exo* ['those outside']" ("Rejoinder" 181). Lewis did not feel he had the gifts for the "direct evangelical appeal of the 'Come to Jesus' type" of evangelism, but he thought that those who could do that sort of thing should "do it with all their might" ("Christian Apologetics" 99). Lewis not only practiced evangelism by writing, but also in his speaking on the radio, speaking for the RAF in World War II, and in personal letters and other contacts. Lewis's commitment to evangelism and the price he paid for it at Oxford are covered brilliantly in the book edited by David Mills, *The Pilgrim's Guide: C. S. Lewis and the Art of Witness*, especially in the late Chris Mitchell's essay, "Bearing the Weight of Glory."

Through all of these varied experiences, Lewis came to have a good understanding of some of the problems with doing effective evangelism in the modern world. One thing he noticed was that "the greatest barrier I have met is the almost total absence from the minds of my audience of any sense of sin.... We have to convince our hearers of the unwelcome diagnosis before we can expect them to welcome the news of the remedy" ("God in the Dock" 243-4; cf. "Christian Apologetics" 95). This was a new situation without precedent in the history of the church. The apostles could assume even in their pagan audience an acute awareness of deserving God's wrath; but that assumption can no longer be made. "Christianity now has to preach the diagnosis—in itself very bad news—before it can win a hearing for the cure" (*PoP* 43). This means not an adjustment to the message, but more work for the evangelist who can no longer easily do his work effectively without help from the apologist. "Christ takes it for granted that men are bad." Until we can feel that about ourselves, we are part of the world He came to save but not of the audience His words can reach (*PoP* 45). There is no hint of the idea that we have to adjust the message to make it more palatable to this new, tougher audience. Rather, we must gird up our loins and do the work required to gain a hearing for this unwelcome diagnosis and the joyous cure that can only makes sense when it follows it.

APOLOGETICS

The evangelist increasingly needs help from the apologist because the diagnosis is no longer self-evident, and it is no longer self-evident partly because the Christian world view is now a foreign country to most modern people. They must be persuaded (the work of the apologist) to try the experiment of looking at the world and their own hearts very differently from the way they habitually do if they are to even understand the relevance of the Gospel to their lives, much less accept it as Good News that is true. The "liberal" approach to this dilemma is to try to accommodate the Gospel to the modern (or now, post-modern) world view, to make it more palatable to the audience that exists. But this approach begs the question. If the Gospel is not *true*, then it is not Good News for anyone; and if it is true, then the modern world view must at points be false. Lewis does not seem to have been tempted at all by the liberal cop-out. He was fully prepared to accept the challenge that, in order to present the Good News today, we must, to an extent that was never necessary before, convince people that not just their behavior and their beliefs but their *thinking* has been mistaken at crucial points.

Apologetics is how we do this. It is the defense of the faith, that branch of theology which asks of the Gospel, "*Why* should we think it is true?" It is the one branch of theology in which Lewis was recognized as an expert, if not a professional. His broad and deep learning, classical, philosophical, and literary, which kept him in touch with the best products of both the human mind and the human heart; his rigorous training in logic and debate by W. T. Kirkpatrick; and the fact that his own conversion was facilitated by reasoned arguments from Chesterton and Tolkien: all these factors combined to make Lewis one of the greatest apologists we have seen. What can he tell us about apologetics as a form of practical theology?

THE NEED FOR APOLOGETICS

Apologetics is needed for many reasons. In the first place it is a biblical mandate: "Sanctify Christ as Lord in your hearts, always being ready to make a defense to everyone who asks you to give an account for the hope that is in you" (1 Pet. 3:15). The word translated "defense" is απολογια (*apologia*), from which we get the English word *apologetics*. It is a courtroom term which refers to the kind of reasoned case a lawyer would make in defense of his client. Lewis was in tune with a number of the reasons why that mandate exists.

One is the very nature of the faith to which the Gospel calls us. Many modern people, Christians included, treat faith as a kind of strange mystical way of knowing unconnected to reason or evidence. They treat it as a zero-sum game in which, the more reason and evidence you have for any given belief, the less of a role is left for faith to play. The New Testament, however, knows nothing of such ideas. For the New Testament writers, faith is simply trust, and salvation is granted to people who put their personal trust in Christ as God's messiah. "If you confess with your mouth Jesus as Lord and believe in your heart that God raised him from the dead, you shall be saved" (Rom. 10:9). In Greek the noun *faith* and the verb *I believe* are built on the same root: πιστισ (*pistis*) and πιστευω (*pisteuo*). You could conceivably have that trust for good reasons or bad reasons or no reasons. It is better to have good reasons. Luke says that

Jesus offered "many convincing proofs" of his resurrection (Acts 1:3), and early preachers like the Apostle Paul were constantly giving reasons and evidence to back up their message. So we could say that apologetics is based on a biblical precept (Peter's command), biblical precedent (the example of the Apostles), and a biblical principle (that the Gospel is *truth* that should be addressed to the whole person, including the mind).

Lewis accepted this biblical perspective fully. This acceptance is shown by his teachings on the nature of truth (see chapter one, above), by his practice of apologetics, and by direct statement. "My faith is based on reason.... The battle is between faith and reason on one side and emotion and imagination on the other" (*MC* 122). The idea is not that emotion and imagination are inherently opposed to faith (one factor leading to Lewis's conversion was the "baptism" of his imagination by George MacDonald), but that in fallen human beings they often are opposed to it. When reason appears to be opposed to faith, on the other hand, this opposition is illusory, because if the Gospel is true, then true reason must support it. We practice apologetics in our evangelism, then, because of the nature of the Gospel as truth and of human beings as whole people who have minds as well as hearts that need to be reached.

The nature of the Gospel and of human beings both make apologetics a necessary part of our theology for every generation. The times in which we live can make the need even more pressing. Lewis lived in such times, and the needs he saw have not diminished since he saw them. A skeptical age will have its effects even on people raised in Christian homes. Lewis describes those effects graphically. He wrote to a Mrs. Lockley on 5 March 1951 that "Skeptical, incredulous, materialistic *ruts* have been deeply engraved in our thought" (*L* 3:93). As a result, even committed Christians like Lewis have moments when Christian truth claims look implausible. What then will be the case for those without his apologetic defenses? In such an age, apologetics is essential equipment for believers wanting to preserve and strengthen their faith just as much as it is when they are proclaiming it to others.

The ruts have not only been dug; they are systematically reinforced. Lewis gives an accurate analysis of the spirit of the age in its resistance to seeing anything but a secular and materialist analysis as being scientific. This habit of looking at every experience only inductively or "from below," of ignoring meaning in favor of mere fact, has a certain inherent plausibility because meaning cannot be put into a test tube. "There will always be evidence, and every month fresh evidence, to show that religion is only psychological, justice only self protection, politics only economics, love only lust, and thought itself only cerebral biochemisty" ("Transposition" 114-5).

The mindset Lewis is describing here is called reductionism: every aspect of reality is reduced to one other thing that is held to explain it exhaustively. For the Marxist, everything is really economics, for the Freudian everything is really just sex, etc. For the materialist, everything is only atoms in motion: so in a materialist age, various forms of reductionism will be the default setting for understanding any aspect of human experience. The reason you can always find real evidence that seems to support reductionism is that thought, for example, does involve cerebral biochemisty. If you only look at it inductively or "from below," that is all you will see. But there has to be more to it than that, because if thought is reduced to brain chemistry, then there is no reason to believe the thought that thought is only brain chemistry. A scientific age only accepts looking "from below" as valid looking. (Looking *from below* here would correspond to looking *at* as opposed to looking *along* in Lewis's essay "Meditation in a Toolshed.") We are pounded by this mentality so consistently that it becomes one of the "ruts" Lewis spoke of above. We have to make a special and concerted effort to counteract the prejudices that result from such habits of how we look at things in order to be reminded that it cannot be the whole story. Apologetics is how we make that effort.

Our age remains as skeptical as Lewis's was, and to that challenge we have now added the ruts of pluralism and its offspring multiculturalism. Lewis's ruts have been worn deeper and new ones have been added. Neither evangelism nor Christian nurture can be conducted effectively without help in navigating around or smoothing out or bridging over those ruts. Therefore, Lewis's advice is even more pertinent today than it was when he gave it:

> To be ignorant and simple now—not to be able to meet the enemies on their own ground—would be to throw down our weapons, and to betray our uneducated brethren who have, under God, no defence but us against the intellectual attacks of the heathen. Good philosophy must exist, if for no other reason, because bad philosophy needs to be answered. ("Learning in Wartime" 58)

APOLOGETIC METHOD

Modern Evangelical apologists tend to group roughly into three camps in terms of methodology: Classical, Evidentialist, and Presuppositionalist. Classical apologists argue first for the existence of God, and then turn to the evidence for the resurrection of Christ to identify who that God is and how He can be known. Evidentialists differ as to how valid the classical arguments (cosmological, teleological, moral, etc.) are, but agree that they only point to an abstract God, not the God of the Bible, and so would prefer to cut to the chase and establish the historicity of the resurrection as pointing to Jesus as being God incarnate. Presuppositionalists say we cannot argue *to* God, but only *from* God. In other words, our philosophical assumptions (presuppositions) determine how we are going to evaluate the evidence, and non-Christians' secular world view and rebellious hearts will not let them hear the evidence objectively and conclude that Christ is Lord. So we have to start by showing that all starting points save one (the existence of the God of the Bible) lead to contradiction. Only after we accept God as God do we have a basis for using reason to evaluate the evidence.

Increasingly people are coming to see these approaches as complementary and indeed mutually interdependent rather than as alternative options. Unless you have reason to believe that a creator God exists, the evidence for the resurrection of Jesus only leads to the conclusion that something really weird might have happened. Unless you see the strength of the evidence for the resurrection, the God of the classical arguments remains only an abstract theory, not a personal savior. Analyzing the world view options and seeing the contradictions of secularism provides a context in which the evidence becomes meaningful. Presenting evidence alone surely does not lead to conversion, but presuppositionalism alone is susceptible to a charge of circularity—and no methodology is successful unless it is blessed and used by the Holy Spirit to bring about conviction and faith. And, despite the purists on all sides, the Spirit has managed to use all three approaches in that way.

C. S. Lewis was not a part of the conversation I've summarized in the two paragraphs above, and he does not discuss the advantages and disadvantages of those approaches. He is best understood as a classical apologist who sometimes argued in ways more typical of evidentialists and presuppositionalists. He was, in other words, an eclectic realist with some common sense. Purists in the three approaches will not find an ally in Lewis, but practical apologists will find much good advice in how to approach their task.

Lewis followed what Groothuis calls the "cumulative case approach" (*Christian Apologetics* 59). He uses many types of arguments: classical (the moral argument, the ontological argument), evidential (the trilemma), presuppositional (the argument from reason), and existential (the argument from desire). His case is not ultimately dependent on any one of them so much as on the fact that they all point to the same conclusion. He explains,

> Authority, reason, experience; on these three, mixed in varying proportions, all our knowledge depends. The authority of many wise men in many different times and places forbids me to regard the spiritual world as an illusion. My reason, showing me the apparently insoluble difficulties of materialism and proving that the hypothesis of a spiritual

world covers far more of the facts with far fewer assumptions, forbids me again. My experience even of such feeble attempts as I have made to live the spiritual life does not lead to the results which the pursuit of an illusion ordinarily leads to, and therefore forbids me yet again. ("Religion: Reality or Substitute" 41).

Authority, reason, experience: when they agree, one can proceed with a certain amount of confidence.

There are then a number of arguments pointing to the truth of the Christian faith, some of them quite strong. We will look at some of the ones Lewis was known for below. But Lewis realized that having good arguments is not enough. We also need to influence the general climate of opinion. In a secular age, unexamined attitudes and ideas influence our minds in ways that do not affect the validity of the reasons we have always had for believing in God, but may have a powerful effect on their plausibility. For example, Ransom insists that "What we need for the moment is not so much a body of belief as a body of people familiarized with certain ideas. If we could even effect in one per cent of our readers a change-over from the conception of Space to the conception of Heaven, we should have made a beginning" (*OOTSP* 154). Space is a vast unpopulated emptiness in which life is an anomaly; heaven is a vibrant matrix of being pulsating with life and light. How we imagine the world has an influence on how we think about it, the kinds of arguments we will be drawn to, and the kind of conclusions we will draw about it.

Lewis's arguments were effective then partly because he knew that more than arguments were needed. In Lewis's apologetic they were supplemented by attempts to imagine what the world would look like if Christianity were true as well as arguments that were not directly about apologetic issues. Lewis wanted Christians to pursue intellectual excellence in general in order to create a situation in which people were not so unused to seeing things from the perspective of the Christian world view as they were already becoming in his generation. "What we want," he said, "is not more little books about Christianity, but more little books by Christians on other subjects" ("Christian Apologetics" 93). When the best available treatments of art, literature, politics, philosophy, ethics, science, etc. all speak as if Christianity were true (without directly mentioning it), then when the time comes to make the case for its truth directly, a receptive audience will have been created. We have much work left to do in this area.

Lewis was also an effective apologist because he was winsome and intelligent. One of my favorite passages is one in which he slyly turns the tables on the skeptics. As an atheist Lewis had had to believe that the great majority of the human race was wrong; "When I became a Christian," he remarks, "I was able to take a more liberal view" (*MC* 43). Here he steals a favorite buzz word, "liberal," and a favorite stance, that of tolerant open-mindedness, from his opponents and stands them on their heads to be used against them. Who is really open minded? Lewis makes his point, but he doesn't rub it in; he makes it and moves on. We could learn a lot from him in manner as well as in message.

Lewis had a unique gift for being able to express the most profound Christian ideas that apologetics needs to defend in language that normal human beings can understand. This was a gift, but it is also a skill that can be cultivated. Lewis wrote to John Beddow on 7 Oct. 1945 that it had always seemed strange to him that missionaries sent by the church to evangelize the Bantus were required to learn Bantu, but the same church was constantly assigning priests to teach the English who "simply don't know the vernacular language of England" (*L* 2:674). He also stressed that you do not really even understand a concept if you cannot translate it into the vernacular. He thought such translation ought to be a compulsory paper for every ordination examination ("Christian Apologetics" 98-99). It was good advice for the apologist as well as the pastor and the evangelist. Sadly, today in Academia there is a prejudice to the effect that writing cannot be intellectual if it is intelligible. Lewis's entire corpus gives the lie to that erroneous notion. It would be good if a host of theologians and apologists following his example could give the lie to it too.

Lewis was also careful not to claim too much. He gives multiple arguments to the best explanation and does not typically claim to have a slam-dunk proof. He wrote to Sheldon Vanauken on 23 Dec. 1950, "I do not think there is a *demonstrative* proof (like Euclid) of Christianity, nor of the existence of matter, nor of the good will & honesty of my best & oldest friends. I think all three are ... far more probable than the alternatives" (L 3:75). Not only does this approach relieve us of the burden of trying to prove more than we can, it is also consistent with the nature of the response we are looking for. As he further explained to Vanauken, God does not give us a demonstrative proof because a response of mere intellectual assent is not what He is after. "Are *we* interested in it in personal matters?" Even fairy tales know better. Othello accepted Desdemona's innocence and Lear Cordelia's love—when they were proved. But by then it was too late (L 3:75). Faith—personal trust—is interested in evidence; it is not indifferent to it. But we do not value faith very highly when it is given only if there is no intellectual alternative, or when it wavers with every fluctuation in the ebb and flow of circumstances conducive to it.

Lewis would have agreed with Francis Schaeffer that "the final apologetic" is a life lived as if the Christian message were true (*The God Who is There* 152; cf. *The Mark of the Christian*). Lewis noted, "If Christianity should happen to be true, then it is quite impossible that those who know this truth and those who don't should be equally well equipped for leading a good life" ("Man or Rabbit?" 109).

Christians so equipped should indeed be leading a life that not only exhibits human thriving from the application of Christian truths but also a sacrificial commitment to showing the love of Christ to each other and the world. Without this "final apologetic," no argument will be finally compelling to people from whom we are asking not just intellectual assent but life commitment. And to some, it will be the only argument that can speak. As Lewis wrote to a Miss Gladding on 7 June 1945, "When a person... has lost faith under so very great and bewildering a trial, no intellectual approach is likely to avail. But where people can resist and ignore arguments, they may be unable to resist *lives*" (*L* 2:659).

The final point in the practice of apologetics is the realization that it is a form of spiritual warfare, and not one without casualties. The best way to be one of those casualties is to ignore the danger. Lewis did not. He realized that "nothing is more dangerous to one's own faith than the work of the apologist. No doctrine of that faith seems to me so spectral, so unreal, as the one I have just successfully defended in a public debate. For a moment, you see, it has seemed to rest on oneself" ("Christian Apologetics" 103). Part of whatever apologetic method we adopt must be a serious reckoning with the fact that intellectual preparation is not enough. We must stand on a foundation that includes serious spiritual preparation as well. The apologist must be a person who walks with the Lord in such a way that he cannot forget on Whom things truly rest.

SOME APOLOGETIC ARGUMENTS

Lewis's various arguments are unified by the fact that he thought there were several aspects of reality and our experience of it for which the truth of the Christian faith was the best explanation. Some, such as the Trilemma and the Ontological Argument, focus our attention on the reality of Christ and of God. Others, such as the Moral Argument, the Argument from Reason, and the Argument from Desire, seemed to him to best explain what is required for our ability to live a meaningful life as full human beings. (For further information on and rigorous defenses and critiques of the Trilemma, the Argument from Reason, The Moral Argument, and the Argument from Desire, see Gregory Bassham's new book *C. S. Lewis's Apologetics: Pro and Con*.)

THE TRILEMMA

The Trilemma may well be the argument for which Lewis is best known. We devoted a whole special section to it after the chapter on Christology above, so we do not need to say much about it here. One aspect of the evidence for the deity of Christ that did not come up in that earlier discussion was the evidence from prophecy. Messianic prophecy has received less attention in some circles because one so easily gets bogged down in wrestling with arguments over the dating and authenticity of the Old-Testament books or over their interpretation. But Lewis thought that abandonment of that source of evidence was premature. He wrote Sister Penelope, CSMV, on 29 July 1942 that modern apologists have given up the argument from prophecy too easily because even if various passages could be explained away, explaining away the whole body of Messianic prophecy stretches "the arm of coincidence rather far" (L 2:526).

Yes, it does.

The Trilemma itself is not limited to the often-quoted passage in *Mere Christianity*. There is a Narnian Trilemma when Professor Kirk is trying to help the children sort out the contradictory claims about Lucy's adventures in the Wardrobe.

> "Logic!" said the Professor half to himself. "Why don't they teach logic at these schools?" There are only three possibilities. Either your sister is telling lies, or she is mad, or she is telling the truth. You know she doesn't tell lies and it is obvious that she is not mad. For the moment then, and unless any further evidence turns up, we must assume that she is telling the truth." (*LWW* 52)

It is a brilliant adaptation of the argument for the children's story. The only reason not to believe Lucy is that her story does not fit with her siblings' preconceived notions about reality and what is possible. Given strong enough evidence about Lucy's character and sanity, why should those preconceptions be the only thing we are not allowed to question? The only things the professor will not question are the dictates of logic, which are, as Lewis argues elsewhere, the very precondition of thought. So the readers of the Narnia books are prepared to make similar analyses of the case for Christ when they meet Aslan by his other name.

THE ONTOLOGICAL ARGUMENT

We have also already spoken of the Ontological Argument in great detail in chapter four, "Theology Proper." There we noticed the irony that this most sophisticated of the classical argument appears in a passage intended for the least sophisticated audience, the children for whom the Narnia books were written. This fact tells us two things: first, that Lewis did not think it too abstract to be important or too abstruse to be explained. That is, Anselm's argument (that God's being that Being greater than which none can be conceived requires that He exist necessarily in reality and not just in our minds) is not just a semantic trick, but rather the articulation of a true intuition of His transcendence. Therefore, since children are capable of having that intuition, they can be helped by story to see its implications, much as Anselm's logic helps some adults to see them. And the adults may also be helped by the story to see them in Anselm.

EVANGELISM AND APOLOGETICS

Let's be reminded of the passage which Lewis called "the 'Ontological Proof' in a form suitable for children" (*L* 3:1472). Puddleglum tells the Green Witch,

> Suppose we *have* only dreamed, or made up, all those things—trees and grass and sun and moon and stars and Aslan himself. Suppose we have. Then all I can say is that, in that case, the made-up things seem a good deal more important than the real ones. Suppose this black pit of a kingdom of yours *is* the only world. Well, it strikes me as a pretty poor one. And that's a funny thing, when you come to think of it. We're just babies making up a game, if you're right. But four babies playing a game can make a play-world which licks your real world hollow. That's why I'm going to stand by the play-world. I'm on Aslan's side even if there isn't any Aslan to lead it. I'm going to live as like a Narnian as I can even if there isn't any Narnia. (*TSC* 190-1).

Puddleglum is not implying that the existence of Aslan is only a desperate hypothesis for him; he is calling into question the adequacy of the Witch's explanation that the children had simply made Aslan up. Aslan as Puddlegulm and the children have experienced him is not too good to be true; he is too good to be nothing more than a childish fantasy. Philosophers still argue whether this argument works as a deductive proof. It certainly works as a way of bringing the implications of the intuition of transcendence to articulation for those who have experienced it.

Does this line of thinking make sense? It is an application of the realization that water does not naturally rise higher than its source. In a similar vein, Lewis wrote to his student Sheldon Vanauken on 23 Dec. 1950, asking, what if we were wrong about our beliefs after all?

> Then one would have paid the universe a compliment it doesn't deserve. Your error wd. even so be more interesting & important than the reality. And yet how could that be? How cd. an idiotic universe have produced creatures whose mere dreams are so much stronger, better, subtler than itself? (*L* 3:75)

More recent apologists have shown the kinship of this argument with more sophisticated versions of the Teleological Argument by noting the inability of natural processes unaided by intelligent agency to produce specified complexity. To put it simply, if information (e.g., the DNA molecule) has been added to nature, someone had to add it; information is not the kind of thing that can naturally add to itself. If intelligent agency is here, it must have been here from the beginning; it must be transcendent. Or, as Lewis put it less abstractly, "How cd. an idiotic universe have produced creatures whose mere dreams are so much stronger, better, subtler than itself?" It remains a very good question.

THE MORAL ARGUMENT

The Moral Argument appears in the opening chapters of *Mere Christianity*. We find ourselves confronted by a moral law. We did not just make it up: it seems to exist independently of our individual preferences. Every attempt to reduce it to a biological instinct or cultural convention fails. Therefore, the best explanation of this law is that there is a moral Lawgiver. Lewis goes systematically through various attempts to give a naturalistic explanation for this phenomenon and shows that they do not work. If the moral law is an instinct, why do we find it telling us to favor one of our actual instincts over another? Yes, we learned it from our parents and teachers, but so did we learn the multiplication table; it does not follow that the multiplication table is subjective and could be different for different cultures. If it is merely a social convention, like whether we shake hands or bow when we meet someone, then why is there such universal agreement across times and cultures about its most basic features (documented in the appendix to *The Abolition of Man*)? How can cultural relativism be true when such patent absurdities follow from it (e.g., that Western morality is not superior to Nazi morality)? The Moral Argument will be persuasive to the extent that the elimination of alternative explanations for the moral law is convincing. Lewis shows us how to do a good job of eliminating them.

Lewis's presentation of the Moral Argument does need some updating, however. He assumes, no doubt correctly in his time, that people will very seldom reply, "To hell with your standard" (*MC* 17) and that they will agree that, while some societies may be monogamous and some polygamous, "they have always agreed that you must not simply have any woman you liked" (*MC* 19). It is not at all uncommon to run into people who will oppose us on such points today. They say relativistic things and think that they believe them.

While our apologetic task may be more difficult than the one Lewis envisioned, he had provided the response to the new situation already. Whenever you meet a person who denies the existence of a real right and wrong, "you will find the same man going back on this a moment later" (*MC* 19). People say they are relativists not because they have thought it through but because they think it allows them to do what they want and to avoid the onerous burden of having to make moral judgments about others. But offer to do a wrong to them or to someone they love, and they will become absolutists at the drop of a hat. The Moral Argument is still a good argument. We must simply be aware that we may need an extra step or two in using it with our own contemporaries. Its greatest advantage is that it presents the case for God's existence in such a way as to highlight our need for the Gospel because of our sins, thus helping point us, not just to the existence of God in the abstract, but to Jesus Christ, and Him crucified.

THE ARGUMENT FROM REASON

When we think of the argument from reason, we think of the opening chapters of *Miracles* and the debate over them with Elizabeth Anscombe at the Oxford Socratic Club. Lewis argued that naturalism undoes itself because it presents us with a view of the world in which thoughts are reduced to chemical reactions in our heads, which are happening there in obedience to the laws of physics and chemistry rather than the laws of logic and reason. But if this is true, we have no reason to trust the very rational processes by which we concluded that our thoughts are chemical reactions. If my thoughts are determined by the physical state of my brain, by the history of the atoms that randomly ended up in motion there—if there is no free rational agent who can see logical relationships between evidence and conclusions—then all thinking is undermined, including the thought that naturalism (or anything else) is true. How can one chemical reaction be right or wrong about another chemical reaction? If my thought and the thought of the person who disagrees with me are both just chemical reactions in our heads, who is to judge between them? The only answer is another entity whose thoughts are subject to the same difficulty as ours. This leads us nowhere. Therefore, reason must somehow be transcendent, something that stands above deterministic cause and effect. To deny this conclusion is to deny your right to deny it. Therefore (to make a long story short), Christian theism can be affirmed without contradiction, but naturalism and materialism cannot.

Anscombe basically challenged Lewis on a technicality: he had not sufficiently distinguished between non-rational and irrational causes of our thoughts, which he had said that we discount when they can be shown to have irrational causes. He revised the relevant chapter of *Miracles* in subsequent editions to try to meet her objections; philosophers of religion continue to argue about how successfully. (See Reppert, who summarizes the debate and concludes, rightly in my view, that Lewis's argument is sound.) It seems after all this time that Lewis was basically right: you cannot have a philosophy that undermines the transcendence of Reason and the ability of persons to access it and then give reasons for that philosophy or claim that it is in any meaningful sense true. Lewis should have stuck to his original chapter title: not the cardinal difficulty but the self-contradiction of the naturalist. (For more on Anscombe's critique, see Williams, "Printing Error.")

What some may not realize is that the argument from reason exemplifies a basic pattern in Lewis's thinking, in his way of seeing reality in general, not just its relation to reason. The world is a big and wonderful place, and only belief in God as He is revealed in Christianity can account for that largeness. If God exists, there is room for all the facts the Atheist accepts. But if He does not, it is not just God and the spiritual that is excluded, but even the Atheist's world has to go also. There is room in the Christian's world for the Atheist, but the Atheist's universe is not even big enough to include the Atheist himself.

This pattern is evident whether we look at the world from the standpoint of knowing, of meaning, or of morals. In the area of knowing, Lewis noted that "when I accept Theology ... I can get in, or allow for, science as a whole.... If, on the other hand, I swallow the [secular] scientific cosmology as a whole, then not only can I not fit in Christianity, but I cannot even fit in science" ("Is Theology Poetry?" 138-9). What of meaning? It turns out that Atheism is just too simple to account for it. "If the whole universe has no meaning, we should never have found out that it has no meaning.... If there were no light in the universe and therefore no creatures with eyes, we should never know it was dark. Dark would be without meaning" (*MC* 46). In thinking about the world from the standpoint of its relation to morality we get the same result. Lewis wrote to Dom Bede Griffiths on 20 Dec. 1946 that he had to give up using evil as an argument against God when he asked how he knew that the universe was evil. "Whence came the light which discovered this darkness, the straight by which I discovered this crookedness?" (*L* 2:747).

In each of these areas the Christian has a view that explains the world as we experience it, in all its vastness, wonder, and mystery, while the skeptic must posit a world in which he himself (as a significant, meaningful, thinking person) does not exist. Taking the Atheist's world view seriously causes it to self-destruct. He is forced to saw off the very limb on which he is sitting. The Christian, on the other hand, can believe in the Atheist's limb and see it as attached to the tree. As Lewis summarized it, "I believe in Christianity as I believe the Sun has risen, not only because I see it, but because by it I see everything else" ("Is Theology Poetry?" 140).

THE ARGUMENT FROM DESIRE

Though Lewis is better known for the Trilemma, the Moral Argument, and the Argument from Reason, perhaps his most characteristic argument is actually the Argument from Desire. It was after all the experience of *sehnsucht*, or "joy," the intense longing aroused by inexplicable beauty, that drove Lewis to his conversion in such a way that he calls it "the central story of my life" (*SbJ* 17). He called "joy" an unsatisfied desire better than any other having (*SbJ* 17-18). He did not so much conclude directly from the experience of having this desire that God exists and that Jesus is His Son; rather, it was what kept him from being comfortable in Atheism until other arguments, such as Chesterton's and Tolkien's that Christ is the fulfillment of human mythology, led to his conversion (Williams, "G. K. Chesterton" 34-6). He tells us quite explicitly that his conversion was not the direct result of his unfulfilled desires: for all he knew, "the total rejection" of what he called joy might have been "one of the demands" of his new faith (*SbJ* 230). Once he had come to faith, though, he probably went back and thought through the implications of his experience to be able to articulate more clearly how it functions as one of the "signposts" he had come to understand it to be by the end of his quest (238). The fruit of that articulation is what we call the Argument from Desire. It is given in its simplest form in *Mere Christianity*:

> Creatures are not born with desires unless satisfaction for those desires exists. A baby feels hunger: well, there is such a thing as food. A duckling wants to swim: well, there is such a thing as water. Men feel sexual desire: well, there is such a thing as sex. If I find in myself a desire which no experience in this world can satisfy, the most probable explanation is that I was made for another world. (*MC* 120)

The argument is not a deductive proof but an argument to the best ("most probable") explanation. What needs explanation is this apparently unsatisfiable desire. It needs explanation because all other natural desires we encounter do seem to have appropriate objects. Lewis was not the only person to notice this pattern. Philosopher of science Michael Polanyi wrote that "our heuristic cravings imply, like our bodily appetites, the existence of something which has the properties required to satisfy us" (Polanyi 129). Why would this one craving be an exception? Lewis asks, in effect, what if it is not?

The argument assumes two states of affairs that could themselves be questioned. First, is the existence of a desire in fact evidence for the existence of the object of that desire? Lewis answers that being hungry doesn't prove you will be fed, but it does prove that you have a body that needs nourishment and that presumably therefore some kind of food exists. Therefore, the desire for Paradise does not prove that you are going to go there, but it does seem to indicate that such a thing exists ("The Weight of Glory," *WoG* 32-3).

Second, do people really experience real desires that no finite temporal thing can satisfy? Lewis thinks they do. Suppose your experience of desire is awakened by the beauty of the hillside you see in the distance. What will happen if you go there? "An easy experiment will show that by going to the far hillside you will get either nothing, or else a recurrence of the same desire which sent you thither" (*PR* 9).

People who deny that they experience any unsatisfiable desire may have repressed it, or they may still be trying to satisfy it with available objects: what is over the the next hill, or the next woman, they tell themselves, will be what they are really looking for. When a person in honesty reckons with the fact that this final finding is just not going to happen in this world, he is ready to consider the conclusion Lewis reached: a person who followed his desire by pursuing all false objects of it until their falseness became apparent, and who then resolutely rejected them, would at last have to realize that human beings must have been made to enjoy some object that is not only never found but cannot be imagined as being found in this world, i.e.,

> If a man followed this desire, pursuing all the false objects until their falsity appeared and then resolutely abandoning them, he must come out at last into the clear knowledge that the human soul was made to enjoy some object that is never fully given—nay, cannot even be imagined as given—in our present mode of subjective and spatio-temporal experience.... And if nature makes nothing in vain, the One who can sit in this chair must exist. (PR 10)

How good is this argument? It has a couple of weaknesses. First, for people who deny having had the relevant experience, it is simply beside the point. Many of them may have had that experience and do not recognize it, or they may be in denial about the impossibility of satisfying their deepest desires with temporal objects, but it would not be possible to prove that this is true of all of them. And even for those really in denial, the argument will have neither interest nor force. Second, from the existence of unsatisfied desire it does not strictly follow that the object which supposedly exists for it is a god of any kind, much less the Christian God. One could equally spin the same facts to support the Buddhist notion that desire is the source of suffering and that therefore the wise course is to follow the Eightfold Path to its elimination.

I would argue that the Argument from Desire does have value in spite of those weaknesses. Lewis was too wise to claim that in itself it proves the existence of the Christian God. Recall his language: "most probable explanation" ... "pretty good indication." But it does make sense of a common human experience and points to the likely existence of *something* compatible with Christian theism and Christian fulfillment. It is, in other words, one more aspect of human experience that makes sense if Christianity is true and presents a very difficult problem if it is not. For those who recognize in themselves the experience Lewis is describing, it can turn that experience into a signpost, into, at the very least, one more reason to follow the arrow to see where the sign might be pointing.

One conclusion might be that the argument from desire just doesn't work with a certain type of person. Perhaps some of us are just too emotionally undeveloped—or jaded—to be susceptible. But I would suggest that we make a mistake by taking such people's statements at face value. Solomon tells us that "God has set eternity in their hearts" (Eccl. 3:11). Either Scripture is wrong or the denial of transcendent desire is a smokescreen, a defense mechanism designed to protect dwarfish atheists from reality.

People who are still human are not in fact fully satisfied by the temporal and physical, however hard they try to convince themselves that they are. But you probably can't argue them out of their position. You can only try to arouse the desire, to fan it to the point where they cannot ignore it any more. And the best way to do that might be to talk about the foretastes of fulfillment we have already been granted in Christ, or just to live a life of transcendent openness to Joy before them. If you can get them to read Thomas Traherne's *Five Centuries of Meditation*, it wouldn't hurt.

> Things unknown have a secret influence on the soul, and like the center of the earth unseen violently attract it. We love we know not what, and therefore everything allures us.... Do you not feel yourself drawn by the expectation of some Great Thing? ... You never enjoy the world aright till you see how a [grain of] sand exhibiteth the wisdom and power of God.... You never enjoy the world aright till the sea itself floweth in your veins, till you are clothed with the heavens and crowned with the stars. ... Infinite wants satisfied produce infinite joys.... You must want like a God that you may be satisfied like God. Were you not made in his image? (Witherspoon and Warnke 694-8)

Lewis learned the argument from desire from Augustine's Trinity-shaped vacuum and his heart that was "restless until it rest in Thee," as developed by Traherne, George Herbert, and George MacDonald. The argument will have a certain logical cogency for those in whose hearts Desire has been sufficiently aroused. The best service those earlier writers—and Lewis himself— may do for us is to fan that flame. In it, let us burn.

CONCLUSION

Why do we need apologetics? We live in a world filled with people who think like Trumpkin: "I have no use for magic lions which are talking lions and don't talk, and friendly lions though they don't do us any good, and whopping big lions though nobody can see them" (*PC* 156). The only cure for that attitude was for Trumpkin actually to meet Aslan. Well, we are all of us constitutionally unbelieving Narnian dwarfs. "'You see,' said Aslan. 'They will not let us help them. They have chosen cunning instead of belief. Their prison is only in their own minds, yet they are in that prison; and are so afraid of being taken in that they cannot be taken out'" (*TLB* 185-6).

Only the Holy Spirit can take us out of ourselves, out of those internal prisons, to the point that we non-believers can hear the evidence for Christ and respond to it with faith. But the Spirit wants us as believers to be ready and able to present that evidence when He does so. Lewis's friend Austin Farrer put it well: "Though argument does not create conviction, the lack of it destroys belief. What seems to be proved may not be embraced; but what no one shows the ability to defend is quickly abandoned. Rational argument does not create belief, but it maintains a climate in which belief can flourish" (Farrer 26).

Lewis, in other words, well understood that the goal of apologetics is not just to win arguments. It must be what he allowed to Sherwood Eliot Wirt was the goal of all his writing: "to bring about an encounter of the reader with Jesus Christ," the kind encounter Lewis described so well: "There comes a moment when people who have been dabbling in religion ("Man's search for God") suddenly draw back. Supposing we really found him? We never meant it to come to that! Worse still, supposing he found us?" (M 96-7). The purpose of apologetics then is to help people channel the shock of that encounter into a serious consideration of the claims of Christ. It is to ensure that this encounter is with the Christ of history and not a counterfeit, that it is an encounter of the whole person with that Christ, and that the faith we hope these people will put in Him will be a rational and well-considered and well-grounded faith. It is to help believers whose faith is more fragmented and superficial grow into that rational and well-considered and well-grounded faith so that they may be preserved in it. It is to remind them in their inevitable moments of doubt that faith is "the art of holding onto things your reason has once accepted, in spite of your changing moods" (MC 123).

The goal is not just to win arguments. It matters little that we persuade people that theism is true in the abstract unless this enables them to meet God. Lewis reminds us, "We trust not because 'a God' exists, but because *this* God exists" ("Obstinacy" 25). We want to get people to the place where "what would, a moment before, have been variations in opinion, now become variations in your personal attitude to a Person. You are no longer faced [simply] with an argument which demands your assent, but with a Person who demands your confidence" ("Obstinacy" 26). For if indeed they can be brought to see the glory of God in the face of Jesus Christ, they will be ready to say with Orual, "You are yourself the answer. Before your face questions die away" (TWHF 308).

CHAPTER 12

Eschatology
The Second Coming, Heaven, and Hell

> *It was the Unicorn who summed up what everyone was feeling. He stamped his right forehoof on the ground and neighed, and then cried: "I have come home at last! This is my real country! I belong here. This is the land I have been looking for all my life, though I never knew it till now. The reason why we loved the old Narnia is that is sometimes looked a little like this. Bree-heee-hee! Come further up, come further in!"* (TLB 213)

Eschatology (from the Greek, *eschatos*, "last") is the doctrine of "last things." It looks forward to the consummation of the history of salvation when this age gives way to the age to come, when time gives way to eternity, when Christ, as He promised, returns for His own. It has two foci: *Personal Eschatology* is concerned with the future of the individual soul, its personal immortality, bodily resurrection, and final destination in the New Earth or Hell. *General Eschatology* deals with the future of the world, its ultimate judgment, redemption, and recreation, and how the events of Christ's return will play out at the end of history in fulfillment of biblical prophecy.

Lewis was focused mainly on personal eschatology; he speaks of general eschatology only in the most general terms. He will give us no guidance, for example, on whether we should be pre-, a-, or post-millennial, or on whether the rapture will be pre-, mid-, or post-tribulational. There is a good reason for this limitation: Lewis was all about "mere" Christianity, the consensus of the great Tradition common to all historic Christians. There has been little consensus across the communions on either the millennium or the rapture, which is not surprising given that Christ Himself told us very plainly that no one can know the day or the hour of His return (Mark 13:32) and that it is not for us to know the times and epochs which the Father has fixed by His own authority (Acts 1:7). It is not that enquiry into such things is useless, but Lewis was perhaps wise to stick with the consensus expressed in the Creeds: that Jesus will come again in power and glory to judge the quick and the dead.

Lewis has a great deal though to say about personal eschatology, the quest for Aslan's Country. Thus, though he may be weak on the details of biblical prophecy, his eschatology has the virtue of being focused on the ultimate goal to which all of God's work for our salvation tends, our complete redemption from sin and unimpeded union with Christ in the age to come. In that sense Lewis's theology as a whole, like that of the Bible itself, may properly be called "eschatological." It is, in other words, *teleological*: That is, it sees history not as a random series of unconnected events but as being guided by God toward a definite goal which defines the meaning of each thing that happens and lets us see the whole series as a *plot*, a meaningful story with a dramatic structure that is a satisfying unity. How does Lewis work this out?

GENERAL ESCHATOLOGY

Lewis's statements about general eschatology basically boil down to two affirmations: first, an explanation of why Christians believe in the Second Coming of Christ as presented by the Creeds, and second, an explanation of why "mere" Christianity does not commit itself to much more than that.

We believe in the Second Coming of course because Christ promised it and the Bible teaches it. Modern people, however, are hindered from giving this promise the same place in their thinking that the early Christians gave it. The sheer amount of time that has passed since the New Testament period with no apparent interruption to the natural unfolding of history is a stumbling block that the Apostles actually anticipated. "In the last days, mockers will come . . . saying, 'Where is the promise of His coming? For ever since the fathers fell asleep, all continues as it was from the beginning of creation'" (2 Pet. 3:3-4). This feeling is intensified for our contemporaries by the scientific world view, which understands everything as the result of strict cause and effect in a closed system. Even many Christians who are committed to the theoretical possibility of miracles, isolated interferences with the normal outplaying of natural cause and effect by supernatural power, have difficulty imagining a more radical disruption of the whole system than we have ever experienced, leading to the replacement of time and indeed of nature as we have known them by something else: a new Heaven and a new earth.

Lewis understood the impact of modernity on our view of time and worked to counteract it by pointing out that the notion that makes it hard for the Second

Coming to find a place in our minds, that of the world slowly evolving toward perfection, "is a myth, not a generalization from experience" ("World's Last Night" 104). The big picture of how the world works presented by naturalistic evolution—not the process of natural selection as such but the exclusion of any other causes, granting it a feeling of inevitability—is not itself a scientific conclusion. "Natural selection is a process that works in certain ways with certain limited effects" is a scientific observation of nature. "Therefore, nothing else can ever happen" is not. It is a philosophical presupposition brought to the data, not a conclusion drawn from it. And the picture of the world that results from confusing the philosophy with the science has the emotional impact precisely of a myth, that is, a story we use to explain the world to ourselves.

Lewis does not assume, as we have seen, that all myths are false. But the truth of a myth must be determined by experience, that is, by observation of the world. The Christian story is true because Christ rose from the dead in history and was observed by the original eyewitnesses (see the excursus on the Trilemma above). The secular evolutionary story, on the other hand, has no such testimony to depend on. It is philosophy masquerading as science because "Nothing else can ever happen" is by definition not an observable event that science could study if it wanted to. Therefore, naturalistic evolution is a myth that comes to us cloaked in the assumed authority of science. Lewis aids our ability to have faith in the Second Coming by explaining this, thereby giving us permission not to be browbeaten by the confusion between science and philosophy that the modern world has accepted without question.

Lewis concludes then that the Creedal expectation of the Second Coming not only can be believed, but should be. The doctrine of Christ's return then should not be rejected because it conflicts with our modern world view (or mythology), but rather "for that very reason to be the more valued and made more frequently the subject of meditation" ("World's Last Night" 106). If we are justified in believing the Christian claims about Jesus as developed above, then we are justified in trusting His promise to return in power and glory to judge the quick and the dead and to usher in a kingdom that will have no end. And because this faith cuts against the grain of the modernist mythology, we need not only to believe it but to value it and meditate on it; otherwise the hope for the future it gives us will slip from our grasp and we will find ourselves living as if we did not believe it at all.

Lewis then affirms the creedal hope about Christ's promised return. He also limits himself to it. His summary of the consensus that all faithful historic Christians have reached about that promise is lucid, succinct, and accurate: Christ's own teaching about His return can be clearly summarized in three simple statements: "(1) That he will certainly return. (2) That we cannot possibly find out when. (3) And that therefore we must always be ready for him" ("World's Last Night" 107).

That second proposition is reported as accurately and faithfully as the rest. It is not for us to know the times and epochs (Acts 1:7); we cannot know the day or the hour (Mark 13:32). It does not follow that we should make no effort to learn what Christ's return will be like or to discern the signs of the times from the many details we are given in prophecies about the end. (*Full disclosure:* I am personally a classical [non-dispensational] pre-millennialist and a post-tribulationalist—but these are only opinions, not dogmas for me. I would go to the stake for the deity of Christ or the Gospel of Grace, but not for my millennial chart.) It does follow that we should make such efforts rather tentatively, with a certain willingness to be surprised. After all, nobody in the First Century got the First Coming completely right. Nobody was expecting a suffering Messiah, nor a lengthy parenthesis that would make His coming a two-stage event. It was only in hindsight, only after the Resurrection, that the congruence of Christ's career with messianic prophecy could be fully discerned. What makes us think we will do any better with the Second Coming?

Lewis's humility with regards to general eschatology is then a good example for us to follow, a useful corrective to a lot of Evangelical eschatological hubris. But he might have actually had a bit too much of that humility. He claimed, "We do not know the play. We do not even know whether we are in Act I or Act V" ("World's Last Night" 105). But we do know the play. Salvation history is a story with a plot, and we know how it ends. If we want to use the analogy of a five-act play, we could say that act one is the creation and fall of man, act two the Old Testament age, and act three the crisis events of Christ's first Coming, His incarnation, virgin birth, life, death, resurrection, and ascension. Act four could be the age of the church, and act five the world to come. That is just a rough sketch. People have divided the story into two parts, three, or seven. Arguing over those schemas misses the point. The point is that we do know something about the play, and we know who we are and what we are to be about precisely by knowing our place in its plot. we are in act four, faithfully fulfilling the Great Commission and waiting for our Lord's return so that He may find us faithful when He appears. Lewis certainly knew that much, and should have encouraged us to think we can know it too. He misspoke in the passage quoted in this paragraph. But his three-point summary of general eschatology (He is coming; we can't know when; we must be ready) is simply spot on.

PERSONAL ESCHATOLOGY: THE GREAT DIVORCE

When it comes to Lewis's view of personal eschatology, the overriding emphasis is one we could express with one of his book titles: *The Great Divorce*. As he explains in the preface, that title is a response to Blake's "Marriage of Heaven and Hell" and the general tendency it represents to deny that reality ever "presents us with an absolutely unavoidable 'either-or'" (5). Rather, Lewis echoes the biblical motif that "It is appointed unto men once to die, and after that the judgment" (Heb. 9:27). *The Great Divorce* is ambiguous about whether the choice can be made after death. George MacDonald's spirit replies to that question, "Ye were not brought here to study such curiosities." But Lewis is always clear that the great business of life is to choose between God and anything else, with eternal consequences depending on that choice. MacDonald continues, "What concerns you is the nature of the choice itself: and that ye can watch them making" (69). Lewis's mind is never far from two ideas: the inescapability of the Choice, and how much it matters.

Ultimately what we are choosing is either God or an idol. But while that choice may be made in a moment of spiritual crisis, as in many Evangelical paradigms, it may for Lewis also be made slowly and unaware throughout our lives, and we may not even realize what we have chosen until the end. Here is how the Narnians face their Day of Judgment in *The Last Battle*:

> As they came right up to Aslan, one or other of two things happened to each of them. They all looked straight in his face. . . . And when some looked, the expression of their faces changed terribly—it was fear and hatred. . . . All the creatures who looked at Aslan in that way swerved to their right, his left, and disappeared into his huge black shadow. . . . The children never saw them again. . . . But the others looked in the face of Aslan and loved him. . . . And all these came in at the Door, on Aslan's right. (*TLB* 192-3)

One is reminded of Jesus' language about the sheep and the goats (Mat. 25:31-46). There are but two paths, two destinations, and there is a final and irrevocable separation between them. How one relates to Jesus (or Aslan) is the final determination of which path one is on, sometimes not finally revealed until the end. One either ends up in Aslan's Country or in the Shadow.

Evangelicals tend to be conversionists; that is, they expect conversion to be a very conscious decision, to involve a crisis experience when the sinner turns overtly and consciously from sin to Christ as the outcome of the process of conviction and calling. While Evangelicals would not insist that a stereotyped conversion experience is necessary to salvation, the expectation of something very like one tends to be their default setting. Lewis did not deny the role of such a conversion. Indeed, he seems to have had at least two such moments in his own journey to faith, one very definite one when he "gave in," laid down his arms and surrendered and "admitted that God was God" and became a theist, and another more subtle one when he realized after a trip to the zoo that he now believed that Jesus was the Son of God (*SbJ* 228, 237). But he put more emphasis on the smaller cumulative decisions that may add up to those larger changes that define a life trajectory.

> Every time you make a choice you are turning the central part of you, the part of you that chooses, into something a little different from what it was before.... All your life long you are slowly turning this central thing into a heavenly creature or into a hellish creature.... Each of us, at each moment, is progressing to the one state or the other. (*MC* 87)

We noted the problems with this passage in the chapter on the atonement. One does not, indeed cannot, "turn" oneself into a heavenly creature; only the grace of God can do that. And one does not need to change oneself into a hellish one; we are already on that trajectory at birth unless the grace of God intervenes. But Lewis is correct to note that "each of us, at each moment, is progressing to the one state or the other," and that the choices we make flow from and confirm us in one trajectory or the other. He is therefore right to notice how significant those choices, even the small ones, are. The fruit of them will indeed be the experience either of Heaven or Hell. Perhaps someone's sins—a hot temper or jealously or lust—are getting very gradually worse, so gradually that the change in seventy years would not be very noticeable. "But it might be absolute Hell in a million years: in fact, if Christianity is true, Hell is the precisely correct technical term for what it would be" (*MC* 73). Hell, in other words, is not just an arbitrary judgment on our sins; it is the revelation of what they are in their essence, what they will become and make of us if unchecked by grace.

Lewis labors long and hard to make sure his readers understand that there is an unavoidable fork in the road of life, that we have to choose one path or the other, that we do so choose whether we realize it or not, and, finally, how cosmic the stakes of those choices are. He wants us to realize that the destiny of individual human beings is terribly important, much more so than the fate of even a nation or a civilization:

> If individuals live only seventy years, then a state or a nation or a civilization, which may last for a thousand years, is more important than an individual. But if Christianity is true, then the individual is not only more important but incomparably more important, for he is everlasting, and the life of a state or a civilization, compared with his, is only a moment. (*MC* 73)

Our very humanity is one of the things at stake: in Heaven you will be more truly human than you ever could be on earth, and in Hell you are essentially excluded from humanity (*PoP* 113). But even greater than that, looming over all other concerns, is the relationship we human beings will have—or not have—with God. Lewis explains what he had portrayed in the passage from *The Last Battle* we quoted above, where the Narnians meet Aslan: "In the end that Face which is the delight or the terror of the universe must be turned upon each of us either with one expression or the other, either conferring glory inexpressible or inflicting shame that can never be cured" ("Weight of Glory" 38). The miserific or the beatific vision: the difference is too great to be put into words, but Lewis comes as close as perhaps as we can:

> In some sense as dark to the intellect as it is unendurable to the feelings, we can be both banished from the presence of Him who is present everywhere and erased from the knowledge of Him who knows all. We can be left utterly and absolutely outside—repelled, exiled, estranged, finally and unspeakably ignored. ("Weight of Glory" 41)

Or we can be finally and forever welcomed home. This is a "great divorce," a great separation or distinction, indeed!

Lewis wants us to understand the great parting of the ways that lies ahead in eternity, but he also wants us to grasp the way in which this vision reaches back to illuminate our life in time. Not only is this life the arena in which such great matters will be decided, but our daily lives are also filled with meaning by that vision here and now. Lewis thought that earth, if preferred to Heaven, would be eventually discovered to have been only part of Hell all along; while if it were put second to Heaven it would eventually be discovered to have always been the vestibule of Heaven itself (*GD* 7). Heaven—or Hell—does not have to wait for eternity. Foretastes of them begin already in this world. Like Jewel the Unicorn, when we reach Aslan's Country (or the other place), we will realize that the reason we loved—or hated—the old Narnia is that sometimes it reminded us of this (*TLB* 213).

Let us then take a look at Lewis's portraits of the great alternatives of both Hell and of Heaven—but first, we must clear out of the way the problematic question of Purgatory.

PURGATORY

Lewis scandalized his fellow Protestants by saying that he thought Purgatory probably existed, though he did not think it proper to hold it as a dogma. He wrote to a Mr. Allcock on 24 March 1955 that he thought Purgatory to be one of those doctrines held by the church of Rome which he thought likely to be true; "but which, since it is not clearly stated in Scripture nor included in the early creeds, I do not think they have any warrant for enforcing" (*L* 3:588). If it is in neither Scripture nor the early creeds, why believe in it?

The problem is that obviously sin cannot enter into Heaven, but most of us die with the process of sanctification incomplete; that is, we do not die sinless. How then are we to enter into Christ's direct presence in Heaven as we are? According to Scripture, the experience of seeing Christ face to face will itself, in its profundity, complete the process of sanctification, purging any remaining sin and making us fit for Heaven immediately. The promise is that "when He appears, we shall be like Him, because we shall see Him just as He is" (1 Jn. 3:2). If you miss this promise, and do not see with complete clarity that it is *Christ's* righteousness, not our own, which gains us entry to Heaven, then it makes sense to posit a place or time of final cleansing after death before entrance into Heaven. More consistent Protestants object to the idea of Purgatory not only because it is not taught in Scripture but because it tends to put focus back on the attainments of righteousness by the believer himself, rather than justification as a free gift granted only to faith in Christ (Rom. 3:24, etc.).

One of Lewis's theological weaknesses, as we have seen, is that while he often depicts well the biblical doctrine of salvation by grace alone through faith alone in Christ alone, he did not fully grasp the absolute necessity of grace alone as a soteriological principle. Toying with the idea of Purgatory is symptomatic of that failing. But in Lewis's defense, we should realize that his speculative version of Purgatory was very different from the traditional Catholic notion of an extended place of punishment and purgation. It was in fact much closer to the biblical picture we gave above. He speculated, "I hope that when the tooth of life is drawn and I am 'coming round,' a voice will say, 'Rinse your mouth out with this.' *This* will be Purgatory" (*LtM* 109). It was a mistake to call this moment Purgatory, but, in fairness, Lewis's idea was actually not as problematic either soteriologically or eschatologically as the Roman Catholic doctrine it unfortunately conjures up.

HELL

If then the great business of this life is to choose the path leading either to Heaven or to Hell, it remains to discover what we can know about these two destinations. We will consider Lewis's perspectives on Hell first and save the best for last.

Consistent with Lewis's emphasis on The Great Divorce is his view that people are in Hell because that is what they have chosen. They might not have known they were choosing it; they might have thought they were choosing something else; but Hell is precisely the grand summation of all that they have chosen. As the George MacDonald character in *The Great Divorce* explains, there are finally only two kinds of people in the world: "those who say to God 'Thy will be done,' and those to whom God says, in the end, '*Thy* will be done.' All that are in Hell choose it" (*GD* 72). They probably did not say to themselves, "I think I shall opt for eternal punishment." But, like Claudius in Hamlet, who wants to repent of murder and receive God's forgiveness but cannot bring himself to give up the effects for which he did the murder, the crown, his own ambition, or the queen, they choose other things which they will not un-choose and which do in fact entail damnation. To choose self over God is in fact to choose Hell, as Lewis explains:

> Be sure there is something inside you which, unless it is altered, will put it out of God's power to prevent you from being eternally miserable. While that something remains there can be no Heaven for you, just as there can be no sweet smells for a man with a cold in the nose, and no music for a man who is deaf. It's not a question of God "sending" us to Hell. In each of us there is something growing up which will of itself *be Hell* unless it is nipped in the bud. ("The Trouble with X" 154-5)

What is this hellish thing growing up inside us? The biblical designation for it is sin, the essence of which is rebellion against God. If Heaven is the enjoyment of God's presence and His favor, then the refusal of God's will, the preference of our own—rebellion, sin—clearly excludes us from that enjoyment by its own nature. Hell then really is God saying, after all His efforts to reclaim us have failed, "Alright, fine, *thy* will be done." He will not redeem us by simply overriding our wills. That is why Lewis says, "I willingly believe that the damned are, in one sense, successful rebels to the end; that the doors of Hell are locked on the *inside*" (*PoP* 115). There comes a point where the will's choice of itself over God is fixed and irrevocable, and that state is Hell. That is why the faces in Hell are "all fixed faces, full not of possibilities but of impossibilities" (*GD* 25).

The spirit of George MacDonald notes that "the whole difficulty of understanding Hell is that the thing to be understood is so nearly nothing" (*GD* 75). This does not mean that choosing Hell is inconsequential or anything less than a colossal tragedy. Behind MacDonald's statement, no doubt, lies Augustine's doctrine of evil as a privation of the good: Hell is the good of existence trying to return to nothingness and nearly succeeding. Also lurking in the background is Augustine's definition of sin as being *incurvatus in se*, "turned in upon oneself," rather than oriented outward to God. God is the Creator and Source of good, that is, of reality. To reject Him and turn inside oneself in one's search for the good is to turn toward nothingness, to turn away from a larger world. That is what MacDonald means when he later says,

> A damned soul is nearly nothing: it is shrunk, shut up in itself. Good beats upon the damned incessantly as sound waves beat on the ears of the deaf, but they cannot receive it. Their fists are clenched, their teeth are clenched, their eyes fast shut. First they will not, in the end they cannot, open their hands for gifts, or their mouths for food, or their eyes to see. (*GD* 123)

Surrounded by God's loving presence (for none can escape it), such people are able to experience it only as judgment. The most chilling picture of Hell may then be the Narnian Dwarfs, in Aslan's country but cut off from the enlarging vistas of "further up and further in" because they are convinced that they are still in the dirty Stable. Offered violets, they reject them as filth and straw. "You see," said Aslan. "They will not let us help them. They have chosen cunning instead of belief. Their prison is only in their own minds, yet they are in that prison; and are so afraid of being taken in that they cannot be taken out" (*TLB* 185-6). A more profound picture of Augustine's phrase could hardly be imagined. These dwarfs are *incurvatus in se* indeed.

The notion of Hell as self-inflicted and the idea of earthly life as a preparation either for Hell or for Heaven are combined in *Till We Have Faces* in the character of Orual as she hardens herself against her brief vision of Psyche's palace, choosing ironically to walk by unbelief rather than by sight. Fortunately she realizes her mistake at the end; but until then her life is a systematic attempt to turn herself into one of those lost dwarfs. "The nearest thing we have to a defence against [the gods]," she says, "is to be very wide awake and sober and hard at work, to hear no music, never to look at earth or sky, and (above all) to love no one" (*TWHF* 81). Looking back on her life, she explains, "I locked Orual up or laid her asleep as best I could somewhere deep down inside me; she lay curled there. It was like being with child, but reversed; the thing I carried in me grew slowly smaller and less alive" (*TWHF* 226). It is as if she had been reading the analysis in *The Four Loves*: "The only place outside of Heaven where you can be perfectly safe from all the dangers and perturbations of love is Hell" (*FL* 169). Augustine's doctrines of evil as privation and of sin as being *incurvatus in se* could not be pictured more brilliantly, not just as abstract ideas, but here as life processes leading to a damnation which is their natural fruition.

The hardest thing to accept about the traditional Christian doctrine of eternal punishment is perhaps its justice. How, skeptics ask, can *unending* punishment be just, no matter what the crime? Lewis takes this problem seriously and attacks it from multiple directions. First, as we have seen, he presents Hell as self-inflicted, not as the arbitrary imposition of punishment by a vengeful Deity so much as the natural fruition of clinging to the choice of allegiance to self. Then he also tries to spin Hell as actually merciful. From Uncle Andrew to the dwarfs to Orual, he consistently pictures God as giving people all the mercy they are able to receive. God actually wants to prevent us from experiencing the kind of damnation Milton's Satan undergoes:

> Which way I fly is Hell; myself am Hell;
> And in the lowest deep a lower deep
> Still threat'ning to devour me opens wide
> To which the Hell I suffer seems a Heav'n. (*PL* IV:75-78)

To protect us from such a fate, Lewis thinks God has created Hell as a limit below which we cannot sink. "The walls of the black hole are the tourniquet on the wound through which the lost soul would bleed to a death she never reached. It is the Landlord's last service to those who will let him do nothing better for them" (*PR* 181). Or, as Lewis describes it poetically,

> God in His mercy made
> The fixed pains of Hell.
> That misery might be stayed.
> God in His mercy made
> Eternal bounds and bade
> Its waves no longer swell.
> God in His mercy made
> The fixed pains of Hell. ("Divine Justice," *Ps* 98)

There comes a point, we said above, at which the soul's rejection of God for self becomes fixed. Actually, according to the Bible, that point has already been reached by all of us apart from God's grace. "A natural man does not accept the things of the Spirit of God" (1 Cor. 2:14); we are not mortally ill but already spiritually "dead in our trespasses and sins" (Eph. 2:1) until we are made alive by Christ (2:5). Does God simply override our wills in changing this situation? No; He *enables* them to choose what otherwise they could not; in removing our stony hearts He gives us a new nature which now naturally desires what before it would have rejected. This involves a change of one's nature that enables one to make a choice in favor of God consistent with that new nature.

How God does so is a great mystery, as we saw in the chapter on the atonement. Lewis did not always make this distinction as carefully as he might have. What he should have said was that there comes a point at which the natural fixedness of our wills in sin is confirmed and the possibility of their rescue from themselves by grace is removed. However we define it, though, he was right to think that such a moment can come, that Hell is its result, and that understanding this is helpful in seeing the rightness of the classical doctrine. He expresses it with one of his classically helpful analogies:

> I believe that if a million chances were likely to do good, they would be given. But a master knows, when boys and parents do not, that it is really useless to send a boy in for a certain examination again. Finality must come sometime, and it does not require a very robust faith to believe that omniscience knows when. (*PoP* 112)

People who object to the doctrine of eternal punishment are understandably horrified by it. But in their objection, they often do not realize what they are asking. What would they have God do with those who persist in their rebellion? Lewis asks, pertinently, "Can you really desire that such a man, remaining what he is... should be confirmed forever in his present happiness—should continue, for all eternity, to be perfectly convinced that the laugh is on his side?" (*PoP* 109). The MacDonald character explains that what "lurks behind" the feeling that the damnation of one soul would render Heaven imperfect is "the demand of the loveless and the self-imprisoned that they should be allowed to blackmail the universe" (*GD* 120). For Lewis, the meaning of human choice is the bottom line. If choice is to be significant, it must be allowed to be significant. Lewis was always very clear about that. Those who choose against submission to God must be allowed to have what they have chosen, and to discover that "length of days with an evil heart is only length of misery" (*TMN* 208).

Lewis then was not a universalist. He believed that there is a Hell and that some human beings will spend eternity in it. He wisely upholds biblical teaching on Hell's existence, but does not speculate too much about what it is actually like (beyond the "suppositions" about the misanthropic ghost town in *The Great Divorce*). Lewis not only defends the justice of Hell, but he argues that Hell is ironically an expression of God's mercy. In many contexts he presents it as the only form of mercy that stubborn sinners (Uncle Andrew, the Narnian Dwarfs, etc.) are able to accept. This is perhaps one of his most useful insights. By and large, Lewis sticks to what Scripture demands and refrains from going beyond it. He leaves the mystery of the eternal fate of the wicked intact while portraying it convincingly as the natural fruition of their rejection of God as their supreme Good.

HEAVEN

If Lewis writes much about Hell, it is because it is a real possibility for human destiny, a place to which human beings can go—and they mustn't. But he is far more interested in Heaven. Indeed, he notes, "We know much more about Heaven than Hell, for Heaven is the home of humanity . . . : but Hell was not made for men" (*PoP* 115). Hell was prepared for the Devil and his angels. Human beings have been enticed there, but it was never meant for them. To go there is to lose an essential part of what it means to be human. To go to Heaven, on the other hand, is to find the fulfillment of all that is best in human nature.

If Lewis knew that any description of Hell could be nothing more than a "supposal," he knew that the same thing is even more true of Heaven. Scripture says that the things God has prepared for those who love Him "have not entered into the heart of Man" (1 Cor. 2:9) except in so far as they have been revealed by the Spirit. Lewis took this truth seriously: all of the biblical images such as harps, crowns, and golden streets, are symbolic attempts to describe the indescribable. "People who take these symbols literally might as well think that when Christ told us to be like doves he meant that we were to lay eggs" (*MC* 121). Therefore, we must take the mountains of Aslan's Country or of the heavenly realm of *The Great Divorce* not as attempts to describe the afterlife but merely as suggestions of its majesty and splendor. As such, they are among the best hints we have outside of Scripture itself. A particularly brilliant symbolic touch is the hard-edged reality of the heavenly grass and even water in *The Great Divorce*, which convey graphically the idea that the realm of the Spirit is *more* real than that of matter.

Lewis does not carefully distinguish the "Intermediate State," the abiding of the "unclothed" soul with Christ in Heaven awaiting the Second Coming and the Resurrection, from the New Heavens and the New Earth which are actually the eternal state of the resurrected believer afterwards. He lumps it all together as "Aslan's Country," much as most popular eschatology does. But he was aware that the Christian hope includes the Resurrection of the body as an essential element. He notes that Christianity is unique among the major religions in its positive attitude toward the body and approval of matter as God's creation. It "believes that matter is good, that God Himself once took on a human body, that some kind of body is going to be given to us even in Heaven and is going to be an essential part of our happiness, our beauty, and our energy" (*MC* 91). Technically, the resurrection body is to be enjoyed on the New Earth, not in Heaven. But Lewis is right about its importance, not only to Christian eschatology but to the whole Christian conception of reality and of what humanity is.

The resurrected body will presumably be like the one Christ had after His resurrection: a "glorified" body with capacities our current model lacks. What exactly it will be like is one of those things we cannot yet quite imagine. Lewis wisely wrote to a Mr. Young on 31 Oct. 1963, "We shall know what a glorified body is when we have one ourselves" (*L* 3:1476). But Professor Kirk shows a practical appreciation for his that will appeal to any of us mortals who find ourselves advancing in years: "I think you and I, Polly, chiefly felt that we'd been unstiffened" (*TLB* 174). We know that the resurrected body will lack the frustrations, the corruption, and the mortality of the current model. But while it will be an essential element of life in Aslan's Country, it is not the chief reward that awaits us.

Heaven for Lewis is most of all the place where our heart's deepest desires, the longings, the *sensucht* of *Surprised by Joy*, will find their ultimate fulfillment in the vision of God. If we find in ourselves desires that nothing in this world can satisfy, that must mean we were made for another world (*MC* 120). The Good News is that it turns out that this in fact is so: "Joy is the serious business of Heaven" (*LtM* 93).

This is not a longing that leaves us dissatisfied with the pleasures of this world, but rather one that sanctifies them and fills them with a meaning beyond themselves. Psyche says, interestingly, that "it was when I was happiest that I longed most" (*TWHF* 74). She explains,

> Because it was so beautiful it set me longing, always longing. Somewhere else there must be more of it. Everything seemed to be saying, "Psyche come!" But I couldn't (not yet) come and I didn't know where I was to come to. It almost hurt me. I felt like a bird in a cage when the other birds of its kind are flying home. (*TWHF* 74)

Recognizing Aslan's Country as our true home does not cause us to despise earth, but to learn to value it truly. The painter ghost is told, "When you painted on earth—at least in your earlier days—it was because you caught glimpses of Heaven in the earthly landscape. The success of your painting was that it enabled others to see the glimpses too" (*GD* 80). Likewise, the old Professor Kirk explains that the old Narnia was "only a shadow or copy of the real Narnia," just as England itself is of "something in Aslan's Country." "It's all in Plato," he characteristically concludes (*TLB* 211-12). That is, the idea of this world as being the reflection or image of a greater Idea was in Plato, who sadly did not know where those true Ideas were to be found. Now the children do. The reason they had loved the old Narnia is that it reminded them of this.

Lewis had concluded that joy or longing, the central experience of his life, was meant as a signpost, and in the Christian hope of eternal life with Christ he thought he had found what the sign was pointing to. We don't just want to behold beauty, he explains, though even that is a great gift. "We want something else which can hardly be put into words—to be united with the beauty we see, to pass into it, to receive it into ourselves, to bathe in it, to become part of it" (*WoG* 42). The Christian doctrine of Heaven is precisely the fulfillment of that desire because it is a doctrine of union with Christ, the Source of all that is good, true, or beautiful. The children in Narnia understand this: it is not the fact that they won't be coming back to Narnia that makes them sad but the fact that (as they first assume) Aslan is not in their own world. "We shan't meet *you* there. And how shall we live, never meeting you?" (*VDT* 269). The spirit from the Mountains in *The Great Divorce* puts it well: "We know nothing of religion here: we think only of Christ. We know nothing of speculation. Come and see. I will bring you to Eternal Fact, the Father of all other facthood" (*GD* 44).

Heaven, then, is not just extended existence or even being reunited with lost loved ones, though it will of course involve all of that. It is union with Christ conceived as the one thing that fills Augustine's heart vacuum that keeps us restless until we rest in God. It is the fulfillment of all our longings. If the Christian doctrine of who Christ is be true, what else could it be? It is no wonder that Lewis concludes that, while at times he wonders if we do desire Heaven, "more often I find myself wondering whether, in our heart of hearts, we have ever desired anything else" (*PoP* 133).

Aslan's Country is the complete fulfillment of our human nature, of all it was meant to be. This involves our deepest longings for beauty, but it fulfills what may be deeper needs than that. Jesus had said, "Blessed are they who hunger and thirst after righteousness, for they shall be filled" (Mat. 5:6). Lewis's exposition of righteousness as being not just conformity to external rules but to the will of Christ whom we love (see chapter 9 above) then also finds its fruition here. Lewis wrote to Dom Bede Griffiths on 8 Jan. 1936, "What indeed can we imagine Heaven to be but unimpeded obedience?" (*L* 2:177). The line echoes Aristotle's discussion of *eudaemonia*, happiness, as the unimpeded pursuit of virtue. It is typical that Lewis would frame the Greek wisdom as true but incomplete. Personal obedience offered to the Lord of Glory who gave Himself for us, offered finally from a pure heart, unimpeded, is the true happiness that the Greeks stumbled toward at their best but did not know where to find. Lewis captures the freedom and the exhilaration of such a state when Aslan reassures Caspian, "You cannot want wrong things any more, now that you have died" (*TSC* 254). Peter has a similar moment on reaching Aslan's Country: "I've a feeling we've got to the country where everything is allowed" (*TLB* 172).

Three passages from *Mere Christianity* sum up Lewis's most profound meditations on the nature of the Christian's hope for consummation of his faith. Just as sin unimpeded would be Hell even if God's justice did not punish it, so holiness unimpeded—unimpeded union and fellowship with Christ—is the essence of Heaven.

It is not that God will refuse you admission to His eternal world if you have not got certain qualities of character: the point is that if people have not got at least the beginnings of those qualities inside them, then no possible external conditions could make a "Heaven" for them—that is, could make them happy with the deep, strong, unshakeable kind of happiness God intends for us. (*MC* 78)

That deep happiness precisely is unimpeded union with Christ:

If you want joy, power, peace, eternal life, you must get close to, or even into, the thing that has them. They are not a sort of prize that God could, if He chose, just hand out to anyone. They are a great fountain of energy and beauty spurting up at the very centre of reality. If you are close to it, the spray will wet you: if you are not, you will remain dry. Once a man is united to God, how could he not live forever? Once a man is separated from God, what can he do but wither and die? (*MC* 153)

Even Lewis cannot describe the results of being immersed in that Fountain; but he gives it a go:

He will make the feeblest and filthiest of us into a god or goddess, a dazzling, radiant, immortal creature pulsating all through with such energy and joy and wisdom and love as we cannot now imagine, a bright stainless mirror which reflects back to God perfectly (though of course on a smaller scale) His own boundless power and delight and goodness. (*MC* 175)

This is the Fountain to which Lewis's wife Joy turned in the last moment of her earthly life: "She said not to me but to the chaplain, 'I am at peace with God.' She smiled, but not at me. *Poi si torno all' eternal fonatana*" (*GO* 60). "Then she turned to the eternal Fountain." The quotation from Dante's *Paradiso* which ends *A Grief Observed* is the greatest reaffirmation of faith Lewis could have put as the period to that honest account of the deepest spiritual struggle.

Because that Fountain is inexhaustible, we can spend all of eternity getting more thoroughly wet by it with no thought of the experience ever getting old or tiresome. But let's give Jewel the last word on the matter as he arrives in Aslan's Country:

"I have come home at last! This is my real country! I belong here. This is the land I have been looking for all my life, though I never knew it till now. The reason why we loved the old Narnia is that is sometimes looked a little like this. Bree-heee-hee! Come further up, come further in!" (*TLB* 213)

CONCLUSION

Lewis's theology is properly and biblically eschatological, that is, teleological—or, in what has become a popular phrase, "purpose-driven." It will not help us navigate the minutiae of prophecy, but it will help us see the big picture perhaps better than any other: we are all headed to one of two great Destinations, one of which is the frustration, and the other the fulfillment, of everything we were created to be. All the beauties, joys, and gifts of this life can be taken either as signposts leading us to eternal Joy or distractions keeping us from it. Union with Christ or separation from Christ are the two poles that define those destinies. The business of theology is to sharpen our desire, to whet our appetite for the fulfilling destiny, and to help us understand life as the path that leads to it by God's grace. If that definition is true, then Lewis's description of Christ as the eternal Fountain of Joy welling up at the heart of Reality, and of eternity as a joyous romp with Aslan, "further up and further in," are among the best theological passages in all the church's doctrinal literature.

For those who are enabled to receive the truth in those passages, then, "All their life in this world and all their adventures in Narnia had only been the cover and the title page: now at last they were beginning Chapter One of the Great Story which no one on earth has ever read: which goes on forever: in which every chapter is better than the one before" (*TLB* 228).

CONCLUSION

Map of the Divine
The Theology of C.S. Lewis

"As long as you are content with walks on the beach, your glimpses are far more fun than looking at a map. But the map is going to be more use than walks on the beach if you want to get to America" (MC 136).

Though he was not a professional theologian, C. S. Lewis may have got more theology into more heads than any other writer of the Twentieth Century. I think our survey of his theology has revealed him as the "theologian of wholeness" we promised in the introduction. With the exception of a few technical points in Sanctification, Ecclesiology, and Eschatology, he covers the whole range of topics in a standard systematic theology and some more that should be there. We have tried, from a standpoint of conservative Evangelical Protestantism, to bring out his strengths and weaknesses as a guide to biblical truth. What have we discovered them to be?

First, the weaknesses: They can be summarized in one general problem that manifests itself in a few doctrinal areas. Lewis was not an exegetical theologian. He did not typically start by asking, on any doctrinal question, "what does the Bible teach about this topic?" and then try inductively to find out. Rather, he tried to discern the consensus of Christian thinking across communions and historical periods and then think through the implications of that consensus. This approach served him well in those areas where such a consensus exists: Theology proper, Christology, etc. But it set him up for some problems in other areas.

It is not, of course, that discerning the consensual tradition is a bad thing; it is indeed a necessary thing. But if the only reason we can do theology at all is because God has revealed Himself in nature, history, and Christ, and if Scripture is the final key to and authoritative statement on the meaning of that revelation, then theology has to start with and center on the exposition of the biblical Text.

Exegetical theologians should arrive at their results in the context of the historic consensus and test them against it. If they do not, they will make unnecessary mistakes and find themselves trying to reinvent the wheel. But if we do not begin and end with Scripture, we will be at a loss when the traditions disagree and may miss important truths even when they don't. It is important to do both things. Neither can be safely done without the other.

Lewis's doctrinal errors came ultimately then from insufficient serious attention to what the Bible actually says. He missed Paul's definition of inspiration as applying to the γραφη (*graphe*), the actual writings of Scripture, and so missed the doctrine of plenary verbal inspiration. The kind of "thought inspiration" Lewis substituted for the biblical doctrine does not do an adequate job of accounting for Scripture's claims about its own authority, nor of preserving that authority. Though Lewis had a high view of Scripture, especially the New Testament, it fell short of the biblical and historical position of the church on the Bible's inerrancy. The same weakness shows up in the two other major areas of concern. In soteriology, Lewis failed to give adequate attention to Paul's teaching on justification by faith and vicarious substitution. As a result, while Lewis did not deny those doctrines, and while he portrayed them well in the Stone Table of Narnia, his treatments of salvation did not give them the same central place of importance or the clear exposition that the New Testament does. Finally, with the character Emeth from *The Last Battle*, Lewis went beyond Scripture in speculating about a possible second chance for conversion after death and in leaving the door to inclusivism open in a way that Scripture does not. Fortunately, these are the only major areas in which Lewis deviates from biblical truth, and in soteriology he does not so much deny the biblical doctrines as simply fail at some points to do them justice.

On the positive side of the ledger, Lewis gives a faithful presentation of the truth of historic Christianity in the vast body of material not mentioned as exceptions above. Not only does he faithfully present it, he does so in a manner that is winsome, intelligent, and intelligible. He avoids jargon, but he does not avoid difficult questions. His usually deft use of analogy allows him to make abstruse ideas accessible without oversimplification or condescension. In this area it would be difficult to find anyone who could match him, not just in the Twentieth Century but in the entire history of the church. Only the Lord Himself—the greatest composer of parables in the history of literature—can be said to surpass Lewis here. This skill alone makes Lewis one of the most valuable theological assets we have.

In addition, there are three other reasons for valuing Lewis's contributions to theology. First is his unapologetic supernaturalism. He was blessedly free of the temptation to make the subtle compromises with the modern secular world view that even the most faithful of our Christian intelligentsia are tempted to make due to the pressure they face to maintain academic respectability in a secularist academy. (His defective doctrine of inspiration might be thought an exception to this assertion, but I hope I have shown that it had different causes.) It is not just that he defended the miraculous elements of the Christian story well but that he also shows us what it looks like for an intelligent and learned person to accept them as fully real. Just being in the presence of his mind as preserved in his writings is a bracing experience that can give us courage for the battles on this front that we still face today.

Second, Lewis was and is supremely the theologian of wholeness. All the old classic divisions, oppositions, and rivalries created within our very persons by the Fall—head versus heart, intellect versus emotion, reason versus imagination—are healed in his outlook in a more profound way than I have encountered in any other writer. You see that wholeness manifested on every page of his writings in both message and manner, with rigorous logic and rich imagination walking hand in hand, borne along by an ebullient love of life it is hard not to believe flowed from knowing the Source of life. The wholeness of Lewis's vision cannot be unrelated to its wholesomeness, if I can call it that without being cloying. Lewis was like his master Edmund Spenser in his ability to make good characters as believable as evil ones. From Hyoi's inability to understand the motivation behind earth's wars to Tinidril's innocence to Lucy's simplicity of faith to Puddleglum's dour faithfulness to the chivalry of Reepicheep and the true Narnian kings: it is hard not to believe that behind it all lies real knowledge of One who is not a tame Lion. Safe? Who said anything about safe? But He's good, I tell you!

Finally, this is a theology that is not a mere academic exercise but a theology of commitment. Lewis thought that truth matters and that it matters to the destiny of eternal human souls. The most boring of them that we meet will one day be either a horror, such as we now see only in a nightmare, or a being of such splendor that we would be tempted to worship it, and we are constantly helping each other to one or the other of those fates, whether we know it or not (*WoG* 45). Theology's job is to do that helping toward the better fate consciously, deliberately, truthfully, and well. It is rare that our academic professional theologians allow themselves to say it so starkly or are able to say it so beautifully. But as we have noticed before, Lewis knew that truth matters, and that it matters like this:

> Here is a door, behind which, according to some people, the secret of the universe is waiting for you. Either that's true, or it isn't. And if it isn't, then what the door really conceals is simply the greatest fraud, the most colossal "sell" on record. Isn't it obviously the job of every man (that is a man and not a rabbit) to try to find out which, and then to devote his full energies either to serving this tremendous secret or to exposing and destroying this gigantic humbug? ("Man or Rabbit" 111-12)

Lewis was weak in certain critical areas where our current Evangelical theologians are strong, or stronger, at least. But we are also horribly weak in areas where Lewis was mighty. If we could add his strengths to ours, that is, add it to our practice of theology and the Christian life, not just admire it ... well, then we might be better able to serve the Truth in a manner worthy of its Source.

C. S. Lewis devoted his full energies to serving the tremendous Secret. May we be granted the grace to do the same, through Jesus Christ our Lord.

Amen.

BIBLIOGRAPHY

Abbott, Edwin A. *Flatland: A Romance of Many Dimensions.* 1884. Rpt. N.Y.: Dover, 1992.

Aeschliman, Michael D. *The Restitution of Man: C. S. Lewis and the Case against Scientism.* Grand Rapids: Eerdmans, 1983; rpt. 1998.

Bagget, David, Gary R. Habermas, and Jerry Walls, editors, *C. S. Lewis as Philosopher: Truth, Goodness, and Beauty.* Downers Grove, Il.: InterVarsity Press, 2008.

Barfield, Owen. *Owen Barfield on C. S. Lewis.* ed. G. B. Tennyson. Middletown, Ct.: Wesleyan Univ. Pr., 1989.

Bassham, Gregory, ed. *C. S. Lewis's Apologetics: Pro and Con.* Leiden: Brill/Rodopi, 2015.

Bauckham, Richard. *Jesus and the Eyewitnesses: The Gospels as Eyewitness Testimony.* Grand Rapids: Eerdmans, & Cambridge: Cambridge Univ. Pr., 2006.

Bauman, Michael. *Pilgrim Theology: Taking the Path of Theological Discovery.* Grand Rapids: Zondervan, 1992.

Berkhof, Louis. *Systematic Theology.* 4th revised & enlarged ed. Grand Rapids: Eerdmans, 1939.

Berkouwer, G. C. *Man: The Image of God.* Studies in Dogmatics, vol. 8. Grand Rapids: Eerdmans, 1962.

Beversluis, John. *C. S. Lewis and the Search for Rational Religion.* Grand Rapids: Eerdmans, 1985.

----------. *C. S. Lewis and the Search for Rational Religion*, revised & updated. Amherst, N. Y.: Prometheus Books, 2007.

Blamires, Harry. *The Christian Mind.* London: S.P.C.K., 1963

----------. ."Teaching the Universal Truth: C. S. Lewis among the Intellectuals." David Mills, ed., *The Pilgrim's Guide: C. S. Lewis and the Art of Witness.* Grand Rapids: Eerdmans, 1998: 15-26.

Brazier, P. H. *C. S. Lewis: Revelation, Conversion, and Apologetics.* Vol. 1 of *C. S. Lewis: Revelation and the Christ.* Eugene, Or.: Pickwick, 2012.

----------. *The Christ of a Religious Economy.* Vol. 3 of *C. S. Lewis: Revelation and the Christ.* Eugene, Or.: Pickwick, 2012.

----------. *The Work of Christ Revealed.* Vol. 2 of *C. S. Lewis: Revelation and the Christ.* Eugene, Or.: Pickwick, 2012.

Brown, Devin. *Inside Narnia: A Guide to Exploring* The Lion, The Witch, and the Wardrobe. Grand Rapids: Baker, 2005.

----------. *Inside Prince Caspian: A Guide To Exploring* Prince Caspian. Grand Rapids: Baker, 2008.

----------. *A Live Observed: A Spiritual Biography of C. S, Lewis.* Grand Rapids: Brazos, 2013.

Burson, Scott R. & Jerry L. Walls. *C. S. Lewis and Francis Schaeffer: Lessons for a New Century from the Most Influential Apologists of our Time.* Downers Grove, IL: IVP, 1998.

Calvin, John. *Institutes of the Christian Religion.* Trans. Henry Beveridge. 2 vols. Grand Rapids: Eerdmans, 1975.

Carnell, Corbin Scott. *Bright Shadow of Reality: C. S. Lewis and the Feeling Intellect.* Grand Rapids: Eerdmans, 1974.

Carpenter, Humphrey. *The Inklings.* Boston: Houghton Mifflin, 1979.

----------. *Tolkien: The Authorized Biography.* Boston: Houghton Mifflin, 1977.

Chan, Simon. "Father Knows Best: Language of God's Fatherhood Communicates Something Essential about His Nature." *Christianity Today,* July August 2013:48-51.

Chesterton, G. K. *The Everlasting Man.* NY: Dodd, Mead, and Company, 1925.

----------. *Orthodoxy.* Garden City, N.Y.: Doubleday, 1959.

Christensen, Michael J. *C. S. Lewis on Scripture.* Waco: Word, 1979.

Christopher, Joe R. *C. S. Lewis.* Twayne's English Authors Series. Boston: G. K. Hall, 1987.

Clark, David G. *C. S. Lewis: A Guide to his Theology.* Oxford: Blackwell Publishing, 2007.

Como, James. *Branches to Heaven: The Geniuses of C. S. Lewis*. Dallas: Spence Publishing Co., 1998.

Cunningham, Richard B. *C. S. Lewis: Defender of the Faith*. Philadelphia: Westminster Pr., 1967.

Davis, Stephen T. "The Mad/Bad/God Trilemma: A Reply to Daniel Howard-Snyder." *Faith and Philosophy* 21:4 (Oct. 2004): 480-92.

Downing, David C. *The Most Reluctant Convert: C. S. Lewis's Journey to Faith*. Downers Grove, IL: InterVarsity Press, 2002.

──────. *Planets in Peril: A Critical Study of C. S. Lewis's Ransom Trilogy*. Amherst: Univ. of Mass. Pr., 1992.

Duriez, Colin. *A Field Guide to Narnia*. Downers Grove, IL: InterVarsity Pr., 2004.

Edwards, Bruce L., Jr., ed. *C. S. Lewis: Life, Works, and Legacy*, 4 vols. London: Praeger, 2007.

──────. *Further Up and Further In: Understanding C. S. Lewis's* The Lion, the Witch, and the Wardrobe. Nashville: Broadman, 2005.

──────. *A Rhetoric of Reading: C. S. Lewis's Defense of Western Literacy*. Provo, Utah: Center for the Study of Christian Values in Literature, College of Humanities, Brigham Young University, 1986.

──────, ed. *The Taste of the Pineapple: Essays on C. S. Lewis as Reader, Critic, and Imaginative Writer*. Bowling Green, OH: Bowling Green State Univ. Pr., 1988.

──────. "A Thoroughly Converted Man: C. S. Lewis in the Public Square." In David Mills, ed., *The Pilgrim's Guide: C. S. Lewis and the Art of Witness*. Grand Rapids: Eerdmans, 1998: 27-39.

Erickson, Millard J. *Christian Theology*, 2nd ed. Grand Rapids: Baker, 1988.

Farrer. Austin. "The Christian Apologist." *Light on C. S. Lewis*, ed. Jocelyn Gibb. NY: Harcourt, Brace, & World, 1965: 23-43.

Filmer, Kath. *The Fiction of C. S. Lewis: Mask and Mirror*. N.Y.: St. Martin's Pr., 1993.

Ford, Paul F. *Companion to Narnia: A Complete Guide to the themes, Characters, and Events of C. S. Lewis's Enchanting Imaginary World*. N. Y.: Collier books, 1986.

Gibb, Jocelyn, ed. *Light on C. S. Lewis*. NY: Harcourt, Brace, & World, 1965.

Gilbert, Douglas & C. S. Kilby. *C. S. Lewis: Images of his World*. Grand Rapids: Eerdmans, 1973.

Glaspey, Terry W. *Not a Tame Lion: The Spiritual Legacy of C. S. Lewis*. Nashville: Cumberland House, 1996.

Glover, Donald E. *C. S. Lewis: The Art of Enchantment*. Athens, Ohio: Ohio Univ. Pr., 1985.

Glyer, Diana Pavlac. *Bandersnatch: C. S. Lewis, J. R. R. Tolkien, and the Creative Collaboration of the Inklings*. Kent, Oh.: Black Squirrel Books, 2016.

----------. *The Company They Keep: C. S. Lewis and J. R. R. Tolkien as Writers in Community*. Kent. Oh.: Kent State Univ. Pr., 2007.

Goffar, Janine. *The C. S. Lewis Index: A Comprehensive Guide to Lewis's Writings and Ideas*. Wheaton: Crossway, 1995.

Green, Roger Lancelyn & Walter Hooper. *C. S. Lewis: A Biography*. NY: Harcourt Brace Jovanovich, 1974.

Gresham, Douglas H. *Lenten Lands: My Childhood with Joy Davidman and C. S. Lewis*. NY: MacMillan, 1988.

Groothuis, Douglas. *Christian Apologetics: A Comprehensive Case for Biblical Faith*. Downers Grove, Il.: Intervarsity Press, 2011.

----------. *Truth Decay*. Downers Grove, Il.: Intervarsity Press, 2000.

Grudem, Wayne. *Systematic Theology: An Introduction to Biblical Doctrine*. Grand Rapids: Zondervan, 1994.

Hart, Dabney Adams. *Through the Open Door: A New Look at C. S. Lewis*. University, AL: Univ. of Alabama Pr., 1984.

Hinten, Marvin D. "Approaches to Teaching Mere Christianity." *The Lamp-Post of the Southern California C. S. Lewis Society*, 30:2 (Summer 2006, pub. April 2008): 3-11.

Hodge, Charles. *Systematic Theology*, 3 vols. 1871-3; rpt. Grand Rapids: Eerdmans, 1968.

Holmes, Michael W., ed. *The Apostolic Fathers: Greek Texts and English Translations of their Writings*. Grand Rapids: Baker, 1992.

Hooper, Walter, ed. *Image and Imagination: Essays and Reviews by C. S. Lewis.* Cambridge: Cambridge Univ. Pr., 2013.

----------. *Past Watchful Dragons: The Narnian Chronicles of C. S. Lewis.* NY: Harper Collins, 1971, rpt. 1979.

Horner, David A. "*Aut Deus aut Malus Homo*: A Defense of C. S. Lewis's 'Shocking Alternative.'" *C. S. Lewis as Philosopher: Truth, Goodness, and Beauty.* Ed. David Baggett, Gary Habermas, and Jerry L. Walls. Downers Grove, Il.: IVP Academic, 2008: 68-84.

Howard-Snyder, Daniel. "Was Jesus Mad, Bad, or God?... Or Merely Mistaken?" *Faith and Philosophy* 21:4 (Oct. 2004): 456-79.

Huttar, Charles, ed. *Imagination and the Spirit: Essays in Literature and the Christian Faith Presented to Clyde S. Kilby.* Grand Rapids: Eerdmans, 1971.

----------. "A Lifelong Love Affair with Language: C. S. Lewis's Poetry." *Word and Story in C. S. Lewis.* Ed. Peter J. Schakel and Charles A. Huttar. Columbia: Univ. of Missouri Pr., 1991: 86-108.

Kantzer, Kenneth Sealer. "John Calvin's Theory of the Knowledge of God and the Word of God." Diss. Harvard, 1950.

----------. "Man, Doctrine of." *Baker's Dictionary of Christian Ethics.* Ed. Carl F. H. Henry. Grand Rapids: Baker, 1973: 403-6.

Keefe, Carolyn, ed. *C. S. Lewis: Speaker and Teacher.* Grand Rapids: Zondervan, 1971.

Kilby, Clyde S. *The Christian World of C. S. Lewis.* Grand Rapids: Eerdmans, 1964.

----------. *Christianity and Aesthetics.* Chicago: Inter-Varsity Press, 1961.

----------. *Images of Salvation in the Fiction of C. S. Lewis.* Wheaton: Harold Shaw, 1978.

Kort, Wesley A. *C. S. Lewis, Then and Now.* Oxford: Oxford Univ. Pr., 2001.

Kreeft, Peter. *C. S. Lewis for the Third Millennium: Six Essays on* The Abolition of Man. San Francisco: Ignatius Pr., 1994.

----------. *Fundamentals of the Faith: Essays in Christian Apologetics.* San Francisco: Ignatius, 1988.

Kreeft, Peter, and Ronald Tacelli. *Handbook of Christian Apologetics.* Downers Grove, Il.: InterVarsity, 1994.

Lawlor, John. *C. S. Lewis: Memories and Reflections*. Dallas: Spence Pub. Co., 1998.

Lewis, C. S. *The Abolition of Man*. Ontario: The MacMillan Company, 1947.

----------. "Answers to Questions on Christianity." 1944; rpt. *God in the Dock: Essays on Theology and Ethics*. Ed. Walter Hooper. Grand Rapids: Eerdmans, 1970: 48-62..

----------. "Bluspels and Flalansferes: A Semantic Nightmare." *Selected Literary Essays*, ed. Walter Hooper. Cambridge: Cambridge Univ. Pr., 1969: 251-65.

----------. "Christian Apologetics." 1945. *God in the Dock*, ed. Walter Hooper. Grand Rapids: Eerdmans, 1970: 89-103.

----------. *Christian Reflections*, ed. Walter Hooper. Grand Rapids: Eerdmans, 1967.

----------. "Christianity and Culture." *Theology* 40 (March 1940): 166-79; rpt. *Christian Reflections*, ed. Walter Hooper. Grand Rapids: Eerdmans, 1967: 12-36.

----------. "Christianity and Literature." *Rehabilitations and Other Essays*. Oxford, 1939. rpt. *Christian Reflections*, ed. Walter Hooper. Grand Rapids: Eerdmans, 1967:: 1-11.

----------. *The Collected Letters of C. S. Lewis*, 3 vols., ed. Walter Hooper. San Francisco: HaperSanFrancisco 2004.

----------. "Cross Examination." As "I Was Decided Upon," *Decision* II (Sept. 1963): 3 and "Heaven, Earth, and Outer Space," *Decision* II (Oct. 1963): 4; rpt. *God in the Dock: Essays on Theology and Ethics*. Ed. Walter Hooper. Grand Rapids: Eerdmans, 1970: 258-67.

----------. "De Descriptione Temporum." 1955; rpt. *Selected Literary Essays*, ed. Walter Hooper. Cambridge: Cambridge Univ. Pr., 1969: 1-14.

----------. "*De Futilitate*." *Christian Reflections*, ed. Walter Hooper. Grand Rapids: Eerdmans, 1967: 57-71.

----------. *The Discarded Image: An Introduction to Medieval and Renaissance Literature*. Cambridge: Cambridge Univ. Pr., 1964.

----------. "The Efficacy of Prayer." *The Atlantic Monthly*, Jan. 1959; rpt. *The World's Last Night and other Essays*. N.Y.: Harcourt, Brace & World, 1960: 3-11.

----------. *English Literature in the Sixteenth Century, Excluding Drama. The Oxford History of English Literature.* Oxford: The Oxford Univ. Pr., 1954.

----------. *An Experiment in Criticism.* Cambridge: Cambridge Univ. Pr., 1961.

----------. "First and Second Things." As "Notes on the Way," *Time and Tide* XXIII (27 June 1942): 519-20; rpt. *God in the Dock: Essays on Theology and Ethics.* Ed. Walter Hooper. Grand Rapids: Eerdmans, 1970: 278-81.

----------. *The Four Loves.* N.Y.: Harcourt, Brace & World, 1960.

----------. "God in the Dock." As "Difficulties in Presenting the Faith to Modern Unbelievers," *Lumen Vitae* III (Sept. 1948): 421-6; rpt. *God in the Dock: Essays on Theology and Ethics.* Ed. Walter Hooper. Grand Rapids: Eerdmans, 1970: 240-44.

----------. *God in the Dock: Essays on Theology and Ethics.* Ed. Walter Hooper. Grand Rapids: Eerdmans, 1970.

----------. "Good Work and Good Works." *Catholic Art Quarterly,* Christmas, 1959; rpt. *The World's Last Night and other Essays.* N.Y.: Harcourt, Brace & World, 1960: 71-81.

----------. *The Great Divorce.* N.Y.: MacMillan, 1946.

----------. *A Grief Observed.* N.Y.: Seabury, 1961.

----------. "Historicism." The Month IV (October 1950); rpt. *Christian Reflections,* ed. Walter Hooper. Grand Rapids: Eerdmans, 1967: 100-113.

----------. "Horrid Red Things." *Church of England Newspaper* LI (6 Oct. 1944):1-2; rpt. *God in the Dock,* ed. Walter Hooper. Grand Rapids: Eerdmans, 1970: 68-71.

----------. *The Horse and His Boy.* 1954; NY: HarperCollins, 1982.

----------. "The Humanitarian Theory of Punishment." *20th Century: An Australian quarterly Review* III:3 (1949): 5-12; rpt. *God in the Dock,* ed. Walter Hooper. Grand Rapids: Eerdmans, 1970: 287-94.

----------. "The Idea of an 'English School.'" 1939; rpt. *Image and Imagination: Essays and Reviews by C. S. Lewis,* ed. Walter Hooper. Cambridge: Cambridge Univ. Pr., 2013: 3-20.

----------. "The Inner Ring." 1944. Rpt. *The Weight of Glory and Other Addresses,* ed. Walter Hooper. Grand Rapids: Eerdmans, 1980: 141-57.

----------. "Is Progress Possible? Willing Slaves of the Welfare State." *The Observer* (20 July 1958): 6; rpt. *God in the Dock*, ed. Walter Hooper. Grand Rapids: Eerdmans, 1970: 311-16.

----------. "Is Theology Poetry?" Paper read to the Oxford Socratic Club, 6 November 1944. *The Socratic Digest* 3 (1945); rpt. *The Weight of Glory and Other Addresses*. Ed. Walter Hooper. San Francisco: Harper Collins, 1980: 116-140.

----------. "The Language of Religion." Address from ca. 1953, first pub. in *Christian Reflections*, ed. Walter Hooper. Grand Rapids: Eerdmans, 1967: 129-41.

----------. *The Last Battle*. 1955; NY: HarperCollins, 1984.

----------. "Learning in Wartime." Sermon preached at St. Mary the Virgin, Oxford, 22 Oct. 1939. *The Weight of Glory and Other Addresses*. Ed. Walter Hooper. San Francisco: Harper Collins, 1980: 47-63.

----------. *Letters to an American Lady*. N.Y.: Pyramid Books, 1971.

----------. *Letters to Malcolm: Chiefly on Prayer*. N.Y.: Harcourt, Brace, Jovanovich, 1963.

----------. "Lilies that Fester." *The Twentieth Century*, Apr., 1955; rpt. in *The World's Last Night and Other Essays*. N.Y.: Harcourt Brace & World, 1960: 31-49.

----------. *The Lion, the Witch, and the Wardrobe*. 1950; NY: HarperCollins, 1978.

----------. *The Magician's Nephew*. 1955; NY: HarperCollins, 1983.

----------. "Man or Rabbit?" S.C.M., 1946; rpt. *God in the Dock: Essays on Theology and Ethics*. Ed. Walter Hooper. Grand Rapids: Eerdmans, 1970: 108-113.

----------. "Meditation in a Toolshed." *God in the Dock*, ed. Walter Hooper. Grand Rapids: Eerdmans, 1970: 212-15.

----------. "Membership." *Sobornost* 31 (June 1945); rpt. *The Weight of Glory and Other Addresses*. Ed. Walter Hooper. San Francisco: Harper Collins, 1980: 158-76.

----------. *Mere Christianity*. N.Y.: MacMillan, 1943.

----------. *Miracles: A Preliminary Study*. N.Y.: MacMillan, 1947.

----------. "Modern Theology and Biblical Criticism." *Christian Reflections*, ed. Walter Hooper. Grand Rapids: Eerdmans, 1967: 152-66.

----------. "Myth Become Fact." *World Dominion* XXII (Sept.-Oct. 1944): 267-70; rpt. *God in the Dock: Essays on Theology and Ethics*. Ed. Walter Hooper. Grand Rapids: Eerdmans, 1970: 63-7.

----------. "On Church Music." *English Church Music* XIX (April 1949); rpt. *Christian Reflections*, ed. Walter Hooper. Grand Rapids: Eerdmans, 1967: 94-99.

----------. "On Obstinacy in Belief." *The Sewanee Review*, Autumn, 1955; rpt. *The World's Last Night and other Essays*. N.Y.: Harcourt, Brace & World, 1960: 13-30.

----------. "On the Reading of Old Books." Preface to St. Athanasius, *The Incarnation of the Word of God*, trans. A Religious of C.S.M.V. Bles, 1944; rpt. *God in the Dock*, ed. Walter Hooper. Grand Rapids: Eerdmans, 1970: 200-207.

----------. "On the Transmission of Christianity." Orig. Preface to B. G. Sandhurst, *How Heathen is Britain?* Collins Publishers, 1946; rpt. *God in the Dock*, ed. Walter Hooper. Grand Rapids: Eerdmans, 1970: 114-119.

----------. "On Three Ways of Writing for Children." The Library Association. *Proceedings, Papers, and Summaries of Discussions at the Bournemouth Conference, 29th April to 2nd May 1952*; rpt. *Of Other Worlds*, ed. Walter Hooper. N.Y.: Harcourt, Brace, Jovanovich, 1964: 22-34.

----------. "Our English Syllabus." 1939; rpt. *Image and Imagination: Essays and Reviews by C. S. Lewis*, ed. Walter Hooper. Cambridge: Cambridge Univ. Pr., 2013: 21-33.

----------. *Out of the Silent Planet*. NY: Simon & Schuster Inc., 1996.

----------. *Perelandra*. NY: Simon & Schuster Inc., 1996.

----------. *The Pilgrim's Regress: an Allegorical Apology for Christianity, Reason, and Romanticism*. London: Bless, 1933; rpt. Grand Rapids: Eerdmans, 1960.

----------. *Poems*, ed. Walter Hooper. N.Y.: Harcourt Brace Jovanovich, 1964.

----------. "The Poison of Subjectivism." *Religion and Life* 12 (1943); rpt. *Christian Reflections*, ed. Walter Hooper. Grand Rapids: Eerdmans, 1967: 72-81.

----------. *A Preface to Paradise Lost*. London: Oxford Univ. Pr., 1962.

----------. "Priestesses in the Church?" as "Notes on the Way," *Time and Tide* XXIX (114 August 1948): 830-31; rpt. *God in the Dock*, ed. Walter Hooper. Grand Rapids: Eerdmans, 1970: 234-9.

----------. *Prince Caspian.* 1951; NY: HarperCollins, 1979.

----------. *The Problem of Pain.* N.Y.: MacMillan, 1967.

----------. *Reflections on the Psalms.* N.Y.: Harcourt, Brace, & World, 1958.

----------. "Rejoinder to Dr. Pittenger." *The Christian Century* LXXV (26 Nov. 1958): 1359-61; rpt. *God in the Dock,* ed. Walter Hooper. Grand Rapids: Eerdmans, 1970: 177-83.

----------. "Religion and Rocketry." *Christian Herald* (as "Will We Lose God in Outer Space?"), April, 1958; rpt. *The World's Last Night and other Essays.* N.Y.: Harcourt, Brace & World, 1960: 83-92.

----------. "Religion: Reality or Substitute?" *World Dominion* XIX (Sept.-Oct. 1941); rpt. *Christian Reflections,* ed. Walter Hooper. Grand Rapids: Eerdmans, 1967: 37-43.

----------. "Religion Without Dogma?" *The Socratic Digest,* 4 (1948): 82-94; rpt. *God in the Dock,* ed. Walter Hooper. Grand Rapids: Eerdmans, 1970: 129-46.

----------. "A Reply to Professor Haldane." *Of Other Worlds,* ed. Walter Hooper. N.Y.: Harcourt, Brace, Jovanovich, 1964:74-85.

----------. "Revival or Decay?" *Punch* CCXXXV (9 July 1958): 36-8; rpt. *God in the Dock: Essays on Theology and Ethics.* Ed. Walter Hooper. Grand Rapids: Eerdmans, 1970: 250-53.

----------. *The Screwtape Letters and Screwtape Proposes a Toast.* With a new preface by the author. N.Y.: MacMillan, 1961.

----------. "The Seeing Eye." As "Onward, Christian Spacemen," *Show* III (Feb. 1963); rpt. *Christian Reflections,* ed. Walter Hooper. Grand Rapids: Eerdmans, 1967: 167-76.

----------. *The Silver Chair.* 1953; NY: HarperCollins, 1981.

----------. "Sometimes Fairy Stories May Say Best What's to be Said." *New York Times Book Review, Children's Book Section,* November 1956; rpt. *Of Other Worlds,* ed. Walter Hooper. N.Y.: Harcourt, Brace, Jovanovich, 1964:35-38.

----------. *Surprised by Joy: The Shape of my Early Life.* N.Y.: Harcourt, Brace, and World, 1955.

----------. *That Hideous Strength*. NY: Simon & Schuster Inc., 1996.

----------. *Till We Have Faces: A Myth Retold*. Harcourt Brace & World, 1956; rpt. Grand Rapids: Eerdmans, 1968.

----------. "Transposition." Sermon preached in the chapel of St. Mansfield College, Oxford, 28 May 1944. *The Weight of Glory and Other Addresses*. Ed. Walter Hooper. San Francisco: Harper Collins, 1980: 91-115.

----------. "The Trouble with X." *Bristol Diocesan Gazette* XXVII (August 1948): 3-6; rpt. *God in the Dock*, ed. Walter Hooper. Grand Rapids: Eerdmans, 1970: 151-5.

----------. *The Voyage of the Dawn Treader*. 1952; NY: HarperCollins, 1980.

----------. "The Weight of Glory," Sermon at St. Mary the Virgin, Oxford, 8 June 1941; *Theology* 43 (Nov. 1941); rpt., *The Weight of Glory and Other Addresses*. Ed. Walter Hooper. San Francisco: Harper Collins, 1980: 25-63.

----------. *The Weight of Glory and Other Addresses* (pub. in England under the title *Transposition and Other Addresses*). Ed. with an Introduction by Walter Hooper. N.Y.: MacMillan, 1949; rpt. Grand Rapids: Eerdmans, 1965; expanded edition, San Francisco: Harper Collins, 1980.

----------. "What are We to Make of Jesus Christ?" *Asking Them Questions*, ed. Ronald Selby Wright. Oxford: Oxford Univ. Pr., 1950: 47-53; rpt. *God in the Dock*, ed. Walter Hooper. Grand Rapids: Eerdmans, 1970: 156-60.

----------. "Why I Am Not a Pacifist." *The Weight of Glory and Other Addresses*. Ed. Walter Hooper. San Francisco: Harper Collins, 1980: 64-90.

----------. "The World's Last Night." *Religion and Life* (as "The Christian Hope—Its Meaning for Today"), Winter, 1952; rpt. *The World's Last Night and other Essays*. N.Y.: Harcourt, Brace & World, 1960: 93-113.

----------. *The World's Last Night and Other Essays*. N.Y.: Harcourt, Brace, & World, 1960.

Lewis, Warren H. *Brothers and Friends: The Diaries of Major Warren Hamilton Lewis*. Ed. Clyde S. Kilby and Marjorie Lamp Mead. N.Y.: Ballantine, 1982.

Lindskoog, Kathryn. *Finding the Landlord: A Guidebook to C. S. Lewis's* Pilgrim's Regress. Chicago: Cornerstone Pr., 1995.

----------. *Light in the Shadowlands: Protecting the Real C. S. Lewis.* Sisters, OR.: Multnomah, 1994.

----------. *The Lion of Judah in Never-Never Land.* Grand Rapids: Eerdmans, 1973.

----------. *Surprised by C. S. Lewis, George MacDonald, and Dante: An Array of Original Discoveries.* Macon: Mercer Univ. Pr., 2001.

----------. *The C. S.. Lewis Hoax.* Portland: Multnomah, 1988.

Lucas, J. R. "Restoration of Man: A Lecture given in Durham on Thursday October 22nd, 1992 by J. R. Lucas to mark the Fiftieth Anniversary of C. S. Lewis's *The Abolition of Man*." 7 March 2003. <http://users.ox.ac.uk/~jrlucas/lewis.html>

MacDonald, Michael H. & Andrew Tadie, eds. *The Riddle of Joy: G. K. Chesterton and C. S. Lewis.* Grand Rapids: Eerdmans, 1989.

Manlove, Colin N. *C. S. Lewis: His Literary Achievement.* N.Y.: St. Martin's Pr., 1987.

----------. *The Chronicles of Narnia: The Patterning of a Fantastic World.* N.Y.: Twayne Publishers, 1993.

Markos, Louis. *Lewis Agonistes: How C. S. Lewis can Train us to Wrestle with the Modern and Postmodern World.* Nashville: Broadman & Holman, 2003.

Martin, Thomas L., ed. *Reading the Classics with C. S. Lewis.* Grand Rapids: Baker, 2,000.

McGrath, Alister. *C. S. Lewis: A Life.* Carol Stream, IL: Tyndale, 2013.

Meilaender, Gilbert. *The Taste for the Other: The Social and Ethical Thought of C. S. Lewis.* Grand Rapids: Eerdmans, 1978.

Menuge, Angus J. L., ed. *C. S. Lewis, Lightbearer in the Shadowlands: The Evangelistic Vision of C. S. Lewis.* Wheaton: Crossway, 1997.

Miller, Rod, ed. *C. S. Lewis and the Arts: Creativity in the Shadowlands.* Baltimore: Square Halo Books, 2013.

Mills, David, ed. *The Pilgrim's Guide: C. S. Lewis and the Art of Witness.* Grand Rapids: Eerdmans, 1998.

Milton, John. *Complete Poems and Major Prose.* Ed. Merritt Y. Hughes. Indianapolis: Bobbs-Merrill, 1957.

Mitchell, Christopher W. "Bearing the Weight of Glory: The Cost of C. S. Lewis's Witness." In David Mills, ed., *The Pilgrim's Guide: C. S. Lewis and the Art of Witness.* Grand Rapids: Eerdmans, 1998: 3-14.

Montgomery, John Warwick, ed. *Myth, Allegory, and Gospel: An Interpretation of J. R. R. Tolkien, C. S. Lewis, G. K. Chesterton, and Charles Williams.* Minneapolis: Bethany, 1974.

Morison, Frank. *Who Moved the Stone?* Downers Grove, IL: Inter Varsity Press, n.d.

Nash, Ronald H. *Life's Ultimate Questions: An Introduction to Philosophy.* Grand Rapids: Zondervan, 1999.

Neill, Stephen. *The Interpretation of the New Testament, 1861-1961.* New York: Oxford Univ. Pr., 1966.

Nicholi, Armand M., Jr. *The Question of God: C. S. Lewis and Sigmund Freud Debate God, Love, Sex, and the Meaning of Life.* N.Y.: Free Press, 2002.

Packer, J. I. *"Fundamentalism" and the Word of God.* London: InterVarsity Press, 1958.

----------. "Living Truth for a Dying World: The Message of C. S. Lewis." *Crux* 34:4 (December 1998): 3-12; rpt. *The J. I. Packer Collection.* ed. Alister McGrath. Downers Grove, IL: Inter Varsity Press, 1999: 269-84.

Packer, J. I. and Thomas C. Oden. *One Faith: The Evangelical Consensus.* Downers Grove, IL: InterVarsity Press, 2004.

Patrick, James. "The Heart's Desire and the Landlord's Rules: C. S. Lewis as Moral Philosopher." In David Mills, ed., *The Pilgrim's Guide: C. S. Lewis and the Art of Witness.* Grand Rapids: Eerdmans, 1998: 70-85.

----------. *The Magdalen Metaphysicals: Idealism and Orthodoxy at Oxford, 1901-1945.* Macon, Ga.: Mercer Univ. Pr., 1985.

Payne, Leanne. *Real Presence: The Holy Spirit in the Works of C. S. Lewis.* Westchester, IL: Cornerstone, 1979.

Polanyi, Michael. *Personal Knowledge: Towards a Post-Critical Philosophy.* N. Y.: Harper & Row, 1964.

Purtill, Richard L. *C. S. Lewis's Case for the Christian Faith*. San Francisco: Harper & Row, 1981.

----------. *Lord of Elves and Eldils: Fantasy and Philosophy in C. S. Lewis and J. R. R. Tolkien*. Grand Rapids: Zondervan, 1974.

Reppert, Victor. *C. S. Lewis's Dangerous Idea: In Defense of the Argument from Reason*. Downers Grove, Il.: InterVarsity Press, 2003.

----------. "Interview: Dr. Victor Reppert on 'The Argument from Reason.'" Quality Christian Internet. 5 March, 2003. <http://go.qci.tripod.com/Reppert-interview.htm>

----------. "The Lewis-Anscombe Controversy: A Discussion of the Issues." *Christian Scholar's Review* 19:1 (Sept., 1989): 32-48.

----------. "Pro: The Argument from Reason Defended." Bassham, Gregory, ed. *C. S. Lewis's Apologetics: Pro and Con*. Leiden: Brill/Rodopi, 2015: 75-89.

Richardson, Cyril C., ed. *Early Christian Fathers*. Vol. 1 of *The Library of Christian Classics*, ed. John Baillie, John T. McNeill, and Henry P. Van Dusen. Philadelphia: Westminster, 1953.

Ricke, Joe and Lisa Ritchie, eds. *Exploring the Eternal Goodness: Selected Writings of David L. Neuhouser*. Hamden, CT.: Winged Lion Press, 2016.

Root, Jerry and Mark Neal, *The Surprising Imagination of C. S. Lewis: An Introduction*. Nashville: Abingdon, 2015.

Ruud, Jay. "Aslan's Sacrifice and the Doctrine of Atonement in *The Lion, the Witch, and the Wardrobe*." *Mythlore* 23:2 (Spring 2001): 15-22.

Ryken, Leland and Marjorie Lamp Meade. *A Reader's Guide Through the Wardrobe: Exploring C. S. Lewis's Classic Story*. Downers Grove, Il.: InterVarsity Press, 2005.

Sayer, George. *Jack: A Life of C. S. Lewis*. Wheaton: Crossway, 1994.

Sayers, Dorothy L. *The Mind of the Maker*. 1941. Rpt. San Francisco: Harper & Row, 1979.

Schaeffer, Francis. *The God Who is There: Speaking Historic Christianity into the Twentieth Century*. Downers Grove, IL.: Inter-Varsity Press, 1958.

----------. *The Mark of the Christian*. Downers Grove, IL.: Inter-Varsity Press, 1970.

Schaff, Philip, ed. *The Creeds of Christendom*, vol. III: *The Evangelical Protestant Creeds with Translations*. 4th ed. 1919; rpt. Grand Rapids: Baker, 1966.

Schakel, Peter J. "The 'Correct' Order for Reading the Chronicles of Narnia." *Mythlore* 23:2 (Spring 2001): 4-14.

----------. *Imagination and the Arts in C. S. Lewis: Journeying to Narnia and Other Worlds*. Columbia: Univ. of Missouri Pr., 2002.

----------., ed. *The Longing for a Form: Essays on the Fiction of C. S. Lewis*. Grand Rapids: Baker, 1977.

----------. *Reading with the Heart: The Way into Narnia*. Grand Rapids: Eerdmans, 1979.

----------. *Reason and Imagination in C. S. Lewis: A Study of* Till We Have Faces. Grand Rapids: Eerdmans, 1984.

Schultz, Jefferey D. & John G. West, Jr., eds. *The C. S. Lewis Reader's Encyclopedia*. Grand Rapids: Zondervan, 1998.

Shaw, Luci. "C. S. Lewis: The Light in the Kilns." *Christianity and Literature* 52:1 (Autumn 2002): 34.

Shakespeare, William. *Shakespeare: The Complete Works*. ed. G. B. Harrison. N.Y.: Harcourt, Brace, & World, 1968.

Sims, John A. *Missionaries to the Skeptics: Christian Apologists for the Twentieth Century--C. S. Lewis, Edward John Carnell, and Reinhold Niebuhr*. Macon, GA.: Mercer Univ. Pr., 1995.

Skinner, B. F. *Beyond Freedom and Dignity*. N.Y.: Bantam, 1971.

Smith, Roger Houston. *Patches of Godlight: The Pattern of Thought of C. S. Lewis*. Athens: The Univ. of Georgia Pr., 1981.

Spenser, Edmund. *The Faerie Queene*. 1590. 2 vols. ed. J. C. Smith. Oxford: Oxford Univ. Pr., 1909.

Stock, R. D. "The Tao and the Objective Room: A Pattern in C. S. Lewis's Novels." *Christian Scholar's Review* 9:3 (1980): 256-66.

Sturgis, Amy, ed. *Past Watchful Dragons: Fantasy and Faith in the World of C. S. Lewis*. Altadena, Ca.: The Mythopoeic Press, 2007.

Tetreault, James. "Parallel Lives: C. S. Lewis and T. S. Eliot." *Renascence: Essays on Value in Literature* 38:4 (Summer 1986): 256-59.

Thorson, Stephen. "Barfield's Evolution of Consciousness: How Much Did Lewis Accept?" *SEVEN: An Anglo-American Literary Review* 15 (1998): 9-35.

----------. "'Knowledge' in C. S. Lewis's Post-Conversion Thought: His Epistemological Method." *SEVEN: An Anglo-American Literary Review* 9 (1988): 91-116.

----------. *Joy and Poetic Imagination: Understanding C. S. Lewis's "Great War" with Owen Barfield and its Significance for Lewis's Conversion and Writings.* Hamden, CT: Winged Lion Press, 2015.

----------. "Lewis and Barfield on Imagination." *Mythlore: A Journal of J. R. R. Tolkien, C. S. Lewis, and the Genres of Myth and Fantasy* 17:2 (Winter 1990): 12-18.

----------. "Lewis and Barfield on Imagination, Part II." *Mythlore: A Journal of J. R. R. Tolkien, C. S. Lewis, and the Genres of Myth and Fantasy* 17:3 (Spring 1991): 16-21.

Tolkien, J. R. R. "Beowulf: The Monsters and the Critics." *Proceedings of the British Academy* 22 (1936): 245-295; rpt. *An Anthology of Beowulf Criticism.* Ed. Lewis E. Nicholson. Notre Dame, Indiana: Univ. of Notre Dame Pr., 1963, pp. 51-103.

----------. *The Fellowship of the Ring.* New York: Ballantine Books, 1982.

----------. *The Hobbit.* New York: Ballantine Books, 1982.

----------. *The Letters of J. R. R. Tolkien.* Selected and edited by Humphrey Carpenter, with the assistance of Christopher Tolkien. Boston: Houghton Mifflin, 1981.

----------. "On Faerie Stories." *The Tolkien Reader.* NY: Ballantine, 1966, pp. 3-84.

----------. *The Return of the King.* New York: Ballantine Books, 1982.

----------. *The Silmarillion.* Boston: Houghton Mifflin Co., 1977.

----------. *The Two Towers.* New York: Ballantine Books, 1982.

Vaus, Will. *Mere Theology: A Guide to the Thought of C. S. Lewis.* Downers Grove: InterVarsity Press, 2004.

----------. Speaking of Jack: A C. S. Lewis Discussion Guide. Hamden, Ct.: Winged Lion Press, 2011.

Veith, Jr., Gene Edward. "A Vision, Within a Dream, Within the Truth: C. S. Lewis as Evangelist to the Postmodernists." In Menuge, Angus J. L., ed., *C. S. Lewis, Lightbearer in the Shadowlands: The Evangelistic Vision of C. S. Lewis.* Wheaton: Crossway, 1997: 367-87.

Walsh, Chad. *C. S. Lewis: Apostle to the Skeptics.* NY: MacMillan, 1949.

----------. *The Literary Legacy of C. S. Lewis.* NY: Harcourt Brace Jovanovich, 1979.

Weaver, Richard. *Ideas Have Consequences.* Chicago: Univ. of Chicago Pr., 1948.

Wenham, John W. *Christ and the Bible.* Downers Grove: InterVarsity Press, 1972.

Werther, David and Susan Werther, eds. *C. S. Lewis's List: The Ten Books that Influenced him Most.* N.Y.: Bloomsbury, 2015.

White, Roger, Judith Wolfe, and Brendan Wolfe, eds. *C. S. Lewis and his Circle: Essays and Memoirs from the Oxford C. S. Lewis Society.* Oxford: Oxford University Press, 2015.

White, William Luther. *The Image of Man in C. S. Lewis.* Nashville: Abingdon, 1969.

Williams, Donald T. "The Abolition of Talking Beasts: Christian Perspectives on the Human in The Chronicles of Narnia." *Past Watchful Dragons: Fantasy and Faith in the World of C. S. Lewis* (Proceedings of the 2005 "Past Watchful Dragons" conference at Belmont University, Nashville, Tn.), ed. Amy H. Sturgis (Altadena, CA.: The Mythopoeic Press, 2007): 23-40.

----------. "Anselm and Aslan: C. S. Lewis and the Ontological Argument." *Touchstone: A Journal of Mere Christianity* 27:6 (Nov.-Dec. 2014): 36-39.

----------. "An Apologist's Evening Prayer: Reflecting on C. S. Lewis's *Reflections on the Psalms.*" *C. S. Lewis: Life, Works, and Legacy,* 4 vols. Ed. Bruce L. Edwards. London: Praeger, 2007: 3:237-56.

----------. "The Argument from Desire Revisited." *The Lamp-Post of the Southern California C. S. Lewis Society* 32:1 (Spring 2010): 32-33.

----------. "A Closer Look at the 'Unorthodox' Lewis." *Christianity Today* (Dec. 21, 1979): 24-27.

----------. *Credo: Meditations on the Nicene Creed.* St. Louis: Chalice, 2007.

----------. "'For the Sake of the Story': Doctrine and Discernment in Reading C. S. Lewis." *Modern Reformation* 18:3 (May-June, 2009): 33-36.

----------. "G. K. Chesterton, *The Everlasting Man.*" *C. S. Lewis's List: The Ten Books that Influenced Him Most.* Ed. David Werther and Susan Werther. N.Y.: Bloomsbury, 2015: 31-48.

----------. "Identity Check: Are C. S. Lewis's Critics Right, or Is His 'Trilemma' Valid?" *Touchstone: a Journal of Mere Christianity* 23:3 (May-June 2010): 25-29.

----------. *Inklings of Reality: Essays toward a Christian Philosophy of Letters.* Toccoa Falls, GA.: Toccoa Falls College Pr., 1996; 2nd edition, revised and expanded, Lynchburg: Lantern Hollow Press, 2012.

----------. "'Is Man a Myth?': Mere Christian Perspectives on the Human." *Mythlore* 23:1 (Summer/Fall 2000): 4-19.

----------. "Lacking, Ludicrous, or Logical? The Validity of Lewis's 'Trilemma.'" *Midwestern Journal of Theology* 11:1 (Spring 2012): 91-102.

----------. "A Larger World: C. S. Lewis on Christianity and Literature." *Mythlore* 24:2 (Spring 2004): 45-37.

----------. "Lions of Succession: On Being a Free Narnian & the Joy of Subordination." *Touchstone: a Journal of Mere Christianity* 18:3 (April 2005): 15-17.

----------. *Mere Humanity: G. K. Chesterton, C. S. Lewis, and J. R. R. Tolkien on the Human Condition.* Nashville: Broadman, 2006.

----------. "'The Mind is its Own Place': Satan's Philosophy and the Modern Dilemma," *Proceedings of the Georgia Philological Association* 2 (December 2007): 20-34.

----------. "The Objectivity of Value: Properties, Values, and Moral Reasoning." *The Bulletin of the Evangelical Philosophical Society* 16 (1993): 49-58.

----------. *The Person and Work of the Holy Spirit.* Nashville: Broadman & Holman, 1994.

----------. "Printing Error: Anscombe's Final Word on Lewis and Naturalism," *Touchstone: A Journal of Mere Christianity* 29:3 (May/June 2016): 20-22.

----------. "Pro: A Defense of C. S. Lewis's 'Trilemma.'" Bassham, Gregory, ed. *C. S. Lewis's Apologetics: Pro and Con.* Leiden: Brill/Rodopi, 2015: 171-89.

----------. *Reflections from Plato's Cave: Essays in Evangelical Philosophy.* Lynchburg: Lantern Hollow Press, 2012.

----------. "Reflections from Plato's Cave: Musings on the History of Philosophy" (Evangelical Philosophical Society Presidential Address, 1996). *Philosophia Christi* 20:1 (Spring, 1997): 71-82.

----------. "Repairing the Ruins: Thoughts on Christian Higher Education." *Christian Educators Journal* 41:4 (April, 2002): 19-21.

----------. Review of *C. S. Lewis's Dangerous Idea*, by Victor Reppert (Downers Grove, IL: IVP, 2003), *Philosophia Christi*, 6:2 (2004): 375-77.

----------. Review of *Into the Region of Awe: Mysticism in C. S. Lewis*, by David C. Downing (Downers Grove, Il.: IVP, 2005). *Trinity Journal* 27:1 (Spring 2006): 179-80.

----------. Review of *Lewis Agonistes: How C. S. Lewis Can Train us to Wrestle with the Modern and Postmodern World*, by Louis Markos (Nashville: Broadman, 2003). *Mythprint* 43:9 (September 2006): 11-12.

----------. Review of *Mere Theology: A Guide to the Thought of C. S. Lewis*, by Will Vaus (Downers Grove, IL: InterVarsity Pr., 2004), *Mythprint* 42:4 (April, 2005): 5.

----------. Review of *The Pilgrim's Guide: C. S. Lewis and the Art of Witness*, ed. David Mills (Grand Rapids: Eerdmans, 1998) in *The Lamp-Post* 23:2 (Summer 1999): 36-37.

----------. "Text *Versus* Word: C. S. Lewis's View of the Inspiration and the Inerrancy of Scripture." *I am Put Here for the Defense of the Gospel: Dr. Norman L. Geisler: A Festschrift in his Honor*. Ed. Terry L. Miethe. Eugene, Or.: Pickwick Publications, 2016: 152-68.

----------. "Wardrobe Accessories": Review of Bruce Edwards, *Further up and Further In: Understanding C. S. Lewis's The Lion, the Witch and the Wardrobe* (Nashville: Broadman & Holman, 2005), Devin Brown, *Inside Narnia: A Guide to Exploring The Lion, the Witch and the Wardrobe* (Grand Rapids: Baker, 2005), and Leland Ryken and Marjorie Lamp Meade, *A Reader's Guide through the Wardrobe: Exploring C. S. Lewis's Classic Story* (Downers Grove, Il.: InterVarsity Pr., 2005). *Touchstone: A Journal of Mere Christianity* 19:1 (Jan.-Feb. 2006): 45-6.

----------. "Writers Cramped: Three Things that Evangelical Authors can Learn from Flannery O'Connor." *Touchstone: a Journal of Mere Christianity* 20:7 (September, 2007): 15-18; rpt. as "Why Evangelicals Can't Write, and How Flannery O'Connor can Help us Learn Better." *Inklings of Reality: Essays toward a Christian Philosophy of Letters*, 2nd ed. Lynchburg: Lantern Hollow Press, 2012: 207-14.

Willis, John Randolph. *Pleasure Forevermore: The Theology of C. S. Lewis*. Chicago: Loyola Univ. Pr., 1983.

Witherspoon, Alexander M. and Frank J. Warnke. *Seventeenth-Century Prose and Poetry*, 2nd ed. N.Y.: Harcourt Brace Jovanovich, 1982.

Wright, Marjorie Evelyn. "The Vision of Cosmic Order in the Oxford Mythmakers." in Charles Huttar, ed., *Imagination and the Spirit: Essays in Literature and the Christian Faith Presented to Clyde S. Kilby*. Grand Rapids: Eerdmans, 1971: 259-76.

Wright, N. T. "Simply Lewis: Reflections on a Master Apologist after 60 Years." *Touchstone*, 20:2 (March, 2007): 28-33.

SCRIPTURE PASSAGES CITED

Genesis 1–3 105
Genesis 1:1 .... 80, 88
Genesis 1:4 94
Genesis 1:28 106
Genesis 2:15 106
Exodus 3:14 79–80
Deuteronomy 6:5 205
Deuteronomy 6:6–9 73
Psalm 1:2 72
Psalm 19:1 42
Psalm 23:5 67
Ecclesiastes 3:11 230
Isaiah 6:1–3 98
Isaiah 53:12 154
Joel 2:32 170
Matthew 5:6 247
Matthew 16:13–18 .... 120, 145
Matthew 22:37 205
Matthew 24:36 121–2
Matthew 25:31–46 237
Matthew 28:18–20 170
Mark 13:32 .... 233, 236
Luke 5:21 135
John 1:5 114
John 3:16 .... 43, 125
John 3:36 155
John 6:44 159
John 8:58 80
John 10:11 154
John 15:13 154
John 15:16 53
John 17:17 54
Acts 1:7 .... 234, 236
Acts 16:30–31 ..... 57, 158, 168–9
Romans 1:18 155
Romans 1:20 .... 42, 170
Romans 1:21–2:1 170
Romans 3:22–28 165
Romans 3:24 240
Romans 3:25 155
Romans 3:26 .... 117, 156
Romans 4:4 165
Romans 5 155
Romans 5:8 154
Romans 5:9 155
Romans 5:18 169
Romans 6:2, 11 156
Romans 10:9–10 .... 158, 169
Romans 10:11–14 170
Romans 12:4–8 178

Romans 13:1–7 212	2 Thessalonians 1:8 155
1 Corinthians 1:8 177	2 Timothy 3:16 .... 60, 149
1 Corinthians 2:9 245	Hebrews 4:15 122
1 Corinthians 2:14 ... 157, 159, 243	Hebrews 6:4–6 167
1 Corinthians 2:15 114	James 2:14–26 165
1 Corinthians 7:10 196	James 2:18 165
1 Corinthians 12:12–27 178	James 2:21 165
2 Corinthians 3:7 193	1 Peter 1:8 196
2 Corinthians 5:19 43	1 Peter 2:9–10 173
2 Corinthians 5:21 154	1 Peter 2:24 155
Galatians 3:13 155	1 Peter 3:15 217
Galatians 5:4 .... 165, 167	2 Peter 3:3–4 234
Ephesians 1:4 53	2 Peter 3:8 69
Ephesians 2:1–9 165	2 Peter 3:16 60
Ephesians 2:1 .... 159, 243	1 John 1:5 96
Ephesians 2:5 243	1 John 2:2 155
Ephesians 2:8–9 157–8	1 John 2:19 167
Ephesians 2:10 165	1 John 3:2 240
Ephesians 4:4–16 178	1 John 4:2–3 121
Ephesians 4:12 215	1 John 4:10 .... 100, 155
Philippians 2:13 161	1 John 4:19 .... 41, 56
Philippians 4:7 196	
1 Thessalonians 1:10 155	

GENERAL INDEX

absolute 39–40, 80–81, 85, 89, 96, 112, 145, 151, 211, 238, 240

abstract, abstraction 20, 36, 51, 56, 78, 81, 85, 92, 100–101, 106, 142–143, 145, 190, 219–220, 224, 226, 232, 243

aesthetics 1, 7, 125, 201, 259

allegory 11, 17, 43, 51, 84, 267

analogy 16, 29, 38, 56, 62, 84, 88–90, 147, 166, 179, 181–182, 199, 236, 252

anthropology 7, 103–104

anti-intellectualism 204–205

antithesis 30, 50

apologetics 7, 13–14, 16, 19, 25, 48, 77, 129, 184, 215–223, 231–232, 255–256, 258–260, 268, 272

Apostle, apostolic 57, 60, 65–66, 136, 149, 160, 170, 183, 218, 258, 271

Arminian, Arminianism 173

art 1, 6, 70, 86, 120, 169, 195, 199, 201–202, 205–209, 216, 221, 232, 255, 257–258, 261, 266–267, 273

aseity 78

atonement 7, 95, 98, 112–113, 117–118, 127, 149–158, 165, 167–168, 171, 173, 238, 244, 268

attributes, attributes of God 42, 51, 75, 88, 94, 96, 98, 117, 122, 131, 151–152, 154

authority 39, 49, 51–52, 60, 67–68, 72, 86–87, 119, 122, 131, 140, 142, 150, 170–171, 182–184, 205, 220–221, 234–235, 252, 294, 314

baptism 162, 180, 188, 218

beauty 9, 15–16, 26, 31, 40, 43, 78, 85, 96, 105–106, 125, 180, 201, 205–207, 228–229, 245–248, 255, 259

Bible 23, 60–72, 78, 80–81, 86, 93, 97, 143, 159, 168, 183, 194–195, 213, 220, 234, 243, 251–252, 271

bibliology 7, 13, 59, 149

bios 162, 187–188

Body of Christ 174, 178–179, 187

calling 19–20, 84, 94–95, 98, 116, 158–161, 163, 171, 173, 175, 185, 187, 203, 225, 237

Calvinism, Calvinist 160, 163, 173

catholic 17, 23, 68, 175, 181–183, 201, 240, 261

Christ 7, 14, 16–20, 23–24, 42–43, 45–47, 53, 55–57, 59, 61, 63–64, 70–71, 75–76, 86–87, 90, 95, 103, 107, 113, 117–132, 136, 139, 141, 143, 145–147, 150–159, 161–163, 166–170, 173–179, 181, 184, 187–191, 193, 197–199, 213, 215–217, 219–220, 223–224, 226, 228, 231–237, 240, 243, 245–249, 251, 254, 256, 265, 271

Christ, deity of 118, 120–121, 129–131, 145, 147, 153, 223, 236

Christ, humanity of 23

Christianity 7, 9, 11, 14, 16, 18, 20, 23, 27, 37–38, 43, 45, 47–48, 50, 54, 57, 84, 95, 99, 103–104, 113, 118, 123–124, 129–130, 133, 137–138, 146–147, 149, 152–154, 156, 158, 166, 169, 173–177, 181, 183, 185, 191, 201–206, 210–211, 214–216, 221–222, 224, 226–230, 233–234, 238, 245, 247, 252, 256, 258–260, 262–263, 268–269, 271–274

christology 7, 13, 117, 120, 124–125, 128, 149, 153, 223, 251

church 1, 7, 14, 19, 23–24, 28, 30, 38, 57, 60, 67–68, 72, 86, 90, 124, 136, 156, 167, 173–185, 187, 195, 199, 205, 209–210, 212, 214–216, 222, 236, 240, 249, 252, 261, 263

civilization 104, 201, 206–207, 209, 211, 238

common grace 115, 201, 207

communion 162, 173, 176–178, 181, 188, 199–200

community 54, 84, 129, 174, 178–180, 182, 185, 194, 258

concrete 20, 30, 81, 142, 177, 199

confession 118, 136, 183, 199–200

congregation 174–177, 180

contradiction 15, 30–32, 66, 93, 118, 168, 220, 227

conversion 39, 44, 57, 125, 159–164, 181, 187, 189, 193, 201, 215, 217–218, 220, 228, 237–238, 252, 256, 270

correspondence theory 26, 29, 32, 34–35

creation 23, 43, 45, 54–55, 59, 81, 87–90, 92, 94, 99–100, 103, 105–108, 111, 116, 126, 157, 203, 205–206, 214, 234, 236, 245

Creeds 23, 44, 66, 117, 124–125, 184, 234, 240, 269

critic, criticism 1, 11, 28, 67, 131–137, 257, 261–262, 270

culture 7, 71, 132, 135, 201–211, 214, 260

damn, damnation 162, 166–167, 241, 243–244

death 14–15, 30–31, 37, 42–43, 63, 72, 89, 95, 106, 109, 114, 117–118, 124, 149–150, 152–156, 158, 163, 169, 174, 188–189, 193, 208, 210, 236–237, 240, 243, 252

deconstruction 26–27

denomination 38, 176, 181

depravity 115–116

devotion 36, 109, 190, 194–196, 199

doctrine 1, 6–7, 9, 13, 19–20, 24, 28, 38, 41, 44–45, 51, 53–54, 56, 59, 61–62, 65, 67–70, 72, 75, 82–85, 88, 91, 97–100, 103–105, 108, 112, 115–118, 122, 124–125, 149–150, 153–154, 156, 159–160, 167, 171, 173, 176, 183, 185,

GENERAL INDEX 279

187–188, 198, 201, 203, 207, 213, 223, 233, 235, 240, 242–244, 247, 252–253, 258–259, 268, 271

dogma, dogmatics 25, 33, 36, 54, 184, 201, 240, 255, 264

ecclesiology 7, 173–174, 181, 251

education 32, 112, 205, 208–210, 214, 273

emotion 16, 55, 84, 125, 196–197, 199, 218, 253

epistemology 79

eschatology 7, 233–234, 236–237, 245, 251

essence 52, 110, 158, 199, 238, 241, 247

eternal, eternity 30, 48, 53, 75, 80, 82, 87–88, 92, 96, 98, 107, 124–125, 140, 142–143, 146, 155, 164, 167, 174–175, 201, 206–207, 230, 233, 237, 239, 241, 243–249, 253, 268

ethics 25, 131, 139–141, 221, 259–264

Evangelical 1–2, 9, 13, 16–17, 61, 69, 150, 154, 165, 167–168, 184–185, 188, 196, 201, 216, 219, 236–237, 251, 254, 267, 269, 272–274

Evangelicalism 69

evangelism 7, 174, 214–216, 218–219

evidentialism, evidentialist 219

evolution 44–45, 64, 104–105, 111, 113, 136, 235, 270

exclusivism 168–169

exegesis, exegetical 24, 139, 143, 149, 165, 251–252

experience 16, 23, 29, 31, 34–35, 39, 49, 52, 54–57, 76, 79, 83–84, 89, 95, 98, 110, 112, 115, 125–127, 139–140, 143, 154, 156, 160, 163–164, 166, 168, 176, 183, 187–189, 195–200, 205, 207, 209–210, 216, 218–221, 223, 228–230, 235, 237–238, 240, 242, 246, 248, 253

fact 17–18, 20, 26–28, 30–32, 35–39, 42–43, 46–48, 50–55, 57, 59, 62, 64–66, 77, 79, 81–82, 86, 88, 92–93, 105–107, 109–112, 114–115, 120, 123, 131, 134, 137, 139, 141, 147, 149–151, 153–154, 156, 175, 181, 189, 194, 198–201, 210, 217–218, 220–221, 223–224, 227, 229–231, 238, 240–241, 246–247, 263

faith 1, 13–14, 19, 23, 25, 30–31, 37–39, 44, 46, 48–49, 54–57, 65, 68, 70, 76, 79, 89, 91, 95, 99–100, 109, 114, 116–118, 120, 122–123, 127, 134, 145–146, 153–154, 156–160, 162–163, 165–171, 173–175, 177–178, 180–185, 188–190, 193, 196–197, 199–200, 202, 205, 215, 217–218, 220–223, 229, 231–232, 235, 238, 240, 244, 247–248, 252–253, 257–259, 261, 267–269, 271, 274

Fall 7, 21, 31, 43, 59, 68, 72, 83, 94, 96, 103, 106–113, 115–117, 119, 126, 130–131, 144, 150–152, 157, 167, 193, 203, 213, 236, 253, 272

Father, fatherhood 43, 51, 55–56, 71, 75, 83–87, 95, 99, 118–120, 122–125, 140, 142, 154, 159, 175–176, 183, 185, 195, 200, 234, 247, 256

fiction 14, 17–19, 30–31, 40, 62, 152, 171, 257, 259, 269

finite 20, 23–24, 26, 29, 41, 53, 55–56, 75, 78, 84, 88, 117, 119, 122, 126, 141, 229

forgiveness 158, 197–198, 241

Fundamentalism 1, 68–69, 72, 267

general eschatology 233–234, 236

generation 30, 48, 104, 113, 125, 208–210, 218, 221

genre 68, 70, 72

glory 11, 26, 40, 42, 48, 67, 78, 80, 85, 88, 104, 107, 109, 164, 180, 189, 195, 202, 216, 229, 232, 234–235, 239, 247, 261–262, 265, 267

goodness 9, 26, 40, 78, 85, 94–100, 105–107, 109, 112, 115–116, 143, 180, 189, 191–192, 205, 248, 255, 259, 268

Gospel 9, 19, 30, 57, 107, 113, 132–133, 145, 158–159, 162, 168–170, 179, 185, 196, 216–218, 226, 236, 267, 273

government 173–174, 211–214

grace 55, 66, 83, 114–115, 151, 155–156, 158–160, 162–168, 185, 187–189, 193–194, 199–201, 207, 236, 238, 240, 243–244, 249, 254

growth 178, 189, 212

hamartiology 1, 7, 103, 108

Heaven 7, 21, 37, 39, 50, 81–82, 86–87, 90, 95, 97, 120, 124, 155, 164, 170, 189, 202–203, 207, 211, 221, 233–234, 237–242, 244–248, 257, 260

Hell 7, 21, 37, 50, 53, 71, 119, 126, 130, 162, 164, 169, 202–203, 226, 233, 237–239, 241–245, 247

hermeneutics 71

high church 176

history 1, 11, 14, 24, 28, 32, 36, 42–48, 51, 57, 59, 61–70, 76, 86, 88, 98, 111, 113, 128, 140, 149, 173, 175, 188, 209, 216, 227, 232–236, 251–252, 261, 273

holy, holiness 31, 60–62, 75, 81–83, 85, 87, 98–99, 107, 113, 115, 122, 125, 145, 157, 159, 162, 164, 173, 179, 184, 188, 197, 220, 231, 247, 267, 272

Holy Spirit 60–62, 83, 85, 113, 122, 125, 145, 157, 159, 179, 188, 197, 220, 231, 267, 272

homeschooling 210

human 15, 23–24, 26, 31–33, 35–36, 39, 41–42, 45–46, 49, 51, 53, 59–64, 66–67, 69, 71, 84, 88–89, 92, 96–98, 103–111, 114–117, 119, 121–124, 126, 128, 130–131, 135–136, 140–142, 146, 151–152, 159–160, 163, 169, 171, 175, 179, 191, 194–195, 200–205, 207–208, 211–212, 214, 217–219, 221–223, 228, 230–231, 238–239, 244–245, 247, 253, 271–272

humanity 23, 36, 39–40, 59, 99, 101, 104–105, 107, 112, 114, 119, 121–122, 126, 207, 209, 213, 239, 245, 272

illumination 71

image of God, /imago Dei 45, 104, 114–115, 255

imagination 1, 15–16, 21, 29–32, 35, 39, 43, 46–47, 57–58, 64, 88, 214, 218, 253, 259, 261, 263, 268–270, 274

incarnation 18, 43, 61–63, 71, 86, 117–119, 121–128, 155, 175, 199, 236, 263

inclusivism 169, 252

incorporeal 82

inerrancy 9, 60, 65–70, 72, 252, 273

infallibility 60, 71

infinite, infinity 23, 29, 41–42, 48, 50, 56, 81, 85, 92, 100, 119, 122, 126, 141, 205, 231

inspiration 9, 59–72, 105, 122, 149, 252–253, 273

interpretation 23, 66, 70, 72, 132, 134, 182, 224, 267

jargon 28, 252

justice 96–98, 117, 126, 150–152, 155–156, 158, 218, 243–244, 247, 252

justification 133, 188, 240, 252

knowledge 23, 32, 36, 39–40, 44, 49–50, 52, 55, 61, 92, 95, 115–116, 132, 149, 151, 158, 162, 183, 190, 208, 220, 230, 239, 253, 259, 267, 270

language 14, 20, 24, 29, 31, 34–35, 40–42, 51, 61, 64–65, 81–82, 85–87, 100, 108, 111–112, 124–125, 147, 152–154, 157, 159, 165, 179, 216, 222, 230, 237, 256, 259, 262

learning 54, 66, 99, 147, 182, 192, 201–203, 208–209, 217, 219, 262

leisure 208–209

liberalism 23, 176

life 2, 7, 11, 13–16, 35–38, 40, 42–43, 47, 52, 56–57, 63, 71, 77, 82–83, 85, 87, 89, 92–93, 96, 99–100, 104, 107, 109, 112, 114, 123, 125, 127, 133, 138, 140, 147, 154–155, 157, 162–163, 166, 175, 178–179, 181, 185, 187–189, 191–194, 196, 198, 200, 202–205, 208–213, 221–223, 228, 231, 233, 236–243, 246, 248–249, 253–254, 257, 263–268, 271

literal 51, 68, 105, 111, 121, 162

literalism 68–69

literature 1, 11, 15, 25, 51, 62, 70, 202, 205–209, 221, 249, 252, 257, 259–261, 269, 272, 274

liturgy, liturgical 176, 180

logic 14–15, 33–34, 49, 79, 91, 93–94, 209, 217, 224, 227, 253

love 9, 11, 14–15, 20, 41, 46, 56, 83–84, 93, 98–100, 108–109, 112, 117, 125–126, 139, 142, 151–152, 154–156, 160, 166, 179–180, 185, 190–195, 198, 203–204, 206, 208–209, 218, 222–223, 226, 231, 242, 245, 247–248, 253, 259, 267

low church 176

man 7, 11, 14–15, 17–18, 21, 24, 26–28, 36–42, 44–48, 62, 64, 69–70, 90, 95–98, 101, 103–108, 110–111, 114–115, 117–124, 126–127, 129–130, 133, 138, 141, 144–146, 150–152, 155–157, 159–160, 162–163, 169, 176, 179, 188–189, 191, 193, 195, 198, 206, 210–215, 222, 226, 230, 232, 236, 241, 243–245, 248, 254–257, 259–260, 262, 266, 271–272

materialism 28, 33, 44, 52, 220, 227

meaning 1, 18, 24, 29–32, 42–44, 46, 50, 61, 71, 81–82, 84, 91, 93, 98–99, 107, 110–111, 117, 131–133, 136, 142–143, 155, 157, 163, 177–178, 182, 218, 228, 234, 239, 244, 246, 251, 265, 267

mechanical dictation theory 61, 68–69

meditation 77, 133, 194–195, 219, 231, 235, 262

mercy 97–98, 117, 143, 151–152, 173, 243–244

"mere" Christianity 16, 181, 233–234

merit, meritorious 44, 97, 116, 160, 166, 202

Messiah, messianic 132, 139, 217, 223–224, 236

Metaphor 35–36, 51, 62, 69, 72, 82, 127, 156, 178

millenial, millennium 57, 233, 236, 259

mind 15, 18–20, 26–27, 29, 36–37, 39–40, 43, 45, 49, 52, 54, 58–61, 64, 69, 73, 80–81, 84, 108, 114, 125–126, 136, 139–140, 144, 195, 204–205, 209, 217–218, 237, 253, 255, 268, 272

ministry 19, 87, 193, 215

miracle, miraculous 68, 91, 105, 111, 253

modernism 28, 34

moral argument 25, 220, 223, 226, 228

morality 98, 226, 228

myth, mythology 11, 25, 31–32, 42, 44–49, 51, 57, 59, 62–65, 70, 88, 105, 111, 123, 132, 228, 235, 263, 265, 267, 270, 272

Narnia 11, 14–15, 17–18, 54–55, 59, 78–80, 95, 101, 106–108, 126–127, 157, 168, 189, 193–194, 211, 224–225, 233, 239, 246–249, 252, 256–257, 266, 269, 271, 273 naturalism 32–34, 104, 227, 272

Nature 7, 18, 24–26, 28–29, 33, 36, 39–40, 42–44, 46–49, 51, 57–60, 62–63, 70, 75–76, 78, 80–82, 84–87, 91–94, 99–100, 103–104, 106–107, 112, 115, 119–120, 122, 124, 126, 130, 132, 140–142, 146, 151–152, 155–156, 161, 173–174, 178, 184–185, 190, 195, 203, 206, 217–218, 222, 225, 230, 234–235, 237, 241, 243–245, 247, 251, 256, 294, 314

neighbor 195, 198, 203

New Testament 31, 55, 60, 63–64, 66, 71, 118, 131, 134, 136, 155, 157, 168, 170, 182–183, 190, 196, 202, 217, 234, 252, 267

obedience 36, 46, 52, 54, 72, 109, 113, 127, 152, 184, 190–194, 200, 227, 247

objectivity 26, 272

Old Testament 62–64, 68, 87, 105, 138–139, 236

omnipotence 80, 88, 90–91, 93, 122

omnipresence 80, 88, 90

omniscience 80, 85, 88, 92, 122, 244

ontological argument 9, 76–80, 220, 223–224, 271

ontology 79

pain 11, 68, 109, 115, 125, 152, 264

passion 83, 179

pastor, pastoral 100, 215, 222

penal 97, 152, 154–158

perseverance 167–168

person 6–7, 15, 26–27, 30, 33, 37–40, 43, 47, 54, 58, 61, 67, 72, 82–85, 89, 91, 97, 99, 101, 104, 106–107, 109, 117–118, 120, 122–127, 129, 131, 137–140, 142–147, 151, 156, 158–159, 161–162, 165, 167, 170, 190, 192, 195, 197, 199, 213, 218, 223, 226–230, 232, 253, 272

personal eschatology 233–234, 237

philosophy 9, 14–15, 25, 27–28, 37, 45, 49, 55, 86, 99, 114, 136, 210, 219, 221, 227, 235, 257, 259, 267–268, 272–274

physical 33, 37, 81–82, 104–107, 111, 121–122, 125–126, 227, 231

pneumatology 13

poetry 16, 19, 40–41, 51, 63, 69, 100, 206–208, 228, 259, 262, 274

poimenics 7, 25, 215

politics, politics 62, 208, 211–214, 218, 221

Pope, papal 182

post-modernism 26–27

prayer 11, 52, 67, 76, 89, 100, 124, 163–164, 169, 174, 180, 194–196, 198–200, 260, 262, 271

predestination 53, 163–164, 171, 200

presuppositionalism, presuppositionalist 219–220

pride 55, 204, 207

prolegomena 7, 23–25, 41, 57–58

prophet, prophetic 87, 119, 294, 314

propitiation 155

proposition 27, 30, 34, 68, 144–145, 191, 236

Protestant 17, 23, 160, 181–183, 185, 201, 269

punishment 97–98, 152, 155, 240–241, 243–244, 261

Purgatory 184, 239–240

ransom 31–32, 105, 107–110, 150, 152–153, 157, 163, 166, 191, 221, 257

rapture 233

reading 15–16, 45, 70–72, 90, 105, 131, 134–136, 142–143, 183, 195, 206, 208, 212, 242, 257, 263, 266, 269, 271

reality 26–40, 42, 46–47, 49–52, 55–56, 58, 63, 76, 78–79, 81–82, 89, 92, 95–96, 100, 103, 107, 109–110, 121, 123–125, 127–128, 140–141, 143, 153, 161, 174–176, 189, 192–194, 197–199, 207, 211, 213, 219, 221, 223–225, 227, 230, 237, 242, 245, 248–249, 256, 264, 272, 274

reason 13–14, 16, 18, 21, 23, 25, 27, 29–35, 39, 43–44, 47, 49–50, 52–53, 55–58, 68, 71–72, 78, 85–87, 93, 95, 99, 106, 109, 111–112, 118, 122–123, 128, 139, 142–143, 145, 182, 190–191, 204–206, 217–221, 223–224, 227–228, 230, 232–233, 235, 239, 246, 248, 251, 253, 263, 268–269

reductionism 40, 79, 125, 219

Reformation 6, 61, 154, 164, 182, 185, 203, 271

relation, relational 1, 18, 28, 36, 39, 41, 47–48, 85, 87, 89, 123, 126, 171, 182, 190, 195, 198, 227–228

relativism, relativism 27, 34, 113, 226

religion, religious 18, 33, 36, 38–39, 41–42, 44, 46–47, 52, 54–57, 64, 87, 93, 98, 106, 120, 134, 169, 176, 184, 191, 195–199, 202, 204, 206, 208–209, 218, 221, 227, 232, 247, 255–256, 262–265

repentance 21, 112, 151, 154, 156–157, 159, 161–162, 170, 196, 199–200

resurrection 31, 42–43, 63, 81, 106, 143, 145–146, 158, 189, 218–220, 233, 236, 245

revelation 13, 24, 41–44, 47–55, 57, 59, 61, 63–64, 72, 76, 80, 86–87, 105, 126, 170, 182, 199, 238, 251, 256

Rome, Roman Catholicism 19, 174, 181–184, 240

GENERAL INDEX

sacrament 181

saint 6, 184

salvation 7, 23, 55, 57, 59, 86, 115–116, 149–152, 158, 160–161, 164–171, 173, 176–177, 185, 193, 196, 202–203, 217, 233–234, 236–237, 240, 252, 259

sanctification 7, 162, 187–188, 197, 200, 240, 251

science 49, 66, 68, 122, 128, 204, 221, 228–229, 235

Scripture 7, 9, 24–25, 42–44, 47, 51, 57, 59–72, 76, 83–84, 86–88, 115, 122, 126, 136, 143, 149–150, 153, 157, 159, 164–165, 167–168, 170–171, 177, 182–184, 188, 192, 230, 240, 244–245, 251–252, 256, 273, 275, 294, 314

second coming 7, 121, 174, 233–236, 245

sehnsucht 26, 44, 228

sin 67, 96, 103, 107–110, 112–115, 117–118, 122, 124, 151–152, 154–156, 158–159, 192, 216, 234, 237, 240–242, 244, 247, 294, 314

skeptical 32–34, 43–44, 66, 125, 134–135, 137, 210, 218–219, 228

Son 17, 30, 43, 46, 75, 83–86, 88, 99, 107, 110, 117, 119–123, 125–127, 130–131, 136, 145, 154–155, 169, 177–178, 183–185, 228, 238

soteriology 1, 7, 149–150, 152, 173, 185, 252

soul 31, 61, 82, 87, 106, 114–115, 151, 201–202, 230–231, 233, 242–245

space 14, 17–19, 33, 36, 63, 75, 80, 82, 88, 90, 92, 175, 212–213, 221, 260, 264

spiritual, spiritual 2, 16, 21, 37, 51–52, 60–62, 64, 71, 75, 80–87, 98–99, 104, 106, 108, 110, 113–114, 122, 124–126, 145, 157, 159, 162–163, 176, 179, 181, 185, 187–188, 190, 194, 197, 201–204, 207–208, 212–213, 218, 220–221, 223, 227, 231, 237, 241, 243, 245, 247–248, 256, 258–259, 267, 272, 274

subcreation 201

subjectivity 26–27, 70

substance 25, 51, 125, 184

substitution 18, 144, 152–158, 202, 252

supernatural 55, 61, 81, 121–122, 136, 176–177, 203–204, 234

supposals 17

teleological 219, 225, 234, 249

text 9, 34, 60–61, 63–68, 71–72, 86–87, 123, 143, 149–150, 182, 251, 273

theism 25, 29, 46, 56, 99, 227, 230, 232

theodicy 25

theology 1–3, 5, 7, 9, 13–14, 16–21, 23–26, 41–44, 47–61, 66–67, 72, 75–76, 83–86, 90, 93, 96, 98, 100–101, 103, 105, 107, 115–116, 121–122, 124, 126, 133–135, 137, 149–150, 154, 159, 161, 167, 173, 178, 182, 185, 187, 200, 215, 217–218, 224, 228, 234, 249, 251, 253–258, 260–265, 270, 272–274, 294, 314

thought 13, 18–19, 21, 27–28, 30, 32–35, 38–39, 44, 47, 49, 55, 61, 77, 81, 86, 91, 93–96, 111–112, 115, 118, 120, 125, 139–140, 145, 153, 161, 167, 175–176, 180, 189, 197–198, 207–210, 216, 218–219, 222–224, 226–227, 229, 239–241, 246, 248, 252–253, 266, 269–270, 273

time 15–16, 18, 27–28, 32–33, 36, 40, 44, 48, 50, 53, 61, 64, 70–71, 75–76, 78, 80, 88–90, 92, 95, 100, 105–107, 119, 121, 123, 125, 129, 134, 136, 149–152, 156, 158–159, 164, 168, 171, 174–175, 180, 182, 193–195, 197, 200, 202, 207–208, 210, 221, 226–227, 233–234, 238–240, 256, 261, 263

tradition 19, 25, 27, 54–55, 57, 66, 69, 71, 91, 97, 100, 165, 167, 176–177, 180, 182–184, 188, 209, 233, 251–252

transcendence 80–81, 88, 92, 98, 106, 142, 224–225, 227

transformation 99, 188–191, 193, 200

transubstantiation 183

trilemma 7, 9, 16, 119–120, 129–131, 133, 135, 137, 139, 141–147, 220, 223–224, 228, 235, 257, 272

Trinity 75, 83–85, 99–100, 117, 125–126, 273

truth 7, 9, 14, 17–20, 23–41, 43, 45–49, 52–54, 56–59, 62, 64–66, 68–69, 85, 89, 92–94, 103, 105–106, 114, 120, 127, 130–131, 133, 139, 142–146, 153, 157, 160, 162, 164–165, 177, 180, 182–183, 187, 191, 198, 201, 204, 206–207, 211, 215, 218, 221–224, 235, 245, 249, 251–255, 258–259, 267, 271

universalism 169

value 18, 20, 37, 54, 94, 97, 169, 201–203, 209, 212, 222, 230, 235, 246, 269, 272

vicarious, vicariousness 152, 154–157, 252

will 1–2, 13–14, 16–17, 20–21, 23, 25, 31, 35, 37, 39–40, 44, 48–51, 53–54, 56–59, 61–63, 65, 68–72, 78–80, 83–84, 86, 90–91, 93–94, 96–98, 104–105, 107, 109–110, 112–113, 116–117, 120–121, 125, 127, 129–131, 133, 135, 137–138, 140, 145–146, 150–152, 154–157, 159–171, 174–179, 181–182, 184–185, 191–193, 196, 198–200, 203–204, 206, 209–212, 214–215, 218–224, 226, 229–236, 238–249, 252–253, 264, 270, 273, 294, 314

Word 9, 20, 23, 29, 36, 42, 59–72,
   81–83, 86, 93, 109, 116, 129, 142,
   150, 159, 165, 178, 183, 194, 204,
   215, 217, 221, 248, 256, 259, 263,
   267, 272–273

works 1, 6, 16, 18–19, 28, 46–47, 49,
   60, 118, 126, 129, 143, 146, 153,
   155, 158–161, 165–167, 171, 175,
   188, 196, 205–206, 208, 225, 235,
   257, 261, 267, 269, 271

worship 43, 53, 87, 96, 98, 104, 107,
   109, 164, 174, 180, 194–195, 199,
   253

wrath 96–98, 100, 155, 216

zoe 162, 187–188, 196

MORE SQUARE HALO BOOKS ABOUT
C.S. LEWIS

C.S. LEWIS AND THE ARTS: CREATIVITY IN THE SHADOWLANDS

"Helpful and worthwhile. Anyone seeking to understand Lewis's approach to the arts will profit from this array of interesting perspectives."
—Dr. Michael Ward

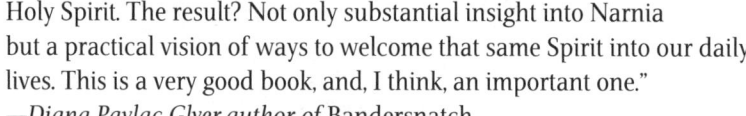

ASLAN'S BREATH: SEEING THE HOLY SPIRIT IN NARNIA

"I've read lots of books that unpack spiritual themes in Narnia: this one is different. Rather than offering a wide catalog of observations, Dickerson dives deep into one key concept: portrayals of the Holy Spirit. The result? Not only substantial insight into Narnia but a practical vision of ways to welcome that same Spirit into our daily lives. This is a very good book, and, I think, an important one."
—Diana Pavlac Glyer, author of Bandersnatch

A COMPASS FOR DEEP HEAVEN: NAVIGATING THE C.S. LEWIS RANSOM TRILOGY

"The essays collected in A Compass for Deep Heaven are a much-needed resource for both scholars and casual readers alike. The careful analysis and enriching insights help unravel the rich tapestry of meaning that links Out of the Silent Planet and Perelandra with That Hideous Strength. If you want to gain deeper understanding of Lewis's beliefs about God, humanity, and our role in His Kingdom while at the same time enjoying tales of adventure, the Ransom Trilogy and this companion book are a must read."
—Steven Elmore, President of the C. S. Lewis Foundation

SQUAREHALOBOOKS.COM